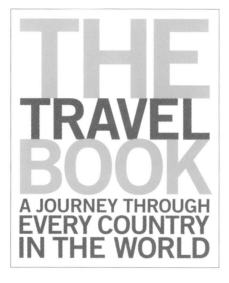

THE TRAVEL BOOK

A JOURNEY THROUGH EVERY COUNTRY IN THE WORLD

MELBOURNE ° OAKLAND ° LONDON

THE STORY OF
THE TRAVEL BOOK

This book contains some 1140 images and 100,000 words, and covers 231 countries. Every country, large or small, is featured and we have sought to evoke each destination through a unique mix of images and original text. The effect is a series of tantalising glimpses, which somehow gather their own momentum with every page turned and combine to present an awesome picture of our vast and kaleidoscopic world.

We started this book with a seemingly simple proposition – *to represent every country in the world in amazing images and inspirational text in an accessible A to Z format.* A few obstacles soon stood in our way. Firstly, the possible answers to the question 'what is a country?' Secondly, the fact that we set out to create a travel book, not an exhaustive reference book of the world. We viewed the world through the lens of the traveller, focusing on places to visit for their beauty, fascination or singularity, even if this sometimes conflicted with the world as it is defined by political or geographical borders. And lastly, sheer logistics – the world is a breathtakingly big place, and to cover it all in one book is a big ambition.

WHAT IS A COUNTRY?

Our first port of call was the United Nations' list of defined countries – all 193 of these had an automatic ticket for entry into this book. The UN list does not include the foreign dependencies of these countries, whether self-governing or Crown colony, but we wanted to feature some of these places because they are ever-popular traveller hang-outs. In this category we included some, but not all, Caribbean islands and groups, as well as Bermuda, New Caledonia, the Cayman Islands and French Polynesia, all dependencies of geographically far-flung entities.

We decided, based on traveller interest more than political correctness, to feature the component parts of Britain – England, Scotland and Wales – as separate entities. Arch enemies and old friends, England, Scotland and Wales all have rich and distinctive histories and cultures, which hold enduring appeal for travellers, and we wanted to reflect that in this book. Other destinations, such as vibrant and colourful Hong Kong, Macau and Taiwan, which are all parts of China, have historic identities that separate them from their present-day political situation. For the traveller, they are often experienced as separate and different, and so we featured them that way.

Antarctica and Greenland are not countries, strictly speaking, but these vast lands are not only extremely photogenic, they are also fascinating to visit, a fact not lost on adventure travellers who make tracks there in ever-increasing numbers.

At the end of the book, you will find 13 'bonus' destinations that we couldn't bear to leave out, but could not justify as full entries. These places were selected because they are fascinating, often beautiful and remote places that are fast gathering focus on the insatiable explorer's map. Visit these places and you may find yourself competing with our illustrious founder, Tony Wheeler, for recognition as Lonely Planet's best-travelled person.

LONELY PLANET'S PERSPECTIVE

In spite of our dilemmas about what to include and what not to include, the structure and organisation of the book was never in doubt. The A to Z format allowed us to view the world with a pleasing kind of egalitarianism, giving equal weight to superpowers like the United States of America and less high-profile nations like Burkina Faso or Belarus. It creates a sense of exhilaration and wonderment as such dramatically diverse and different places follow one after another – Afghanistan, Albania, Algeria, Andorra, Angola – the arbitrary linking of countries by letters of the alphabet belying the deeper connections that are shared across nations and humanity.

Having finally selected our official list of countries, we sent out the call to everyone at Lonely Planet to help us compile text and images for each destination. We had an amazing response from the avid travellers among our own staff, all of whom are passionate about the world and their favourite parts of it.

The guiding philosophy for us in writing this book was to present a subjective 'Lonely Planet' view of the world which gets under the skin of the place, showing a slice of life in every single country in the world. With just two pages per country, we could never hope to cover everything, so we chose instead to evoke the spirit of the place by focusing on the senses – what might you expect to see, what might you hear people say in conversation or greeting, what kind of food or drink can you expect to taste, and what sort of music, books or film would help open up your imagination to each country? In this sense, the book is much more about impressions than dry statistics – impressions that we hope will whet your appetite to find out more.

The same applied to image selection: we could never illustrate every aspect of every country in this book, so we again focused on capturing the spirit of a place and its people. Our image researchers avoided clichéd icons and picture-postcard views, beautiful as they often are, in favour of the icons of everyday life – people together and alone relaxing, eating, walking, reading, praying, working, sleeping, laughing and living.

THE WHOLE WORLD IN YOUR HANDS

Hundreds of Lonely Planet staff gave their time to be involved in this book, from writing text and selecting images to editing, checking, proofing and scanning pictures. It is their passion and their perspectives on our world which make for the wonderful, vibrant and breathtaking book which you now hold in your hands.

We hope that you will enjoy using this book to rediscover your favourite places, plan your next adventure, or dream about the places you may never go...

ROZ HOPKINS
Trade and Reference Publisher – Lonely Planet Publications

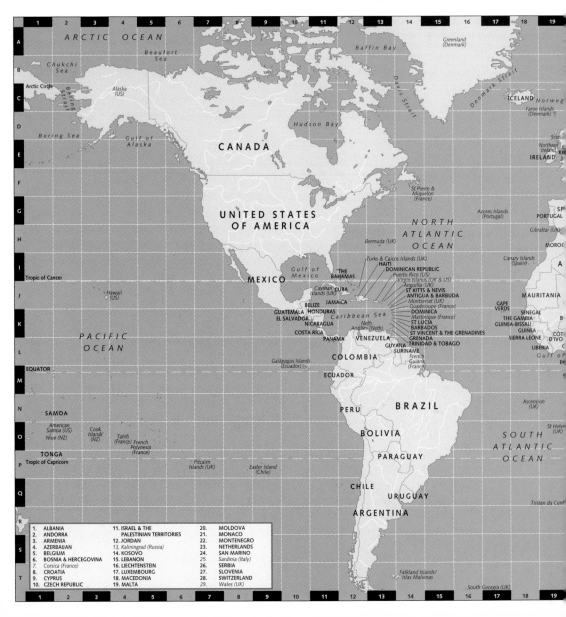

ARCTIC OCEAN

Beaufort Sea

Chukchi Sea

Arctic Circle

Alaska (US)

Bering Strait

Baffin Bay

Greenland (Denmark)

Davis Strait

Denmark Strait

ICELAND Norweg

Faroe Islands (Denmark)

Bering Sea

Gulf of Alaska

Hudson Bay

CANADA

Scotla

Northern Ireland KIN
IRELAND

St Pierre & Miquelon (France)

NORTH

Azores Islands (Portugal)

SP

PORTUGAL

UNITED STATES OF AMERICA

ATLANTIC

Bermuda (UK)

OCEAN

Gibraltar (UK)

MORO

Tropic of Cancer

Hawaii (US)

Gulf of Mexico

MEXICO

THE BAHAMAS

Turks & Caicos Islands (UK)

HAITI
DOMINICAN REPUBLIC
Puerto Rico (US)
Virgin Islands (UK & US)
Anguilla (UK)
ST KITTS & NEVIS
ANTIGUA & BARBUDA
Montserrat (UK)
Guadeloupe (France)
DOMINICA
Martinique (France)
ST LUCIA
BARBADOS
ST VINCENT & THE GRENADINES
GRENADA
TRINIDAD & TOBAGO

Canary Islands (Spain)

A

MAURITANIA

CAPE VERDE

SENEGAL
THE GAMBIA
GUINEA-BISSAU
GUINEA
SIERRA LEONE

B

Cayman Islands (UK)

CUBA

JAMAICA

BELIZE

GUATEMALA HONDURAS
EL SALVADOR
NICARAGUA

Caribbean Sea

Neth.
Antilles (Neth)

CÔTE
D'IVO

LIBERIA

Gulf of
E

PACIFIC

OCEAN

COSTA RICA

PANAMA

VENEZUELA

GUYANA

SURINAME

COLOMBIA

French Guiana (France)

Galápagos Islands (Ecuador)

EQUATOR

ECUADOR

SAMOA

American Samoa (US)
Niue (NZ)

Cook Islands (NZ)

Tahiti (France) French Polynesia (France)

PERU

BRAZIL

Ascension (UK)

St Hele
(UK)

TONGA

Tropic of Capricorn

Pitcairn Islands (UK)

Easter Island (Chile)

BOLIVIA

PARAGUAY

SOUTH

ATLANTIC

OCEAN

CHILE

URUGUAY

Tristan da Cunf

ARGENTINA

Falkland Islands/ Islas Malvinas

South Georgia (UK)

Blessed with a stark natural beauty, venerable history, and rich and diverse culture, Afghanistan has of late been blighted with more than its share of troubles. This landlocked country, at the crossroads of Central Asia, has seen armies and empires, merchants and mendicants, poets and prophets come and go over millennia. Images of a war-torn landscape do not do justice to a country that once hosted Silk Road caravans and used to be the ultimate destination on the hippy trail.

BEST TIME TO VISIT

April to June for clement weather – or the 1380s, the artistic zenith of the Timurids

ESSENTIAL EXPERIENCES

» Shopping for bargains in the bazaar in Herat, seat of Persian culture
» Climbing the Chihil Zina (40 steps) carved into the hillside near Kandahar
» Gazing at the dizzyingly high Minaret of Jam – what's it doing in the middle of nowhere?
» Joining the pilgrims flocking around the blue domes of the Shrine of Hazrat Ali in Mazar-e Sharif
» Soaking in the mineral-rich waters of the Band-e Amir lakes

GETTING UNDER THE SKIN

» **Read** Robert Byron's *The Road to Oxiana* or Eric Newby's *A Short Walk in the Hindu Kush*, both all-time travel classics; Idris Shah's *Afghan Caravan* – a compendium of spellbinding Afghan tales, full of heroism, adventure and wisdom
» **Watch** *Osama*, directed by Sidiq Barmak, a poignant tale of a young girl forced to assume a male identity to survive, and one of Afghanistan's first post-Taliban movies

2.

3.

4.

» **Eat** *qabli pulao* (seasoned rice with mutton, almonds, grated carrots and raisins); apricots dried in mountain villages

» **Drink** green tea scented with cardamom

IN A WORD

» *Salām alekum* (peace be with you), a ubiquitous greeting and blessing; *Borou bekheir* (travel well)

TRADEMARKS

» Men with moustaches and turbans; women in head-to-toe veils; opium poppies; snow-topped mountain vistas; intricate weaves of tribal rugs; horseborne swashbucklers playing polo with a headless goat carcass instead of a ball; oasis cities looming on the horizon

SURPRISES

» Overwhelming hospitality and spontaneous generosity; historical treasures; skies as perfectly blue as azure tiles; melons and mulberries

MAP REF H,27

(1.) Men stroll in front of the majestic Shrine of Hazrat Ali (Blue Mosque) in Mazar-e Sharif
(2.) Curious children stand above a cultivated valley in Ghor Province
(3.) The last of the sunlight glows on a house in the riverside town of Chaghcheran
(4.) Destroyed buildings loom above a road in Kabul
(5.) Lost for words, a man sits in front of a heavily inscribed marble wall in Mazar-e Sharif
(6.) A widow in a burkha begs at the Shrine of Hazrat Ali (Blue Mosque) in Mazar-e Sharif

1.

This pint-sized, sunny slice of Adriatic coast was ground down for years by poverty and blood vendettas, but Albania now manages to pack a wild punch of traditional Mediterranean charm and Soviet-style inefficiency. It's a giddy blend of religions, styles, cultures and landscapes, from Sunni Muslim to Albanian Orthodox, and from idyllic beach or rocky mountain to cultivated field. Relics from one of the longest dictatorships in Eastern Europe rub shoulders with citrus orchards, olive groves and vineyards.

BEST TIME TO VISIT

May to September

ESSENTIAL EXPERIENCES

» Admiring the beauty and mystique of Albania's mountains
» Getting lost in the ancient city of Durrës, founded in 627 BC
» Visiting the stunning and well-preserved Roman ruins at Butrint
» Beach-hopping from one gorgeous sun-soaked spot to another
» Being overwhelmed by the strikingly picturesque museum town of Gjirokastra, perched on the side of a mountain above the Drino River
» Wandering around Berat – sometimes called 'the city of a thousand windows' for the many windows in its red-roofed houses

GETTING UNDER THE SKIN

» **Read** *Broken April* by Albania's best-known contemporary writer, Ismail Kadare, which deals with the blood vendettas of the northern highlands before the 1939 Italian invasion. *Biografi* by Lloyd Jones is a fanciful story set in the immediate post-communist era, involving the search for Albanian dictator Enver Hoxha's alleged double.
» **Listen** to *Albania, Vocal and Instrumental Polyphony*, a great recording of traditional Albanian music

11

2.

» **Watch** *Lamerica*, a brilliant and stark look at Albanian post-communist culture

» **Eat** *fërgës* (a rich beef stew), or *rosto me salcë kosi* (roast beef with sour cream)

» **Drink** the excellent red wine Shesi e Zi from either Librazhd or Berat, or *raki* (a clear brandy distilled from grapes), taken as an aperitif

IN A WORD

» *Tungjatjeta* (hello)

TRADEMARKS

» Polyphony; shish kebabs; a former communist state; baggy pants and colourful scarves

SURPRISES

» As much as 20% of the labour force currently works abroad, mainly in Greece and Italy; Albanians shake their heads to say 'yes' and usually nod to say 'no'

MAP REF G,22

(1.) Muslim men gathered for prayer time at Ethem Bey Mosque in Tirana
(2.) An artillery bunker – one of many similar structures around the country – in Gjirokastra
(3.) A bird's-eye view of the historic Mangalem quarter in Berat
(4.) Grabbing a *burek* (meat-filled pastry) to go at a streetside food stall

13

1.

Despite continued political violence and a history of instability, Algeria is beginning to show signs of a more secure, positive environment. Independent travel can be difficult here, so outside the cities travellers are better off joining an organised tour to see such sights as the dunes of the Sahara and the majestic Atlas ranges. In Algiers there are French-influenced buildings and the majestic Turkish palaces of the medina to explore, while mountain villages and oasis towns are rich in Berber culture.

BEST TIME TO VISIT

March to April or October to November; Saharan temperatures can be ferocious in the summer months

ESSENTIAL EXPERIENCES

» Taking in the views over Algiers from the edge of the medina
» Exploring the exceptional Roman ruins at Timgad
» Drinking the sweetest water of the Sahara, specific to the oasis town of El-Goléa
» Shopping for carpets amid the bustle of the daily market in Ghardaïa
» Catching a sunrise in the scenic mountains of Assekrem
» Enjoying magic moonlit views over the salt lake at Timimoun

GETTING UNDER THE SKIN

» **Read** *Between Sea and Sahara: An Algerian Journal* by Eugene Fromentin, Blake Robinson and Valeria Crlando, a mix of travel writing and history; or *Nedjma* by Algerian writer Kateb Yacine, an autobiographical account of childhood, love and Algerian history
» **Listen** to *Algeria: The Diwan of Biskra*, a collection of traditional Algerian rhythms

15

2.

3.

4.

5.

JEAN ROBERT

» **Watch** Brigitte Rouan's *Outremer* (Overseas), a story of revolution and the social change that disrupts the privileged life of three sisters in French-colonial Algeria

» **Eat** chickpea fritters, couscous in both savoury and sweet dishes, and lamb *tagine* (casserole) spiced with cinnamon

» **Drink** rejuvenating fresh mint tea or robust Turkish coffee

IN A WORD

» *Marhaba* or *salam* (hello)

TRADEMARKS

» Sand dunes; the Atlas Mountains; magnificent views; searing heat; colourful carpets; mosques; breathtaking scenery; desert nomads; Tuareg swords; the old quarter in Algiers

SURPRISES

» The museum overflowing with mosaics at Djemila; soft drinks made from the inescapable salty water at In Salah

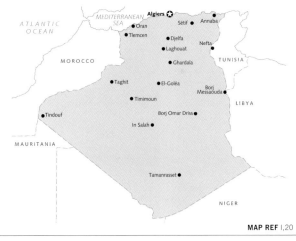

MAP REF I,20

(1.) A stone dwelling in Assekrem blends into the surrounding landscape
(2.) Sisters cast sibling shadows on a wall in Algiers
(3.) A group of desert travellers break their journey for a drink and a chat
(4.) A man leads a train of pack camels over rocky ground
(5.) The dignified bearing of a local man dressed for the desert

1.

2.

3.

All but lost between France and Spain, like the fairytale pea in the mattresses, Andorra comprises just a handful of mountainous landscapes and meandering rivers. Though it is tiny, it contains some of the most dramatic scenery – and the best skiing – in the Pyrenees. There are plenty of good hiking opportunities in the high, remote parts of the country, away from the overdevelopment and heavy traffic that plague Andorra's capital.

BEST TIME TO VISIT
Ski season from December to March

ESSENTIAL EXPERIENCES
» Skiing at Pas de la Casa-Grau Roig, Soldeu-El Tarter and La Massana
» Wandering the narrow cobblestone streets between stone houses in the Barri Antic (Historic Quarter), in Andorra la Vella
» Relaxing at Caldea – an enormous complex of pools, hot tubs and saunas fed by natural thermal springs, enclosed in what looks like a futuristic cathedral
» Hiking around the hamlet of Llorts, set amid fields of tobacco and backed by near-pristine mountains

GETTING UNDER THE SKIN
» **Read** *Andorra* by Peter Cameron, a darkly comic novel set in a fictitious Andorran mountain town. *Approach to the History of Andorra* by Lídia Armengol Vila is a solid work published by the Institut d'Estudis Andorrans.
» **Listen** to classical violinist Gérard Claret
» **Watch** *Dies d'Hivern* (Days of Winter) directed by Andorran Josep Duran, about young delinquents on a voyage of self-discovery
» **Eat** *trinxat* (bacon, potatoes and cabbage) or *escudella* (a stew of chicken, sausage and meatballs)

4.

» **Drink** mulled red wine to which lemon, apple, cinnamon, raisins and cognac are added

IN A WORD

» *Hola* (hello)

TRADEMARKS

» Ski resorts; duty-free shopping; the Pyrenees; a pocket-sized princedom; tax haven

SURPRISES

» True to logic-defying form, Andorrans are a minority in their own country, forming only about a quarter of the total population of 69,000, the majority of whom are Spaniards. Democratic Andorra is a 'parliamentary co-princedom' – the bishop and president are joint, but nominal, heads of state. Until the 1950s, Andorra's population hovered around 6000.

MAP REF G,20

(1.) Spectacular views from the the the ski gondola to Arinsal, Andorra
(2.) Glass spires pierce the sky at Caldea, Europe's largest thermal spa, Escaldes-Engordany
(3.) Old meets new – a modern steel sculpture and an ancient watchtower, Andorra la Vella
(4.) A snowy landscape in the mountainous province of La Massana

For most outsiders this Sub-Saharan giant means bloody war, bloodier diamonds and bubbling crude (oil, that is). This, with its long, nasty marriage and messy split from Portugal has had more than a few labelling it an African basket case. But this land and its people are not to be underestimated. Angolans are unshockable, resilient and resourceful. They're fighters – but they're lovers too. Portuguese is a great language for singing about love, which is perfect for these music-mad romantics.

BEST TIME TO VISIT

June to August during the dry season, or any time in peace time

ESSENTIAL EXPERIENCES

» Weaving your way through Luanda's potholed, palm-fringed streets alongside Rastas, streetkids, flash wheeler-dealer types and fashion-obsessed girls
» Going wild in Kissama's grassland park among giraffes, ostriches, and the antelope unique to Angola, the palanca
» Dancing in the wake of a fast-moving *kizomba* dancer, or busting a move to accordion-fuelled dance music, *rebita*
» Soaking it up on your own stretch of beach in Namibe
» Taking in the dizzying heights at Tunda-Vala volcanic fissure, 2600m above sea level

GETTING UNDER THE SKIN

» **Read** *Angola Beloved* by T Ernest Wilson, the story of a pioneering Christian missionary's struggle to bring the gospel to an Angola steeped in witchcraft
» **Listen** to anything by Bonga Kwenda, former world record–holding runner and soccer player who became a musical legend
» **Watch** *Rostov-Luanda*, which documents the journey of a returning refugee across Angola in search of an old friend

» **Eat** *calulu de peixe* (fish stew)
» **Drink** local coffee: Angola was one of the largest producers of coffee worldwide prior to the civil war

IN A WORD

» *Tudo bom?* (how's things?)

TRADEMARKS

» Mass population displacement, starvation, landmines – all the trophies of war; sparkling beaches; mineral wealth; poverty

SURPRISES

» Luanda is the fourth-most expensive city in the world (all that imported food); much of the large national park areas are devoid of animals, because most have been eaten by starving people during recent periods of conflict

MAP REF N,22

(1.) President José Eduardo dos Santos keeps watch over Ilha de Luanda
(2.) The notable pink façade of the colonial Portuguese Banco Nacional de Angola in Luanda
(3.) An Angolan drummer pounds out the rhythm at Fortress of Sao Miguel in Luanda
(4.) Church of Nossa Senhora dos Remedios, Rua Rainha Ginga

1.

MARK & AUDREY GIBSON

Anguilla, the most northerly of the British Leeward Islands, retains the laid-back character of a sleepy backwater. It's small and lightly populated, and the islanders are friendly and easy-going. It also has some of the finest beaches in the Caribbean. The interior of the island is flat, dry and scrubby, pockmarked with salt ponds and devoid of dramatic scenery, but it is fringed by beautiful beaches, aquamarine waters and nearby coral-encrusted islets, which offer great swimming, snorkelling and diving.

BEST TIME TO VISIT

December to February

ESSENTIAL EXPERIENCES

» Lazing on Shoal Bay, one of the finest beaches in the Eastern Caribbean
» Snorkelling and having a picnic on Prickly Pear Cays
» Taking a sunset stroll along Meads Bay – a lovely mile-long sweep of white sand with calm turquoise waters
» Diving one of Anguilla's many shipwrecks
» Hanging out in Sandy Ground, with its casual beach bars and old saltworks
» Riding around the island on a scooter and checking out the numerous salt ponds

GETTING UNDER THE SKIN

» **Read** *Green Cane and Juicy Flotsam: Short Stories by Caribbean Women*, or check out the island's history in Donald E Westlake's *Under an English Heaven*
» **Listen** to Bankie Banx, a celebrated Anguillan singer-songwriter
» **Watch** *Pirates of the Caribbean* – it has nothing to do with Anguilla, but you can pretend. There is no local film industry.

SLIM PLANTAGENATE

» **Eat** a crayfish or lobster – don't forget to suck out the tasty brains
» **Drink** Guinness or rum

IN A WORD
» *Limin'* (hanging out with friends and passing the time)

TRADEMARKS
» Tranquil; crystal-clear water and white-sand beaches; wild goats running amok; ganja; snorkelling

SURPRISES
» During the two-year rebellion against the British there were no fatalities; Anguillans are fanatic boat racers and on Sunday you'll see plenty of boats cutting up the ocean

LAYNE KENNEDY

ATLANTIC OCEAN

Prickly Pear Cays

The Valley ✪

Sandy Island

CARIBBEAN SEA ● Sandy Ground

Meads Bay

Blowing Point ●

MAP REF J,13

(1.) Beachside, a wooden fishing boat waits for its next excursion out to sea
(2.) Lazy days by the crystal-clear waters of Shoal Bay
(3.) Future cricket champions keep their eyes on the ball at a church party
(4.) Just a few final tweaks before the Carnival boat races in Island Harbour

1.

Antarctica is spectacular, a wilderness of landscapes reduced to a pure haiku of ice, rock, water and sky, filled with wildlife still unafraid of humans. A land of extremes, it is described by a bevy of superlatives: the driest, coldest, most inhospitable and isolated continent on Earth. Vast and ownerless, Antarctica is unique, and a journey here is like no other.

BEST TIME TO VISIT

November to February for 'summer' – or in time for a solar eclipse

ESSENTIAL EXPERIENCES

» Bathing in Deception Island's thermally heated Pendulum Cove
» Taking a cruise on a rubber dinghy among the icebergs
» Scuba diving in McMurdo Sound
» Visiting the historic explorers' huts in the Ross Sea region for a taste of the Heroic Era
» Having postcards stamped at the Dome, South Pole

GETTING UNDER THE SKIN

» **Read** Ernest Shackleton's *Aurora Australis*, the only book ever published in Antarctica, and a personal account of the 1907–09 *Nimrod* expedition; Nikki Gemmell's *Shiver*, the story of a young journalist who finds love and tragedy on an Antarctic journey
» **Listen** to Doug Quin's *Antarctica* – a collection of nature recordings, including seals, penguins and creaking glaciers. Icestock is an annual rock festival held by staff at McMurdo station, and recordings are often available online.
» **Watch** Koreyoshi Kurahara's *Antarctica*, the story of sled dogs on a 1958 Japanese expedition. David Attenborough's *Life in the Freezer* is a BBC documentary series with excellent wildlife footage.
» **Eat** an Antarctic barbecue, set up on deck or even on the ice; early explorers had to make do with penguin and seal

» **Drink** an Antarctic Old Fashion, a blend of bourbon, LifeSavers sweets and snow; travellers may prefer to stick to adding a little glacier ice to their whisky

IN A WORD

» The 'A-factor' (the local term for the unexpected difficulties caused by the Antarctic environment)

TRADEMARKS

» Icebergs; penguins; freezing cold; geologists; explorers; the South Pole; glaciers; seals; 24-hour sunlight (or 24-hour darkness depending on the time of year)

SURPRISES

» No polar bears (that's the Arctic); penguins smell terrible; dehydration and sunburn are real risks

- Bouvetoya
- Zavodovski Island
- South Georgia
- South Orkney Islands
- Deception Island
- Paradise Harbor
- Lemaire Channel
- Antarctic Peninsula
- Weddell Sea
- Vinson Massif 4897m
- Geographic South Pole
- Amundsen-Scott Station
- Ross Ice Shelf
- McMurdo Station
- The Dry Valleys
- Wilkes Land
- South Magnetic Pole 64°42'S - 138°36'E
- SOUTHERN OCEAN

MAP REF T,30

(1.) A lone figure walks across the icy terrain of Coats Land
(2.) A friendly Weddell seal surfaces from an opening in the ice
(3.) A courtship ritual at the Dawson Lambton Glacier, Weddell Sea
(4.) Passengers witness the *Kapitan Khlebnikov* ice-cutter at work in the Ross Sea

1.

2.

3.

HOLGER LEUE

Antigua's tourist office boasts that the island has 365 beaches, 'one for each day of the year'. It has great reefs and wrecks for diving and snorkelling. On neighbouring Barbuda you can track the island's fabled frigate birds and visit the Caribbean's largest rookery. Barbuda is a quiet, single-village island that attracts very few independent visitors, mainly ardent birdwatchers and yachties enjoying its clear waters and tranquil beaches. Antigua is a bit more happening, but the pace is still deliciously slow.

BEST TIME TO VISIT

December to mid-April

ESSENTIAL EXPERIENCES

» Exploring colonial-era sights, including a working sugar mill at Betty's Hope and the 18th-century Nelson's Dockyard
» Kicking back on the island's white-sand beaches
» Diving coral canyons, wall drops and sea caves with marine life such as turtles, sharks and barracuda
» Touring the Caribbean's largest rookery, in Barbuda
» Taking the scenic route along Fig Tree Drive
» Snorkelling the coral-encrusted wreck of the *Andes*, lying in the middle of Deep Bay, its mast poking up above the water
» Poking around the overgrown churchyard of Antigua's first church, St Paul's Anglican Church – one of the island's oldest buildings, dating to 1676

GETTING UNDER THE SKIN

» **Read** Jamaica Kincaid's *Annie John*, which recounts growing up in Antigua. Desmond Nicholson, president of the Antigua historical society, has published several works on the country's history, including *Antigua, Barbuda and Redonda: A Historical Sketch.*

4.

RICHARD CUMMINS

- » **Listen** to steel band, calypso and reggae music
- » **Watch** *No Seed* by Antiguan husband-and-wife team, director Howard Allen and producer Mitzi Allen
- » **Eat** *duckanoo* (a dessert made with cornmeal, coconut, spices and brown sugar) or black pineapple, purported to be the sweetest of them all
- » **Drink** the island's locally brewed rum Cavalier or English Habour, or try the local lager, Wadadli

IN A WORD

- » *Fire a grog* (drink rum)

TRADEMARKS

- » Cricket players; rum; endless pristine white-sand beaches; dancing; calypso music; black pineapples

SURPRISES

- » Barbuda has less than 2% of the nation's population; the black pineapple is not black; most of Barbuda's 1100 people share half a dozen surnames and can trace their lineage to a small group of slaves brought to the island in the late 1600s.

MAP REF J,13

(1.) A chat and a chuckle at the Antigua Yacht Club and Marina
(2.) Stairway to heaven at St John's Anglican Cathedral, St John's
(3.) The distinctive tones of steel drums ring out across the waters of Falmouth Harbour
(4.) Shopping couldn't get much brighter on Newgate Street, St John's

1.

From its tropical north to its glacial south, Argentina boasts more diversity and beauty than its fair share, and it takes time to grasp the multitude of environments and experiences that are on offer. Despite the country's tumultuous political heritage, the people of Argentina remain friendly, open and willing to share a laugh with a new amigo. Do as the Argentines do – accept the concept of time as fluid, and draw in all that life brings to greet you.

BEST TIME TO VISIT
March to May (autumn) – or before 1516 when Spanish navigator Juan Díaz de Solís first probed the region

ESSENTIAL EXPERIENCES
» Being enchanted by street tango at the Sunday antique market in San Telmo
» Listening to the deafening roar of the spectacular Iguazú Falls
» Indulging your chocolate cravings in Bariloche
» Taking in the dizzy heights of Cristo Redentor in the Central Andes
» Getting friendly with a Magellanic penguin at the Península Valdés wildlife sanctuary
» Staying at a gaucho ranch in Las Pampas

GETTING UNDER THE SKIN
» **Read** Patricia Sagastizabal's *A Secret for Julia*, which won Argentina's equivalent to the Pulitzer Prize in 2000. For a humorous account of Buenos Aires life, pick up Miranda France's *Bad Times in Buenos Aires*.
» **Listen** to the legendary tangos of Carlos Gardel and the contemporary folk music of Mercedes Sosa of Tucumán
» **Watch** the magic realism of Luis César D'Angiolillo's *Killing Grandpa*

4.

5.

6.

» **Eat** *empanadas* (turnovers stuffed with savoury fillings), *alfajores* (a popular sweet) and *facturas* (sweet pastries)

» **Drink** maté (pronounced mah-tay), *licuados* (milk-blended fruit drinks) and *chopp* (lager)

IN A WORD

» *¿Qué tal?* (how are things?)

TRADEMARKS

» Tango; maté-drinking rituals; Spanish colonial architecture; the Péróns; glaciers; the Andes; gauchos; charmingly inflated egos; hearty steaks; wine; *cumbia* music

SURPRISES

» Delicious *helado* (ice cream); locals enjoying maté on the bus (and just about everywhere!); gauchos still in traditional dress

MAP REF R,13

(1.) The dazzling Perito Moreno Glacier in Los Glaciares National Park
(2.) A cardon cactus in the arid landscape of San Juan
(3.) Street musicians inspire spontaneous dancing in Buenos Aires
(4.) Setting sun casts long shadows over Diagonal Roque Sáenz Peña, Buenos Aires
(5.) Works of art for sale beneath the brightly painted houses of La Boca, Buenos Aires
(6.) Thundering falls form a curtain of mist above the grasslands

1.

BILL WASSMAN

Fate placed Armenia at the point where the European and Middle Eastern continental plates collide, with a resulting mix in fortunes. Geography has brought the natural beauty of the Caucasus – majestic mountain ranges, snowy peaks, alpine lakes and forests. History, however, has seen Armenia suffer at the hands of conquering armies passing through – Roman, Persian, Arab, Ottoman Turk and Russian. These factors define the Armenians, a nation of artists, merchants, poets and stonemasons, fiercely proud of their language, culture and homeland.

BEST TIME TO VISIT
» March to June – or the 10th century, the golden age of Armenian literature and art

ESSENTIAL EXPERIENCES
» Photographing the domes and cupolas of the national treasury in Echmiadzin
» Enjoying cosmopolitan Yerevan's choice of opera, concerts, museums and dining
» Visiting the reconstructed temple to Helios, Roman god of the sun
» Imagining life on the ancient Silk Road at Selim Caravanserai
» Travelling to dramatic Tatev Monastery, rising high above the Vorotan Canyon

GETTING UNDER THE SKIN
» **Read** Phillip Marsden's *The Crossing Place* – a thought-provoking journey through the Armenian diaspora
» **Listen** to *Black Rock* by Djivan Gasparian, master of the *duduk* (traditional reed flute), the quintessential Armenian sound
» **Watch** Sergei Paradjanov's *The Colour of Pomegranates*, a visually striking Armenian epic, dizzy with colour and symbolism

43

» **Eat** *khoravatz* (lamb or pork, skewered and barbecued) and *lavash*, the wafer-thin bread that accompanies every meal
» **Drink** strong and gritty coffee; vodka; Armenian cognac – a national speciality

IN A WORD

» *Genats!* (cheers!)

TRADEMARKS

» Solitary churches on rocky peaks; intricate stonemasonry; medieval manuscripts; bracing breezes from snow-capped mountains; rich vestments on bearded priests; vital people said to have their minds in the West but their hearts in the East

SURPRISES

» Toasts (lots of them) before, during and after every meal; a culture imbued with literature and poetry; the delights of summer fruits

MAP REF G,25

(1.) Friends enjoy an outdoor meal and plenty of wine
(2.) An elderly woman from Yerevan enjoys a quiet moment
(3.) Shoppers at the entrance to the indoor Hayastan Market in Yerevan
(4.) Exquisite tile work covers the grand dome of Gok Jami mosque in Yerevan
(5.) The mysterious Sanahin Monastery rising above the surrounding woodlands

1.

It's possible that the Netherlands Antilles is the most concentrated area of multiculturalism in the world. Papiamento, spoken throughout the Netherlands Antilles, is testament to this fact – the language is derived from every culture that has impacted on the region, including traces of Spanish, Portuguese, Dutch, French and local Indian languages. The islands are diverse – there are the cutesy houses of Curaçao, ruggedly steep Saba, Sint Maarten with its large resorts and casinos, and the delightfully slow pace of Sint Eustatius.

BEST TIME TO VISIT
Year-round

ESSENTIAL EXPERIENCES
» Hiking to the top of Mt Scenery on Saba, for a close-up view of an elfin forest with its lush growth of ferns, tropical flowers and mahogany trees, and a panoramic view of Saba and neighbouring islands
» Diving in Bonaire with hawksbill turtles, peacock flounders, sting-rays and seahorses
» Exploring the strange volcanic Hooiberg ('haystack') on Aruba – the parched scrub and cacti landscape are classic Spaghetti Western country
» Kicking back in Sint Eustatius, a tranquil little Dutch outpost where islanders strike up conversations and stray chickens and goats mosey in the streets
» Cycling around Simpson Bay Lagoon on Sint Maarten
» Wandering around Willemstad on Curaçao – the maze of streets and lanes wiggling back from the waterfront are lined with houses running the gamut from pastel and spruce to crumbling and spooky

4.

GETTING UNDER THE SKIN

» **Read** Andrew Holleran's *Nights in Aruba*, the story of a gay man who spends his early years on Aruba
» **Listen** to lyric-heavy calypso, beat-based soca, or reggae
» **Eat** cornmeal johnny cakes and *yambo* (green soup of okra, salt pork, onions, celery and sometimes fish)
» **Drink** Saba Spice (a rum-based liqueur spiced with a 'secret concoction') or Amstel beer on Aruban beaches

IN A WORD

» *Bon bini* ('welcome' in Papiamento)

TRADEMARKS

» Palm-fringed white-sand beaches; tourism; diving; Dutch colonialism

SURPRISES

» Only about 20% of all residents were born on Sint Maarten

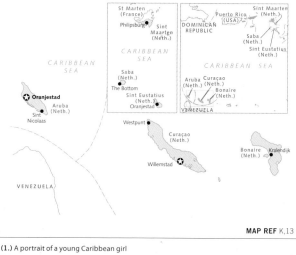

MAP REF K,13

(1.) A portrait of a young Caribbean girl
(2.) A man splitting bananas on the floating market in Willemstad
(3.) Deep in the waters of Bonaire a long lure frogfish conceals itself from a curious diver
(4.) The architecture of Curaçao's towns reflects Dutch, Spanish and Portuguese colonial styles

1.

From endless sunbaked horizons to dense tropical rainforest and wild southern beaches, Australia's biggest attraction is its natural beauty. Scattered along the coasts, its cities blend a European enthusiasm for art and food with a passionate love of sport and the outdoors. Visitors expecting to see an opera in Sydney one night and meet Crocodile Dundee the next day will have to re-think their grasp of geography in this huge country. It is its sheer vastness that gives Australia – and its diverse population – much of its character.

BEST TIME TO VISIT

Any time is a fine time – and definitely before 1788 when Europeans arrived

ESSENTIAL EXPERIENCES

» Watching the dramatic changing colours of sunrise or sunset over Uluru (Ayers Rock)
» Exploring the underwater world of the Great Barrier Reef
» Sampling the exquisite wines of the Barossa Valley
» Discovering the natural beauty of tropical Fraser Island by 4WD
» Viewing Sydney Harbour after climbing to the top of the 'coathanger', Sydney Harbour Bridge
» Meeting the native wildlife on Kangaroo Island

GETTING UNDER THE SKIN

» **Read** *Remembering Babylon* by David Malouf, a compelling insight into the social dynamics of early-colonial Australia; Bruce Chatwin's controversial *Songlines* for a look at the Aboriginal lay of the land
» **Listen** to Slim Dusty's 'Pub with No Beer', a classic Australian country tune; Paul Kelly's *Songs from the South* greatest hits compilation

2.

3.

4.

» **Watch** *The Castle*, about an 'Aussie battler' who takes on the big guys and wins

» **Eat** kangaroo or emu – if you can bring yourself to eat the animals represented on Australia's coat of arms! Try the fresh seafood – local specialities are always your best choice.

» **Drink** ice-cold beer; Australia's superb wines

IN A WORD

» G'day mate!

TRADEMARKS

» Bronzed Aussies; dangerous creatures; endless beaches; friendly locals; Outback pubs; sizzling barbecues; Aussie Rules football

SURPRISES

» Kangaroos don't hop down city streets; it isn't always hot and sunny; it has the oldest continuing culture in the world

MAP REF P.34

(1.) The Hills Hoist clothesline, an iconic Australian invention, Cape York Peninsula
(2.) A mob of kangaroos on the alert for whizzing golf balls at Anglesea Golf Club, Victoria
(3.) Two Queensland boys enjoy a swim to cool down
(4.) An architectural feature of Federation Square, Melbourne
(5.) The station boss at Bow River Station in the eastern Kimberly region relaxes with a rollie
(6.) Uluru at sunrise, Northern Territory

1.

2.

3.

Austria is an environmentally responsible land of mountains and impressive architecture with an unrivalled musical tradition that even *The Sound of Music* couldn't sully. Vienna is the capital, hub of the country's musical life and littered with beautiful buildings. Music, art and architecture reach baroque perfection in Salzburg, Mozart's birthplace. Innsbruck's snow-capped peaks frame its fascinating historic buildings. The rhythm of daily life throughout Austria has a musical beat and music festivals fill its calendar.

BEST TIME TO VISIT
Year-round

ESSENTIAL EXPERIENCES
» Enjoying the wine in a *Heurigen* or an evening of high culture in the Staatsoper
» Wandering your way through Vienna's Christmas markets
» Strolling through Salzburg – one perfect view after another
» Gawking at the oddities of the Josephinum, Vienna's medical history museum
» Marvelling at the unfolding scenic magnificence of the Grossglockner Road
» Hobnobbing with jetsetter skiers in upmarket Lech
» Gorging at the Giant Chocolate Festival of Bludenz

GETTING UNDER THE SKIN
» **Read** *The Left-Handed Woman* by Peter Handke; the *Nibelungenlied*, an epic poem of passion, faithfulness and revenge in the Burgundian court at Worms; or Wittgenstein's *Tractatus,* a seminal book in the field of linguistic philosophy
» **Listen** to Beethoven, Mozart, Haydn, Schubert and Falco

4.

» **Watch** *The Third Man*, set in postwar Vienna
» **Eat** *Wiener Schnitzel* with *Knödel* (dumplings) followed by *Mohr im Hemd* for dessert (chocolate pudding with whipped cream and chocolate sauce)
» **Drink** *Sturm* (new wine) in autumn, and *Glühwein* (hot, spiced mulled wine) at Christmas

IN A WORD

» It is customary to greet people, even shop assistants, with the salute *Grüss Gott* and to say *Auf Wiedersehen* when departing

TRADEMARKS

» Strauss waltzes; strudel; *Inspector Rex;* edelweiss; Sigmund Freud; dirndls (traditional peasant dresses)

SURPRISES

» The *Föhn*, a hot, dry wind that sweeps down the mountains in early spring and autumn, which causes – according to folk wisdom – restless animals, increased car crashes and suicides

MAP REF F,21

(1.) The abstract façade of Friedensreich Hundertwasser's Spittelau incinerator in Vienna
(2.) View of St Michael's dome from Kohlmarkt, Vienna
(3.) The mighty Grossglockner flanks the Pasterze Glacier in Salzburg province
(4.) Julie Andrews could appear at any moment, Tirol

1.

Azerbaijan is exotic by the standards of its more European neighbours. The click of *nard* (backgammon) through the hot summer nights; the endless sweet tea, jam and cigarettes; the entire herds of cattle wandering aimlessly across motorways – it's clear that while Georgia and Armenia look to Europe, Azerbaijan is very much part of Asia. This ancient land of Zoroastrianism displays a history and scenery that are equally dramatic – from Albanian churches and Baku's old walled city to the extraordinary beauty of the High Caucasus Mountains.

BEST TIME TO VISIT

May to June and September to October

ESSENTIAL EXPERIENCES

» Visiting Xınalıq, a remote village high in the Caucasus Mountains
» Exploring Baku, Azerbaijan's cosmopolitan capital, packed full of crumbling oil-boom mansions and Soviet and Islamic architecture, and with an impressive walled city
» Hiking near the ancient Persian mountain hamlet of Lahıc and exploring its pretty village
» Strolling around the hunter-gatherers' caves of Qobustan, home to a unique reserve of Stone- and Bronze-Age petroglyphs

GETTING UNDER THE SKIN

» **Read** Mehmed bin Suleyman Fuzuli's sensitive rendition of the classic *Leyli and Majnun*, which influenced many Azeri writers right up to the 19th century. Also recommended is Kurban Said's classic novel *Ali and Nino*.
» **Listen** to *mugam*-jazz pianist and composer Aziza Mustafazade
» **Watch** *The Bat*, directed by Ayaz Salayev, and Samil Aliyev's *The Accidental Meeting*

- » **Eat** shashlyk (lamb kebab) or *dograma* (a cold soup made with sour milk, potato, onion and cucumber)
- » **Drink** a traditional restorative cup of tea at a *çayxanə* (teahouse)

IN A WORD

- » *Salam* (hello)

TRADEMARKS

- » Oil; carpets; wine; Zoroastrianism; tea plantations; saffron; caviar; kebabs

SURPRISES

- » Noruz Bayramı (New Year Festival) marks the return of spring and the start of the New Year, according to the Persian solar calendar; traditions associated with Noruz Bayramı include spring-cleaning the house, preparing special rice dishes and jumping over bonfires to cleanse the spirit

MAP REF G,25

(1.) The magnificent exterior of Baku's Palace of Shirvan Shah reveals intricate carved insets
(2.) Thrilling rides at Primorky Park, Baku
(3.) Azerbaijan's best-known landmark, Maiden's Tower, rises above old bath houses in Baku
(4.) A few familiar faces try to blend in with the crowd of traditional painted babushka dolls
(5.) Playing to win – backgammon masters in Baku

1.

GREG JOHNSTON

The Bahamas has successfully promoted itself as a destination for US jet-setters, and a lot of it is Americanised. Yet there are still places among its 700 islands and 2500 cays to disappear into a mangrove forest, explore a coral reef and escape the high-rise hotels and package-tour hype. The 18th-century Privateers' Republic has now become the 21st-century banker's paradise, at least on New Providence and Grand Bahama. On the other islands – once known as the Out Islands but now euphemistically called the Family Islands – the atmosphere is more truly West Indian.

BEST TIME TO VISIT
» June to August when it's hottest and wettest

ESSENTIAL EXPERIENCES
» Listening to a rake 'n' scrape band in a bar on a backwater cay
» Hiking in Abaco National Park
» Watching flocks of flamingos in Inagua National Park
» Swimming with sharks while they feed at Stella Maris and Walker's Cay
» Staying at Pink Sands on Harbour Island and enjoying the charming historic village of Dunmore Town

GETTING UNDER THE SKIN
» **Read** Brian Antoni's *Paradise Overdose*, about the 1980s drug- and sex-addled Bahamian highlife
» **Listen** to Tony Mackay's 'Natty Bon Dey' on his *Canaan Lane* album. The Obeah Man, alias Tony Mackay, is a flamboyant performer and musical superhero from Cat Island.
» **Watch** James Bond in action in *For Your Eyes Only, The Spy Who Loved Me* and *Never Say Never Again* for the Bahamas backdrop

» **Eat** conch (a mollusc served pounded, minced and frittered; marinated and grilled; or even raw as a ceviche) or duff (a fruit-filled jelly pudding served with a rum-flavoured sauce)

» **Drink** Kalik beer or Bacardi rum

IN A WORD

» Hey man, what happ'nin'?

TRADEMARKS

» Casinos; luxury yachts; rum; drug trading; sun, sand and 'sin'

SURPRISES

» Many Bahamians believe that if you take the 'bibby' (mucus) from a dog's or horse's eye and put it in your own, you can actually see a spirit; conch is considered an aphrodisiac capable of 'givin' men a strong back'

MAP REF I,12

(1.) A local woman sells straw hats and bags from her house on Cat Island
(2.) A pink flamingo preens itself with contortionate expertise
(3.) A young woman from Nassau
(4.) A local girl sits in a colourful window sill at the straw market on Harbour Island

1.

PHIL WEYMOUTH

The only island-state in the Arab world, Bahrain comprises 33 islands and was once the seat of one of the ancient world's great trading empires. It's a fascinating and diverse place, offering travellers an easy and hassle-free introduction to the Gulf. There are alleys to explore, coffeehouses in which to sit and watch the world go by, magnificent desert landscapes, basket weaving with palm leaves and every kind of souq (market) your shopping heart could wish for.

BEST TIME TO VISIT

November to February (for warm days and cool nights)

ESSENTIAL EXPERIENCES

» Absorbing 7000 years of Bahrain's history at its excellent National Museum in Manama
» Entering the Al-Fatih Mosque in Manama, a rare opportunity for non-Muslims
» Spotting an Arabian oryx at the Al-'Areen Wildlife Sanctuary
» Visiting the seven layers of excavated material at the Qala'at al-Bahrain archaeological site
» Watching the local weavers at work in the village of Bani Jamrah
» Sipping Arabic coffee in the funky souq and viewing the traditional houses on Muharraq Island
» Wandering through the impressive Royal Tombs at A'ali

GETTING UNDER THE SKIN

» **Read** Geoffrey Bibby's *Looking for Dilmun*, an archaeologist's account of early excavations in Bahrain. It also paints a fascinating picture of life there in the 1950s and 1960s.
» **Listen** to *Desert Beat*, an album of ambient rhythms and Arabic songs by the young Bahraini musician and composer Hashim al-Alawi

2.

3.

4.

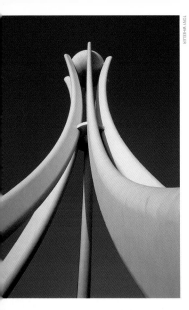

» **Watch** *Al Za'ir* (Visitor), Bahrain's first ever thriller, directed by Bassam Al Thawadi

» **Eat** *machbous* (rice served with meat or fish), *shawarma* (spit-roasted lamb or chicken wrapped in pita bread) or *sambousak* (cheese- or meat-filled filo pastry)

» **Drink** coffee, coffee and more coffee – cardamom-infused Arabic-style

IN A WORD

» *Salām 'alaykum* (common greeting; literally, 'peace be upon you')

TRADEMARKS

» Amazing archaeological excavations; palm trees; dates; carpet weaving; embroidered ceremonial gowns; ancient temples and forts; colourful souqs; burial mounds; drinking tiny cups of tea at the teahouses; dhows (fishing boats); baklava

SURPRISES

» Scuba diving in the warm, shallow waters, which offer over 200 species of fish; snorkelling among Bahrain's coral reefs

MAP REF I,25

(1.) A large mosque near Beit Sheikh Isa bin Ali
(2.) A potter in his workshop in the small village of A'ali
(3.) An incongruous billboard on the wall of the Beit al-Quran in Manama
(4.) The ornately engraved wooden doors of Manama's old High Court building
(5.) The Pearl Monument in Manama – a well-known landmark
(6.) A smiling resident of Manama

1.

JERRY GALEA

Bangladesh may have had its share of floods, famines and cyclones but this visually stunning destination has much to offer. The world's most crowded country has friendly people, luxuriously fertile land, a rich history, a broad mix of cultures and a tropical atmosphere that is unique to Bangladesh. Away from the noise and bustle of the capital, Dhaka, there are magnificently lush rural hill regions just waiting to be explored, plus archaeological sites, the longest beach on the planet and cruises along the country's countless rivers.

BEST TIME TO VISIT
» October to February (winter) – or the 16th century, when this region was the wealthiest part of the subcontinent

ESSENTIAL EXPERIENCES
» Wandering through the dilapidated 19th-century mansions of the maharajas
» Watching the panorama of river-life in Dhaka's old city
» Taking a ride in one of Dhaka's 600,000-plus rickshaws
» Visiting Sompapuri Vihara – an 11-hectare Buddhist monastery
» Spotting a Royal Bengal tiger in Sundarbans National Park
» Enjoying a refreshing dip in Kaptai Lake in the Chittagong Hill Tract

GETTING UNDER THE SKIN
» **Read** *Gitanjali* by Rabindranath Tagore, the great Bengali poet and winner of the 1913 Nobel Prize for Literature; James J Novak's *Bangladesh: Reflections on the Water*, a good all-round introduction to the country
» **Listen** to *Garo of the Madhupur Forest*, a collection of traditional Bengali music
» **Watch** the *Apu-Trilogy* by Satyajit Ray, one of the fathers of Bengali cinema

2.

3.

4.

» **Eat** dhal (yellow lentils) and rice; fish or meat with vegetables cooked in a spicy, mustard-oil spiked sauce; crispy *bhaja*, fried morsels of vegetables dipped in spicy chickpea batter

» **Drink** yogurt *sharbat*, a chilled spicy yogurt drink flavoured with chilli, mint, coriander and cumin

IN A WORD

» *Asalam walekum* (hello)

TRADEMARKS

» Green rice fields; rivers; manicured tea plantations; palm trees; rickshaws; stupas; mosques; Hindu temples; tribal villages; forests full of monkeys and spectacular bird life; terracotta sculpture; Royal Bengal tigers; Asiatic elephants

SURPRISES

» The Bangladeshi habit of staring at the unusual means that foreigners can draw a fixed gaze just by walking out on the street

MAP REF I,29

(**1.**) A group of women stand with their cattle in Pabna
(**2.**) A farmer harvests jute in Tangail
(**3.**) A neglected *rajbari* (Raj-era palace) in Painam Nagar village, Sonargaon
(**4.**) Sacrificial Eid ul-Adha cows in Dhaka
(**5.**) Rickshaws and baby taxis fight for space on the streets of Dhaka
(**6.**) A passenger peeks through the back window of a rickshaw in Dhaka

1.

Barbados is the 'Little England' of the Caribbean, but not to the point where the locals have given up rotis for kidney pies, or rum for bitter ale. Bajans, as the islanders call themselves, are as West Indian as any of their neighbours, and have tended to appropriate rather than adopt English customs. Nonetheless, old stone Anglican churches are in every parish, horse races are held on Saturdays and portraits of Queen Liz hang on plenty of walls.

BEST TIME TO VISIT

February to May

ESSENTIAL EXPERIENCES

» Taking a tram ride through Harrison's Cave, an astonishing network of limestone caverns and subterranean waterfalls
» Revelling in lush tropical plants in the natural wilderness of Welchman Hall Gully or the cultivated botanical gardens of the Flower Forest
» Exploring the Barbados Museum and the adjacent history-laden Garrison area
» Bodysurfing at Crane Beach, a scenic stretch of pink-tinged sand
» Encountering local fauna at the Barbados Wildlife Reserve, which features green monkeys, red-footed turtles, caimans, brocket deer, iguanas and agoutis

GETTING UNDER THE SKIN

» **Read** the novel *In the Castle of My Skin* by Bajan author George Lamming, an account of growing up black in colonial Barbados
» **Listen** to calypso artist the Mighty Gabby, whose songs on cultural identity and political protest speak for emerging black pride throughout the Caribbean
» **Watch** *The Tamarind Seed,* which stars Omar Sharif and Julie Andrews, a romance-cum-spy thriller set partly in Barbados

2.

3.

4.

» **Eat** *cou-cou* (a creamy cornmeal and okra mash, often served with saltfish) or *souse* (a dish made out of pickled pig's head and belly, spices and a few vegetables, commonly served with a pig-blood sausage called 'pudding')

» **Drink** Mount Gay rum or Banks, a good locally brewed beer

IN A WORD

» Workin' up (dancing)

TRADEMARKS

» Cricket fanatics; elderly women in prim hats; calypso music; rum; nightlife

SURPRISES

» Barbados boasts more international cricket players on a per capita basis than any other nation; women are the head of the household in many families, and a majority of children are born outside of wedlock

ATLANTIC OCEAN

Speightstown

Bathsheba

Holetown

Boarded Hall

Bridgetown

Oistins

CARIBBEAN SEA

Silver Sands

MAP REF K,14

(1.) A bright beer mural on a wall in Bridgetown
(2.) You definitely need a hat to play at this table
(3.) He sells sea shells by the sea shore, St Lucy
(4.) The exotic Bird of Paradise spreads its spectacular blossoms, St James
(5.) King of groove, Crop-Over Festival in Bridgetown
(6.) Young faces at Pollard's Bar on Manhole Road, Bridgetown

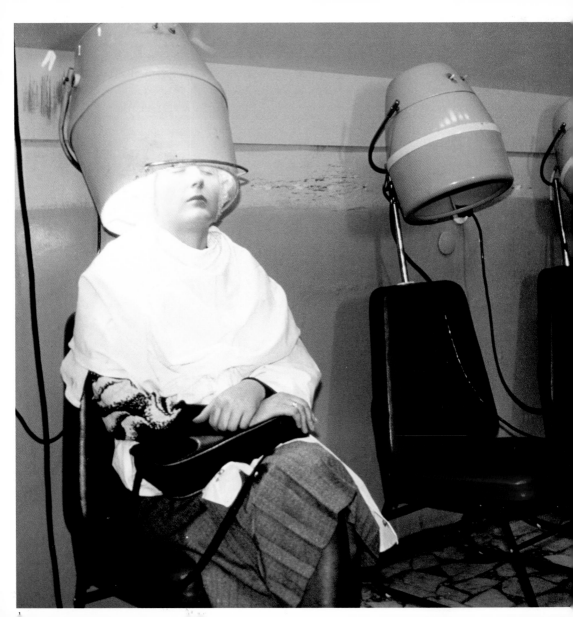

JEFF GREENBERG

Geography has played a major role in the history of Belarus, as the low-lying country straddles the shortest route between Moscow and the Polish border. The land has consequently been ravaged by war and controlled by Soviet dictatorship, but has emerged a survivor. A welcome detour from the madding tourist trail, Belarus has more to see than you might suspect. Wide stretches of unbroken birch groves, vast forested marshlands, and wooden villages amid rolling green fields give it a haunting beauty; and the hospitality of the Belarusian people is legendary.

BEST TIME TO VISIT

» It's always low season in Belarus but best from April to May (spring) or September (late summer) – but not during the 1930s when Stalin ruled

ESSENTIAL EXPERIENCES

» Downing a pint in the shadow of the KGB building in Minsk
» Catching a glimpse of European bison, the continent's largest mammal, at the Belavezhskaja Pushcha National Park
» Walking in Marc Chagall's footsteps through Vitsebsk
» Eating and drinking with friendly locals in cosmopolitan Brest, the lively, bustling bordertown
» Marvelling at Minsk's neoclassical Stalinist architecture

GETTING UNDER THE SKIN

» **Read** Maxim Haradsky's *Two Souls*, a poignant expression of the repressed state of Belarus after WWI
» **Listen** to *Kupalinka: Folk Music of Belarus*
» **Watch** *Kojak: The Belarus File*, conspiracy-theory intrigue where Kojak investigates the deaths of Russian émigrés

2.

» **Eat** mushrooms – mushrooming is a traditional expedition in Belarus. Try the mushroom and barley *hribnoy sup* (soup) and *kotleta pokrestyansky* (pork cutlet covered in mushroom sauce).
» **Drink** *kvas*, an elixir made of malt, flour, sugar, mint and fruit

IN A WORD

» *Dob-ree dzhen* Добры джень (hello)

TRADEMARKS

» Onion-dome architecture; the last dictatorship in Europe; splendid isolation; mountain villages; hearty peasant food and sweet, strong liqueurs; freezing-cold temperatures; furry hats; monasteries, churches and cathedrals

SURPRISES

» Belarus beat the Swedes in the 2002 Winter Olympics hockey tournament; there are still some working collective farms in the Belarusian countryside

MAP REF E,23

(1.) Pausing for pleasure in a Minsk beauty salon
(2.) Reconstructed 10th- and 13th-century Russian Orthodox churches near the Dzvina River
(3.) A farm worker tosses hay with a pitchfork
(4.) The dramatic star-shaped entrance to the Brest Fortress WWII Memorial

1.

Despite being home of the EU, Belgium's spotlight on the European stage remains a little dim, but only because its people are rarely boastful. Belgium has more history, art and architecture inside its tiny borders than many of its bigger, louder neighbours. For a start, it claims some of Europe's finest medieval cities: Antwerp, Brussels, Bruges, Ghent and Leuven. Festivals and celebrations keep the locals occupied year-round, and eating well or lingering over a beer in good company are national pastimes.

BELGIUM

CAPITAL BRUSSELS POPULATION 10,089,088 AREA 30,510 SQ KM OFFICIAL LANGUAGES DUTCH, FRENCH, GERMAN

BEST TIME TO VISIT

May to September (summer), Christmas and Carnival (January to February)

ESSENTIAL EXPERIENCES

» Stepping back in time in dreamlike Bruges
» Sampling the country's 800-odd beers and world-renowned chocolates
» Creeping through corridors and dungeons at the Château de Bouillon
» Visiting Ypres' poppy-clad WWI battlegrounds
» Wining, dining and indulging in lively and atmospheric Antwerp
» Warming up on hot wine at a Christmas market

GETTING UNDER THE SKIN

» **Read** *A Tall Man in a Low Land* by Harry Pearson for a humorous look at the country; Hugo Claus' *The Sorrow of Belgium* – wartime Belgium through the eyes of a Flemish adolescent
» **Listen** to Jacques Brel's poetic oeuvre or tunes from dEUS, Arno, Vaya con Dios and K's Choice
» **Watch** Van Dormael's charming *Le Huitième Jour* and *Toto le Héros*, or the Dardenne frères' *Rosetta* – they're all shot locally

» **Eat** *mosselen/moules* (mussels), *gegratineerd witloof/gratin au chicon* (chicory au gratin), grey North Sea *garnalen/crevettes* (shrimps), *waterzooi* (a chicken or fish stew)

» **Drink** Duvel, Westmalle, Hoegaarden or even Kriek (cherry) *bieren/bières* (beers), or some excellent 'young' or 'old' *jenevers/genièvres* (gin) from distilleries like Smeets and Filliers

IN A WORD

» *Schol!/santé!* (cheers!)

TRADEMARKS

» Beer; chocolates; lace; the linguistic divide; the European Union; Rubens, Breugel & Van Eyck; kisses on the cheek; Tintin; *frites* (hot chips) with mayonnaise; pigeon-racing; confusing placenames; Manneken Pis; elegant town squares; waffles; Hercule Poirot

SURPRISES

» Alcohol-free beer does exist; the saxophone was invented in Belgium

MAP REF F,20

(1.) Crimson doors and window frames adorn the façade of an appealing triangular barn
(2.) The psychedelic St Anna tunnel built under the Schelde River in the 1930s, Antwerp
(3.) Pride of the kingdom, the Grand Place in Brussels
(4.) Costumed act Gilles performs clog stomping at the Carnival of Binche
(5.) Delicious chocolate pralines await consumption

1.

Belize embraces a beguiling mix of Caribbean and Latin cultures, infused with a colonial history brought to its shores by British settlers. English-speaking, Creole-dominated and with a thoroughly coup-free history, this tiny country has an atmosphere that couldn't be more laid-back. Tourism may be unashamedly big business, but visitors rarely feel commodified. The local people are friendly, open and relaxed, and everyone here seems to know how to have a good time.

BEST TIME TO VISIT
» It rains less in the first half of the year, but you'll probably be too relaxed to care either way

ESSENTIAL EXPERIENCES
» Flying into Belize City, then hightailing it out to the beaches as quickly as possible
» Ordering a Belikin beer, then ordering another one
» Riding the bus into Belmopan, Belize's capital city, still wondering if you've arrived as you drive out the other side
» Snorkelling in the impossibly warm waters of the Caribbean Sea
» Exploring Belize's many beautiful Mayan ruins

GETTING UNDER THE SKIN
» **Read** *Belizious Cuisine*, a collection of 200 dishes that demonstrate the richness of Belize's multicultural past
» **Listen** to the Garifuna rhythms, culture and politics of Andy Palacio's *Til Da Mawnin*
» **Watch** *The Mosquito Coast*, starring Harrison Ford and River Phoenix, which flaunts the lush beauty of Belize's interior (though the setting is supposed to be neighbouring Honduras)

2.

3.

4.

» **Eat** the two main dishes on a Belizean menu: 'rice and beans' and 'beans and rice' – either way, it tastes great with a dash of Marie Sharp's famous hot sauce

» **Drink** Belize's famous Belikin beer, which always goes down a treat

IN A WORD

» You better Belize it! (cringeworthy but ubiquitous)

TRADEMARKS

» Mayan ruins; 'surf-and-turf'; diving the Blue Hole; Marie Sharp's famous hot sauce

SURPRISES

» Listening in on a conversation in a curious language, only to realise the language is English; it is actually possible to fill an entire day doing absolutely nothing

MAP REF J,10

(1.) A young girl from the Maya Mountains shows off her teeth and her Sunday best
(2.) An Atlantean statue of Jesus greets a diver in the mysterious depths off Ambergris Caye
(3.) A hieroglyphic frieze adorns the imposing Mayan structure, El Castillo, in Xunantunich
(4.) A sailing vessel glides through the glassy waters off Glover's Atoll
(5.) Nose first, a tamandua (three-toed anteater) eats his way up a sapling
(6.) A Caye Caulker islander keeps the hair out of his eyes Belize-style

1.

As the birthplace of voodoo and the seat of one of West Africa's most powerful kingdoms, Benin once had a historical renown that extended far beyond its borders. More recently the country has shrugged off Marxism to embrace democracy and capitalism with characteristic fervour. Visitors to surprising Benin will find remnants of the vast palaces of the formidable Dahomey empire, take boat rides through villages built entirely on stilts, see hippos eyeballing them from murky rivers, stop off at deserted beaches where slave ships once sailed and see stunning indigenous architecture.

BEST TIME TO VISIT

January and February (the dry season)

ESSENTIAL EXPERIENCES

» Witnessing the life-affirming ceremonies of traditional Beninese dance
» Visiting the ancient capital of Abomey, home to one of West Africa's largest palaces
» Bowing before Legba upon entering the Sacred Forest of Ouidah
» Boating to Ganvié, an extraordinary stilt village in the middle of Lake Nokoué
» Spying elephants, hippos and lions at Parc National de la Pendjari
» Relaxing on the long, palm-fringed beaches of Grand Popo

GETTING UNDER THE SKIN

» **Read** Bruce Chatwin's *The Viceroy of Ouidah*, which tells the story of a Brazilian trader stranded on the 'Slave Coast' in the 17th century
» **Listen** to Angélique Kidjo, Gnonnas Pedro, Nel Olivier and Yelouassi Adolphe

91

2.

- » **Watch** *Globe Trekker: West Africa – Mali, Benin and Burkina Faso* for a visual tour of the region
- » **Eat** *pâte de maïs* (mashed maize) with either meat, cheese or *gombo* (okra) sauce
- » **Drink** La Béninoise, the local beer, or *sodabe*, the local rocket fuel

IN A WORD

- » *Neh-àh-dèh-gbòhng?* (how are you? in the local language, Fon)

TRADEMARKS

- » Voodoo fetishes; smiling faces; fishing villages on stilts; poachers; multiple coups; elephants and hippos

SURPRISES

- » The name of the de facto capital, Cotonou, means 'mouth of the river of death' in Fon, referring to the role the town played in the exportation of slaves; on Voodoo Day (10 January) people meet on Ouidah's beaches to pray for good health

MAP REF K,20

(1.) Get your motor running – taxis outside Notre Dame Cathedral, Cotonou
(2.) A boy reflects on life in Koko village, Atakora
(3.) A woman strolls past a mosque in Porto Novo
(4.) Paddling through the still waters of Lake Nokoume in a pirogue

1.

BERMUDA

Visitors from the USA find this most isolated of island groups to be quaintly English with its cricket matches and afternoon teas. Brits, on the other hand, find it has an American flavour. Whatever your point of origin, you can't fail to appreciate that Bermuda is far enough from urban pollution to offer clear skies and turquoise waters. Bermuda is sometimes erroneously associated with the Caribbean, which lies nearly 1000 miles to its south.

BEST TIME TO VISIT

Year-round

ESSENTIAL EXPERIENCES

» Strolling along the crooked streets in Town of St George and poking into its churches, museums and historic sites
» Watching the boats cross the harbour from Hamilton's Front St, a harbourfront road lined with turn-of-the-century Victorian buildings in bright pastel lemon, lime, apricot and sky blue
» Visiting the Royal Naval Dockyard, where the inner fort has been turned into the island's leading historic museum, the Bermuda Maritime Museum
» Lazing in the sun on the dazzling pink-sand beaches at South Shore Park
» Splashing about in the turquoise waters of Horseshoe Bay

GETTING UNDER THE SKIN

» **Read** *Bermuda's Story* by Terry Tucker, the island's most highly regarded historian
» **Listen** to reggae, calypso and Bermuda's most rocking band, the Kennel Boys
» **Watch** *The Deep*, an underwater thriller of drug lords and treasure set off the coast of Bermuda

2.

3.

4.

GREG JOHNSTON

» **Eat** fish chowder (a tasty reddish-brown chowder commonly made with rockfish or snapper and flavoured with local black rum and sherry peppers sauce) or a traditional Sunday codfish breakfast (codfish, eggs, boiled Irish potatoes, bananas and avocado, with a sauce of onions and tomatoes)

» **Drink** Gosling's Black Seal Rum (a dark rum) or dark 'n' stormy (a two-to-one mix of carbonated ginger beer with Black Seal Rum)

IN A WORD

» De rock – the rock (meaning Bermuda)

TRADEMARKS

» Bermuda shorts; tidy pastel cottages; pink-sand beaches; the Bermuda Triangle

SURPRISES

» Bermuda held 'witch' trials in the 17th century; Bermuda has the world's northernmost coral reefs

ATLANTIC OCEAN

Town of St George

St David's

Bailey's Bay

Castle Harbor

Nonsuch Island

Tucker's Town

Harrington Sound

South Channel

Flatts Village

Somerset Village

Hamilton

Great Sound

Little Sound

MAP REF H,13

(1.) A motorcyclist whizzes past a lime-green Victorian shopfront on Front Street, Hamilton

(2.) The bells and bellows of St George's town crier

(3.) The bleached walls of a church in the city of Hamilton

(4.) Over 100 years old, St David's Lighthouse is a prominent landmark on the eastern coast

1.

IZZET KERIBAR

The Kingdom of Bhutan teeters between contemporary and medieval: monks transcribe ancient Buddhist texts into laptop computers, traditionally dressed archers use alloy-steel bows and arrows, and its farsighted leaders maintain Bhutan's pristine environment and unique culture. Since Bhutan's doors opened in 1974, visitors have been mesmerised by spectacular Himalayan scenery, impressive architecture and hospitable people.

BEST TIME TO VISIT

September to November when skies are clear and the high mountain peaks visible

ESSENTIAL EXPERIENCES

» Experiencing the extraordinary friendliness and warm hospitality of the Bhutanese people
» River-rafting down remote, stunningly beautiful rivers, from small alpine runs like the Paro Chhu to the big-water Puna Tsang Chhu
» Exploring ancient and precious Buddhist sites at Bumthang
» Marvelling at the Trashi Chhoe Dzong (Fortress of the Glorious Religion) at Thimphu and visiting 'the painting school' below it
» Spotting black-necked cranes at the glacial valley of Phobjika on the western slopes of the Black Mountains

GETTING UNDER THE SKIN

» **Read** *A Baby in a Backpack to Bhutan*, an engaging, amusing adventure by Bunty Avieson, who quit her job and travelled with her newborn baby to Bhutan
» **Listen** to *Music to Meditate By: Tibetan Buddhist Rites From the Monasteries of Bhutan, Vol. 1: Rituals of the Drukpa* by the Thimphu Monastic Orchestra
» **Watch** *Little Buddha*, directed by Bernardo Bertolucci and starring Keanu Reeves – partly set and filmed in Bhutan; *The Other*

2.

3.

4.

JULIA WILKINSON

Final, a documentary about a football match between Bhutan and Montserrat, the world's worst soccer teams in 2002

» **Eat** Tibetan-style *momos* (filled steamed dumplings), yak meat, and *ema datse* (chillies and cheese) – but not all at once!

» **Drink** XXX Bhutan Rum

IN A WORD

» *Dzong* (the iconic white, fortress-style monastery)

TRADEMARKS

» The last Himalayan Buddhist kingdom; colourful textiles; unsurpassed beauty; ancient myths and legends; a hair-raising descent into Paro airport; a place for inspiration and solitude; prayer flags, beads and wheels; *datse* (archery) enthusiasts

SURPRISES

» Thimphu is the only world capital without traffic lights. One set was installed, but residents complained that it was too impersonal.

ALISON WRIGHT

CHINA (Tibet)

Laya Lunana
Gasa
Punakha Bumthang Kurtoe
Thimphu ✪ Jakar
Wangdue Phodrang
Paro
Ha Kheng Mongar Trashigang
Chhukha Pemagatsei
Damphu Samdrup Jongkhar
Samtse Sarpang

INDIA

MAP REF I,29

(1.) The monks' room at the National Memorial Chorten in Thimphu
(2.) Dancers re-enact legendary religious stories in front of the National Library, Thimphu
(3.) School children vie for attention in Thimphu
(4.) Rice fields on the way to Paro and Thimphu
(5.) One of the temples of Kurjey Lhakhang in the Choskhor Valley
(6.) A Bhutanese boy from Paro in traditional dress

1.

Bolivia isn't called the Tibet of the Americas for nothing: it's the western hemisphere's highest, most isolated and most rugged nation. It's also South America's most traditional realm: the majority of the population claim pure Amerindian blood. The geography of this landlocked, Andean country runs the gamut from jagged peaks and hallucinogenic salt flats to steamy jungles and wildlife-rich pampas. Bolivia is often left off travellers' itineraries, making it the perfect off-the-beaten-track destination.

BEST TIME TO VISIT
May to October (winter)

ESSENTIAL EXPERIENCES
» Strolling along the cobblestoned streets surrounding Iglesia de San Francisco in La Paz
» Visiting the spectacular ice caves and turquoise lakes of the Zongo Valley
» Choosing one of Lake Titicaca's 36 islands and sailing through the clear sapphire-blue waters to get there
» Taking a jungle trip to the rainforest surrounding Rurrenabaque, on the Río Beni
» Finding out that seeing is believing – Salar de Uyuni, the southwest's salt deserts, have spurting geysers and eerie lagoons

GETTING UNDER THE SKIN
» **Read** *The Fat Man from La Paz: Contemporary Fiction from Bolivia*, a collection of 20 short stories edited by Rosario Santos
» **Listen** to *Charango* masters Celestino Campos, Ernesto Cavour and Mauro Núñez, or local pop outfit Azul Azul
» **Watch** *Sexual Dependency*, directed by Bolivian Rodrigo Bellott, dealing with the loss of sexual innocence

2.

3.

4.

» **Eat** *salteña* (a pastie filled with meat and vegetables); *surubí* (catfish), the lowlands' most delicious freshwater fish
» **Drink** the favourite alcoholic drink *chicha cochabambina*, obtained by fermenting corn; *mate de coca* (coca leaf tea), the most common boiled drink

IN A WORD
» *Buenos días sopita. ¿Qué tal?* (good day, how are you?)

TRADEMARKS
» Bowler hats; altitude sickness; Lake Titicaca; La Paz; cocaine guerrillas; colourful hand-woven shawls; llamas; chewing coca

SURPRISES
» Legendary outlaws Butch Cassidy and the Sundance Kid supposedly met their demise in San Vicente

MAP REF 0,13

(1.) A local takes a walk in downtown La Paz
(2.) An Aymara woman and her dog rest in colourful La Paz
(3.) The beautiful, high-terrain landscape is reflected in a saline lake in in the far southwest
(4.) A shy llama peeks between the cacti on the Isla de los Pescadores
(5.) Between Potosí and Sucre, a young girl stops at the roadside
(6.) The shoreline of Lake Verde with the majestic volcano Licancabur in the background

5.

6.

1.

Sandwiched between Croatia and Serbia, the small mountainous country of Bosnia and Hercegovina has been a zone of contention since Occident and Orient first began arm-wrestling for it nearly two millennia ago. The devastating war of the 1990s destroyed much of its heritage, but progress since then has been substantial and Bosnia and Hercegovina shows proud resilience through its scars. Gorgeous Sarajevo is coming back to life and a drive through the craggy, dramatic countryside is unforgettable.

BEST TIME TO VISIT

Year-round – the weather is agreeable except for summer and winter extremes

ESSENTIAL EXPERIENCES

» Taking a tram ride and drinking Turkish coffee in Sarajevo
» Clambering among the cobblestones in the walled city of Jajce
» Visiting the medieval castle, Many-Coloured Mosque and natural springs at Travnik
» Discovering Islamic culture and Turkish souvenir shops in Mostar, nestled in the valley of the aqua-green Neretva River
» Making a pilgrimage to Međugorje to search for an apparition of the Virgin Mary
» Skiing on quaint Mt Jahorina, site of the 1984 Winter Olympics

GETTING UNDER THE SKIN

» **Read** Misha Glenny's *The Fall of Yugoslavia: The Third Balkan War*, a British journalist's first-hand account of the disintegration of the former Yugoslavia
» **Listen** to *Bosnian Breakdown: the Unpronounceable Beat of Sarajevo (Yugoslavia)* by Kalesijki Zvuci – a mix of pop and folk tunes
» **Watch** *No Man's Land* by Sarajevo-born Danis Tanović, depicting

2.

3.

4.

the relationship between a Serb and a Muslim soldier during the time of siege in Sarajevo

» **Eat** *sirnica* (cheese pie) or *tufahije* (apple cake topped with cream and walnuts)

» **Drink** *šljivovica* (plum brandy) or *loza* (grape brandy)

IN A WORD

» *Živjeli* ('cheers!' when toasting)

TRADEMARKS

» Old cobbled streets; medieval forts and castles; mountain villages; excellent Turkish food; war memorials; hilly countryside and forests; bronze artisans; beautiful natural springs

SURPRISES

» Rafting the rapids of the Una River at Bihać; the Dervish monastery *(tekija)* at Blagaj; homemade wines for sale at Cevrići

MAP REF G,22

(1.) Two women walk down a war-scarred street in Sarajevo
(2.) Time to break out from the feathered frenzy in the Turkish Quarter, Bascarsija
(3.) The reconstructed Mostar Bridge spans the Neretva River at Mostar's Ottoman Quarter
(4.) Peaceful moments for prayer at Gazi-Husrevbey Mosque in Sarajevo
(5.) A man bathed in Sarajevo's golden dawn
(6.) The Moorish grandeur of the City Hall and Library in Sarajevo

1.

An African success story, Botswana achieved independence from Britain in 1966 and, immediately thereafter, discovered three of the world's richest diamond mines. And like a good mystery story, it takes time to unravel the country's secrets. Beyond the narrow eastern corridor, where the majority of the population is concentrated, Botswana is a largely roadless wilderness of savannas, deserts, wetlands and salt pans. As freedom of speech and equality are guaranteed under the country's constitution, the main threat to Botswana's stability is the AIDS virus.

BEST TIME TO VISIT

April to August (the dry season), for wildlife viewing

ESSENTIAL EXPERIENCES

» Travelling by *mokoro* (traditional canoe) on the Okavango River
» Seeing the incredible gallery of ancient San paintings in the remote and mystical Tsodilo Hills
» Wildlife spotting in Chobe National Park – marvel at lions, cheetahs, hippos, giraffes, zebras and several species of birds
» Camping with the wild things at Moremi Game Reserve
» Keeping a lookout for buried treasure in the Gcwihaba Caverns, with their gargantuan stalagmites and stalactites

GETTING UNDER THE SKIN

» **Read** *Bayeyi & Hambukushu: Tales from the Okavango* (edited by Thomas J Larson), a compilation of oral poetry and stories from the Okavango Panhandle region; or Alexander McCall Smith's popular mystery series, *The No 1 Ladies' Detective Agency*
» **Listen** to Nick Nkosanah Ndaba's *Dawn of Bojazz* and Rastafarian Ras Baxton's 'Tswana reggae'
» **Watch** *The Gods Must Be Crazy* and *March of the Flame Birds*

2.

3.

4.

» **Eat** *mabele* (sorghum) or *bogobe* (porridge made from sorghum), which form the basis of most Batswana meals
» **Drink** *bojalwa*, a sprouted-sorghum beer that's brewed commercially as Chibuku

IN A WORD

» *Dumêla* ('hello' in Tswana)

TRADEMARKS

» National parks; the San people; the Kalahari desert; salt pans

SURPRISES

» Okavango is the world's largest inland delta; baobab trees with a circumference of over 30m could be as much as 4000 years old; one of the highest rates of HIV/AIDS infection in the world

MAP REF P.22

(**1.**) Ostriches await an approaching thunderstorm in Savute marsh, Chobe National Park
(**2.**) Travelling along the Delta river in a *mokoro* boat hollowed from a tree trunk
(**3.**) A red-billed oxpecker helps maintain a zebra's coat
(**4.**) A female cheetah surveys her surroundings
(**5.**) Baobabs, known as the Sleeping Sisters, in Makgadikgadi
(**6.**) A Ngambiland local enjoys a pipe

1.

TOM COCKREM

From the frenzied passion of Carnaval to the immensity of the dark Amazon, Brazil is a country of mythic proportions. Encompassing half the continent, South America's giant has stretches of unexplored rainforest, islands with pristine beaches and endless rivers. After decades of internal migration and population growth, Brazil is also an urban country; more than two out of every three Brazilians live in a city, and São Paulo is among the world's most populous metropolises.

BEST TIME TO VISIT
There is no bad time to visit Brazil

ESSENTIAL EXPERIENCES
» Dancing through the streets of Salvador da Bahia during Carnaval
» Escaping to Ilha Grande, the perfect island getaway, blending tropical beach and Atlantic rainforest
» Experiencing the mad spectacle of football at Maracanã
» Partying till dawn at sexy samba clubs in Lapa
» Watching *capoeira* (an Afro-Brazilian martial art) on the beach
» Taking a jungle tour into the heart of the Amazon

GETTING UNDER THE SKIN
» **Read** *The Alchemist* by novelist Paulo Coelho, or *The Masters and the Slaves: A Study in the Development of Brazilian Civilization* by Gilberto Freyre, the most famous book on Brazil's colonial past
» **Listen** to bossa nova's founding father, guitarist João Gilberto; for something more contemporary, the punk-driven Legião Urbana
» **Watch** Hector Babenco's *Pixote*, the tale of a street kid in Rio that won the best film award at Cannes in 1981. *Cidade de Deus* (City of God) is an honest, disturbing portrayal of life in a Rio *favela* (slum).
» **Eat** *feijoada* (pork stew served with rice and a bowl of beans) or *acarajé* (peeled brown beans, mashed in salt and onions, and

2.

RUA
PACHECO LEÃO

3.

4.

5.

then fried – inside is dried shrimp, pepper and tomato sauce)
» **Drink** *cafezinho* (coffee, served as an espresso-sized shot with plenty of sugar and without milk) and *sucos* (juice from the incredible variety of Brazilian fruits)

IN A WORD

» *Bacana* (cool)

TRADEMARKS

» Carmen Miranda; 'The Girl from Ipanema'; Carnaval; the Amazon; soccer; beaches; bossa nova

SURPRISES

» Candomblé gods are known as *orixás* and each person is believed to be protected for life by one of them. Millions of Brazilians go to the beach at New Year to pay homage to Iemanjá, the sea goddess, whose alter ego is the Virgin Mary.

MAP REF N,14

(1.) A capoeira dancer pulls a stunt on the cobbled streets of Salvador da Bahia
(2.) Soft-drink vendors help beachgoers cool off in Rio de Janeiro
(3.) One of the many colourful houses in Rio de Janeiro's Jardim Botanico district
(4.) A family from the Amazonas region
(5.) Sunset over Ipanema Beach with its dramatic backdrop of the Dois Irmãos mountain

1.

The Islamic sultanate of Brunei is one of the world's smallest countries – and richest, thanks to its treasure trove of oil. It's known chiefly for the astounding wealth of its sultan and for its tax-free, subsidised society. The country's full name is **Negara Brunei Darussalam**, translated as 'Brunei – the Abode of Peace', and with alcohol virtually unobtainable, no nightlife or active political culture, it's certainly peaceful. The capital, Bandar Seri Begawan, has retained its fringe of traditional, river-dwelling stilt villages as an enduring vision of the past, and away from the coast the landscape is taken over by largely pristine tropical forest.

BEST TIME TO VISIT

March to October – or 1929 when oil was discovered, Brunei's most memorable payday

ESSENTIAL EXPERIENCES

» Racing through the waterways of Sungai Brunei in a longboat
» Contemplating the shadows and light on the capital's Omar Ali Saifuddien Mosque as the sun goes down
» Getting lost in the maze of plank-walks linking the water villages of Kampung Ayer
» Trekking though Brunei's Peradayan Forest Reserve
» Feasting on an abundance of satay, barbecued fish, and pancakes filled with peanuts, raisins and sugar at a local food market

GETTING UNDER THE SKIN

» **Read** *Time and the River* by Prince Mohamed Bolkiah, penned by the sultan's youngest brother
» **Listen** to the Brunei national anthem, a cheery tribute to the sultan and to prosperity

4.

» **Watch** any number of pirated DVDs – Brunei's film industry is virtually nonexistent and censorship is entrenched, but video piracy is booming

» **Eat** *roti chanai* for breakfast – flaky flat bread accompanied by coconut curry dipping sauce

» **Drink** fresh fruit juices and luridly coloured soy drinks

IN A WORD

» *Panas* (hot)

TRADEMARKS

» Flamboyant sultans; exotic waterways; excellent medical and education services; a place for your liver to recuperate; strict drug laws; a tax haven

SURPRISES

» Daily oil production: 163,000 barrels; the oil supply is predicted to run out in 2030

MAP REF L,32

(1.) A fisherman paddles along the mangrove swamps beside the Brunei River
(2.) The magnificent Sultan Omar Ali Saifuddien Mosque in Bandar Seri Begawan
(3.) Children play on the verandah of their home in Bandar Seri Begawan
(4.) Boats speed through the floating villages of Kampung Ayer

1.

BULGARIA

Since the early 1990s Bulgaria has morphed into a more modern version of itself, attracting tourists with its cheap skiing, beach holidays on the Black Sea coast, bustling capital Sofia, dramatic mountains, havenlike monasteries, Roman and Byzantine ruins, and excellent coffee. In the villages you can still find folk who ride a donkey to work, eat homegrown potatoes and make their own cheese – the difference now is that dinner is eaten in front of a satellite TV.

BEST TIME TO VISIT

» April to mid-June (spring) – and in 863 to help saints Kiril and Metodii create the Cyrillic alphabet

ESSENTIAL EXPERIENCES

» Skiing down Bulgaria's affordable snowy peaks
» Sipping full-bodied aromatic coffee in a Sofia café
» Walking through the strikingly beautiful Rila Mountains, encountering deers, wild goats, eagles and falcons among the forests of fir trees and beechwoods
» Basking on the beach at Burgas on the Black Sea coast
» Sampling a glass of dark red wine at Melnik in a centuries-old wine bar cut into the rocks
» Reflecting and contemplating life at revered Rila Monastery, a significant symbol of national identity

GETTING UNDER THE SKIN

» **Read** *Bulgarian Rhapsody: The Best of Balkan Cuisine* by Linda J Forristal – an informative cookbook with delicious recipes and snippets of Bulgarian culture and history
» **Listen** to Orthodox chants sung by a 100-strong choir at the Aleksander Nevski Church, Sofia
» **Watch** *Under the Same Sky,* an award-winning film of the Sofia International Film Festival directed by Krasimir Krumov, about a

2.

15-year-old girl who goes in search of her father

» **Eat** *kyopolou*, baked eggplant with garlic and walnuts, a Varna speciality

» **Drink** a glass of red wine, a tradition in Bulgaria since the 6th century BC

IN A WORD

» *Blagodarya, mersi* (thank you)

TRADEMARKS

» Monasteries; feta; rose petals; ancient ruins; hearty meat and vegetable stews; kooky festivals; traditional fire-dancing

SURPRISES

» There are over 160 monasteries; rose oil is a major export; Bulgaria is the world's fifth-largest exporter of wine

MAP REF G,22

(1.) Two elderly women observe the street from the steps of a house in southwest Bulgaria
(2.) The majestic Hrelyu Tower and church domes of the Rila Monastery, Rila Mountains
(3.) Women in a donkey and trap clatter their way into the town of Veliko Târnovo
(4.) A street vendor is nicely framed among the stars at a Sofia newsstand

1.

ERIC WHEATER

Between Sahelian empires and coastal kingdoms, between Muslim and animist Africa, between Saharan desertscapes and southern waterfalls, Burkina Faso weaves many of Africa's diverging strands into a fascinating and thoroughly seductive fabric. In the markets, turbaned traders on camels mix with farmers on donkey-drawn carts in a colourful swirl of diverse ethnic groups. The Burkinabé are descended from a long line of regal emperors who have suffered the plebeian indignities of colonialism and blackbirding, but this has only served to strengthen and preserve their cultural identity.

BEST TIME TO VISIT

November to February

ESSENTIAL EXPERIENCES

» Strolling through Ouagadougou by day and then dancing the night away
» Marvelling at the intricate decoration of Bani's seven mosques
» Kicking back in the languid charm of Bobo-Dioulasso, with its old quarter and distinctive Grande Mosquée
» Exploring the other-worldly landscapes of the Sindou Peaks
» Wandering amid the colour of Gorom-Gorom's Thursday market
» Swimming in the Karfiguéla waterfalls in the dry season

GETTING UNDER THE SKIN

» **Read** *The Maxims, Thoughts and Riddles of the Mossi* by Dim-Dolobsom Ouedraogo, which offers a glimpse of Burkina Faso barely 30 years after the French colonised it
» **Listen** to Idak Bassave's *Les Mêmes Problèmes*
» **Watch** *Les Etrangers* by Mamadou Kola Djim, or *Samba Traoré* by Idrissa Ouedraogo – both are excellent Burkinabé directors

127

2.

ANTHONY HAM

3.

4.

» **Eat** *pintade grillé* (grilled guinea fowl) or *riz sauce* (rice with sauce)
» **Drink** *Brakina* or *So.b.bra* – popular lager-type beers

IN A WORD
» Start the day with some Moré (the language of the Mossi):
yee-bay-roh (good morning)

TRADEMARKS
» The Pan-African Film Festival; a 'don't worry be happy' attitude;
one of the world's poorest countries

SURPRISES
» Burkina Faso literally translates as 'Homeland of the Incorrupt-
ible', or 'Country of Honest Men'. As a means of fostering unity
among an ethnically diverse people, the name was coined from
two of the country's most widely spoken languages: the Moré
word for 'pure' and the Dioula word for 'homeland'.

MAP REF K,20

(1.) The thoughtful stare of a young Burkinabé boy
(2.) Burkinabé lads play table soccer, a popular pastime in Burkina Faso
(3.) A street scene of downtown Ouagadougou, the nation's capital
(4.) Peul women wearing bright colours and smiles at the Gorom-Gorom market, Oudalan
(5.) A young herdsman squints at the sun from beneath a traditional straw hat
(6.) The traditional mud architecture of the Grande Mosquée of Bobo-Dioulasso

1.

Wedged between Tanzania, Rwanda and the Democratic Republic of Congo (Zaïre) is the tiny mountainous nation of Burundi. A turbulent history of tribal wars and factional struggles has left its scars on the beautiful landscape, and colonisation has only complicated the conflict. Civil war is synonymous with the nation and gunfire is not uncommon in the capital, Bujumbura.

BEST TIME TO VISIT

Avoid the extremes of the wet season (May to September) and dry season (June to August and December to January)

ESSENTIAL EXPERIENCES

» Going on safari to spot monkeys and chimpanzees in Parc National de la Kibira, the largest rainforest in Burundi
» Getting in before the curfew after a night drinking in Bujumbura's vibrant restaurants and bars
» Cruising across Lake Tanganyika all the way to Tanzania
» Lazing by the lake at Plage des Cocotiers (Coconut Beach)
» Investigating Source du Nil, the country's claim to the origin of Africa's celebrated river
» Getting historical at La Pierre de Livingstone et Stanley – the alleged site of the legendary 'Dr Livingstone, I presume?' encounter

GETTING UNDER THE SKIN

» **Read** Ahmedou Ould-Abdallah's *Burundi on the Brink 1993–95*, a heart-rending account by the former UN ambassador about his efforts to bring peace
» **Listen** to *Drummers of Burundi: Live at Real World*, a truly skin-splitting performance
» **Watch** *Gito the Ungrateful*, the story of a cosmopolitan young Burundian's return to his homeland

131

5.

» **Eat** *busoma*, a cereal made from corn, soybeans and sorghum
» **Drink** *impeke*, a beer brewed from sorghum, which is commonly served at family gatherings

IN A WORD

» *Bwa* ('hello' in Kirundi)

TRADEMARKS

» Safaris through dense jungle; civil war raging through the streets; Lake Tanganyika dwarfed by surrounding mountains; colonial explorers in pith helmets; the 'Heart of Africa' nickname; abundant chimps and gorillas

SURPRISES

» Secluded in the mountains and forests, the Twa tribal group still live an uninterrupted hunter-gatherer lifestyle just as their ancestors have for thousands of years

RWANDA

• Kirund

Muyinga •

• Kayanza

DEMOCRATIC
REPUBLIC
OF CONGO
(ZAÏRE)

• Muramvya

Cankuzo •

🏵 **Bujumbura**

• Gitega

*Lake
Tanganyika*

TANZANIA

• Bururi

• Makamba

MAP REF M,23

(1.) Open wide and say 'Aaahhh' – hippos in Lake Tanganyika
(2.) Taking some time out in the shade of a picnic shelter on the shores of Lake Tanganyika
(3.) A uniformed band member blows his horn at a peace march in Bujumbura
(4.) Women draped in vibrant fabrics share a giggle on the streets of Bujumbura
(5.) Skilful families of the Twa tribe create durable traditional pots

1.

JULIET COOMBE

The spectres of Pol Pot and the Khmer Rouge still haunt Cambodia, but peace and optimism are slowly returning and there's a frontier-style excitement and entrepreneurial zing to the place. Take saffron-robed monks, lichen-covered ruins, hard-core *moto* traffic and clouds of dragonflies, and mix with jasmine-scented sunsets, gracious colonial boulevards, gorgeous silks and rioting bougainvilleas, garnish with the zest of Buddhism and serve at steaming temperatures.

BEST TIME TO VISIT

November to January, when humidity levels are low

ESSENTIAL EXPERIENCES

- » Gliding down the Mekong River past houseboats and villages
- » Gazing at the beautiful temples of Angkor, among the foremost architectural wonders of the world, at sunset or sunrise
- » Trekking in Bokor National Park and swimming in its waterfall
- » Joining in the mayhem of the Water Festival in Phnom Penh
- » Taking a *moto* trip through the capital in the jasmine-and-pepper scented air of sunset, taking you past the Royal Palace and down to the waterfront

GETTING UNDER THE SKIN

- » **Read** *The River of Time*, by John Swain – a journalistic memoir of the Khmer Rouge and the tragedy of people who find themselves in situations beyond their control
- » **Listen** to the unmistakable sound of monks chanting
- » **Watch** *The Killing Fields* – the gut-wrenching account of the reign of the Khmer Rouge, and of ordinary Cambodians caught up in the madness
- » **Eat** sticky banana – a baked banana wrapped in rice, inside a banana leaf; fish *amok* – a coconut fish curry, served in a coconut;

2.

3.

4.

5.

fried spiders – by all accounts they taste like…chicken

» **Drink** soda and fresh lime – nothing beats the heat quite as well; Angkor beer, the award-winning local beer

IN A WORD

» *Niak teuv naa?* (where are you going?)

TRADEMARKS

» Monks in saffron robes with yellow umbrellas; manic traffic; Apsara dancers; street urchins; ceiling fans; meticulously clean cyclos; beautiful silks; the Mekong; trucks crowded with people from the provinces; rice paddies; coconut palms; the smell of jasmine

SURPRISES

» Cambodia is not as cheap as other destinations in the region; the sun goes down between 5pm and 6pm regardless of the time of year; luxury items such as French wines are available in supermarkets

MAP REF K,31

(1.) Traditional Khmer dancing taught in a Siem Reap classroom for both boys and girls
(2.) Saffron-robed monks queuing during an event at the ancient site of Angkor
(3.) Sunlight illuminates the face of a man holding incense, Angkor
(4.) Angkor Wat at dawn
(5.) Massive roots frame the entrance to the mysterious Ta Prohm Temple

1.

At the crossroads of West Africa and Central Africa, Cameroon is one of the most culturally diverse countries on the continent – rich in indigenous cultures, vibrant artistic and musical traditions, and wonderful Cameroonian hospitality. The country is made up of a network of ancient tribal kingdoms, and offers visitors the choice of rainforests and relaxing beaches in the south; rocky outcrops, terraced hillsides and hobbit-like villages in the north; and the wildlife of Parc National de Waza.

BEST TIME TO VISIT
» March and April, for wildlife viewing before the rains come

ESSENTIAL EXPERIENCES
» Bargaining for local crafts at Foumban's artisans market
» Dining on grilled fish on the beaches around Limbe and Kribi
» Exploring the mountains and picturesque villages around Maroua
» Climbing Mt Cameroon, West Africa's highest peak
» Watching wildlife at Parc National de Waza
» Hiking among ancient tribal kingdoms and striking mountain scenery in the Ring Road area near Bamenda

GETTING UNDER THE SKIN
» **Read** *The Poor Christ of Bomb*, Mongo Beti's cynical recounting of the failure of a missionary to convert the people of a small village, or Kenjo Jumban's novel *The White Man of God,* which deals with the country's colonial experience
» **Listen** to Manu Dibango's hit album *Soul Makossa*
» **Watch** *Afrique, Je Te Plumerai* (Africa, I Will Fleece You), directed by Jean-Marie Teno, an outstanding documentary about modern Cameroon life
» **Eat** delicious sauces accompanied by *riz* (rice), or with *pâte* or *fufu*, both thick mashed potato-like staples made from corn,

2.

DAVID WALL

manioc, plantains or bananas; *feuille* (manioc leaves)

» **Drink** tea served with loads of sugar in a small glass or, if you're feeling brave, tackle a white *mimbo* (local brew)

IN A WORD

» *No ngoolu daa* (hello)

TRADEMARKS

» Tribal kingdoms; Pygmies; black rhinos; trekking; great food; *makossa* music

SURPRISES

» When travelling to areas that see few outsiders, it's always best to announce your presence to the local chief (known as the *fon* in western Cameroon, and *lamido* in parts of the north). The ruler of the Bamoun is known as the sultan, and the Bamoun can trace the lineage of their sultan back to 1394.

CAMEROON

ANTHONY HAM

MAP REF L,21

(1.) Pipers play in front of the Sultan's Palace in Foumban
(2.) Giant volcanic plugs in Rhumsiki
(3.) A Rhumsiki man known as the Crab Sorcerer displays some of the tools of his trade
(4.) Trees dot the arid landscape of Rhumsiki and the surrounding Mandara Mountains

141

1.

JEFF GREENBERG

CAPITAL OTTAWA POPULATION 32,207,113 AREA 9,984,670 SQ KM OFFICIAL LANGUAGES ENGLISH, FRENCH

Canada's wild northern frontier has etched itself into the national psyche, and its distinct patchwork of peoples has created a country that is decidedly different from its southern neighbour. It's the sovereignty of Canada's indigenous, French and British traditions that gives the nation its complex three-dimensional character. Add to this a constant infusion of US culture and a plethora of traditions brought by immigrants, and you have a thriving multicultural society.

BEST TIME TO VISIT

March to November – spring, summer and autumn

ESSENTIAL EXPERIENCES

» Gorging on a whopping big lobster supper on the delectable Prince Edward Island
» Checking out fog-bound Halifax, one of the world's largest natural harbours
» Chilling out in the old town of Montréal – the streets are filled with musicians, restaurants, groovy shops and a general atmosphere of *bonhomie*
» Spotting arctic wildlife in Churchill – from polar bears and beluga whales to caribou and arctic foxes
» Hiking in Auyuittuq National Park, a pristine wilderness of mountains, valleys, fjords and meadows
» Visiting the historic Viking settlement at L'Anse aux Meadows
» Canoeing in Algonquin Provincial Park

GETTING UNDER THE SKIN

» **Read** Margaret Atwood's Booker Prize–winning *Blind Assassin*, and Michael Ondaatje's *In the Skin of a Lion*, both set in 1930s Canada
» **Listen** to Leonard Cohen, Neil Young, Rufus Wainwright and the Cowboy Junkies

2.

3.

4.

FRANK CARTER

» **Watch** Bruce Macdonald's *Dance Me Outside* about contemporary Native American Indian life
» **Eat** Oka cheese from Quebec or maple syrup (best served on pancakes with ice cream)
» **Drink** VO ('Very Own') rye whisky, or a cherry cider

IN A WORD

» *Parlez-vous anglais?* (do you speak English?)

TRADEMARKS

» Moose and bears; the Rockies; smoked salmon; Bryan Adams; maple trees

SURPRISES

» Halifax was the base of rescue operations for the *Titanic* tragedy. The plains people, such as the Cree and Blackfoot, were forced into the Europeans' world by the virtual extinction of the buffalo.

MAP REF E,8

(1.) Dancer in traditional costume, Wanuskewin Heritage Park
(2.) Young baseball players watch a game unfold in Calgary
(3.) Families stroll through the sea mists at Long Beach, Pacific Rim National Park Reserve
(4.) Grain silos in early morning light, Denholm, Saskatchewan
(5.) Picnic area in autumn at Waterton Lakes National Park
(6.) Old shop fronts along Rue de la Commune, Montréal

1.

On the islands of Cape Verde you can find lush valleys and mountains, long stretches of white sand, smoking volcanoes and dusty deserts, and pretty towns with cobbled streets. Additionally, there are Portuguese wine and local liquor, sad songs alongside those with a frenetic Latin beat, and exciting diving and windsurfing, hiking and fishing. Islanders mix up African, Portuguese, Mediterranean and Latin influences and come out with a flavour that's distinctly 'Cabo'.

BEST TIME TO VISIT

August to October

ESSENTIAL EXPERIENCES

» Vanishing into the verdant valleys and forests of beautiful Santo Antão island
» Gorging on Cape Verde's delicious fresh fish or famous lobsters
» Losing yourself in the colour and chaos of Mindelo's Mardi Gras, the country's most vibrant festival
» Plunging into the open waters of the Atlantic and seeking out sharks, manta rays and whales
» Huffing and puffing to the top of Mt Fogo, an active volcano, still spouting its stuff
» Cooing over a *coladeira* or two sung by a talented local singer

GETTING UNDER THE SKIN

» **Read** poet Jorge Barbosa's *Arquipélago*, which is laden with melancholic reflections on the sea, and longings for liberation
» **Listen** to the undisputed star of *mornas* and *coladeiras* Cesária Évora
» **Watch** *O Testamento do Senhor Napumoceno* (Napumoceno's Will), a comedy about social and sexual mores among Cape Verde's bourgeoisie

2.

3.

4.

» **Eat** the national dish, *cachupa* (a tasty stew of several kinds of beans plus corn and various kinds of meat)

» **Drink** *grogue* (grog), the local sugar cane spirit; *ponch* (rum, lemonade and honey), or Ceris, a decent bottled local beer

IN A WORD

» *Bom-dee-ah* ('good morning' in Crioulo)

TRADEMARKS

» Portuguese cultural legacy; volcanic islands; high literacy rate; *mornas*; *coladeiras* and *funaná* music

SURPRISES

» The razo lark (*Alauda razae*) is one of the rarest birds in the world (only 250 are thought to remain). Many indigenous inhabitants have left Cape Verde and now expats outnumber the islanders.

MAP REF J,17

(1.) The imposing Mt Fogo volcano (last eruption 1995), Ilhas do Sotavento region
(2.) Every man and his dog help launch a fishing boat in Sao Pedro village
(3.) The small town of Paul on Santo Antão island, perched on the tip of the Atlantic
(4.) Children play table football in Ponta do Sol
(5.) A Cape Verde local gives a wry smile
(6.) Colourful boats line the beaches

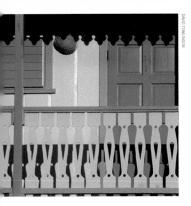

DAVID TOMLINSON

STEVE ROSENBERG

JEFF GREENBERG

The Cayman Islands are dotted with deal-cutting characters with briefcases and mobile phones, scuba divers in wetsuits and English folk checking the cricket scores. The islands are colourful: coral reefs, bright orange frogfish, sociable stingrays and reggae beats on the street. As a result of the islands' mellow charms, resorts and condos have sprung up all over. But if you want to get away from it all there are lots of places to escape satellite dishes and slickness, not least of them underwater.

BEST TIME TO VISIT

June to October to avoid the peak season

ESSENTIAL EXPERIENCES

» Diving famous dive spots such as the Bloody Bay Wall and Jackson Point on the northwestern coast of Little Cayman

» Strolling the mile-long trail that winds through the Queen Elizabeth II Botanic Park – lush terrain, orchids, iguanas and parrots

» Treasure-hunting on Cayman Brac – spelunkers can go caving along the northern shore, where legend has it pirates used to stow away their loot

» Meandering through Mastic Trail – the old-growth forest that once supplied early settlers with timber

» Sightseeing on Cayman Brac, which is covered in fruit trees, orchids and cacti, and surrounded by good beaches

GETTING UNDER THE SKIN

» **Read** *The Cayman Islands: The Beach and Beyond* by Martha K Smith – excellent for those who think being a beach bunny is boring

» **Listen** to West Indian soca, calypso and reggae

» **Watch** the action beneath the waves if you happen to be in the Caymans for the annual International Underwater Film Festival
» **Eat** local specialties at the annual cooking festival, known simply as The Cook Off, in May, or the Taste of Cayman festival in June
» **Drink** a cold beer after a day's diving, or sip on a gin and tonic

IN A WORD

» *Brac* (actually a Gaelic word meaning bluff)

TRADEMARKS

» Shipwrecks; pirate history; condos; resorts; snorkelling and diving, diving, diving

SURPRISES

» The Booby Pond Nature Reserve is home to one of the hemisphere's largest breeding populations of red-footed boobies. Cayman Turtle Farm is the only one of its kind in the world. This government-run operation raises green turtles to increase their population in the wild and – slightly more disturbing – sell their meat and shells.

MAP REF J,11

(1.) A studious school of schoolmaster snapper
(2.) The colourful door and balcony of a house in George Town
(3.) A green turtle finds its way through the coral labyrinth of The Maze on Grand Cayman
(4.) A craft shop vendor in East End posing beneath coconut bird feeders
(5.) An empty jetty awaits the threatening approach of a hurricane

1.

TONY WHEELER

A country of rare natural beauty, with some of the world's most amazing wildlife, Central African Republic (CAR) is nonetheless underdeveloped, fragmented and poverty-stricken. It's a country that has important mineral deposits and great natural resources, yet precious little of the wealth generated seeps down to the population. For centuries CAR has endured rapacity, first from invaders, later from its own leaders, and the situation doesn't look like changing any time soon. True to the spirit of 'real' Africa, however, the people of this plundered nation are open, friendly and generous.

BEST TIME TO VISIT

November to April (dry season)

ESSENTIAL EXPERIENCES

» Buying ebony sculptures, leathergoods and batiks at Bangui's artisans centre
» Taking a guided tour of 'Emperor' Bokassa's former palace outside the capital, past lion cages and other gruesome relics of his time in power
» Spotting wildlife at St Floris and Bamingui-Bangoran parks
» Visiting the spectacular Chutes de Boali (Boali Waterfalls) during the rainy season
» Trekking through the Dzanga-Sangha Reserve

GETTING UNDER THE SKIN

» **Read** *The Central African Republic: The Continent's Hidden Heart*, a social history by Thomas E O'Toole
» **Listen** to *Aka Pygmy Music*, a Unesco recording
» **Eat** the staples, which are rice, fermented cassava (manioc root) and bananas

» **Drink** a jug of home-brewed palm or banana wine

IN A WORD
» *Bara ala kwe* (hello in the Sango language)

TRADEMARKS
» Forest elephants; lowland gorillas; Pygmies; dictators; political chaos

SURPRISES
» Hunting safaris are still huge business in CAR, and have been ever since the French arrived a century ago and began parcelling up the land into hunting estates. Big-game hunting grounds near the Sudanese border were personally sponsored by former French president, Giscard d'Estaing.

MAP REF L,22

(1.) A group of Ba'Aka pygmies makes its journey into the Dzanga-Sangha National Park
(2.) A blue duiker is divided up and prepared by Ba'Aka pygmies after a successful hunt
(3.) A domesticated goat rests beside a mud hut on the road from Bangui to Kembe Falls
(4.) A group of children gathers outside brightly painted store doors in Sangha

With one of the most painful histories in Africa, Chad is a nation with its foundations built on conflict. The harsh climate, geographic remoteness, poor resource endowment and lack of infrastructure have combined to create a weak economy susceptible to political turmoil. There's the promise of a more optimistic future though – Chad's position as one of the world's poorest nations may change if the country's oil industry takes off.

BEST TIME TO VISIT

December to mid-February, when the days are dry and warm and the nights quite cool

ESSENTIAL EXPERIENCES

» Living it up in Chad's capital, N'Djaména, with markets, bars and a thriving live-music scene
» Photographing the country's best wildlife inside Zakouma National Park
» Chilling out in Moundou's riverside bars with an icy beer
» Haggling yourself hoarse in the frontier markets of Mao
» Witnessing the cultural clash of the old town of Abéché, the gateway to exploring the Sudan
» Dancing the night away in Sarh, the capital of the south

GETTING UNDER THE SKIN

» **Read** *Chad: A Nation in Search of Its Future* by Mario J Azevedo and Emmanuel U Nnadozie, presenting an economic, political and social view of the nation
» **Listen** to the lute, a long-necked guitar popular in Chad and heard on *Africa: Anthology of the Music of Chad*
» **Watch** *Abouna* (Our Father), a heart-rending feature filmed in Chad in which two boys search for their lost father

CHAD

CAPITAL N'DJAMÉNA POPULATION 9,253,493 AREA 1,284,000 SQ KM OFFICIAL LANGUAGES FRENCH, ARABIC

» **Eat** a hearty dish of *nachif* (finely minced meat in sauce)

» **Drink** a Gala beer in Moundou, straight from the brewery

IN A WORD

» *Harmattan* (dry, dusty Saharan wind)

TRADEMARKS

» Desert expanses; unpaved roads; unsettled relationship with Libya; impoverished citizens; mud-brick architecture

SURPRISES

» To (legally) take photos in Chad, visitors need a permit from the Ministry of Information; an estimated one billion barrels of oil could be extracted from the Doba Basin

MAP REF K,22

(1.) Children fetch water and women wash clothes as their herds drink from the lake at Adré
(2.) The impressive exterior of the cathedral in N'Djaména, built in French colonial times
(3.) A fluffy cloud of harvested cotton in southern Chad
(4.) A young herdsman rides his water-laden donkey between Abéché and Adré
(5.) A man waits outside a mud-brick building in Gaoui Village, N'Djaména

1.

It may look like a long string bean but Chile is among South America's richest countries, both economically and culturally. For years exploited internally by unsavoury leadership and externally by the great powers of the northern continent, Chile has surfaced as vibrant, economically stable and resilient. It boasts myriad sights and cultures, and is well recognised as a safe destination for travellers, who feel right at home thanks to the Chileans' warmth and generosity.

BEST TIME TO VISIT

September to December (spring)

ESSENTIAL EXPERIENCES

» Driving a 4WD across the sand dunes of the Atacama desert
» Watching cosmopolitan life in Santiago go by from the Terraza Neptuno on Cerro Santa Lucia
» Skiing the slopes of the high Cordillera in Middle Chile
» Standing next to one of the colossal *moai* of Easter Island (Rapa Nui), and wondering how the heck they got there
» Travelling to Chile's rugged southern tip, considered to be 'the end of the world', to watch the breaching whales

GETTING UNDER THE SKIN

» **Read** Isabel Allende's *House of the Spirits*, the story of a Chilean family depicted with modern-day realism and a dose of the supernatural
» **Listen** to Victor Jara, murdered after Pinochet's 1973 coup, who sang about political issues of the time; local singer Nicole, who is signed to Madonna's Latin music label
» **Watch** Cristián Galaz's *El Chacotero Sentimental* (The Sentimental Teaser), a popular and highly awarded film about love stories on the radio

2.

3.

4.

- » **Eat** *empanadas fritas* (fried pasties with ground beef and spices)
- » **Drink** Mistral beer or try a foamy pisco sour (brandy with lemon juice, powdered sugar and egg white)

IN A WORD
- » *Ah, que rico(a)* – normally used when describing a tasty dish (but just as applicable when referring to a good-looking person)

TRADEMARKS
- » The Andean condor; cowboys; the Allendes; Pinochet; micro buses; magic realism; street vendors; great wine; Michelle Bachelet (Chile's first female president)

SURPRISES
- » Reality TV is an unexpected hit in Chile; Chileans often work six days a week, but are always ready for a *carrete* (party)

MAP REF Q,12

(1.) Lush marshlands carpet the foreground of Parinacota volcano in Lauca National Park
(2.) The mysterious *moai* of Ahu Akivi wait under brooding sky on Easter Island
(3.) El Tatio Geysers on the Chilean north plains in the light of dawn
(4.) Fishing boats packed like sardines at the harbour in Antofagasta
(5.) Sisters in Temuco share a favourite doll
(6.) The benign face of a hardcore rodeo competitor in Rancagua

1.

Recent times have seen a ceaseless drama of energetic development and economic contortions unfold in China. Emerging from the austerities and craziness of the Mao era, the country is now a full member of the World Trade Organization, and is home to the 2008 Beijing Olympics. Massive investment has radically improved transport quality, and travel has become steadily speedier and more comfortable. China has never been so transformed, except perhaps when the Mongols passed through with their own blueprints for change.

BEST TIME TO VISIT

March to May and September to November are best, avoiding the extremes of winter and summer

ESSENTIAL EXPERIENCES

» Adding the Great Wall sites near Beijing to your must-sees
» Paying a mandatory visit to the ancient Forbidden City and Summer Palace in Beijing
» Parading through the Army of Terracotta Warriors, grand reminders of China's imperial past
» Enjoying the more-familiar Western atmosphere of Shanghai
» Chilling out in Xishuangbanna's lush, subtropical rainforest

GETTING UNDER THE SKIN

» **Read** Jonathan D Spence's *The Search for Modern China* – perhaps the most readable attempt to encompass Chinese modern history in a single volume; the novels of Pearl S Buck, including *The Good Earth* and *Imperial Woman*
» **Listen** to *Moon Rising in the Rosy Clouds*, a selection of classical and modern works featuring traditional instruments by the Chinese National Orchestra

2.

3.

4.

» **Watch** the films of Zhang Yimou, of the 'Fifth Generation' film movement, including *Shanghai Triad* and *Raise the Red Lantern*

» **Eat** Peking duck in Beijing; anything with four legs in Guangzhou

» **Drink** *chá* (tea); as political surveillance relaxes, China's teahouses, traditional centres of gossip and intrigue, are making a comeback

IN A WORD

» *Tài guì le!* (too expensive!)

TRADEMARKS

» Pandas; unchecked development; students practising English on tourists; Tiananmen Square; noodles; the Great Wall

SURPRISES

» The one-child policy is open to interpretation: rural families may have two children (so long as the first is a girl)

MAP REF H,30

(1.) School children prepare to clean the streets of Shenyang
(2.) The spice markets come to life at night in Guangzhou
(3.) Monks ascend stairs in the Dongcheng district of Beijing
(4.) The sun touches the ancient Great Wall of China and surrounding hills
(5.) A Zhuang girl works in the water-soaked rice terraces of Long Ji, Guangxi
(6.) Bicycles flood Beijing's streets during rush hour

1.

For many, Colombia is unknown territory – a place of cocaine barons, guerrillas and mysterious lost cities. It is the land of Gabriel García Márquez and his *One Hundred Years of Solitude* – a tale as magical as the country itself. Far from being a place to avoid, complex and hospitable Colombia offers some of South America's most varied landscapes, flora and fauna. As you travel through this diverse country, you'll discover a changing panorama of climate, architecture, topography, wildlife, crafts and music.

BEST TIME TO VISIT

January to March (the dry season)

ESSENTIAL EXPERIENCES

» Visiting Cartagena – this is a living museum of Spanish colonial architecture
» Beachcombing at coastal Parque Nacional Tayrona
» Photographing the enigmatic stone statues at San Agustín – a pre-Hispanic ceremonial funeral site
» Hanging out in the great cosmopolitan metropolis of Bogotá
» Hiking to Ciudad Perdida, one of the greatest pre-Hispanic cities found in the Americas, hidden in a lush rainforest

GETTING UNDER THE SKIN

» **Read** *One Hundred Years of Solitude* by Nobel prize winner Gabriel García Márquez, or anything by poet José Asunción Silva
» **Listen** to Colombia's most famous musical export Shakira, whose album *Laundry Service* stormed charts in 2002. For some traditional Afro-Caribbean tunes check out Totó La Momposina.
» **Watch** *Ilona Arrives with the Rain* or *Time Out* by Colombian film director Sergio Cabrera

5.

» **Eat** *ajiaco* (chicken and potato soup); or, for the more adventurous, *hormiga culona* (a dish consisting largely of fried ants)

» **Drink** coffee, the number one drink – *tinto* (a small cup of black coffee) is served everywhere. Other coffee drinks are *perico* or *pintado*, a small milk coffee, and the larger, milkier *café con leche*.

IN A WORD

» *Chévere* (cool)

TRADEMARKS

» Coffee; emeralds; lost cities; El Dorado; football

SURPRISES

» Colombia claims to have the highest number of species of plants and animals per unit area of any country in the world; Laguna de Guatavita, the sacred lake and ritual centre of the indigenous Muiscas, is where the myth of El Dorado originated

MAP REF L,12

(1.) The spiny trunks of Colombia's national tree, La Palma de Cera, protrude from a Quindío hillside
(2.) Bathers transform themselves into living statues in the muddy Volcán de Lodo El Totumo
(3.) A leering megalithic statue guards the entrance to San Agustín Archaeological Park
(4.) High-stepping street performers entertain crowds in Plaza de Bolívar, Bogotá
(5.) The primary colours and vacant streets of Ráquira make it resemble a model village

1.

Studding the Indian Ocean between the African mainland and Madagascar, the islands of Comoros and Mayotte offer an amazing diversity of people and cultures. Despite a succession of political coups and civilian riots, the islands boast cobblestoned medinas, ports bustling with dhows, tropical moon-rises over white-sand beaches and blazing ocean sunsets that set the sky on fire. All this is wrapped in the fragrant aroma of ylang-ylang oil, African warmth, French chic and Arabic aesthetics, and a colourful history of sultans, eloping princesses and plantation owners.

BEST TIME TO VISIT

May to October (dry season)

ESSENTIAL EXPERIENCES

- » Discovering the coral reefs and white sandy beaches at Chiroroni
- » Breathing in the scents of the ylang-ylang distillery at Bamboa
- » Walking through the decaying palaces at Hari ya Moudji
- » Fishing, diving and boating in the waters of Mayotte
- » Finding the perfect hand-crafted souvenir at Mitsoudjé
- » Green sea turtle–watching at Chissioua Ouénéfou
- » Hiking past majestic waterfalls and beautiful deserted beaches
- » Swimming in the pristine waters on Anjouan

GETTING UNDER THE SKIN

- » **Read** *The Comoros Islands: Struggle Against Dependency in the Indian Ocean*, by Malyn Newitt, which outlines the turbulent recent history of the region
- » **Listen** to a performance by the Maalesh Group, a group of musicians led by Comoran-born Maalesh who sing songs of injustice and hope in Comoran, Swahili and Arabic

2.

3.

4.

» **Eat** *langouste à la vanille* (lobster cooked in vanilla sauce) or rice and meat infused with cardamom, vanilla, cinammon, cloves and nutmeg, or fish with coconut

IN A WORD

» *Habari* or *salama* ('hello' in Comoran)

TRADEMARKS

» Magnificent blue-green clear ocean waters; fields of ylang-ylang, jasmine, cassis and orange flower; blazing sunsets; long, white beaches; beautiful rainforests; political turmoil; excellent seafood; mosques; scuba diving; big-game fishing

SURPRISES

» Swahili-inspired architecture with arcades, balustrades and carved wooden latticework; Comoran women with faces applied with a yellowish paste of sandalwood and coral *(m'sidzanou)*

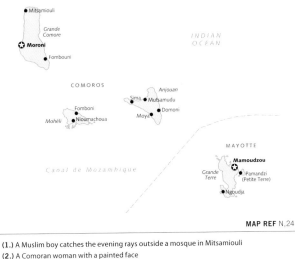

MAP REF N.24

(1.) A Muslim boy catches the evening rays outside a mosque in Mitsamiouli
(2.) A Comoran woman with a painted face
(3.) A man outside a rural mosque made of corrugated iron
(4.) The crater lake of Dziani Dzaha, Mayotte
(5.) Children share a joke in Moroni
(6.) Markets burst with colour on Grande Comore Island

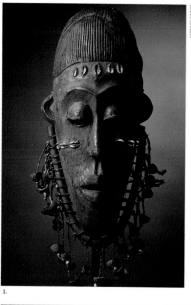

1.

2.

3.

LEANNE LOGAN

Almost as large as Western Europe, the Democratic Republic of Congo is a sprawling mass of rainforest, fast-running rivers, red clay and dust – the epitome of Joseph Conrad's *Heart of Darkness*. Formerly called Zaïre, and now often shortened to DRC, it remains intoxicatingly mysterious and largely cut off to visitors, thanks to civil war, lack of development, and naturally impenetrable terrain. The country clings to a fragile ceasefire after decades of brutal civil war and neglect, but if the situation stabilises it has the potential to reclaim its mantle as Africa's most adventurous destination.

BEST TIME TO VISIT

December to February (north of the equator), April to October (south of the equator)

ESSENTIAL EXPERIENCES

- » Experiencing hectic, confusing and colourful Kinshasa
- » Playing with bonobos (pygmy chimps) and enjoying the lakes at Chutes de Lukia
- » Perusing the fish market at Kinkole – constructed by Mobutu to honour the country's fishermen
- » Travelling by barge from Kinshasa to Kisangani along the Congo River – the real highway of Central Africa

GETTING UNDER THE SKIN

- » **Read** about Mobutu's looting as a form of government in Michaela Wrong's *In The Footsteps of Mr Kurtz*; or *The Catastrophist* by Ronan Bennett, a novel built around Patrice Lumumba, the charismatic leader of the fight for independence from Belgium
- » **Listen** to the *soukous* of Africa's Elvis Presley, Papa Wemba
- » **Watch** Ngangura Mweze's *Life is Rosy* – a celebration of the

4.

CONGO, DEMOCRATIC REPUBLIC OF (ZAÏRE)

Congolese culture and folklore, starring Papa Wemba
» **Eat** barbecued goat and manioc from street vendors, and *liboke* (fish stewed in manioc leaves)
» **Drink** beer from a roadside stall

IN A WORD
» *Mbóte* (hello)

TRADEMARKS
» Virgin jungle; bustling rivers; primates; political and military strife; *Heart of Darkness*

SURPRISES
» Bonobos are the closest relatives to humans; the recent civil war fought between rival Congolese militias (the proxy armies of Uganda and Rwanda) has caused the death of an estimated 2.5 million people

CENTRAL AFRICAN REPUBLIC
SUDAN
Gbadolite
CAMEROON
Bumba
Lake Albert
Kisangani
REP. OF CONGO
GABON
Mbandaka
Lac Tumba
UGANDA
Lac Mai-Ndombe
Goma
Bukavu
RWANDA
Kindu
BURUNDI
Kinshasa
Ilebo
Kikwit
Matadi
Kananga
Boma
Tshikapa
Mbuji-Mayi
Kalemie
TANZANIA
Lake Tanganyika
Lake Mweru
ATLANTIC OCEAN
ANGOLA
Kolwez
Likasi
Lubumbashi
ZAMBIA

MAP REF M,22

(1.) This striking work of art portrays the elongated head of a Mangbetu ruler
(2.) A tribal pygmy woman sits with her family as her hair is styled in Mount Hoyo
(3.) A stylish balancing act walks with ease down the market road
(4.) Gentle giant – a mountain gorilla enjoys a light snack in the Virunga volcanoes

1.

The Republic of Congo is a former French colony on the west Atlantic coast of central Africa. The countryside around Brazzaville is all rolling hills and lush greenery; further north, there's bright orange earth and untamed tropical rainforest bristling with wildlife – the Congo boasts Africa's largest lowland gorilla population. After three devastating civil wars in less than a decade, this is a nation of people eager for a laugh and luckily, as the country regains its stability, there's something to smile about.

BEST TIME TO VISIT

June to September, when the season is dry and the temperatures are uniform

ESSENTIAL EXPERIENCES

» Being inspired by the intoxicating blend of Congolese food, culture and music
» Trawling Brazzaville's colourful markets to pick up useful items such as caterpillars, bats, palm wine and aphrodisiacs
» Eating croissants in a Brazzaville café while watching water hyacinths float down the Congo River and black marketeers paddle their pirogues (traditional canoes)
» Spotting a lowland gorilla at Odzala National Park
» Playing a game of *babyfoot* (table football) with friendly locals

GETTING UNDER THE SKIN

» **Read** *Congo Journey* by naturalist Redmond O'Hanlon, who explores the swamplands of the Congo with descriptive style
» **Listen** to *Brazzaville*, an atmospheric compilation of jazz, samba and soul fusion tracks
» **Watch** *Congo*, directed by Frank Marshall and based on a Michael Crichton novel about an unknown race of killer apes – certainly not to be taken seriously

2.

» **Eat** *maboke*, river fish cooked with chilli and wrapped in manioc (cassava) leaves

» **Drink** a huge bottle of refreshing Ngok ('crocodile') beer

IN A WORD

» *Bonjour* (hello)

TRADEMARKS

» A nation of lively, enthusiastic conversationalists; riotous colour and glorious chaos; beaches; Denis Sassou Nguesso; gorillas, chimps and all things monkey; baguettes; a country in recovery; candlelit night markets; Congo River; elephants; civil war; towering office blocks housing foreign oil companies

SURPRISES

» Even Brazzavillois don't know the street names of their city! Instead, everyone makes reference to landmarks.

MAP REF M,21

(1.) A sea of eager young faces at a rainforest school in the town of Pokone

(2.) A Ba'Aka pygmy family outside its temporary leaf house near the Cameroon border

(3.) A fashionable local woman strolls past colourful goods for sale at a market in Pokone

(4.) Ba'Aka pygmies glide through the waters in a dugout canoe

1.

MANFRED GOTTSCHALK

Wafer-thin cays and far-flung atolls, blue lagoons and superb reef snorkelling, white-sand beaches and verdant volcanic mountains, a slow pace and friendly people – what's not to like about the Cook Islands? Lascivious dancing and beer bashes in the bush have survived years of missionary zeal. Rarotonga, the gorgeous main island, has been a Maori hang-out for at least 1500 years and it's easy to see why. Get yourself stranded on an outer island and hope your return-trip freighter doesn't come back any time soon.

BEST TIME TO VISIT
April to November (the dry season)

ESSENTIAL EXPERIENCES
» Hiking the lush, craggy mountains of Rarotonga
» Taking a dip in the turquoise lagoon of Aitutaki
» Dancing and feasting the night away at an 'island night' theme party on Rarotonga or Aitutaki
» Whale-watching from any of the main islands
» Spelunking the various caves of 'Atiu, Ma'uke, Mitiaro and Mangaia
» Photographing the island from Rangimotia, the highest point on Mangaia

GETTING UNDER THE SKIN
» **Read** *An Island to Oneself,* the account of hermit Tom Neale, who lived on Suwarrow Atoll
» **Listen** to *Drums, Songs and Chants of the Cook Islands*, a great sampler of local music
» **Watch** *The Other Side of Heaven*, a delightful coming-of-age tale that was mostly filmed on Rarotonga

2.

3.

4.

5.

DALLAS STRIBLEY

- » **Eat** island fare such as *ika mata* (raw fish in coconut sauce) or *anga kuru akaki ia* (stuffed breadfruit)
- » **Drink** at a *tumunu* (or bush beer-drinking session), akin to the ancient Polynesian kava-drinking ceremonies in Fiji or Samoa

IN A WORD

- » *Kia orana!* (may you live long!) – a greeting

TRADEMARKS

- » Saucy traditional dancing; pandanus-thatched roofs; rich Maori culture; deserted atolls ripe for diving; breadfruit served at every meal; tax haven for well-tanned fat cats

SURPRISES

- » The stunning black pearl jewellery for sale; soulful Christian hymns sung in churches everywhere

Pukapuka

Nassau

Northern Group

SOUTH PACIFIC OCEAN

Aitutaki

Mitiaro

Southern Group

'Atiu

Ma'uke

Rarotonga ✪ **Avarua**

Mangaia

MAP REF 0,3

(1.) A cloud hovers over the island of Rarotonga and Muri lagoon
(2.) Flower-clad school children from Rarotonga
(3.) A local fisherman displays his catch on the island of Aitutaki
(4.) The tropical frangipani flower, native to the Cook Islands
(5.) A student on Rarotonga

1.

For decades, Costa Rica was a forgotten backwater, a country so laconic it couldn't be bothered having an army, even though it was sandwiched between war-torn Nicaragua and Canal-plagued Panama. Then North American retirees discovered its charms and its *poco a poco* (little by little) lifestyle, and Costa Rica became hot property. With its luxuriant rainforests, pristine white beaches, diverse wildlife, to-die-for coffee, relaxed hospitality and full-on eco-tourist trade, Costa Rica is definitely one of the destinations *de jour*.

BEST TIME TO VISIT
December to April (the dry season)

ESSENTIAL EXPERIENCES
» Soaring across the jungle canopy on a flying fox at Monteverde
» Taking time out to sit and ponder the majestic rainforest at Parque Nacional Manuel Antonio
» Making a nocturnal visit to Arenal volcano, followed by a hot spa
» Learning to surf at Tamarindo
» Doing the Fortuna to Saint Elena route by jeep and horseback

GETTING UNDER THE SKIN
» **Read** *Costa Rica: A Traveler's Literary Companion*, 26 short stories that capture the soul of the county
» **Listen** to *Costa Rica: Calypso*, happy calypso tunes for the road, from rootsy trad to pop
» **Watch** *1492: Conquest of Paradise*. This Hollywood version of Colombus' discovery of the New Americas was always going to be problematic – a Frenchman playing an Italian-born employee of the Spanish army interacting with Mayans is asking for trouble. The location shots are stunning though.

COSTA RICA

CAPITAL **SAN JOSÉ** POPULATION **3,896,092** AREA **51,100 SQ KM** OFFICIAL LANGUAGE **SPANISH**

2.

3.

4.

» **Eat** *la olla*, a stew of potatoes, beef, maize, beans and tomatoes
» **Drink** coffee – Costa Rica is possibly the only country in the world where even a takeaway coffee in a Styrofoam cup from a fast-food burger joint tastes like ambrosia

IN A WORD

» *Pura vida* (literally 'pure life', a national expression that sums up the desire to live the best and most pure existence)

TRADEMARKS

» Dripping rainforests; toucans and macaws; erupting volcanoes; La Negrita (or the Black Madonna); dead-keen soccer fans; foaming waterfalls; the aroma of coffee

SURPRISES

» A former president (Oscar Arias Sánchez) is the winner of a Nobel Peace Prize; there are great surfing beaches, but hordes of sharks

MAP REF K,11

(1.) A carnival-coloured keel-billed toucan
(2.) Three boys playing football outside a row of painted buildings, Puerto Limón
(3.) A white-faced capuchin monkey reclines on a branch in his rainforest home
(4.) The dry bed of El Limbo lagoon in Parque Nacional Santa Rosa
(5.) A family gathers in the doorway of their home in Fray Casiano
(6.) Mother and child walk past a run-down wooden church near Puerto Limón

1.

Côte d'Ivoire's most powerful attraction is its people, so if you're interested in African history, art or music, this is the place to be. There's also a whole lot of physical beauty, from towering mountains to fishing villages. For many years Côte d'Ivoire was the jewel of West Africa. Its strong economy attracted thousands of workers from neighbouring countries, and sizeable French and Lebanese communities established themselves in Abidjan. In more recent times, the country has been rocked by huge debts, a military coup and ongoing security problems.

BEST TIME TO VISIT

November to February

ESSENTIAL EXPERIENCES

- » Exploring Grand Bassam's faded colonial charm
- » Experiencing the warmth and friendliness of Ivoirians
- » Taking in a live performance of exhilarating music and masked dance in the Man area
- » Goggling at Yamoussoukro's colossal basilica
- » Soaking up the sun at rainforest-clad beaches, such as Grand Béréby, Grand Lahou or Monogaga
- » Communing with chimpanzees in the Parc National de Taï or with hippos at Parc National de la Comoë

GETTING UNDER THE SKIN

- » **Read** Bernard Dadié's *Climbié*, an autobiographical account of his childhood, or Maurice Bandaman's novel *Le Fils de la Femme Mâle*
- » **Listen** to *Apartheid is Nazism* by Côte d'Ivoire's best-known reggae star, Alpha Blondy
- » **Watch** *Visages des Femmes* (Faces of Women), directed by Côte d'Ivoire's Désiré Ecaré

4.

» **Eat** *kedjenou* (chicken, or sometimes guineafowl, simmered with vegetables in a mild sauce), or snack on *aloco* (ripe bananas fried with chilli in palm oil – it's a popular street food)

» **Drink** *bangui* (a local palm wine), or try it distilled as *koutoukou* (a skull-shattering spirit)

IN A WORD

» *I-ni-cheh. I-kah-kéné* ('Hello. How are you?' in Dioula, the market language)

TRADEMARKS

» Violence-plagued elections; eating out in *maquis*; coups; Korhogo cloth, Dan masks

SURPRISES

» Côte d'Ivoire lost 42% of its forest and woodland from 1977 to 1987 – the highest rate of loss in the world; Côte d'Ivoire is the largest producer of cocoa in the world

MAP REF L,19

(1.) Two performers from La Troupe Artistique Sangbe in Grand Bassam
(2.) A young girl carries her baby sister in Sassandra
(3.) Fishermen mend their nets on a lazy afternoon in Sassandra
(4.) Women enter a small *banco* (baked mud) mosque in Kong

1.

Croatia has the best that Eastern Europe has to offer in a nutshell: forested hills, rustic villages, idyllic islands, walled medieval cities, Roman ruins, Adriatic coastline and a vibrant culture. Sitting on the fault line where Western and Eastern Europe meet, Croatia has weathered its share of difficulties, but has absorbed Latin, Venetian, Hapsburg and Slavic influences to create its own distinctive whole.

BEST TIME TO VISIT
» April to September for the good weather – or the 15th century in independent Ragusa (Dubrovnik)

ESSENTIAL EXPERIENCES
» Wandering through the walled medieval city of Dubrovnik – a rhapsody in limestone, cobbled streets and terracotta tiles
» Fossicking in Split, a city built around Roman Emperor Diocletian's palace
» Sunning yourself in the Venetian harbour town of Hvar, where the sun shines 300 days a year
» Visiting the country's surprisingly cosmopolitan capital, Zagreb
» Watching the tumbling cascades at Plitvice Lakes National Park

GETTING UNDER THE SKIN
» **Read** Rebecca West's *Black Lamb and Grey Falcon*, a classic account of a 1930s trip through the region; Slavenka Drakulić's *Café Europa,* an insightful series of essays on Croatia and Eastern Europe
» **Watch** *How the War Started on My Island* by Vinko Brešan, a contemporary black comedy
» **Eat** *ćevapčići* (grilled, spiced meatballs), a Balkan classic; *pašticada* (beef stuffed and roasted in wine and spices)
» **Drink** *šljivovica*, plum brandy with a kick; wines from Istria or Kvarner

2.

3.

4.

IN A WORD

» *Na zdravlje* (to your health)

TRADEMARKS

» Untouched fishing villages on the Dalmatian coast; European café culture; terracotta rooftops and baroque cathedrals; paprika and garlic; crystal-clear seas and beachside promenades; dining al fresco – meat on the grill

SURPRISES

» Shakespeare's *Twelfth Night* is set in Dalmatia; cravats and ballpoint pens were invented by Croatians; there are few spotted dogs in Dalmatia

MAP REF F,22

(1.) The famed Lovrjenac Fort, Dubrovnik, newly repaired since the Balkan conflict
(2.) The walls of St Nicholas in Nin rise imposingly above an ancient burial mound
(3.) A view of the terracotta rooftops of Dubrovnik
(4.) Fans of the all-over tan, sunbathers in Cavtat set to work on their complexions
(5.) The sun comes out for washing day in the old town of Rovinj, Istria
(6.) An old sea dog presides over the harbour in Split

1.

CUBA

CAPITAL **HAVANA** POPULATION 11,263,429 AREA 110,860 SQ KM OFFICIAL LANGUAGE SPANISH

In an amazing balancing act, Cuba is at once poor and broken, and rich and thriving. From the beat of the music echoing through towns and villages to the hustle of Havana's glorious, crumbling streets, Cuba challenges and enchants all who venture in. Its political isolation has prevented a tourist flood, and locals are sincerely friendly to visitors. While Fidel's infrastructure has seen better decades and the food is, well, best not spoken about, the last great bastion of communism enchants with its intoxicating human spirit. Or was that the rum?

BEST TIME TO VISIT
» November to May to avoid the heat and hurricanes – or before Fidel goes, and whenever you want to shake your booty

ESSENTIAL EXPERIENCES
» Walking along Havana's Malecón on a warm night
» Pretending you can salsa in a nightclub
» Taking a photo of a '50s Cadillac on your first day
» Speaking Spanish to the locals – even if you can't!
» Taking in a baseball game in Cuba's Major League
» Smoking a cigar…just because
» Drinking *mojitos*…just because

GETTING UNDER THE SKIN
» **Read** *Trading with the Enemy: A Yankee Travels Through Castro's Cuba* by Tom Miller – it's a rich feast of Cuban lore, and a great travel book about Cuba
» **Listen** to Polo Montañez's *Guajiro Natural*. Montañez died tragically in 2002, but the raspy, mellow strains of this album will leave you feeling full of life
» **Watch** everyone's favourite, *Fresa y Chocolate*, 1995's hit Havana comedy directed by Tomás Gutiérrez and Juan Carlos Tabío

DOUG MCKINLAY

2.

NoCarteles

3.

4.

» **Eat** something home-cooked, such as an *ajiaco* stew, made from potatoes, meat, corn, old beer and anything else lying around

» **Drink** a minty, sweet rum *mojito* as the sun goes down

IN A WORD

» *No es fácil* ('it's not easy', applied to virtually everything)

TRADEMARKS

» Cigars; communists; rum; salsa; Fidel; poverty; sex; the *Buena Vista Social Club*

SURPRISES

» Even if you *know* the food is bad, it's actually much worse; many people actually like communism; everything is priced in US dollars, and more expensive than you'd think; TV soap operas are the biggest show in town

MAP REF J,11

(1.) Fidelity to Fidel – a Havana local smokes on his doorstep
(2.) Trinidad street scene, Sancti Spiritus
(3.) In the late afternoon, a denizen of the capital takes time out
(4.) A gracefully decaying car blends into the peeling wall of a colonial building in Havana
(5.) Dressed to impress, two gentlemen hit the streets of Old Havana
(6.) A simple advertisement for Cuban rum adorns a wall in Old Havana

1.

CAPITAL **NICOSIA** POPULATION **771,657** AREA **9250 SQ KM** OFFICIAL LANGUAGES **GREEK, TURKISH**

STELLA HELANDER

Culturally European but geographically almost Middle Eastern, Cyprus is a blend of Turkish and Greek, Muslim and Christian influences, viewed through the perspective of 9000 years of constant invasion. Crusader castles rub shoulders with ancient vineyards, frescoed monasteries overlook citrus orchards, and sandy, sun-soaked feet tread Roman mosaic floors. Politically, Cyprus has remained a divided island since 1974 and, although unity is now on the EU's agenda, the wounds caused by 30 years of division will not be easily healed.

BEST TIME TO VISIT
April to May and September to October to avoid the heat and crowds

ESSENTIAL EXPERIENCES
» Visiting the magnificent Byzantine frescoed churches of the Troödos Mountains
» Cycling through the almost-deserted Karpas Peninsula
» Wandering around the castles of the Girne (Kyrenia) Range
» Skin diving at Cape Greco and swimming at deserted beaches
» Hiking the Mt Olympus trails in the Troödos Mountains

GETTING UNDER THE SKIN
» **Read** *Journey Into Cyprus* by Colin Thubron, a classic Cyprus travelogue
» **Listen** to Pelagia Kyriakou's *Paralimnitika* recordings, a superb collection of Cypriot demotic songs from the beginning of the 19th century and sung in the original Cypriot dialect
» **Watch** *The Wing of the Fly*, directed by Hristos Siopahas, or *The Slaughter of the Cock*, directed by Andreas Pantazis – both deal with the Turkish invasion of Cyprus in 1974

» **Eat** *kleftiko* (oven-baked lamb) or *mezedes* (dips, salads and other appetisers)

» **Drink** *raki* (Turkish) or *zivania* (Greek), the local firewater made from distilling the leftovers of grape crushings

IN A WORD

» *Yasas* (hello) for Greek Cypriots; *merhaba* (hello) for Turkish Cypriots

TRADEMARKS

» Strong, thick coffee; Turkish and British military camps; British pubs at Agia Napa; the Green Line; citrus orchards

SURPRISES

» Richard the Lionheart married Berengaria at Lemesos Castle in the 12th century; there was once a rail system in Cyprus that ran the length of the island

MAP REF H,23

(1.) A goat herder near Agia Marina protects his flock with a big stick and an intent look
(2.) The Byzantine stones of Kantara Castle gaze from the Girne mountain range
(3.) Distinguished only by its architecture – a mosque next to a Christian orthodox church
(4.) We all knead each other – a family gets together to make bread
(5.) Limpid waters reveal a wealth of gleaming pebbles near Aphrodite's Rock

1.

RICHARD NEBESKÝ

Most visitors to the Czech Republic spend their time in its near-mythical capital, Prague. Granted, the Golden City does exert a siren pull, and you could spend endless hours there – roaming through the maze of its Old Town, discovering its back-street secrets, getting to know each stone saint on the Charles Bridge. But don't miss out on the rest of the country, with its stately old spa towns, fanciful castles, spruce forests and subterranean caves. The Czech Republic is a feast of art, history and heart-attack food – abandon your vowels and tuck in.

BEST TIME TO VISIT

April to June (spring) – or during the halcyon Prague Spring of 1968 (preferably before the Soviet tanks rolled in)

ESSENTIAL EXPERIENCES

» Getting up early to cross Prague's Charles Bridge at dawn
» Drinking *slivovice* at an all-night party on the Day of the Witches
» Hiking through the crenellated sandstone pinnacles of the Adršpach-Teplice Rocks
» Contemplating your mortality under the bone chandelier in the Ossuary Chapel of All Saints in Sedlec
» Catching a classical music concert in the underground caves of the Moravian Karst

GETTING UNDER THE SKIN

» **Read** Milan Kundera's *The Book of Laughter and Forgetting*, in which the absurdity of the communist era is woven with themes of love, memory and music; or Bruce Chatwin's *Utz*, a novella about porcelain and alchemy set in Prague's Jewish quarter
» **Listen** to Dvořák, everyone's favourite Czech classical composer; or *The Plastic People of the Universe*, the psychedelic but oppressed heroes of the Prague Spring

2.

3.

4.

RICHARD NEBESKY

» **Watch** *Divided We Fall*, Jan Hrebejk's uneasily funny film about a Czech couple who hide a Jewish man in their apartment during the Nazi occupation; Jan Sverák's *Kolya,* about an aging Czech musician who has to care for a small Russian boy

» **Eat** *smažený květák s bramborem* (cauliflower fried in bread-crumbs, served with boiled potatoes and tartare sauce)

» **Drink** Budvar (the original version of Budweiser) or absinthe

IN A WORD

» *Ahoj* (hello, informal)

TRADEMARKS

» Beer; castles; crystal; dumplings; folk art; impenetrable language

SURPRISES

» The word 'defenestration' is derived from incidents in Czech history where Catholic and Hapsburg councillors were flung out of windows during disputes in Prague; it *is* possible to eat vegetarian

JONATHAN SMITH

GERMANY · POLAND · Ústi nad Labem · Liberec · Hradec Králové · ✪ Prague · Plzeň · Ostrava · Olomouc · Brno · České Budějovice · GERMANY · AUSTRIA · SLOVAKIA

MAP REF F,21

(**1.**) Speed and light streak the ultra-modern Můstek station, Nové Město, Prague
(**2.**) Heavenly light illuminates a pub in Kampa, Prague
(**3.**) Snow and silence fall in a bright corner of Český Krumlov
(**4.**) Under the gaze of vigilant statues, the early-morning set crosses Charles Bridge, Prague
(**5.**) A rainbow emerges from a gilded field of mustard-seed plants
(**6.**) Roof and façade of the Town Hall, Prague

CZECH REPUBLIC

1.

Cute and compact, Denmark is a harmonious blend of the old and the new. Ancient castles and Viking ring forts exist side-by-side with lively cities and sleek modern design. Over a millennium ago Danish Vikings brought the country to the world's attention when they took to the seas and ravaged half of Europe, but these days they've filed down their horns and forged a society that stands as a benchmark of civilisation, with progressive policies, widespread tolerance and a liberal social welfare system.

BEST TIME TO VISIT

May and June or AD 900 if pillaging is your thing

ESSENTIAL EXPERIENCES

» Knocking back a local beer while enjoying a summer evening on Nyhavn canal
» Letting your hair down at northern Europe's largest rock festival, Roskilde Festival
» Being charmed by the cobbled streets and well-preserved buildings of Ribe, Denmark's oldest town
» Building (and destroying) your own mini-empire at Legoland
» Dipping a toe at Skagen, where the waters of Kattegat and Skagerrak clash
» Cycling across this flat landscape on the extensive bike routes
» Exploring a Viking ring fortress at Trelleborg

GETTING UNDER THE SKIN

» **Read** *Miss Smilla's Feeling for Snow* by Peter Høeg, a suspense set in Copenhagen; or for a change of pace, Kierkegaard's philosophical works or Hans Christian Andersen's fairy tales
» **Listen** to the pop of Aqua, dance beats of Junior Senior, or the sweet sounds of Tina Dico

2.

3.

4.

» **Watch** anything by Lars Von Trier, particularly *The Idiots*

» **Eat** *smørrebrød* (the famous Danish open-faced sandwich), *frikadeller* (Danish meatballs of pork mince, served with potatoes and gravy), *sild* (pickled herring), and of course Danish pastries, known locally as *wienerbrød* (literally, Vienna bread)

» **Drink** *øl* (beer), or *akvavit* (schnapps) – swallow it in one swig

IN A WORD

» *Det var hyggeligt!* (that was cosy!)

TRADEMARKS

» Butter cookies; brightly coloured plastic bricks; 'The Little Mermaid'; Bang & Olufsen stereos; Royal Copenhagen plates and Georg Jensen jewellery; Arne Jacobsen's egg chair

SURPRISES

» Denmark has virtually no downhill skiing because its highest 'mountain' is 147m; not all Danes are blonde and blue-eyed

MAP REF E,21

(1.) The Tilsandede Kirke smoulders in the glow of sunset in Skagen, North Jutland
(2.) The dim light of streetlamps glistens on a dark canal in Nyhavn, Copenhagen
(3.) A mantle of frost transforms a woodland in northwest Zealand into a frozen tableau
(4.) Mummy gets delivered to the headquarters of a major travel agency in Copenhagen
(5.) Yellow flowers blaze in a dazzling rapeseed plantation in west Zealand
(6.) Shielding the sun from his eyes, a tourist inadvertently salutes a Royal Palace Guard

1.

Djibouti's strangely seductive blend of African, Arab, Indian and European influences is seasoned with a hefty dose of khat, the mildly intoxicating herb that is chewed by most males and sets the country's pace to unhurried. The capital may be little more than a minor port filled with peeling colonial buildings, but its streets are unforgettable, shared by traditionally robed tribesmen and French legionnaires, hennaed women and Somali refugees, and filled with the aromas of French cuisine and seedy bars. Away from the coast, the hinterland is a bizarre treat of eerie volcanic landscapes and vast salt lakes. Djibouti could well be one of East Africa's best-kept secrets.

BEST TIME TO VISIT

November to mid-April, when the weather is coolest

ESSENTIAL EXPERIENCES

» Exploring the great salt lake of Lac Assal
» Visiting the weird, lunar landscape of Lac Abbé at dawn
» Snorkelling the stunning coral reefs off Djibouti's Red Sea coast
» Spotting birds and animals in the Fôret du Day national park
» Trekking behind the Afar nomads and their caravans along the ancient salt route
» Sharing a *poisson yéménite* (fish supper) with the locals

GETTING UNDER THE SKIN

» **Read** *Khamsine*, a collection of lyrical, sometimes semi-erotic, poems by Djiboutian poet William JF Syad
» **Listen** to solo guitarist Aïdarous and Guux musician Taha Nahari
» **Watch** *Total Eclipse*, which was made in part in Djibouti
» **Eat** local *foie* (liver) for breakfast and *cabri farci* (stuffed kid) for lunch

2.

3.

4.

FRANCES LINZEE GORDON

» **Drink** the fizzy and slightly salty local bottled water or tea

IN A WORD

» *Salam 'alekum* (greetings)

TRADEMARKS

» Nomads; men chewing khat; arid deserts; the Red Sea; the civil war; camels

SURPRISES

Many Afar nomads file their front teeth into ferocious-looking points; Afar huts are usually spherical, while Somali huts are more quadrangular in design

FRANCES LINZEE GORDON

MAP REF K,24

(**1.**) An Afar tribesman awakens beside his mobile dwelling on the stony banks of Lac Abbé
(**2.**) Afar tribesmen gather natural salt from Lac Assal
(**3.**) Unforgiving terrain surrounding the Bay of Ghoubbet shimmers in the midday heat
(**4.**) The palms of a young woman bear stunning henna tattoos at a festival in Djibouti City
(**5.**) Two elegant Somali women observe the proceedings of a wedding in Hol Hol, Ali Sabieh
(**6.**) Fishermen drag in their ropes

1.

MICHAEL LAWRENCE

Dominica is largely rural, uncrowded and unspoiled. It has a lush mountainous interior of rainforests, waterfalls, lakes, hot springs and rivers, many of which cascade over cliff faces en route to the coast. Apart from its natural splendours, including the highest mountains in the Eastern Caribbean, the island has an interesting fusion of British, French and West Indian cultural traditions, and is home to the Eastern Caribbean's largest Carib Indian community.

BEST TIME TO VISIT

December to February

ESSENTIAL EXPERIENCES

» Enjoying scenic Roseau, with its colonial architecture and Creole food and culture
» Exploring Cabrits National Park, with fine views from the ruins of Fort Shirley
» Taking in the unsurpassed mountain and rainforest scenery
» Hiking to Boiling Lake, the world's second-largest natural boiling lake
» Kicking around Scotts Head, a tiny fishing village of only 800 souls on the gently curving shoreline of Soufrière Bay (the rim of a sunken volcanic crater)
» Diving at Scotts Head Drop, a shallow coral ledge that drops abruptly to a depth of over 50m (160ft) and has a wall of tube sponges and soft corals

GETTING UNDER THE SKIN

» **Read** *Voyage in the Dark* by Dominica's most celebrated author, Jean Rhys, or Dominica's other noted novelist, Phyllis Shand Allfrey, who is best known for *The Orchid House*
» **Listen** to African *soukous*, Louisiana zydeco and a variety of local bands at the World Creole Music Festival held in Roseau

2.

MICHAEL LAWRENCE

3.

4.

» **Watch** Dominican filmmaker Pauline Marcelle's animation films *Burn*, *The Snake Steps* or *Paradogs*

» **Eat** callaloo soup (a creamy soup made with dasheen leaves) and mountains of delicious fresh fruit

» **Drink** fruit punch made with fresh fruit and rum, or the locally brewed beer Kubuli

IN A WORD

» Lime about (lazing about)

TRADEMARKS

» Diving; Rasta colours; rainforests; cricket; Creole culture

SURPRISES

» Dominica's national bird, the Sisserou parrot, is the largest of all the Amazon parrots; there are more than 200 rivers in Dominica

Guadeloupe Channel

ATLANTIC OCEAN

Portsmouth

Marigot

Salisbury

Castle Bruce

St Joseph

Massacre

Roseau ✪

CARIBBEAN SEA

Soufriere

Martinique Channel

MAP REF K,13

(1.) Nestled amongst the greenery, a house overlooks the Roseau Valley
(2.) A young fisherman casts his line into shallow waters
(3.) A declaration of devotion emblazoned on a beachside banner, Scotts Head
(4.) Infernal vapours issue from the craters of Boiling Lake, St Patrick
(5.) Dusk light captures three boys at play
(6.) With stripes in his stride a policeman marches past a vivid building

1.

Is there a better definition of paradise than palm-fringed white-sand beaches, turquoise waters and rum-and-merengue-soaked nights? Santo Domingo offers architectural charm and historical gravitas, while the rugged mountain interior greatly satisfies adventure-seekers with world-class rafting, trekking and wildlife-watching opportunities. Above all, however, it's Dominicans who make the DR tick: fun-seekers throw themselves wholeheartedly into all manner of neighbourhood parties, surfing and windsurfing contests, music festivals and not one but two annual Carnival celebrations.

BEST TIME TO VISIT

December to April

ESSENTIAL EXPERIENCES

» Discovering the New World in Santo Domingo's Zona Colonial
» Whale-watching on the Península de Samaná
» Cheering for *beisbol* champions in San Pedro de Macorís
» Windsurfing in Caberete, the DR's hippest beach town
» Hiking, rafting and birdwatching in the interior's mountainous national parks
» Taking part in a Dominican fiesta: one part rum, one part Presidente beer, one part *sancocho* and three parts dancing (salsa, merengue and the countryfied *bachata*)

GETTING UNDER THE SKIN

» **Read** Julia Alvarez's *In the Time of the Butterflies*, the lyrical tale of 1960s political martyrs, the Mirabal sisters; or *Feast of the Goat* by Mario Vargas Llosa, about the Trujillo regime
» **Listen** to 1960s and '70s tunes by merengue legend Johnny Ventura; Juan Luis Guerra's *Bachata Rosa*, a revolutionary album

by the DR's most celebrated contemporary artist; anything by prolific *bachateros* Antony Santos and Raulín Rodriguez
» **Watch** *1492: The Conquest of Paradise*, the lavish Columbus-meets-New World epic
» **Eat** *sancocho de siete carnes*, hearty soup with manioc, plantain and seven (count 'em!) types of meat, *the* soup for a family gathering
» **Drink** rum or Presidente, the country's beloved local beer

IN A WORD
» *¡Que chulo!* (great!)

TRADEMARKS
» Palm-lined beaches; plantains; merengue; rum; cigars that are better than but not as famous as those from Cuba; Sammy Sosa

SURPRISES
» Dominicans are amazingly polite and tend to dress quite formally; Dominicans often refer to their island by its Taino name, Quisqueya

MAP REF J,12

(1.) A boy carries a heavy load through Duarte Street, Santo Domingo
(2.) A local of Bayahibe, La Romana, enjoys her relaxation equipment with matching house
(3.) All grins and giggles, cheeky children peer from a shuttered window
(4.) Eyes on the prize, a soldier checks his slip outside a betting shop in Santo Domingo
(5.) Relaxation is obligatory at Balneario Los Platos, a river-fed public pool in Paraíso

1.

In May 2002 East Timor became the first new nation of the 21st century. Independence from Indonesia, however, brought mixed fortunes to this recovering conflict zone. Political turmoil, violence and riots in March 2006 returned chaos to the country. Hopefully the future will see a time when tourists flock to this nation to enjoy its fine beaches, colonial towns, rugged mountains and lush interiors.

BEST TIME TO VISIT

May to November for the weather

ESSENTIAL EXPERIENCES

» Walking up to the towering Christ Statue at Cape Fatucama to take in the view over the bay to Dili
» Diving the crystal waters off Atauro Island amid turtles, dugongs and colourful reef fish
» Climbing lofty Mt Matebian (2315m), East Timor's holy mountain
» Overnighting in Maubisse's historic *pousada* (Portuguese inn)
» Visiting the crumbling Portuguese garrison of Fatusuba

GETTING UNDER THE SKIN

» **Read** Timothy Mo's *The Redundancy of Courage*, which uses the fictional country of Danu to depict East Timor's struggle during the Indonesian occupation. Luis Cardoso's *Crossing: A Story of East Timor* is a memoir of growing up in East Timor under Portuguese and Indonesian rule.
» **Listen** to *Liberdade Viva East Timor,* the benefit album for the newly created nation
» **Watch** *Death of a Nation: The Timor Conspiracy*, John Pilger's exploration of the international abandonment of the tiny nation
» **Eat** fresh seafood – East Timor's crystal-clear seas are teeming with gourmet goodies, which find their way onto restaurant tables cooked in Indonesian, Chinese and Portuguese styles

2.

3.

4.

» **Drink** rich, flavoursome Arabica coffee or *sopi*, a potent brew distilled from the pandanus plant

IN A WORD

» *Ba nebé?* (where are you going?)

TRADEMARKS

» Xanana Gusmão; José Ramos-Horta; UN convoys; freedom fighters; colourful woven lengths of *tais* (traditional cloth)

SURPRISES

» A small patch of East Timor (the Oecussi Enclave) sits nearly 100km removed from the rest of the country, sharing its land borders with Indonesian West Timor; the Greater Sunrise oilfield between Australia and East Timor is believed to be a rich source of both oil and gas and its bounty should provide the struggling nation with income for years to come

MAP REF N,33

(1.) In a flurry of feathers, men perform a Timorese dance
(2.) The afternoon sun gleams on playful children on the shores of Dili
(3.) Children scavenge for coral and other collectibles on Dili's beach
(4.) Peak hour traffic in the hill village of Maubisse
(5.) A young traditional dancer from the mountain town of Ainaro
(6.) The iconic statue of the Virgin gazes from Mt Ramelau, the highest point in East Timor

1.

A wealth of vibrant indigenous cultures, colonial architecture, otherworldly volcanic landscapes and dense rainforests are packed into the borders of tiny Ecuador. You can change your surroundings here as fast as you can change your mind – one day your cold fingers are picking through handwoven woollen sweaters at a chilly indigenous market in the Andean highlands, and the next they're slapping mosquitoes on a tropical beach. Then there are the Galápagos Islands, lauded as one of the world's greatest natural history treasures.

BEST TIME TO VISIT

From May to December on the mainland, or January to April for the Galápagos

ESSENTIAL EXPERIENCES

» Travelling to the Galápagos Islands to snorkel with harmless sharks, stare at iguanas and scuba dive with manta rays
» Wandering through the splendid colonial streets of Cuenca
» Outdoor pursuits in the Oriente – where you can hike, visit indigenous communities, fish for piranhas and spot caimans
» Bouncing around the spectacular high Andean road known as the Quilotoa loop, stopping to hike, buy indigenous crafts and visit Ecuador's most stunning crater lake, Laguna Quilotoa
» Journeying down the Río Napo to the Amazon River by canoe and cargo boat from Coca in the Oriente to Iquitos, Peru

GETTING UNDER THE SKIN

» **Read** Jorge Icaza's *Huasipungo*, a naturalistic tale of the miserable conditions on Andean haciendas in the early 20th century. Kurt Vonnegut's *Galápagos* is a comic, cautionary tale.
» **Listen** to Marco Villota, who plays with the band Pueblo Nuevo

2.

3.

4.

» **Watch** *Talking with Fish and Birds*, directed by Rainer Simon, documenting the life and death of a shaman
» **Eat** *ceviche* (uncooked seafood marinated in lemon and served with popcorn and onion) or *patacones* (fried plantain chips)
» **Drink** the good local *cervezas* (beer), or *aguardiente* (sugar cane alcohol) – a more acquired taste

IN A WORD

» *Bacán* (cool)

TRADEMARKS

» The Galápagos Islands; panama hats; panpipes; the Andes; eating roasted guinea-pigs

SURPRISES

» Ecuador has one of the highest deforestation rates in Latin America; the oldest tools found in Ecuador date to 9000 BC

MAP REF M,11

(1.) Herders follow a flock of sheep down the flanks of Cotopaxi Volcano
(2.) Dark clouds loom above a team of climbers descending Cotopaxi Volcano
(3.) Marine iguanas let their tails down at Punta Suárez
(4.) Ramshackle houses of the Las Peñas district, Guayaquil
(5.) An unimpressed chicken takes a tour on the back of a local girl in Otavalo
(6.) A vendor flashes a golden-toothed smile at the Otavalo Indian Market

1.

Egypt has captured the imagination of travellers since ancient times. It is a multilayered history lesson, with relics left by pharaohs, Greeks, Romans, Christians and Arabs alike. Mud-brick villages rub shoulders with modern buildings of steel and glass, the call of the muezzin with the blare of city traffic. It's also a diver's dream dip or a visitor's perfect trek across the sands on a camel. And through everything, the majestic River Nile flows on, Egypt's lifeblood since the dawn of history.

BEST TIME TO VISIT

October to May to avoid the heat – or the 3rd century BC, when Alexandria was the cultural and intellectual capital of the world

ESSENTIAL EXPERIENCES

» Battling tour buses and camel drivers to see the Great Pyramids at Giza – because you know you have to
» Taking a lazy afternoon drift along the Nile in a felucca at Aswan
» Feeling very small in Karnak's Great Hypostyle Hall
» Sipping tea and smoking a *shisha* (waterpipe) with a thousand and one others at Cairo's landmark coffeehouse, El-Fishawi
» Diving, snorkelling or trekking the Sinai, where the desert meets the Red Sea

GETTING UNDER THE SKIN

» **Read** Max Rodenbeck's *Cairo: The City Victorious*, a fascinating history and first-person travelogue. For true insight into Egyptian culture, nothing tops Naguib Mahfouz's epic and sometimes ponderous *The Cairo Trilogy*.
» **Listen** to Umm Kulsoum, forever Egypt's diva
» **Watch** *Cleopatra*, an over-the-top romp starring Elizabeth Taylor
» **Eat** *fuul* and *taamia* – salty fava-bean paste and felafel, rumoured to taste better the lower the hygiene standards. For dessert, try

LEANNE LOGAN

2.

3.

4.

besboussa, a sweet, sticky pastry, and *kunafa*, crispy strands of dough layered over sweet cheese.

» **Drink** fresh fruit juice, like mango, strawberry and lemon – cheap and delicious. An icy gin and tonic really does the trick when it's hot out there.

IN A WORD

» *Inshallah* (God willing), an all-purpose disclaimer, as in 'See you tomorrow at 9, *inshallah*'

TRADEMARKS

» Camels; pyramids; deserts; fezzes; turbans; baksheesh; incessant honking; tour guides; tacky King Tut souvenirs

SURPRISES

» The pyramids at Giza get all the attention, but Egypt boasts dozens of pyramids; visit the massive Bent Pyramid at Dahshur and you might have it all to yourself

MAP REF I,23

(**1.**) Passengers test the limits of luxury on a 2nd-class train across the Arabian Desert
(**2.**) Arabian splendour gleams from a festive tent in the market district of Islamic Cairo
(**3.**) A goose-vendor sells poultry, dead or alive, along Bab Zuweila, Cairo
(**4.**) The hulking façade of a pyramid rises like a mirage behind a lone camel rider, Giza
(**5.**) A weather-beaten face and toothy grin emerge from the headdress of a local man
(**6.**) Paper decorations adorn Coptic Cairo's narrow streets

1.

El Salvador's name still evokes images of the brutal civil war fought throughout the 1980s in its tangle of mountains and farmlands. The war, however, is over and the volcanic landscape remains the most turbulent aspect of the country. Now El Salvador is making headlines once again, thanks to its degraded environment. The people of El Salvador are its richest resource, and the best reason to come: direct, friendly and unjaded by mass tourism.

BEST TIME TO VISIT

November to April (the dry season)

ESSENTIAL EXPERIENCES

» Hiking in the mountains surrounding the former guerrilla stronghold of Perquín
» Stepping off the Ruta de las Flores to visit the string of charming little towns in the cool western highlands
» Visiting the weekend food fair at Juayúa
» Checking out the laid-back vibe and happening arts scene in Suchitoto
» Catching the bus from Metapán to El Poy through El Salvador's spectacular mountain scenery

GETTING UNDER THE SKIN

» **Read** *Cuentos de Barro* (Tales of Mud) by Salarrué (one of El Salvador's most famous writers); the poetry of Manlio Argueta and Francisco Rodriguez
» **Listen** to the underground movement of *canción popular* (folk music), which draws its inspiration from current events
» **Watch** *Salvador*, the story of a war correspondent directed by Oliver Stone, for Hollywood's insights into the civil war
» **Eat** *pupusas* (cornmeal dough stuffed with farmer's cheese, refried beans or fried pork fat) or *panes* (French breads sliced

5.

open and stuffed with chicken, salsa, salad and pickled vegetables)

» **Drink** *licuados* (refreshing blended fruit and milk) or Torito (a vodka-like spirit made from sugar cane)

IN A WORD

» *Cheque* (all right)

TRADEMARKS

» Bitter civil war; liberation theology; coffee; surfing; volcanoes; circling vultures; lush cloud forest

SURPRISES

» El Salvador enjoys the highest minimum wage in Central America; 9% of Salvadorans are considered of full European ancestry, while only 1% is indigenous

MAP REF K,10

(**1.**) Child leans against a gaudy turquoise wall
(**2.**) Fishermen haul their catch in Bahia de la Unión, once El Salvador's busiest port
(**3.**) Rich colours form appealing contrasts on the wall of a house in Suchitoto
(**4.**) Cowboy-hatted characters shoot the breeze at a Suchitoto handicraft stall
(**5.**) An easy rider of the Cuscatlan region prepares to hit the mean streets of Suchitoto

England is where world-renowned institutions and symbols remain cherished and intact – from Big Ben at Westminster to Canterbury Cathedral, Wembley Stadium to Lord's Cricket Ground, Stonehenge to Tower Bridge. But the load is carried with panache as this tiny entity strides into the 21st century offering designer fashion, cutting-edge clubbing, and fine wining and dining as never before. England's presence on the global stage remains large, one of the many legacies of an empire long gone but not quite forgotten.

BEST TIME TO VISIT

May to September (summer) – or, for the free-spirited, the swinging 1960s

ESSENTIAL EXPERIENCES

» Climbing to the top of St Paul's Cathedral for an alternative view of London
» Marvelling at the prehistoric ruin of Stonehenge and the sheer effort involved in its creation
» Revelling in the sense of achievement on reaching the peak of Scafell Pike, England's highest mountain, in the Lake District
» Mixing Roman and Georgian history in the elegant town of Bath
» Eating fish and chips on a pebbly beach, and willing the sun to shine
» Exploring Cornwall's coastline of cliffs and bays

GETTING UNDER THE SKIN

» **Read** *The English* by Jeremy Paxman, an exploration of the English psyche by one of the country's toughest TV interviewers
» **Listen** to the Kinks' *Waterloo Sunset*, a great introduction to the many songs written about the capital; or anything by the Beatles

2.

3.

4.

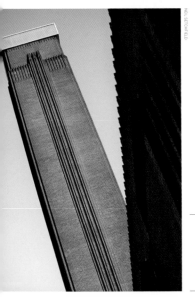

» **Watch** *Sense and Sensibility*, a film of a thoroughly English novel in a thoroughly English setting

» **Eat** Sunday roast dinner – typically beef with roast potatoes, Yorkshire pudding, carrots, peas and gravy

» **Drink** real ale – England is the home of proper beer

IN A WORD

» 'Oright?

TRADEMARKS

» The weather; the Royal Family; Lords, Ladies and big hats at Ascot; Cockney rhyming slang; Brit Pop; jellied eels; warm beer; page three girls; fry-ups; football

SURPRISES

» It doesn't actually rain that much; most of the best things on offer in England are free

MAP REF E,20

(1.) The pebbled shores of Brighton, the natural sunbathing habitat of the English
(2.) Cricketers enjoy a quiet game outside Warkworth Castle, Northumberland
(3.) The enigmatic Stonehenge on Salisbury Plain
(4.) How much is that doggy? Everything is for sale at the Brick Lane Market in London
(5.) A tube station sign leads to a subterranean world of speed, light and mute commuters
(6.) The towering Tate Modern, repository of England's finest collection of 20th-century art

1.

2.

3.

SEAN SPRAGUE

While most of Equatorial Guinea's two regions remain densely covered with the type of forest that made Tarzan swing, the recent discovery of underwater oil looks set to change the face of the country. Bioko Island has been thoroughly taken over by oil money and an influx of foreign workers, but a trip to the mainland (Rio Muni) is still like taking a step back in time. The only way to get from A to B is to hack and bribe and hold on tight to bush taxis making their way through the jungle. This is real adventure travel, with amazing rewards – rainforest, beaches, traditional African villages and, with some hard hiking and good luck, you might get to spend some time with gorillas.

BEST TIME TO VISIT

December to February for slightly drier weather

ESSENTIAL EXPERIENCES

» Hiking in search of gorillas, elephants, chimpanzees, crocodiles and whatever else turns up in the Monte Alen National Park
» Beachcombing around Luba and other deserted beach towns on Bioko Island
» Taking a pirogue across the estuary between Gabon and Equatorial Guinea to the village of Cogo
» Wandering around vibrant Malabo – a town in the heart of the African tropics – with its outdoor bars, thriving nightclubs and colourful markets

GETTING UNDER THE SKIN

» **Read** Mary Kingsley's 1897 classic *Travels in West Africa*, which details her trip spent slogging through the rainforest to gather specimens for a natural history museum

4.

» **Listen** to a traditional orchestra of drums, wooden xylophones, *sanzas* (a small thumb piano made from bamboo), bow harps and even zithers

» **Eat** wonderful seafood and fresh fruit

» **Drink** beer, locally brewed palm wine and *malamba*, made from sugar cane

IN A WORD

» *Mbôlo* (hello)

TRADEMARKS

» Corrupt officials; oil; dense rainforest; hardcore travellers; small villages with mud-wattle houses; gorillas

SURPRISES

» Sorcerers are still among the most important community members here; among the country's most fascinating celebrations is the *abira*, a ceremony that helps cleanse the community of evil

MAP REF L,21

(1.) Wide smiles from children playing in front of a church in Ebebiyin
(2.) A wooden church in need of restoration in Batete
(3.) A young boy quenches his thirst at a local well
(4.) A community dresses in its Sunday best for local festivities in Malabo

1.

Perched on the horn of Africa, Eritrea is a tiny country with a strong sense of identity. Torrid deserts, fertile highlands and arid plains are all crowded together within the diminutive confines of its borders. Its richness and beauty did not escape the attention of the outside world and the country was a colony of Italy for more than fifty years. Evidence of Italy's imperial rule can still be seen in the magnificent architecture of the capital, Asmara. Modern Eritrea is a lively country with an exuberant and optimistic population.

BEST TIME TO VISIT

October to May, when the mercury settles at an agreeable temperature

ESSENTIAL EXPERIENCES

» Strapping on a snorkel and marvelling at the unspoiled underwater treasures around the Dahlak Archipelago
» Exploring Eritrea's remarkable archaeological ruins in Qohaito
» Surveying war-torn Nakfa, once the heart of Eritrean resistance
» Discovering the lunar landscape of Dankalia, one of the most desolate areas on earth
» Enjoying a pastry at one of Asmara's Italian-style cafés
» Climbing up to one of the isolated Orthodox monasteries

GETTING UNDER THE SKIN

» **Read** *Eritrea at a Glance*, edited by Mary Houdek and Leonardo Oriolo, for a fantastic introduction to the country, particularly the capital Asmara. For a gripping yarn of the struggle for independence read *Even the Stones Are Burning* by Roy Pateman.
» **Eat** *legamat*, a deep-fried dough sold hot in newspaper cones by little boys in the lowlands. A popular dish in the west is *sheia*,

CAPITAL ASMARA POPULATION 4,362,254 AREA 121,320 SQ KM OFFICIAL LANGUAGES TIGRINYA, ARABIC,

PATRICK HORTON

2.

3.

4.

JEAN-BERNARD CARILLET

lamb drizzled with oil and herbs then barbecued on very hot stones until it sizzles

» **Drink** excellent espresso, macchiato or ginger coffee

IN A WORD

» *Selam* (hello)

TRADEMARKS

» Yellow Fiat taxis; politeness; excellent coffee; classic architecture; stark landscapes; relaxed attitudes

SURPRISES

» Legend credits Eritrea as the El Dorado of Africa. The Egyptian pharaohs held the land comprising present-day Eritrea in awe, referring to it as The Land of Punt. From over its borders came a seemingly endless stream of gold, frankincense, myrrh, slaves, ostrich feathers, antelopes, ebony and ivory.

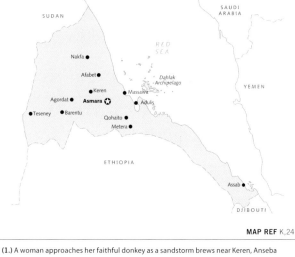

MAP REF K,24

(1.) A woman approaches her faithful donkey as a sandstorm brews near Keren, Anseba

(2.) A novice monk at the Debre Libanos monastery beams a prayer across the valley

(3.) Young men strut down the main drag of Assab

(4.) Two saltbushes stand watch over the empty waters of the Red Sea

(5.) Chilling out for a chat on the steps of the Khulafa Al Rashidin (Great Mosque) in Asmara

(6.) The striking face of a Tigre tribeswoman

1.

A forgotten gem strategically placed between Russia and Scandinavia, this former Soviet Republic has undergone a rapid transformation since independence. The internet and mobile phone revolutions in particular have taken the nation by storm. The influence of modern technology co-exists happily with a people that are strongly connected to nature, and whose land – almost half of which is forest – is home to countless traditions and folk tales.

BEST TIME TO VISIT
May to July for the good weather

ESSENTIAL EXPERIENCES
» Rejuvenating in a mud bath at one of Pärnu's health spas
» Trying to walk across the icy cobbled streets of wintry medieval Tallinn
» Catching a ferry to the outlying island of Saaremaa
» Exploring Tartu, Estonia's spiritual capital, where locals claim a *vaim* (spirit) inhabits its 19th-century streets and mingles with its large student population
» Seeking out brown bear, lynx, wolves and, if you're lucky, the rare European flying squirrel

GETTING UNDER THE SKIN
» **Read** anything by Lydia Koidula – Estonia's first lady of poetry; or Jaan Kross's *The Czar's Madman*
» **Listen** to *Miserere Litany* by Arvo Pärt
» **Watch** animated films from Estonia such as the bizarre creations of Priit Pärn and Mati Kütt that verge on surreal and absurd
» **Eat** *suitsukala* (smoked fish), *verivorst* (blood sausage), *verileib* (blood bread) and, for true vampires, *verikäkk* (balls of blood rolled in flour and eggs with pig fat thrown in for taste)
» **Drink** Vana Tallinn (a syrupy liqueur) or Saku (beer)

ESTONIA

CAPITAL TALLINN POPULATION 1,408,556 AREA 45,226 SQ KM OFFICIAL LANGUAGE ESTONIAN

259

4.

5.

6.

JOHN NOBLE

IN A WORD

» *Ma olen taimetoitlane* (I'm a vegetarian)

TRADEMARKS

» Quiet, reserved people; mobile phone addicts; White Nights, midsummer evenings that remain in twilight till dawn; grand limestone buildings; open-air song festivals; stag night weekends

SURPRISES

» Estonia received the attention of 160 million TV viewers when it hosted the 2002 Eurovision Song Contest; it is home to one of Europe's few accessible meteorite craters at Kaali on Saaremaa Island; it has a centuries-old shamanistic tradition

MAP REF D,23

(1.) Window shopping for hand-crafted toys in Town Hall Square, Tallinn
(2.) The onion domes of the Russian Orthodox Alexander Nevski Cathedral gleam in the sun
(3.) Rebel Rebel – pinhead punks in Tallinn
(4.) A stroller steps into the sunlight in the Old Town district of Tallinn
(5.) Austere stone fortresses preside over the city walls of Tallinn
(6.) Empty rowing boats moored at a jetty in Triigi, Saaremaa

1.

Rich in history, wildlife and cultural traditions, Ethiopia deserves the aura and fame of Egypt. To many it remains synonymous with famine and war, but the relative obscurity has its rewards, flavouring travel with a sense of adventure and discovery. The landscape is littered with rock-hewn churches, mighty castles and isolated monasteries. Nature lovers come away with memories of waterfalls, mountains and wildlife. Travel here can be tough but also hugely satisfying – and you won't have to worry about crowds of tourists, yet...

BEST TIME TO VISIT

October to January, when rains have turned the land into its lush, blooming best

ESSENTIAL EXPERIENCES

» Walking around the rock-hewn churches at Lalibela at dawn
» Trekking into the Bale Mountains in search of the elusive Ethiopian wolf
» Exploring Gonder's castles and the colourful interior of Debre Beirhan Selassie Church
» Visiting the ruins of Aksum, once home to a mysterious and mighty ancient civilisation
» Taking a boat to Lake Tana's island monasteries, then visiting the Blue Nile Falls

GETTING UNDER THE SKIN

» **Read** Graham Hancock's *The Sign and the Seal*, a historical detective story which traces the Ark of the Covenant to Ethiopia, while providing an overview of the country's history and culture
» **Listen** to anything by Mahmoud Ahmud, a legend of Ethiopian music with his soulful and funky Amharic sound. Start with his *Live in Paris* set.

ETHIOPIA

CAPITAL **ADDIS ABABA** POPULATION **66,557,553** AREA **1,127,127 SQ KM** OFFICIAL LANGUAGES **AMHARIC,**

5.

» **Eat** *injera*, a phenomenally bouncy bread that is found throughout the country. Try it with fiery *kai wat* sauce.

» **Drink** the excellent Ethiopian beer, especially Harar. Delicious fruit juice mixtures known as *spris* shouldn't be missed.

IN A WORD

» *Denkenesh* (you are wonderful), the Ethiopian Amharic name given to Lucy, the oldest complete hominid skeleton ever found, on display at the National Museum in Addis Ababa

TRADEMARKS

» Ancient churches; Live Aid; Haile Selassie; Radio Ethiopia

SURPRISES

» Ethiopia is home to one of the oldest Christian civilisations in the world; Ethiopians believe their country is the resting place of the Ark of the Covenant; the country is at peace

MAP REF L,24

(1.) Amhara boy herders tending their flock in Simien Mountains National Park
(2.) A proud woman of the nomadic Karo tribe is adorned with bright beaded necklaces
(3.) It's all here in black and white – a herd of Burchell's zebras in Nechisar National Park
(4.) First coat of the elaborate body painting that many tribal groups wear while dancing
(5.) Two men chat outside a rock-hewn church that dates back to the 12th century

1.

JULIET COOMBE

Just next door to South America and Antarctica, the Falklands are curiously British through and through, with peat fires burning in every hearth and jolly tea times to set your clock by. With only a scattering of inhabitants (most are British military personnel), it's hardly Touristville. The remote islands briefly rocketed to international importance during the 1980s, when Britain took them back after an invasion by Argentina and everyone learnt their alternative name: the Islas Malvinas.

BEST TIME TO VISIT
October to April

ESSENTIAL EXPERIENCES
» Admiring ramshackle Stanley, a town that appears to have been pieced together from flotsam, stone and a lot of bright paint
» Wildlife-watching on the aptly named Sea Lion Island
» Paying court to breeding pairs of king penguins at Volunteer Beach
» Snacking on the South Sandwich Islands and seeing more than five million pairs of breeding chinstrap penguins

GETTING UNDER THE SKIN
» **Read** *The Battle for the Falklands*, a cool assessment of the politics and strategy of the 1982 war by Max Hastings and Simon Jenkins
» **Listen** to the Fighting Pig Band
» **Watch** *Falklands – Taskforce South*, a gritty account of the British defence of the islands aboard a British naval vessel
» **Eat** hydroponically grown vegetables in Stanley, but pack your own lunch anywhere else (British explorer Shackleton didn't and almost starved to death)
» **Drink** tea during a regular smoko (traditional mid-morning tea break)

CAPITAL STANLEY · POPULATION 2967 · AREA 12,173 SQ KM · OFFICIAL LANGUAGE ENGLISH

FALKLAND ISLANDS/ISLAS MALVINAS

2.

IN A WORD

» Cuppa (usually a cup of tea, the most warming thing on a freezing-cold day)

TRADEMARKS

» British-Argentine battlefield; penguin mating grounds; snow-covered islands; near-dark winters; snow, snow and even more snow

SURPRISES

» The Falklands War, for which the island is still best known, lasted only 72 days, but saw casualties of almost a thousand service-men. Anywhere outside of Stanley is known as 'camp', from the Spanish word *campo*, countryside.

MAP REF T,13

(1.) A retired anchor leans against a fence post on Westpoint Island
(2.) King penguins greet one another in the grass
(3.) An Antarctic cruise ship skirts the gorse-covered shoreline of Carcass Island
(4.) A lovingly painted car and house in the well-decorated East Falkland region
(5.) A farmer drives his sheep along the dusty Port Howard-Fox Bay Road near Little Chartres

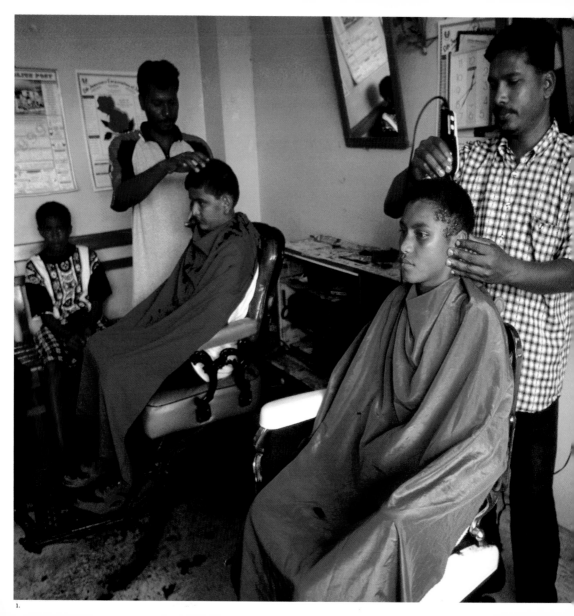

1.

Lapped by warm azure waters, fringed with vibrant coral reefs and cloaked in the emerald green of the tropics, Fiji is a paradise-seeker's dream come true. Its sun-soaked, white-sand beaches and resorts are bliss, but only a slice of the country's allure. Fiji is an exotic blend of Melanesian, Polynesian, Micronesian, Indian, Chinese and European influences – which means visitors can feed on curries and chop suey, visit temples, churches and mosques, hear Urdu and Mandarin, and sip spiced chai or kava.

BEST TIME TO VISIT

May to October, during the 'Fijian winter' when humidity and rainfall are lower

ESSENTIAL EXPERIENCES

» Exploring Suva's waterfront and market, with its exotic fruits and vegetables, seafood and spices
» Snorkelling and diving in Fiji's extraordinary crystal-blue reefs
» Experiencing the hospitality of Fiji's multiethnic inhabitants
» Surfing the fantastic breaks of the southern Mamanucas
» Admiring traditional *bure* architecture in the highlands
» Swimming through the dark chambers of the Sawa-i-Lau caves in the Yasawa group of islands

GETTING UNDER THE SKIN

» **Read** Fiji's most popular coffee-table book, *Children of the Sun*, with photos by Glen Craig and poetry by Bryan McDonald
» **Listen** to the guitar-strumming, crooning songs from *Bula Fiji Bula: Music of the Fiji Islands*
» **Watch** Tom Hanks playing the modern-day Robinson Crusoe in *Cast Away*, featuring Monuriki Island

2.

3.

4.

» **Eat** traditional Fijian foods including *tavioka* (cassava) and *dalo* (taro) roots, and seafood in *lolo* (coconut cream)

» **Drink** a cloudy bowl of lip-numbing *yaqona* (also known as kava), a ritualistic drink prepared from the aromatic roots of the Pacific pepper shrub, originally drunk in honour of the ancestors

IN A WORD

» *Bula* (hello)

TRADEMARKS

» Surfers seeking the big break; honeymooners' paradise; grass skirts; hammocks; woven baskets; white-sand beaches

SURPRISES

» Over 300 islands comprise Fiji's archipelago, and about two-thirds are uninhabited; boiled *beka* (bat) was once a popular indigenous Fijian dish

MAP REF 0,38

(1.) A close shave at a barber shop in Sigatoka
(2.) Noisy boys – traditional dancers leap to the beat on Denarau Island
(3.) A thatched house in Navala village perched above the dramatic Nausori Highlands
(4.) A parrot's-eye view of Qalito Island (Castaway Island) in the Mamanuca archipelago
(5.) Sultry winds tease the fronds of immense palm trees on Yanuca Island
(6.) A warrior dancer on Robinson Crusoe Island wears a battledress of garlands and tattoos

1.

Finland is a quiet, laid-back place, where a ramshackle cottage by a lake and a properly stoked sauna are all that's required for happiness. It's a vast expanse of forests and lakes punctuated by small towns. The exception to this is the country's vibrant yet still intimate capital, Helsinki, which is fast becoming Europe's city break of choice. During the months of the midnight sun, coastal regions are a sailing and fishing paradise; when the nights are cold and long (and they can be very, very long), you can huddle inside with a vodka.

BEST TIME TO VISIT

May to September to avoid the cold and dark

ESSENTIAL EXPERIENCES

» Poking around the harbourside fish market in Helsinki – there's everything from salmon and sausages to handicrafts and all manner of reindeer-related souvenirs
» Spending the afternoon among the ramparts of the historic fortress on Suomenlinna Island
» Boating around the islands of Ekenäs Archipelago National Park
» Staying overnight in one of Hanko's charming Russian villas
» Dancing your heart out at the annual festival of Finnish Tango, Tangomarkkinat
» Seeing the aurora borealis – nature's Arctic light show

GETTING UNDER THE SKIN

» **Read** anything by Aleksis Kivi, who founded modern Finnish literature with *Seven Brothers*, a story of brothers who try to escape civilisation in favour of the forest
» **Listen** to Finnish jazz musician Raoul Björkenheim, or rock group The Flaming Sideburns

2.

» **Watch** Aki Kaurismäki's *The Man Without a Past*, the story of a man who loses his memory and becomes homeless, or the road film *Leningrad Cowboys Go America*

» **Eat** snow grouse, reindeer stew or glowfired salmon

» **Drink** *Salmiakkikossu* (a homemade spirit combining dissolved liquorice-flavoured sweets with the abrasive Koskenkorva vodka), or *sahti* (sweet, high-alcohol beer)

IN A WORD

» *Sisu* (often translated as 'guts', epitomising Finnish resilience)

TRADEMARKS

» Fish; beating oneself with a fragrant branch of birch leaves in a sauna; Nokia phones; reindeers; Sami; Moomin trolls

SURPRISES

» The world's largest smoke sauna is in Kuopio; the world's most popular surf instrumentalists are Laika & the Cosmonauts

MAP REF C,23

(1.) Forest pines lit by the supernatural glow of the aurora borealis near Kuusamo
(2.) Reindeers wandering the streets of Vuotso, Lapland
(3.) From trees to timber, a neat log pile stacked at the edge of a forest in northern Finland
(4.) A sapling pokes its head from beneath a blanket of winter snow in Oulu
(5.) Identical wooden houses in Rovaniemi built in the style of Lapland and the north

1.

With a capital that's synonymous with romance, a culture that's richer than foie gras, and a gene pool of philosophers, revolutionaries and designers, it's no wonder France has status. Fantastic ski slopes, glamorous beach resorts and rural villages complete the picture, while the food and wine score a gastronomic A+. Passionately patriotic, the French believe they live in the best place on earth. And since they invented *joie de vivre*, they might just be right.

BEST TIME TO VISIT

April and May (spring) or September and October (autumn)

ESSENTIAL EXPERIENCES

» Taking a boat down the Seine and marvelling at the Parisian architecture
» Checking out the glitz and glamour of the Le Mans 24-Hour Race
» Paying your respects at the evocative D-Day landing beaches in Normandy
» Enjoying on-piste action and après-ski at Val d'Isère
» Sipping a glass of Dom Perignon in Champagne
» Visiting the imposing châteaux on the Loire

GETTING UNDER THE SKIN

» **Read** Gustave Flaubert's *Madame Bovary*, a 19th-century classic about rural life and deluded passions
» **Listen** to Serge Gainsbourg's 'Je t'aime...moi non plus' – it is impossible not to turn Francophile when you hear this song
» **Watch** *À Bout de Souffle* (Breathless). Jump cuts, long takes, Jean Seberg's gamine look, Jean-Paul Belmondo's smouldering gaze – this is *nouvelle vague* cinema at its best.
» **Eat** bloody steak, croissants, baguettes, Camembert
» **Drink** red Bordeaux from Médoc, dessert wine from Sauternes

2.

3.

4.

IN A WORD

» *Ooh la la!*

TRADEMARKS

» Café society; stinky cheese; the Eiffel Tower; garlic; la guillotine; stripy T-shirts; berets; Cartier; Chanel; Gaultier; Louis XIV; the impressionists; *boules*; red meat; red wine; Gauloises

SURPRISES

» Attitudes can be conservative; bars close at 7pm in rural market towns

MAP REF F,20

(1.) Dancers pause for a breath of air at the tall windows of a Parisian studio
(2.) The enchanting fortified abbey of Mont-Saint-Michel watches over a flock of sheep
(3.) Contrasting styles define the art and architecture of the Musée du Louvre, Paris
(4.) Cabaret any day – the windmill of the Moulin Rouge has been turning in Paris since 1889
(5.) Vineyards form quilted patterns of Van Gogh colours in Beaujolais
(6.) A tourist photographs the Eiffel Tower, an icon of everything French

1.

Modern French Guiana is a land of idiosyncrasies, where European Space Agency satellite launches rattle the market gardens of displaced Hmong farmers from Laos, and thinly populated rainforests swallow nearly all but the country's coastline. Highly subsidised by Mother France, it boasts the highest standard of living of any 'country' in South America, but look beyond the capital city and you'll still find backwoods settlements of Maroons and Amerindians barely eking out a living.

BEST TIME TO VISIT

July to December, or in late February for Carnaval

ESSENTIAL EXPERIENCES

» Observing by moonlight the amazing ritual of giant leather-back turtles storming the beach to lay eggs and their newborn offspring scuttling to the sea
» Visiting the fascinating former penal-settlement islands of Îles du Salut by private catamaran or sailboat
» Learning everything you always wanted to know about rockets but were afraid to ask at Centre Spatial Guyanais (French Guiana Space Center)
» Hanging out in Cayenne and enjoying ethnic diversity, tropical ambience, gorgeous streetscapes and Creole cuisine
» Being overwhelmed by the age-old virgin rainforest in the Trésor Nature Reserve (or just about anywhere in the interior)

GETTING UNDER THE SKIN

» **Read** Henri Charrière's classic *Papillon* for a readable first-person account of the infamous penal colony on Devil's Island
» **Listen** to Caribbean rhythms with a French accent
» **Watch** the legendary Hollywood film *Papillon* starring Steve McQueen and Dustin Hoffman

4.

» **Eat** *crêpe forestière* (a savoury crepe of mushrooms and cheese), Vietnamese noodles or deliciously decadent pastries

» **Drink** rum or fresh fruit juice

IN A WORD

» *Chébran* (cool)

TRADEMARKS

» Penal settlements (particularly Devil's Island); French space rockets; Francophiles; turtles

SURPRISES

» French Guiana's rainforest is 90% intact; Plage Les Hattes contains the highest density of leatherback-turtle nesting sites in the world

MAP REF L,14

(1.) Block rockin' beats on the streets of Cayenne
(2.) Pink defines the interior decoration of an old prison in the Îles du Salut
(3.) Devil's Island caught in the natural frame of a rock formation
(4.) The grim remains of the notorious convict prison on Devil's Island in the Îles du Salut

FRENCH GUIANA

1.

Outside Libreville, its flashy air-conditioned capital, Gabon is a laid-back country of small villages, steamy rainforest, roaring rivers and imposing mountains. It's one of the richest and most stable countries in Africa, but also a place where people know the value of relaxation. The jungle is teeming with wildlife – elephants, leopards, gorillas, hippos, pythons – and new national parks are opening the forests to ecotourism, and closing them to loggers.

BEST TIME TO VISIT

May to September (dry season)

ESSENTIAL EXPERIENCES

» Visiting Albert Schweitzer's jungle hospital in the wildlife-rich lakes region of Lambaréné
» Swimming, exploring, eating and relaxing in Mayumba – an untouristed beach town
» Walking through the forests of Réserve de la Lopé, Gabon's best wildlife park, where you can see elephants, monkeys and, if you're lucky, gorillas
» Camping at the Cirque de Leconi, a spectacular red-rock canyon on the Bateke Plateau

GETTING UNDER THE SKIN

» **Read** *African Silences*, by Peter Matthiessen, in which he focuses on his journeys throughout Gabon and other parts of West Africa
» **Listen** to Oliver N'Goma, the hottest Gabonese musician today
» **Watch** *The Great White Man of Lambaréné,* a film about Albert Schweitzer from an African perspective
» **Eat** manioc paste (or rice) served in a spicy sauce
» **Drink** a Castel – or better yet, a Régab – beer from the Sobraga brewery, but never, ever the tap water

CAPITAL LIBREVILLE POPULATION 1,321,560 AREA 267,667 SQ KM OFFICIAL LANGUAGE FRENCH

2.

IN A WORD

» *Mbôlo* (hello, in Fang)

TRADEMARKS

» The wealthiest nation in sub-Saharan Africa; the slow pace of life; steamy rainforest; Albert Schweitzer

SURPRISES

» The Pont de Liane south of Franceville is a bridge made of vines, which locals use to cross the river; Gabon has been ruled since 1967 by President El Hadj Omar Bongo

CAMEROON

EQUATORIAL
GUINEA

Cocobeach

Bitam
Oyem
Bélinga
Makokou

Libreville

Booué

Equator

Ndjolé

Port-Gentil

Lambaréné

Lastoursville

Iguéla

Mouila

Franceville

*ATLANTIC
OCEAN*

Tchibanga

CONGO

MAP REF M,21

(**1.**) Capture the sun – a fisherman casts his net into the sea at sunset
(**2.**) Patients dance for redemption at Bwiti, an all-night healing ceremony in Gamba
(**3.**) An orphaned baby lowland gorilla enjoys a mango on Evangue Island
(**4.**) Gustave Eiffel's 1887 metal church, Mission Sainte Anne, in Fernan Vaz

1.

Sunshine and golden beaches have long made the Gambia a winter getaway for Europeans. But beyond the European-flavoured resorts are African-style wildlife reserves and the ruins of long-abandoned slaving stations. The Gambia is blessed with so many species of birds in such a compact area that even those who would struggle to identify a pigeon can't fail to be impressed. Its size, people, language and food make the Gambia the perfect gateway to West Africa.

BEST TIME TO VISIT

November to April (dry season)

ESSENTIAL EXPERIENCES

» Being surprised by the colonial elegance and unhurried pace of the capital, Banjul
» Sunning yourself in Serekunda, where there's a beach – and a beach bar – for every taste
» Birdwatching in the Abuko Nature Reserve – home to 250 bird species
» Relaxing in the southern fishing village of Gunjur, much quieter than neighbouring resorts to the north
» Cruising down the Gambia River with an amazing array of birdlife for company
» Soaking up the sleepy, crumbling, ex-colonial atmosphere of Georgetown

GETTING UNDER THE SKIN

» **Read** *Chaff on the Wind* by Gambian author Ebou Dibba, which follows the fortunes of two rural boys who go to work in the city
» **Listen** to the swinging rhythms of ever-popular band Ifang Bondi's album, *Gis Gis*

4.

5.

6.

ANDREW BURKE

» **Watch** *Roots*, by Alex Haley, who traced his origins to Jufureh, a village on the lower Gambia River

» **Eat** *domodah* (peanut stew with rice) or *benechin* (rice baked in a thick sauce of fish and vegetables)

» **Drink** the refreshing local beer, JulBrew

IN A WORD

» *I be ñaading* (hello)

TRADEMARKS

» Beaches; birdwatching; riverboats; night clubs; package tourism

SURPRISES

» It's a taboo in the Gambia to whistle after dark; Banjul International Airport's main runway was partly built by NASA as an emergency runway for space shuttles

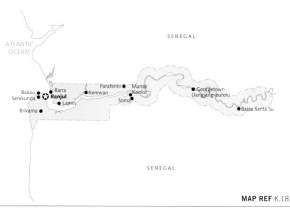

MAP REF K,18

(1.) Musicians beat out traditional tunes at the Roots Homecoming Festival in Banjul
(2.) A man checks his salted fish at a Banjul market
(3.) A woman wearing a traditional head-wrap flashes her teeth and jewellery
(4.) The Waasu Stone Circle, an enigmatic group of megalithic stones on MacCarthy Island
(5.) Using their heads as counter-tops, women sell refreshments in Banjul
(6.) At the close of day, traditional fishing pirogues retire in rows to Bakau beach

1.

CAPITAL TBILISI POPULATION 4,934,413 AREA 69,700 SQ KM OFFICIAL LANGUAGE GEORGIAN

Described variously as part of Europe, Central Asia or the Middle East, Georgia has long been a flash point for cultural and geographical collision. Tourist facilities in this newly independent nation are challenged by Western standards, but as a visitor you'll be fêted, fed, watered, and made to sing and dance, all in the incomprehensible Georgian language. Even if you can't understand much more than your hosts' smiles, the warmth you'll experience here will help you understand why Georgia remains a highlight of many people's travels.

BEST TIME TO VISIT

May, June and September for pleasant weather

ESSENTIAL EXPERIENCES

» Hiking in the magnificent Caucasus Mountains
» Taking a walk in Batumi's fragrant botanical gardens
» Exploring the ancient cave monastery city at Vardzia
» Strolling through the picturesque lanes of Tbilisi's Old Town
» Discovering the religious architecture at Mtskheta
» Chilling out at a pebble-beach resort on the Black Sea coast

GETTING UNDER THE SKIN

» **Read** *Please Don't Call It Soviet Georgia* by Mary Russel, an entertaining travelogue describing the period of upheaval leading to independence, or *Bread and Ashes* by Tony Anderson, a brilliant and up-to-date travelogue about trekking through Georgia
» **Listen** to *Georgian Voices* by the Rustavi Choir, Georgian music performed by a collection of singers from various parts of the country showcasing different styles and brilliant harmonies
» **Watch** *Keto and Kote* by respected Georgian filmmaker Siko Dolidze, filmed in 1949

2.

3.

4.

» **Eat** *khachi* (a breakfast soup made from cow hoof, tripe and garlic), *pkhali* (beetroot or spinach paste mixed with garlic and walnuts), *lobio* (spiced red or green beans), and *tkemali* (tasty wild-plum sauce)

» **Drink** delicious Georgian wines such as Guurdzaani, Tsinandali and Saperavi

IN A WORD

» *Didi madloba* (many thanks)

TRADEMARKS

» The stunning flora and fauna of the Caucasus; impressive cave complexes; elaborate toasting and revelry at a traditional dinner; cakes laden with cream, fruit and sugar; churches, monasteries and pagan temples

SURPRISES

» Until you experience a full Georgian meal, complete with lengthy toasting ceremonies, you can't truthfully claim to have seen the real Georgia

MAP REF G,24

(1.) A villager keeps a careful grip on his chickens as he buses into town on market day
(2.) Wild flowers bloom beneath the ruins of Jvari, an early-7th-century church in Mtskheta
(3.) An oddly artistic lookout point on the Georgian Military Highway near Krestovy Pass
(4.) Lips pursed in concentration, a woman harvests grapes in the Kakheti wine region
(5.) A candle illuminates the pious face of a worshipper at Kashveti Church, Tbilisi
(6.) The face of an elderly woman in Tbilisi etched with history and untold stories

1.

In the heart of Europe, Germany offers small picturesque towns, elegant big-city charm, fine wine and beer and a wealth of art and culture, plus the perennial pleasures of huge tracts of forest and castles along the Rhine. Germany also lies at the crossroads of Continental history. From Charlemagne and the Holy Roman Empire to Otto von Bismarck's German Reich, Nazism and the rise and fall of the Berlin Wall, no other nation has shaped Europe to the same extent as Germany.

BEST TIME TO VISIT

November to April for fewer tourists and surprisingly nice weather

ESSENTIAL EXPERIENCES

» Hiking from *Gasthaus* (hotel) to *Gasthaus* in the Black Forest
» Experiencing Buchenwald or other Holocaust memorials
» Immersing yourself in the urban cultures of Berlin, Munich, Hamburg and Dresden
» Taking a trip down the evocatively scenic Rhine Valley
» Discovering the picturesque walled cities and towns along the Romantic Road
» Enjoying a traditional meal in a *Ratskeller* (basement restaurant)
» Viewing lofty cathedrals such as the Ulm Münster

GETTING UNDER THE SKIN

» **Read** Goethe's *Faust*, which tells of the classic deal with the devil, and Nobel Prize–winning author Günther Grass's novel *The Tin Drum*, which caused an uproar in Germany in the 1950s because of its depiction of the Nazis
» **Listen** to Berlin-style punk symbol Nina Hagen, or tune in to Kraftwerk's '80s techno, and chanteuse Ute Lemper
» **Watch** Wim Wenders' *Wings of Desire* or the more fast-paced *Run Lola Run*

2.

3.

4.

» **Eat** wurst (sausage) with mustard, sauerkraut and potato salad

» **Drink** beer: with 80% of Europe's breweries in Germany, the choice is ample; or sample white wines such as Gewurtztraminer or Riesling

IN A WORD

» *Auf Wiedersehen* (goodbye/farewell/until we meet again)

TRADEMARKS

» *Lederhosen*; the legacy of WWII; good engineering; no speed limits; Oktoberfest; the Berlin Wall; doing what is socially accepted (and expected); BMW, Volkswagen, Mercedes, Audi and Porsche

SURPRISES

» German is a very pretty spoken language; Germans sometimes break the rules; Germans can play as hard as they work

MAP REF F,21

(1.) The perfect fairytale, Neuschwanstein Castle perched 200m above the valley

(2.) Dancers at the Munich Union Move

(3.) Berlin's new Jüdisches Museum (Jewish Museum)

(4.) The surreal architecture of Caligari Hall in Filmpark Babelsberg, Brandenburg

(5.) A serene lookout over the Sylvenstein Reservoir, Lenggries

(6.) The striking Maxim Gorki Theatre in Berlin

1.

Ghanaians have plenty to be proud of. Their country was home to West Africa's mightiest, gold-dripping empire; it was the first to drop colonialism and go it alone; it built the biggest artificial lake in the world; and it produces some of Africa's best highlife music and most famous sculpture. And you won't find a more chilled-out and friendly people. So if you want to sample West Africa's modern and ancient cultures, explore its historic slave forts, toast yourself on its beautiful beaches – and do it all speaking English – it's got to be Ghana.

BEST TIME TO VISIT
October to March, when the weather is cooler and dryer

ESSENTIAL EXPERIENCES
» Browsing Accra's Makola (batik and beads) and Kaneshie (food and spices) markets
» Steeping yourself in Ashanti culture and history at the National Cultural Centre in Kumasi
» Strolling through Accra's peaceful Aburi Botanical Gardens
» Spending the night in an old fort or castle on the Atlantic coast
» Lazing on the long white sandy beach at Busua
» Hiking and wildlife watching at Kakum National Park

GETTING UNDER THE SKIN
» **Read** *Asante: The Making of a Nation* by Nana Otamakuro Adubofour, for an insight into Ashanti history and culture
» **Listen** to *Electric Highlife*, a taste of highlife that will really get you moving; *Master Drummer from Ghana* by Mustapha Tettey Addy, one of West Africa's greatest drumming performers
» **Watch** *Heritage Africa* by the celebrated Ghanaian director Kwaw P Ansah – an exploration of the effects of colonialism in Ghana

2.

3.

4.

» **Eat** groundnut stew; *omo tuo* – mashed rice balls served with fish or meat soup; *kyemgbuma* – crabs with potatoes, meat and cassava dough; *ntomo krakro* – fried sweet potato cakes, a popular street food

» **Drink** *askenkee* – a cool, milky-white nonalchoholic drink made from corn

IN A WORD

» *Hani wodzo* (let's dance)

TRADEMARKS

» Beautiful beaches; vibrant city nightlife; fishing villages; ruins of the slave trade; elephants and antelope; highlife music; ancient forts and castles

SURPRISES

» It's possible to meet the current Ashanti king at Manhyia Palace in Kumasi – inquire politely and bring a gift

MAP REF L,20

(1.) Proud as a statue, a woman surveys her village from the roof of her house in Sirigu

(2.) The sun sets on Larabanga mosque, the oldest religious building in Ghana

(3.) A musical mound of maraccas for sale at a market in Accra

(4.) A decorated pirogue rests on the Volta River in Ada

(5.) Four schoolgirls in Kumasi enjoy iced treats and strike a pose in their uniforms

(6.) A devoted subject of the king bears a golden sceptre at Manhyia Palace in Kumasi

1.

Having exported chaos, drama, tragedy and democracy before most nations stayed up late enough to want souvlaki, Greece boasts an unrivalled legacy. From smoggy Athens to the blindingly bright islands dotting the sea, ancient fragments abound – the belly button of the cosmos at Delphi, fallen columns galore on sacred Delos, frescoed Minoan palaces on Crete and even, quite possibly, the remnants of Atlantis at Santorini.

BEST TIME TO VISIT
» Easter to mid-June for the weather and fewer crowds

ESSENTIAL EXPERIENCES
» Dining out beneath the floodlit Acropolis in Athens
» Taking a walk in spring through the Mani or Arcadia mountains in the Peloponnese
» Island-hopping from Piraeus to Mykonos, Delos and Naxos
» Hiking through Crete's dramatic Samaria Gorge
» Catching that first glimpse of Santorini's sheer cliffs and white-washed buildings

GETTING UNDER THE SKIN
» **Read** *Zorba the Greek* by Nikos Kazantzakis – a tale about living life to the fullest by Greece's most celebrated contemporary author; *Captain Corelli's Mandolin* by Louis de Bernières – a captivating WWII-era love story set on Kefallonia
» **Listen** to Demis Roussos – the larger-than-life singer who spent the 1980s strutting the world stage clad in his kaftan. Yanni is a US-based techno wizard who hails from Greece.
» **Watch** *Eternity and a Day*, directed by Theodoros Angelopoulos – traces the last days of a celebrated Greek writer; *Orgasmos tis Ageladas* (The Cow's Orgasm), a comedy directed by Olga Malea

2.

3.

4.

» **Eat** *spanakopita* (spinach pie), moussaka (layers of eggplant or zucchini, minced meat and potatoes topped with cheese and baked) or baklava (layers of filo pastry filled with honey and nuts)

» **Drink** Greek coffee, the national drink – it is served in a small cup with the grounds and no milk. Ouzo is the aperitif of choice.

IN A WORD

» *Kalimera* (good day)

TRADEMARKS

» The Parthenon; ouzo; plate-smashing; package tourists; beautiful beaches; the birthplace of philosophy; inter-island hopping

SURPRISES

» Greeks wear blue trinkets to ward off the evil eye; gum mastic (from the lentisk bush) has been used since ancient times to cure ailments from stomachache to snake bite

MAP REF G,22

(1.) Shades are strictly orthodox for this hipster priest on Rhodes
(2.) Inky clouds blot out the sky as a ferry approaches the coast of Santorini
(3.) A row of octopus hanging up to dry on Lipsi island
(4.) Pride of Athens, the ancient Parthenon of the Acropolis
(5.) Picturesque Olymbos clings to the ridgeface below Mt Profitis Ilias, Karpathos
(6.) Donkeys pick their way down steps leading from the port of Fira Skala on Santorini

1.

DEANNA SWANEY

Ever since 15th-century explorers returned from the distant north with wild and woolly tales of unicorns and citadels of ice, Greenland has been a semi-mythical destination. And it's still a fantasy land come to life, with the aurora borealis, the vast tundra, monstrous glaciers that calve icebergs into the sea, and a coastline of glacial ice and ancient rock – the oldest on the planet. Its villages are visited by Mercedes in summer and dogsled in winter, and though supermarkets now offer pineapples from Hawaii and tomatoes from Mexico, you can still grab a seal steak from the frozen goods section.

BEST TIME TO VISIT

July to September during the thaw

ESSENTIAL EXPERIENCES

- » Hiking from Narsarsuaq to Kiattuut Sermiat's mountain lake
- » Soaking in the Uunartoq Hot Springs while watching icebergs floating past
- » Wandering around Hvalsey, the best-preserved Norse ruins in Greenland
- » Being awed by the soaring granite ramparts of Uiluit Qaaqa and Ulamertorsuaq at Tasermiut Fjord
- » Taking the ferry to Aappilattoq through sapphire-blue waters
- » Hanging out in Nanortalik – a relaxed and friendly town in scenic countryside

GETTING UNDER THE SKIN

- » **Read** The entertaining account of the country in *Last Places – A Journey in the North*, by Lawrence Millman
- » **Listen** to pop group Qulleq, or check out techno band Hap
- » **Watch** the Oscar-nominated classic *Qivitoq*

2.

» **Eat** fresh *kapisillit* (salmon), or pick your own huckleberries

» **Drink** the local home-brew beer called *imiaq* – but you may need to gather some gumption first

IN A WORD

» Brrrr!

TRADEMARKS

» Whale steaks; Seasonal Affective Disorder ('SAD syndrome'); ice; Inuit people; fishing trawlers; glaciers

SURPRISES

» Greenland has one of the world's lowest rates of cardiovascular disease due to the consumption of unsaturated fatty acids found in marine mammals; Greenlanders believe their children are born with the wisdom, magic and intelligence of their ancestors

MAP REF A,15

(1.) Cheerful matchbox houses nest amongst the rocks of Uummannaq
(2.) Pens, pencils and pennants– national dress is school uniform in Uummannaq
(3.) A fishing boat slices through the freezing waters of Ilulissat Kangualua, Disko Bay
(4.) The setting sun gleams on houses both old and new in Qaqortoq
(5.) A home for gnomes – a traditional sod house in Nanortalik

Dubbed the 'Spice Islands' because of its impressive production of nutmeg, mace, cinnamon, ginger and cloves, Grenada is a heady mix of idyllic tropical rainforests, fecund valleys, terraced gardens and rivers that fall away to white-sand beaches, bays and craggy cliffs. St George's, the beautiful capital, gives Grenada a small-town character, with a dash of dynamic sophistication. Its harbour, known as the Carenage, is one of the prettiest in the Caribbean.

BEST TIME TO VISIT

Temperatures are optimum year-round; Carnival, the second weekend in August, is hard to miss

ESSENTIAL EXPERIENCES

» Swimming at glorious Grand Anse beach
» Taking the ferry over to lazy Carriacou island
» Walking around tiny Petit Martinique island
» Driving through the Grand Etang National Park
» Splashing about on the undeveloped sands of Bathways Beach

GETTING UNDER THE SKIN

» **Read** native Grenadian Jean Buffong's *Under the Silk Cotton Tree: A Novel (Emerging Voices)*, a portrait of her Grenadian girlhood, religion and culture
» **Listen** to local calypso, steel bands and reggae
» **Watch** the documentary *Grenada: The Future Coming Towards Us*, which covers Grenada's early history and looks at contemporary Grenadian society
» **Eat** pigeon peas and rice (pigeon peas are the brown, pea-like seeds of a tropical shrub) or curried *lambi* (conch)
» **Drink** the nonalcoholic fruit juice *mauby* (a bittersweet drink made from the bark of the rhamnaceous tree), rum sprinkled with nutmeg, or the locally brewed beer Carib

4.

IN A WORD

» Small is beautiful – a popular saying in the Caribbean

TRADEMARKS

» The 'Spice Islands'; the invasion led by former US president Ronald Reagan; Grand Anse beach; the *Bianca C* shipwreck; smuggling

SURPRISES

» Grenada produces one third of the world's nutmeg; Scottish heritage on the island of Carriacou is evident in Highland-style cottages and Celtic methods of boat building

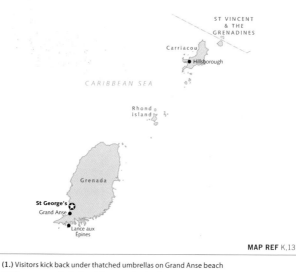

ST VINCENT & THE GRENADINES

Carriacou

● Hillsborough

CARIBBEAN SEA

Rhond island

Grenada

St George's ☆
Grand Anse ●

Lance aux Épines

MAP REF K,13

(1.) Visitors kick back under thatched umbrellas on Grand Anse beach
(2.) A woman carries fruit and flowers on her head
(3.) Boys playing with bicycle wheels, Hermitage
(4.) Out with the family, St George's

MARGIE POLITZER

1.

Guadeloupe's spirited blend of French and African influences goes straight to the heart of the Caribbean's Creole culture. As well known for its sugar and rum as for its beaches and resorts, Guadeloupe mixes modern cities and rural hamlets, rainforests and secluded beaches. There are nine inhabitated islands to choose from, including Grande-Terre, Basse-Terre and Marie-Galant. Bustling Pointe-à-Pitre is the main hub, but the sleepy capital is on Basse-Terre's remote southwestern flank.

BEST TIME TO VISIT
February to April (dry season)

ESSENTIAL EXPERIENCES
» Kicking back on the Frenchified island of Terre-de-Haut and checking out its grand 19th-century fort
» Visiting the sleepy isles of La Désirade and Marie-Galante, with their uncrowded beaches and unspoiled scenery
» Lazing on the beach at Anse à la Gourde, a gorgeous sweep of white coral sands
» Exploring the rainforest in Parc National de la Guadeloupe, on Basse-Terre
» Snorkelling the waters of the Réserve Cousteau
» Hiking up the volcanic summit of Basse-Terre's La Soufrière

GETTING UNDER THE SKIN
» **Read** *Anabase* by local poet Alexis Léger (translated by TS Eliot); *The Tree of Life* by Maryse Condé, centring around the life of a Guadeloupean family
» **Listen** to local zouk group Malavoi or *gwo-ka* master Guy Konket
» **Watch** *Sucre Amer* directed by Christian Lara
» **Eat** *crabes farci* (spicy stuffed land crabs) or *colombo cabri* (curried goat)

319

GREG GAWLOWSKI

JEAN ROBERT

» **Drink** *ti-punch* (white rum, cane sugar and fresh lime, mixed to your own proportions), or locally brewed Corsaire beer

IN A WORD

» *Bonjour!* – best delivered with a big smile

TRADEMARKS

» Sugar; rum; beaches; resorts; fishing villages; Creole food; women in traditional Creole costume

SURPRISES

» Guadeloupe is a member of the EU; about two-thirds of all the bananas eaten in France are from Guadeloupe

MAP REF K,13

(1.) Fishing boats return at sunset
(2.) The tropical Grand Etang lake
(3.) Terre-de-Haut clings to the coastline on the island of Les Santines
(4.) A lone kayaker cruises through the waters off Îles des Saintes

GUADELOUPE

1.

2.

3.

JOHN ELK III

Looking for tribal villages or ancient cultures that are untouched by the modern world? You won't find them in Guam, as this strategic US territory isn't in the 'Tropical Paradise' mould. You'll have more luck in the Northern Marianas, with their turquoise waters, white sands, fine diving, snorkelling and hiking. And if you really want to get away from it all, hop over to laid-back Tinian or rustic Rota. Guam and the Northern Marianas are inextricably linked by history and geography, sharing typhoons, an archipelago, Spanish and US influences, the Mariana Trench and Chamorro culture.

BEST TIME TO VISIT
December to March (the dry season)

ESSENTIAL EXPERIENCES
» Dodging Saipan's golf courses to find that rare secluded beach
» Slowing down to the village pace of Rota
» Communing with monolithic latte stones or bodysurfing the beaches on Tinian
» Whooping it up at a fiesta in Agana's Chamorro Village
» Getting romantic at Guam's Two Lovers Point where two legendary lovers plunged to a precipitous death

GETTING UNDER THE SKIN
» **Read** *Micronesia: Winds of Change*, spanning the history from 1521 to 1951 with accounts of early explorers, missionaries and locals
» **Listen** to *It's Party Time in the Marianas* by the Castro Boyz for a funky mix of English and Chamorro tunes
» **Watch** George Tweed's short film *Return to Guam*, which traces the journey back to the island by a former US serviceman

4.

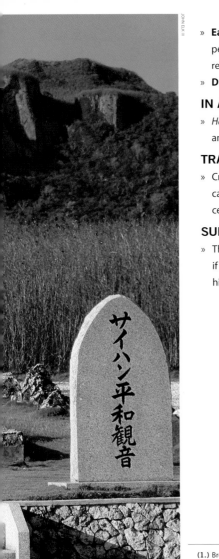

JOHN ELK III

» **Eat** anything with *finadene*, a hot sauce zinging with red peppers, soy sauce, lemon juice and onions that turns dishes into a real Chamorro meal

» **Drink** a major American cola – they're all here

IN A WORD

» *Hafa adai* (a catch-all greeting encompassing 'Hello', 'What's up?' and 'How are you?')

TRADEMARKS

» Crystal-clear blue waters and white-sand beaches; crusty American GIs comparing war wounds; package tourists ambling past centuries-old latte stones; beach bars pouring all day and night

SURPRISES

» The Marianas are at the edge of the deep-sea Mariana Trench, so if measured from their bases the islands are actually the world's highest mountains, dwarfing Mt Everest by 3000m

PHILIPPINE SEA

Ritidian Point

Uruno Beach

Tarague Beach

Tanguisson Beach

Gun Beach

• Yigo

• Tumon

• Tamuning

Apra Harbor

✪ **Hagåtña (Agana)**

NORTH PACIFIC OCEAN

Yona •

Ipan Beach

Cetti Bay

Talofofo Bay

Fort Soledad •

• Inarajan

Cocos Island

MAP REF J,35 & K,35

(1.) Breathtaking views towards the city from Amantes (Two Lovers) Point
(2.) A Giant Moray Eel pops out to greet a visiting diver
(3.) The interior of Dulce Nombre de Maria Cathedral Basilica in Hagåtña
(4.) The Heiwa Kannon Memorial at Banzai Cliff on Saipan Island

1.

Although Guatemala is recovering from the psychic wounds of military dictatorships and guerrilla warfare, it possesses a gritty determination to keep the glorious colours of Mayan culture flying. And what a wealth of masts it has to nail them to. Its volcanoes can seem the highest and most active, its Mayan ruins the most ruinous, its colonial cities the most historic, its jungles the most enigmatic and impenetrable, and its flora and fauna some of the most unusual in the world.

BEST TIME TO VISIT
November through to May (the dry season)

ESSENTIAL EXPERIENCES
» Joining a Spanish-language school in Antigua
» Spending a day in a hammock on lazy Santa Cruz la Laguna
» Hiking to the highest point in Central America (Tajumulco Volcano), camping overnight and watching the sun rise
» Engaging in a spot of bartering at the Sunday Chichicastenango markets
» Spending a day at the Mayan ruins at Tikal

GETTING UNDER THE SKIN
» **Read** *Hombres De Maíz,* by Miguel Ángel Asturias, the Nobel Prize–winning author and long-time exile who combines Mayan mysticism and social consciousness to deliver an indictment of dictatorial rule
» **Listen** to *Guatemala: Celebrated Marimbas*, highlighting the principal instrument of traditional Guatemalan music. Paco Pérez's 'Luna de Xelaju' is the best-known composition for marimbas.
» **Watch** *What Sebastian Dreamt*. Part documentary, part narrative, this rare Guatemalan film offers the rainforests as primary suspect in a murder/mystery thriller.

GUATEMALA

CAPITAL GUATEMALA CITY POPULATION 13,909,384 AREA 108,890 SQ KM OFFICIAL LANGUAGE SPANISH

2.

3.

4.

» **Eat** tortilla, a thin round patty of corn dough cooked on a griddle; frijoles, black beans; *tapado*, a Caribbean casserole of seafood, plantains, coconut milk and vegetables

» **Drink** coffee, hot chocolate, fresh fruit and vegetable juices

IN A WORD

» *Basta que basta* (enough is enough)

TRADEMARKS

» Old Mayan gods and ruins; colourful masks; cheerfully painted buses; the quetzal; brooding volcanoes; rainforests; cornfields; brilliantly coloured textiles; Mayan trouble dolls; tongue-challenging place names; highly wrought iron crucifixes

SURPRISES

» The quality of jewellery; the national passion for football (soccer); the cold in the Highlands; cheap mobile phone calls

MAP REF K,10

(1.) Brassy beats blare in Totonicapán as musicians pull out the stops for a wedding
(2.) Vapours rise from steaming pots of food in the spiritual centre of Chichicastenango
(3.) Hooded figures bless the streets of Antigua with incense on Good Friday
(4.) Mayan colours come out of the closet for market day in San Lucas Toliman
(5.) The crown of Templo I in the lost city of Tikal materialises from the morning mist
(6.) Look, no hands! Cheeky children carrying traditional embroidery in Antigua

1.

2.

3.

GREENSHOOTS COMMUNICATIONS

Guinea was once ruled by one of the most oppressive regimes in Africa, but these days the country exudes a marked energy and growing economic vitality. High on the country's list of attractions is the vibrancy of its cultural traditions, particularly in music and dance, and its natural beauties include lush rainforests and breathtaking highland scenery. Visitors to Guinea can trek through the jungles of the southeast, watch an amazing dance performance in Conakry or browse through one of the many bustling markets.

BEST TIME TO VISIT

November to February (the dry season) – or between the 13th and 15th centuries when Guinea was part of the Empire of Mali

ESSENTIAL EXPERIENCES

» Strolling the streets and taking in the vibrant neighbourhood life in Conakry
» Hiking in the beautiful green hills of Fouta Djalon
» Scouring the enormous Wednesday market at Guéckédou
» Visiting the Grande Mosquée and sculpture workshop at Kankan
» Viewing the Bridal Falls (during the rainy season) at Kindia
» Lying in the sun on the beach at Cape Verga

GETTING UNDER THE SKIN

» **Read** *L'Enfant Noir* by Guinean writer Camara Laye, full of fascinating insights into traditional daily life
» **Listen** to *Bembeya Jazz National* by the popular Guinean group Bembeya Jazz, one of Africa's premier dance bands
» **Watch** *Djembefola* by Laurent Chevallier, the story of Guinean drummer Mamady Keita's return to his remote native village
» **Eat** *kulikuli* – peanut balls made with peanuts, onion and cayenne pepper; grilled fish; brochettes (kebabs)

4.

» **Drink** *café noir* – small cups of espresso-like coffee drunk with lots of sugar

IN A WORD

» *I be di* (hello in Maninka)

TRADEMARKS

» Indigo cloth; vibrant nightlife; gorgeous beaches; traditional music and dance; great street food; French colonial influences; mangrove swamps; rich wildlife

SURPRISES

» The open-air cinema at Mamou; French-style patisseries in Conakry; chimpanzees and hippopotamii in the Parc Transfronalier Niokolo-Badier

MAP REF K,18

(1.) Drumming delirium at a ceremony in Sesse village, north of Beyla
(2.) A local craftsman makes decorated stools on the roadside near Mamou
(3.) Primary school children take their singing lesson out of the classroom
(4.) A Guinean woman deftly juggles brochettes in a frying pan

1.

DAVID ELSE

Tiny, verdant and fractured by waterways, Guinea-Bissau is a gem for those prepared to seek it out. Sleepy towns, quiet beaches and sacred rainforests dot the mainland, while offshore the Arquipélago dos Bijagós has a unique culture and fantastic marine and animal life. Guinea-Bissau is not a well-developed nation – even by African standards it's gut-wrenchingly poor – and it's been badly served by its recent leaders. However, it remains peaceful and its people are some of the most unconditionally hospitable in West Africa.

BEST TIME TO VISIT

Late November to February, when it's dry and cool

ESSENTIAL EXPERIENCES

» Viewing the flora and fauna of the Arquipélago dos Bijagós
» Dancing at Bissau's February Carnival – music, papier-mâché masks and parades
» Hiking and observing wildlife in the south's sacred forests
» Checking out the Portuguese colonial architecture throughout the country
» Relaxing on the archipelago's pristine beaches

GETTING UNDER THE SKIN

» **Read** Susan Lowerre's *Under the Neem Tree*, which tells a vivid story of a Peace Corps volunteer's experiences in the region
» **Listen** to Super Mama Djombo and popular singers Dulce Maria Neves, N'Kassa Cobra and Patcheco
» **Watch** Flora Gomes' *The Blue Eyes of Yonta,* a film about dreams and revolution
» **Eat** *riz gras* (rice with a greasy sauce) at rice bars, or grilled fish and salad at *barracas* (makeshift bar/restaurants)

» **Drink** *caña de cajeu* (cashew rum) – made from the cashew fruit that surrounds the nuts

IN A WORD

» *Bom-dia* (good morning)

TRADEMARKS

» Monkeys; groundnuts; Portuguese colonialism; the Arquipélago dos Bijagós

SURPRISES

» Guinea-Bissau is the world's sixth-largest producer of cashew nuts; the Orango Islands National Park is home to a rare species of saltwater hippopotamus

MAP REF K,18

(1.) Gone fishing – an ocean-going canoe tries its luck along the Guinea-Bissau coast
(2.) A jam-packed ship plies the waters around the Arquipélago dos Bijagós
(3.) A distinctly Mediterranean-influenced Christian church in Bissau
(4.) Brightly painted buildings showcase Bissau's Portuguese colonial history

1.

2.

3.

Dutch and British colonisation made an indelible mark on Guyana, leaving behind a now dilapidated colonial capital, a volatile mix of peoples and a curious political geography. The country's natural attractions, however, are impressive, unspoiled and on a scale that dwarfs human endeavour. Guyana has immense falls, vast tropical rainforest, and grasslands teeming with wildlife. If the government doesn't destroy the environment in a bid to pay off its huge foreign debt, it could be the ecotourism destination of the future.

BEST TIME TO VISIT

At the end of either rainy season: late January or late August

ESSENTIAL EXPERIENCES

» Revelling in the spray of South America's most majestic waterfalls, Kaieteur Falls
» Visiting Iwokrama, a rainforest conservation and development centre
» Trucking on an unforgettable overland crossing from Georgetown to Lethem
» Taking a wildlife-viewing excursion to a local ranch in the Rupununi Savanna, a vast area of grassland, termite mounds and forested hills
» Exploring the gold and diamond fields near Bartica

GETTING UNDER THE SKIN

» **Read** the country's best known work of literature, ER Braithwaite's *To Sir With Love*; or *Ninety-Two Days* which Evelyn Waugh wheezed his way through Guyana's rugged interior to write
» **Listen** to Eddy Grant, who had a hit with 'Electric Avenue' in the early '80s

4.

» **Watch** *The Mighty Quinn* starring Guyanese-born Norman Beaton
» **Eat** pepper pot (a spicy stew cooked in bitter cassava juice), souse (jellied cow's head), or try an East Indian curry and roti
» **Drink** Banks beer, local rum El Dorado 5 Star, or delicious fruit punches

IN A WORD

» Cat a ketch rat, but he a teef he massa fish (good and evil come from the same source)

TRADEMARKS

» Crime; the Jim Jones tragedy; having the worst national football team in South America; internationally renowned cricketer Clive Lloyd

SURPRISES

» An estimated 30% of Iwokrama's flora and fauna is still unidentified; the national indoor pursuit is dominoes

MAP REF L,13

(**1.**) Sitting on the dock of the bay – watching the ferry on the Correntyne River
(**2.**) The giant clocktower looms over shoppers at Stabroek Market
(**3.**) Colourful advertising outside a halal meat shop in Georgetown
(**4.**) One of the world's tallest timber churches, St George's Cathedral, Georgetown

1.

ERIC WHEATER

The modern world's first black-led republic, Haiti boasts a unique culture and an incredible artistic tradition. Its intensely spiritual people are known for their humour and passion, upheld in the face of poverty, civil strife, oppression and urban over-population. Their language, dance and music reflect a unique syncopation between the spiritual and material worlds. Haiti is not yet set up for the Club Med crowd, but the open-minded adventurer will find a country whose contradictions will linger in mind, heart and spirit.

BEST TIME TO VISIT

June to August (the dry season)

ESSENTIAL EXPERIENCES

» Touring Jacmel's Victorian gingerbread homes
» Visiting the Musée National in Port-au-Prince, housing King Christophe's suicide pistol and a rusty anchor reputed to have been salvaged from Columbus' *Santa Maria*
» Strolling past the Spanish-influenced architecture of Cap-Haïtien
» Shopping at Port-au-Prince's Marché de Fer (Iron Market), packed with stalls, vendors and piles of fruit, baskets and religious totems
» Taking the horseback trek to the Bassins Bleu – three cobalt-blue pools joined by spectacular cascades

GETTING UNDER THE SKIN

» **Read** *Beast of the Haitian Hills* by Pierre Marcelin and Philippe Thoby Marcelin, a novel about life in the Haitian countryside; the historical novel *All Souls' Rising* by Madison Smartt Bell
» **Listen** to Cuban-Haitian vocal group Desandann or Lody Auguste
» **Watch** *Lumumba* by acclaimed Haitian director Raoul Peck, or for some classic Hollywood horror from 1932, *White Zombie*

343

» **Eat** *grillot et banane pese* (pork chops with island bananas) or *diri et djondjon* (rice and black mushrooms)
» **Drink** rum, the drink of choice

IN A WORD

» *Pas plus mal* (no worse than before) – the standard answer to 'How are you?'

TRADEMARKS

» *Vodou*; zombies; Papa Doc; slave history; racial discord; shanty towns

SURPRISES

» Orange peels drying on sunny surfaces throughout Cap-Haïtien are destined to one day lend their flavour to luxury liqueurs Grand Marnier and Cointreau; actors in enormous papier-mâché masks act out parables of good versus evil during Jacmel's pre-Lent Mardi Gras festivities

Île de la Tortue

ATLANTIC OCEAN

● Cap du Môle

● Cap-Haïtien

● Gonaïves

Golfe de la Gonâve

Hinche ●

Île de la Gonâve

● Jérémie

● Dame Marie

Petite Rivières de Nippes ●

Port-au-Prince ✪

● Pétionville

Les Cayes ●

● Côtes de Fer

Jacmel ●

Port Salut ●

Île-à-Vache

Caribbean Sea

DOMINICAN REPUBLIC

MAP REF J,12

(**1.**) Water, gossip and washing up – the market well is a one-stop shop for locals in Milot
(**2.**) Floating chefs take a catch of conch down to Lambi harbour where they will be cooked
(**3.**) The cautious eyes of a young girl carrying a tub-load of laundry in Artibonite
(**4.**) Cheerful as a merry-go-round, a bus in Port-au-Prince welcomes passengers aboard
(**5.**) A woman guards the doorway of her home in Les Cayes

1.

Honduras' slow pace, natural beauty and low-profile tourism make it particularly appealing to travellers (well-armed with insect repellent) who enjoy getting off the beaten track. Take your pick from the spectacular Mayan ruins at Copán, the long and lazy Caribbean coastline, the idyllic Islas de la Bahía (Bay Islands), the tropical rainforest of the Mosquitia region, colonial mountain towns, the cool cloud forest of La Tigra National Park, or the manatees and birdlife in the country's protected coastlands, wetlands and lagoons.

BEST TIME TO VISIT

May to June for the festivals

ESSENTIAL EXPERIENCES

» Diving in the warm, crystal-clear waters of Islas de la Bahía
» Fossicking through the pyramids and temples of Copán
» Visiting the Spanish colonial mountain town of Gracias
» Experiencing the spectacular cloud forest of Parque Nacional Celaque
» Exploring the Río Plátano biosphere at La Mosquitia
» Taking the eight-hour boat ride up the Río Plátano to Las Marías through virgin rainforest

GETTING UNDER THE SKIN

» **Read** *El Gran Hotel* by Guillermo Yuscarán (one of Honduras' most celebrated writers) or *The Soccer War* by Ryszard Kapuscinski, which is about the 100-hour war between Honduras and El Salvador known as the Guerra de Fútbol (the Football War)
» **Listen** to Garífuna band *Los Menudos*
» **Watch** *El Espíritu de mi Mama* (Spirit of my Mother) directed by Ali Allie, about a young Garífuna woman

2.

3.

4.

» **Eat** coconut bread or *casabe* (a crispy flat bread common throughout the Caribbean)
» **Drink** Port Royal or Salva Vida beer

IN A WORD

» *Buenos días* (good day)

TRADEMARKS

» The Mosquito Coast; inexpensive diving; Copán; the brief Football War; howler monkeys

SURPRISES

» Islas de la Bahía form part of the second-largest barrier reef in the world; Honduras is experiencing the most rapid urbanisation in Central America

MAP REF K,11

(1.) A young boy and his indignant reptiles pose for show-and-tell
(2.) Cowboy kids relax with snacks in the town of Copán
(3.) Stilt houses creep across the water on the island of Roatán
(4.) A pair of Scarlet Macaws perch on a carving at the archaeological site of Copán
(5.) A mermaid presides over an empty bar in Tela
(6.) The white façade of La Iglesia de La Merced evinces old colonial glory in Gracias

1.

Hong Kong is like no other city on earth. It's a pulsating, densely populated fusion of East and West, lit by neon, fuelled by nonstop yum cha, dressed in faux Dior and serenaded by Canto-pop. And just when you think it's all too much, it's a secluded sandy beach on Lantau or a visit to a Taoist temple in the New Territories. Despite its British colonial past, Hong Kong has always stuck to its roots, and the culture beneath the glitz is pure Chinese – with a vibrant twist.

BEST TIME TO VISIT

October to December (the dry season)

ESSENTIAL EXPERIENCES

- » Crossing the harbour on a crowded Star Ferry
- » Heading out for a night on Lamma Island by *san-pan* or night ferry
- » Sipping cocktails at sunset in a skyscraper bar overlooking the harbour
- » Hopping on the cable car at Ocean Park and enjoying the view of the cliffs down to Deep Water Bay
- » Riding the double-decker bus to Stanley market – try to get a seat in the front row on the upper deck

GETTING UNDER THE SKIN

- » **Read** *An Insular Possession* by Timothy Mo – a novel set in precolonial Hong Kong; *Fragrant Harbour* by John Lanchester – set in the more recent past
- » **Listen** to Canto-pop: treacly pop schmaltz, with stars including Sally Yip, Sammi Cheung and Andy Lau
- » **Watch** *Crime Story*, directed by Che Kirk Wong Chi Keung, a traditional Jackie Chan movie combining good comedy and kung fu; *Young and Dangerous*, directed by Andrew Lau Wai Keung, a film adaptation of a local comic series about Triad society

351

2.

» **Eat** *juk* (breakfast rice porridge), *cha siu bau* (steamed pork buns), *sinning jin yuen gain* (pan-fried lemon chicken), *she gang* (snake soup)

» **Drink** *dong gafe* (chilled coffee soft drink), *bolei* (green tea), Tsingtao (a popular Chinese brand of beer), *mao tai* (Chinese wine)

IN A WORD

» *Nei ho ma?* (hello; how are you?)

TRADEMARKS

» Early morning bargains; crowds jostling for space; designer fakes; Jackie Chan; festivals all year around; expatriates; the Star Ferry; feng shui; dim sum

SURPRISES

» Hong Kong consumes more oranges than anywhere else on earth; the frequently heard new year greeting *kung hei fat choi* literally means 'respectful wishes, get rich'

MAP REF J,32

(1.) Villains and lovers take centre stage in a Cantonese opera performance
(2.) Shoppers cross the bustling intersection of Queen's Road and D'Aguilar Street
(3.) Sweeping and gliding, a girl on rollerskates runs rings around Hong Kong Park
(4.) A rickshaw chauffeur catches his breath and the local news

1.

As piquant as the paprika it's famous for, and romantic as the Roma music that inspired Béla Bartók, Hungary offers visitors a taste of Europe's heart and soul – but at half the price of anywhere in Western Europe. Budapest is the star attraction, fabulously located on the Danube and rich in Art Nouveau and baroque architecture. Elsewhere, there are ruined castles, rejuvenating spas, Roman and Turkish remnants, and exquisite lake and vine country. Now that Hungary has joined the EU, the time is more than ripe to experience Magyarország.

BEST TIME TO VISIT

May to September – or before 1526 and the Battle of Mohács

ESSENTIAL EXPERIENCES

» Soothing away aches and pains in a thermal bath in Budapest
» Letting loose at a resort on Lake Balaton, Hungary's 'inland sea'
» Strolling around the Castle District in Buda
» Cycling along the Danube Bend, particularly around Szentendre
» Birdwatching in the Hortobágy National Park
» Caving in the Aggtelek Karst, a Unesco World Heritage site

GETTING UNDER THE SKIN

» **Read** *Fateless,* by Imre Kertész, an autobiographical novel about the author's experiences in concentration camps in WWII; *Eclipse of the Crescent Moon,* by Géza Gárdonyi, a tale set in the 16th century during the Turkish siege
» **Listen** to *Márta Sebestyén,* whose haunting voice appears on *The English Patient* soundtrack, or Hungarian folk ensemble Cifra
» **Watch** *István a Király* (Stephen the King), written by Levente Szörényi and János Bródy, a stirring rock-opera about the life of the first king of Hungary. *6:3* is Péter Timár's account of the

DAVID GREEDY

2.

impact the 1953 'football match of the century' between England and Hungary had on people's lives.

» **Eat** *töltött káposzta*, cabbage leaves rolled and stuffed with meat and rice; *madártej*, a delicious custard-like dessert

» **Drink** *Tokaji Aszú* – 'the wine of kings and the king of wines'; *pálinka*, a kick-like-a-mule brandy made from stone fruits

IN A WORD

» *Szia* (hello)

TRADEMARKS

» Goulash; salami; Rubik's Cube; water polo; Nobel Prize winners; Zsa Zsa Gabor; Roma music

SURPRISES

» Hungarian surnames appear before their Christian names, as in Asian cultures; the burial place of Attila the Hun and his lost treasure is said to be somewhere in Hungary

MAP REF F,22

(1.) Checkmates – playing chess is a steamy activity at the Széchényi Baths, Budapest
(2.) Swimmers paddle past magnificent columns in the Gellért Thermal Baths, Budapest
(3.) A man enjoys beer, sunflower seeds and warm light in a Csongrád pub
(4.) Fine buildings of Blaha Luiza Square on the Pest side of the capital
(5.) Dusk brings an undersea atmosphere to Budapest's Chain Bridge over the Danube

1.

GRANT DIXON

The big island with the chilly name has become one of Europe's hottest properties, bursting with natural wonders: active volcanoes, valley glaciers, Europe's biggest waterfalls, lava fields, geysers, thermal pools and the aurora borealis. Reykjavík, the world's northernmost capital, is a cultural dynamo with live music, great restaurants and museums squeezed into a small-town environment. Outside the capital there's puffin-watching, whale-gazing, white-water rafting and medieval relics that make those famous Icelandic sagas come to life.

BEST TIME TO VISIT

Early June to the end of August, when the country defrosts

ESSENTIAL EXPERIENCES

» Enjoying Reykjavík's famously uninhibited nightlife
» Swimming in the piping-hot waters of the geothermal field at Nesjavellir
» Snapping a photo of the iceberg-filled Jökulsárlón lagoon
» Checking out Vatnajökull – Europe's biggest icecap
» Cooing over thousands of puffin chicks on Heimaey island
» Dogsledding on the icecaps at Mýrdalsjökull

GETTING UNDER THE SKIN

» **Read** *Independent People* by Halldór Laxness, one of half a dozen brilliant novels by the Nobel Prize winner, or the comic drama *Angels of the Universe*, by Einar Már Gudmundsson
» **Listen** to the Leaves and Emiliana Torrini
» **Watch** *Children of Nature* directed by Friðrik Thór Friðriksson, which tells the story of an elderly couple forced into a retirement home in Reykjavík. *101 Reykjavík*, directed by Baltasar Kormákur and based on the novel by Hallgrímur Helgason, is a dark comedy that explores the life of a loafer in downtown Reykjavík.

» **Eat** *harðfiskur* (haddock), which is cleaned and dried in the open air until dehydrated and brittle. For something sweet, try *pönnukökur* (Icelandic pancakes).

» **Drink** *kaffi* (coffee), Icelandic beer or the traditional Icelandic brew *brennivín*, a sort of schnapps made from potatoes and flavoured with caraway

IN A WORD

» *Skál!* (cheers!)

TRADEMARKS

» Fire and ice; Björk; fish; volcanoes; the aurora borealis; beer guzzling; hot springs; Blue Lagoon

SURPRISES

» At weekends the whole of Reykjavík joins in the great Icelandic pub-crawl, which goes on till dawn; it's forbidden for parents to bestow non-Icelandic or foreign-sounding names on their children

MAP REF C,18

(1.) The hills of Landmannalaugar marbled with gleaming snow, Fjallabak Nature Reserve
(2.) Turf-roofed houses appear half-submerged in grass above the glacial plains of Sandur
(3.) Summer wildflowers bloom in defiance of the bleak landscape of Skeidararsandur
(4.) A game of volleyball in the steamy waters of Laugardalur outdoor pool in Reykjavík
(5.) Like castle ruins, the austere rim of an extinct volcano presides over Vestmannaeyjar

1.

Everyone wants a piece of India. From Aryan, Afghani and Persian invasions to the British era, people from distant lands have sought to possess India's treasures for themselves. But a funny thing always happens: India takes these foreigners and makes them Indians. Defying the doctrine of 'us' and 'them', India weaves races, cultures and philosophies into a tapestry that grows richer and more intricate every day. To experience India is to share in the sorrows, dreams, tribulations and almost unbearable joy of a billion fellow human beings. Fear not: India will make you her own, too.

BEST TIME TO VISIT

November to March, when it's cooler

ESSENTIAL EXPERIENCES

» Watching the sunrise at the Taj Mahal
» Floating to Udaipur's Lake Palace
» Kicking back on a Goan beach
» Taking a camel safari in Rajasthan
» Relaxing in a Shimla hill-station resort

GETTING UNDER THE SKIN

» **Read** Jawaharlal Nehru's *Discovery of India*, tales from the Vedic era to WWII, or VS Naipaul's *India: A Million Mutinies Now*, a Trinidadian's take on India's tribulations and triumphs
» **Listen** to Lata Mangeshkar's *The Greatest Film Songs* – the diva extraordinaire sings Bollywood hits, or to Ravi Shankar's *In Celebration* – the world's greatest sitarist plays classical and fusion
» **Watch** *Mother India,* India's answer to *The Grapes of Wrath*; *Gandhi,* the epic film that made Ben Kingsley famous; or any Bollywood flick

PATRICK HORTON

2.

RICHARD I'ANSON

3.

4.

» **Eat** tandoori chicken, dhal, dosas, samosas, curries

» **Drink** lassi (a sweet or savoury yogurt drink), or toddy (fermented palm sap)

IN A WORD

» *Are vah!* (holy cow! – not literally)

TRADEMARKS

» Cows in streets; snake charmers; world's largest slums; Bollywood; maharajahs in palaces; rickshaws; gods and goddesses; computer geeks

SURPRISES

» Cities have killer nightlife scenes; most food isn't spicy hot; English is the de facto national language; for the most part Hindus and Muslims live together peacefully

MAP REF J,28

(1.) Bathers scrub themselves in the Yamuna River beneath the majesty of the Taj Mahal

(2.) Whoever goes down to a river goes down to the Ganges, Varanasi

(3.) Wanna lift? A taxi driver cruises the busy streets of Kolkata

(4.) All smiles, a young woman of Jaisalmer in a brilliantly coloured sari

(5.) Siblings compete for exposure in a family portrait, Udaipur

(6.) Bollywood beauty emblazons a Kozhikode shopfront where a man reads the newspaper

1.

GREGORY ADAMS

RICHARD I'ANSON

The world's most expansive archipelago dips and rises across the equator from the Indian Ocean to the Pacific. There are around eighteen thousand islands to choose from, six thousand of which are uninhabited, offering adventure that's hard to find in the developed world. Indonesia is endowed with a phenomenal array of wildlife, including tigers and orang-utans, and its fine white-sand beaches, sublime rice fields and exotic temples continue to lure visitors from afar.

BEST TIME TO VISIT
May to September, during the dry season

ESSENTIAL EXPERIENCES
» Climbing Bali's Gunung Batur to see exceptional sunrises
» Taking a Batik course in Yogyakarta, Java
» Eating breakfast at the floating market in Banjarmasin, Kalimantan
» Chilling out on Lombok's Gili Islands
» Watching the Ramayana Ballet full story unfold at the outdoor theatre in Prambanan, Java
» Catching a wave at Pantai Suluban, Bali's surfing mecca

GETTING UNDER THE SKIN
» **Read** Pramoedya Ananta Toer's *The Fugitive*, by the leader of a failed nationalist revolt against Japanese occupation during WWII. Ayu Utami's *Saman* is a story of political repression, extra-marital sex and religious intolerance.
» **Listen** to Iwan Fals, a rock idol who conveys society's sufferings, and Padi, the favourite group at the 2003 Indonesia MTV Video Awards
» **Watch** Garin Nugroho's *Bulan Tertusuk Ilalang* (And the Moon Dances). Joko Anwar's *Arisan* is the first home-grown film showing two men kissing.

4.

- » **Eat** nasi goreng (fried rice), the country's most common dish, and *sate* (skewered meats with spicy peanut sauce)
- » **Drink** *kopi* (coffee), as Indonesia is the world's third-largest coffee producer; black *teh* (tea); or *bir* (beer), especially the domestic Bintang and Anker

IN A WORD

- » *Tidak apa-apa* (no problem)

TRADEMARKS

- » Great surfing; komodo dragons; terraced ricescapes; woodcarvings, textiles, basketwork and beadwork; exotic fruits; political corruption

SURPRISES

- » The Balinese year is only 210 days long; snow is found two degrees south of the equator on 'Puncak Jaya' in Papua

MAP REF M,32

(1.) Like Hindu dolls, a procession of finely robed girls walks back from a Balinese temple
(2.) With a ceremonial sword strapped to his back a boy observes a temple ceremony in Bali
(3.) Lush rice terraces at Ceking near Ubud offer a glimpse into the Garden of Eden
(4.) Buddha among the stupas of Borobudur, an ancient Buddhist monument in Central Java

1.

CLINT LUCAS

The Middle East's best-kept secret, Iran forms a footbridge between Europe and Asia, and has hosted some of the great invaders: Genghis Khan from the east, Alexander the Great from the west, and hippies from all over the world. A visit to Iran is a voyage of contrasts – women clad in black, mosques bejewelled and dazzling, desert towns with twisting laneways, formal gardens and snow-capped peaks. And wherever you go, you are welcomed with a warmth that is astounding.

BEST TIME TO VISIT

March to May or September to November – or during the reign of Shah Abbas, who, with an eye to international tourism, set up a vast network of caravanserais

ESSENTIAL EXPERIENCES

- » Sipping tea at sunset in Emam Khomeini Square, Esfahan
- » Trying to imagine what Persepolis was like during the time of Darius the Great
- » Getting lost in the twisting lanes of Yazd, feeling like you've stumbled onto a *Star Wars* set
- » Goggling at the fantastical exhibits of Tehran's National Jewel Museum, which have inspired war
- » Paying your respects to the dead poets of Shiraz by visiting their mausoleums

GETTING UNDER THE SKIN

- » **Read** *Moonlight on the Avenue of Faith* by Gina Nahai – magic realism set amongst the Jewish community of Tehran; *Persian Pilgrimages* by Afshin Molavi, an expat Iranian journalist who explores both history and current issues, by speaking to locals
- » **Listen** to *Night Silence Desert* by Kayhab Kalhor and Mohammad Reza Shajarian, a fusion of Iranian classical and folk music forms

2.

3.

4.

» **Watch** *The Circle*, Jafar Panahi's story of women who have fallen outside the law
» **Eat** *ābgùsht*, a meat soup stew, or *gaz* – nougat Esfahan style
» **Drink** *chāy* – tea, taken in conjunction with a puff on the hookah pipe. *Dùgh* is a popular cold drink made from yogurt or sour milk and sparkling or still water.

IN A WORD
» *Masha'allah* (God has willed it)

TRADEMARKS
» Chadors, tiled mosques, mullahs, covered bazaars, Persian carpets, controlled borders; Paykan cars (*paykan* means 'arrow')

SURPRISES
» The skiing season lasts through to May; women can pursue higher education; Iran is emphatically not Arabic

MAP REF H,25

(1.) A peacock soars sunward on a dazzling blue mural in Shiraz
(2.) Sweet-toothed women from Tehran enjoy a cooling ice cream and each other's company
(3.) Village houses of Kandovan carved from an eroded volcanic hillside
(4.) The peaks of the Alborz Mountains cast shadows over the snowy valleys beneath
(5.) Brilliant tiles grace the arches and porticos of the famed Masjed-e Emam in Esfahan
(6.) The benevolent face of an Afghani refugee at the Shiraz Bazaar

1.

JANE SWEENEY

In its long and rich history Iraq has played host to great civilisations, such as the Mesopotamian, in which writing, mathematics and astronomy were developed. The medieval Islamic period of great learning and beautiful architecture was ruled over by the legendary city of Baghdad. But recent history has been less kind: the dictatorial reign of Saddam Hussein, war with Iran and Kuwait, and trade embargoes after the Gulf War and the US-led invasion in 2003 have all taken severe tolls, resulting in food and medicine shortages and ongoing social and economic problems for this embattled country.

BEST TIME TO VISIT

April to September, depending on the political state of play and your tolerance to 35°C-plus days

ESSENTIAL EXPERIENCES

» Visiting the Hanging Gardens of Babylon, one the Seven Wonders of the World and Iraq's most famous ancient site
» Winding along mountain roads through dramatic scenery, pleasant towns and waterfalls in the Kurdish Autonomous Region
» Experiencing the extreme and shimmering heat of the Anabar and Al Hajara deserts
» Exploring a lively bazaar with people selling colourful rugs, jewellery and copperware
» Taking a boat ride down the Euphrates River

GETTING UNDER THE SKIN

» **Read** *The New Iraq: Rebuilding the Country for Its People, the Middle East, and the World* by Joseph Braude, a forward-looking and positive account of the country post-Saddam
» **Listen** to Kazem El-Saher singing 'love poetry' on *Abhathu Anki*

» **Watch** *National Geographic – 21 Days to Baghdad*, an insider's look at Operation Iraqi Freedom; *Three Kings*, starring George Clooney and set in post–Desert Storm Iraq

» **Eat** *masgouf*, a traditional dish made from Tigris River fish

» **Drink** sweet, strong black tea; soft drinks made from rose petals or orange blossom

IN A WORD

» *Salām 'alaykum* (peace be upon you)

TRADEMARKS

» One of the world's most high-profile troubled spots; oil interests; arid desert; mosques; long-suffering people; marshes; dust storms

SURPRISES

» The garden of Eden is said to have been located in Iraq; the country is a breeding centre for Arabian horses

MAP REF H,24

(1.) Children linger outside their traditional Marsh Arab reed house
(2.) Men attend a civilised tea party outside the Holy Shrine of the Imam Ali ibn Abi Talib
(3.) The faithful of Samarra flock beneath the golden dome of the Ali el-Hadi Mosque
(4.) Nervous adventurers scale the vertiginous minaret of the Abu Duluf mosque in Samarra

1.

It's said that Ireland, once visited, is never forgotten, and for once the blarney rings true. The Irish landscape has a mythic resonance, the country's history is almost tangible, and a sustained period of investment and economic growth has injected a heady dose of confidence and energy. Thankfully, Ireland hasn't paid the ultimate price for this recent transition as the character, wit and hospitality of the people, the most successful of all Irish exports (except maybe the Irish pub), remains wonderfully intact.

BEST TIME TO VISIT

May to September, when the weather is warmer and the days are longer

ESSENTIAL EXPERIENCES

» Enjoying Dublin's gorgeous old pubs and cutting-edge nightclubs
» Visiting the ancient ring fort of Dún Aengus
» Feeling history come alive at beautifully restored Kilkenny Castle
» Exploring the country's past at County Offaly's Clonmacnoise monastery city
» Checking out the murals in West Belfast for an insight into the history of the Troubles
» Sampling the whiskey at Bushmills Distillery, County Antrim

GETTING UNDER THE SKIN

» **Read** *McCarthy's Bar*, a terrifically funny account of the author's quest to explore his cultural heritage
» **Listen** to anything by U2 and Sinead O'Connor, or more recent offerings by Damien Rice such as *O*
» **Watch** *The Commitments* for good fun and *The Quiet Man* for an all-time classic family favourite

IRELAND

CAPITAL DUBLIN (REPUBLIC OF IRELAND), BELFAST (NORTHERN IRELAND) POPULATION 3,924,140 (REPUBLIC), »

2.

3.

4.

RICHARD CUMMINS

» **Eat** soda bread, a fry-up, smoked salmon and Kimberly biscuits

» **Drink** Guinness, whiskey and red lemonade

IN A WORD

» What's the craic? (what's happening?)

TRADEMARKS

» Potatoes; harps; shamrocks; Guinness; the good people (leprechauns); American tourists; shillelaghs; ceilidh; the Corrs; the Troubles; James Joyce

SURPRISES

» The Irish drink more tea per capita than any other nation in the world; until the 19th century the national colour of the Emerald Isle was blue, as the flag of St Patrick featured a gold harp on a blue background

OLIVER STREWE

MAP REF E,19

(1.) The radiant Celtic features of a young Dubliner
(2.) Twilight casts eerie colours over the ghostly ruins of Athassel Priory in County Tipperary
(3.) The labyrinth at Dublin Castle weaves fabulous patterns over the lawn
(4.) Detail of a thatched roof, typical of the charming cottages of Dunmore East
(5.) Hook Head Lighthouse stands ever watchful over the stormy seas off County Wexford
(6.) A farmer in Antrim herding his flock along a country lane

1.

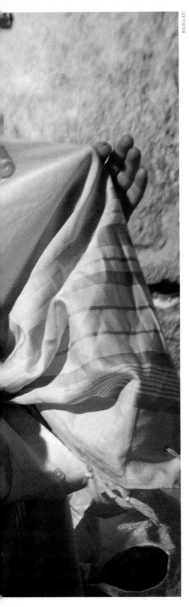

LEE FOSTER

Since its creation as a modern state in 1948, Israel has never been far from international attention. A combination of Promised Land, postcard beaches and political powder keg, everyone has their own perception of what Israel should be. The capital, Jerusalem, is a sacred place to Jews, Muslims and Christians, but it is as much a modern city as a concept, as full of living, breathing people as ghosts and biblical figures. And behind the political headlines is a bustling, noisy, modern country.

BEST TIME TO VISIT

The summer months are warm, but during major Jewish holidays the country fills up with pilgrims, accommodation prices double and travel between cities is impossible

ESSENTIAL EXPERIENCES

» Admiring the magnificent Dome of the Rock, built on the spot where Mohammed ascended to heaven
» Being dazzled by the golden view of Jerusalem's Old City at dawn
» Hitting the clubs or shopping in cosmopolitan Tel Aviv
» Saying a prayer for peace at Jerusalem's Wailing Wall
» Escaping to Hula Valley & Nature Reserve, a beautiful valley with unique wetlands wildlife
» Splashing out at the water-sports capital of Eilat, with coral-fringed beaches for windsurfing, parasailing and water-skiing
» Witnessing the many security fences and walls dividing Israel and Palestine

GETTING UNDER THE SKIN

» **Read** the meditations of Israeli novelist, Amoz Oz, on his country and culture
» **Listen** to pop princess Sarit Hadad, especially her Eurovision hit, 'Let's Light a Candle Together'

383

2.

3.

4.

» **Watch** *Promises*, an honest portrait of seven children from Israel and the Palestinian Territories by Justine Shapiro, BZ Goldberg and Carlos Bolado

» **Eat** *malawach*, a buttery pastry served with fillings or salsa

» **Drink** the ubiquitous *sahlab*, a milky, spicy drink originally from Egypt, but drunk everywhere in Israel

IN A WORD

» *Shalom* (hello, literally 'peace')

TRADEMARKS

» Nobel Peace Prize winner Shimon Peres; the Star of David adorning tanks; troubled war-zone; international kids on kibbutzim; dark-clothed Hasidics sweltering in the heat; diplomatic imbroglio

SURPRISES

» A fifth of Israel's landmass is national parks – there are 300 of them

MAP REF H,24

(1.) A Jewish man praying in Old Jerusalem
(2.) The Al-Aqsa Mosque and Dome of the Rock in the Old City of Jerusalem
(3.) The oldest known harbour, first mentioned by Hiram talking to Solomon, Tel Aviv
(4.) Two local men from the ultra-orthodox Jewish community in Mea She'arim
(5.) The sun sets over the restorative Dead Sea
(6.) An Arab man catches up on the day's news

ISRAEL

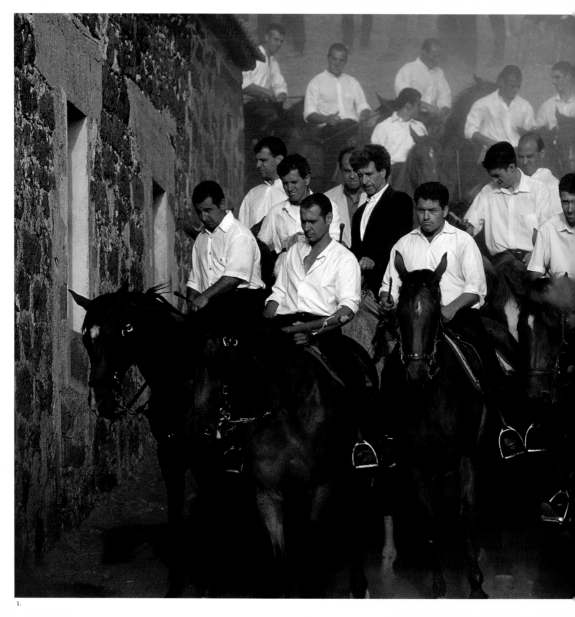

1.

DALLAS STRIBLEY

La dolce vita, il Belpaese...these phrases merely scratch the surface of a country that has beguiled visitors since the days of the Grand Tour and beyond. From design-conscious Milan, Renaissance-rich Florence, cosmopolitan Rome to the more traditional south, Italy is a seductive mix of history, culture, fashion and cuisine. It's impossible not to fall in love with a country which is connected so strikingly to the ancient glories of yesteryear and the sophisticated pleasures of today.

BEST TIME TO VISIT
April to June, when it's not too crowded or hot

ESSENTIAL EXPERIENCES
» Hiring a car and driving through the beautiful Tuscan countryside
» Feeling the history of the ruins of Herculaneum or Pompeii
» Queuing for hours to enter the Uffizi Gallery in Florence
» Venturing offshore to the less-touristy islands of Sicily and Sardinia
» Wandering along the canals of Venice and shelling out the euro for a gondola ride
» Window-shopping in Milan's Golden Quad or Rome's Via del Corso

GETTING UNDER THE SKIN
» **Read** Umberto Eco's masterful *The Name of the Rose*, a medieval whodunnit with a difference. Giuseppe Tomasi di Lampedusa's *The Leopard* charts the demise of Sicilian royalty and rise of Italian nationhood.
» **Listen** to Pavarotti, one of the world's most beloved tenors; Andrea Bocelli, wildly popular for his renditions of popular classics; and Jovanotti, known for his wacky rap stylings
» **Watch** *Roman Holiday* for a romantic fix or try Fellini's classic, *La Dolce Vita*; for a modern view, *L'Ultimo Bacio* explores issues

2.

3.

4.

affecting Italy's 30-somethings

» **Eat** polenta (cornmeal), *baccalà* (salted cod), *risotto nero* (flavoured with squid ink), *sfogliatella* (pastry filled with ricotta), panettone (fruit bread eaten at Christmas)

» **Drink** espresso, chianti (Tuscan wine), Marsala (sweet wine), grappa (grape-based liqueur)

IN A WORD

» *Ciao Bella!* (hi beautiful!)

TRADEMARKS

» Beeping Fiats and screeching Vespas; pizza by the slice; Roman ruins; Michelangelo and Leonardo; La Cosa Nostra, Prada, Gucci and Dolce and Gabbana

SURPRISES

» Cappucinos are considered a breakfast coffee; not every Italian has Mafia connections; pesto originally hailed from Genoa,

MAP REF G,21

(1.) The arrival of white-shirted jockeys at the S'Ardia horse race in Sedilo, Sardinia

(2.) The Leaning Tower of Pizza – a neon sign shares airspace with the Leaning Tower of Pisa

(3.) Cyprus trees zigzag through a golden Tuscan landscape near La Foce

(4.) Ranks of empty café tables bask in the glow of morning at Piazza San Marco, Venice

(5.) A baker hits the pavements of Padova to deliver his pastries

(6.) The distinctive bumblebee behind of a yellow Fiat parked on a zebra crossing in Rome

1.

Ever since Errol Flynn cavorted here with his Hollywood pals in the 1930s and '40s, travellers have regarded Jamaica as one of the most alluring of the Caribbean islands. Its beaches, mountains and carnal red sunsets regularly appear in tourist brochures promising paradise. Jamaica has a diversity that few other Caribbean islands can claim. Stray from the north coast resorts, and you'll discover radically different environments and terrain. Or throw yourself into the thick of the island's life and experience the three Rs: reggae, reefers and rum.

BEST TIME TO VISIT
May to November, during the off-season

ESSENTIAL EXPERIENCES
» Spending the day in Alligator Pond, a deep blue bay backed by dunes
» Clambering up tiers of limestone to get to Dunn's River Falls, which tumble down to the beach in a series of cascades and pools
» Hiking in the Blue Mountains
» Taking a helicopter excursion over the dramatic sculpted limestone plateau of Cockpit Country
» Surfing at Long Bay in the northeast – a crescent-shaped bay with rose-coloured sand and deep turquoise waters

GETTING UNDER THE SKIN
» **Read** Jean Rhys' *Wide Sargasso Sea*, which is a sultry tale of post-emancipation Jamaica
» **Listen** to undisputed king of reggae Bob Marley and early pioneer of ska Tommy McCook
» **Watch** *Bob Marley: Time Will Tell*, a documentary about Bob Marley & the Wailers

2.

3.

4.

» **Eat** *jerk* (meat smothered in tongue-searing marinade, and barbecued slowly in an outdoor pit over a fire of pimento wood, which gives the meat its distinctive flavour)

» **Drink** the famous Jamaican Blue Mountain coffee or try a sky-juice, a cool drink made from shaved ice flavoured with syrup

IN A WORD

» Evert'ing cool, mon? (a common greeting much like 'how are you?')

TRADEMARKS

» Reggae, reefers and rum; Bob Marley; Rastafarianism; Kingston; palm-fringed beaches

SURPRISES

» The national motto of Jamaica is 'Out of Many, One People'; once the major celebration on the slave calendar, Jonkanoo is a Christmas celebration in which revellers parade through the streets dressed in masquerade

MAP REF J,12

(1.) Peanut soup? The owner of a roadside eatery offers the house special to passers-by
(2.) A girl sells bunches of guinep fruit to bathers at Bluefields beach in the St Ann region
(3.) Hanging tuff outside the ghetto-fabulous Tuff Gong Studios in Kingston
(4.) Brisk trade at the Papin Market in the capital
(5.) A dreadlocked denizen of Kingston brandishes a rasta beard
(6.) Pale colours adorn houses in Falmouth

1.

Whether you end up taking photos of a neon-lit skyline, surfing an indoor wave, musing in a Zen temple, shacking up in a love hotel or kipping down in a traditional inn, you'll do best to come to Japan with an open mind and be prepared to be surprised. Somewhere between the elegant formality of Japanese manners and the candid, sometimes boisterous exchanges that take place over a few drinks, between the sanitised shopping malls and the unexpected rural festivals, everyone finds their own vision of Japan.

BEST TIME TO VISIT

March and April; or before 1853, when Japan started opening up to foreigners

ESSENTIAL EXPERIENCES

» Taking a relaxing dip in an *onsen* (hot spring) at Beppu
» Admiring the cherry blossoms in Tokyo's Ueno Park in March
» Drinking in the view of Tokyo from the top of Mt Fuji
» Pretending you're a Samurai warlord at Himeji castle
» Having a zen experience at Kinkakuji (Golden Temple), Kyoto
» Finding out why war sucks at the Hiroshima war museum
» Riding on a slide made entirely of ice at the Sapporo Snow Festival

GETTING UNDER THE SKIN

» **Read** *Inside Japan* by Peter Tasker, a fascinating foray into Japanese culture, society and the economy; *Kitchen* by Banana Yoshimoto is a hauntingly beautiful story set in contemporary Tokyo
» **Listen** to 'Sukiyaki' by Kyu Sakamoto, a 1960s hit and classic Japanese tune, reminiscent of 1950s lounge music; or anything by Morning Musume, an all girl J-pop group of 13(!) members
» **Watch** Kurosawa's *Seven Samurai*, a classic 1954 film set in 17th-century rural Japan, or get a taste for Japan with *Tampopo*,

2.

3.

4.

a witty and insightful film set in a *ramen* (noodle) shop

» **Eat** *ramen* noodles, Japan's fast-food speciality – though you haven't 'done' Japan till you've experienced fresh raw fish

» **Drink** sake (rice wine), Japan's signature drink

IN A WORD

» *Sugoi* (used for surprise, wonder or horror)

TRADEMARKS

» Raw fish; Samurai swords; hard-working salary men; bowing; Hiroshima and the A-bomb; electronic gadgets; geishas; Mt Fuji; karaoke; manga comic books

SURPRISES

» It's polite to slurp loudly when eating soup or noodles; most kitchens don't have ovens; Japan has over 1500 earthquakes a year

MAP REF H,34

(1.) Tokyo's 'CosPlay' culture can mean cross-dressing as your favourite anime character

(2.) Following fashion, a kimono-clad woman walks Kyoto's streets

(3.) Autumn brings out rich hues in Kanto's maple trees

(4.) Stepping out in style – geishas' kimonos and platform shoes

(5.) Cherry blossoms fringe the view of Mt Fuji from Kawaguchi

(6.) Sweet green *kusa-mochi* rice cakes served up to celebrate the New Year

1.

BECCA POSTERINO

Lawrence of Arabia, Bible stories and mysterious lost cities – Jordan is romantic and epic. Better yet, it's one of the most welcoming countries in the world. Where else do total strangers invite you into their homes for a heady brew of tea? It's also home to two of the most spectacular sights in the Middle East: Petra, the ancient Nabatean city, and the startling desert scenery of Wadi Rum that enraptured TE Lawrence.

JOHN ELK III

BEST TIME TO VISIT

April to May or September to October, when you can dodge the baking sun of summer and the freezing winds of winter

ESSENTIAL EXPERIENCES

» Visiting the ancient ruins of Petra
» Pretending you're Julius Caesar at the preserved city of Jerash
» Lolling in the restorative salt, sea and mud of the Dead Sea
» Diving into the scuba-friendly waters around Aqaba
» Camping out under the stars at Wadi Rum
» Finding your inner Richard the Lionheart at Karak, Jordan's best-preserved Crusader castle

MARK DAFFEY

GETTING UNDER THE SKIN

» **Read** *Seven Pillars of Wisdom* by TE Lawrence – it's Lawrence of Arabia straight from the camel's mouth
» **Listen** to *Khaliji*, a collection of tunes and belly dancing hits featuring Jordanian, Naser Musa
» **Watch** *Indiana Jones and the Last Crusade* for the climactic scenes filmed in and around Petra
» **Eat** *mensaf*, the Bedouin speciality – a whole lamb, head included, on rice and pine nuts
» **Drink** tea, because you'll be offered it in bladder-bursting amounts by hospitable Jordanians

IN A WORD

» *Salam* (hello)

TRADEMARKS

» Bedouins in *keffiyah* (head robes); endless tea-drinking; wind-swept deserts; ancient ruins; bubbling nargileh (water pipes); peacemaking King Hussein

SURPRISES

» Not everyone is a Bedouin in Jordan; there's a majority Palestinian population which arrived during times of war in their homeland

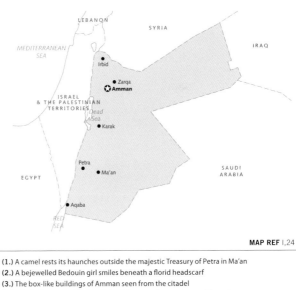

MAP REF I,24

(1.) A camel rests its haunches outside the majestic Treasury of Petra in Ma'an
(2.) A bejewelled Bedouin girl smiles beneath a florid headscarf
(3.) The box-like buildings of Amman seen from the citadel
(4.) A Bedouin woman herds a flock of sheep and goats across arid terrain
(5.) Tourists enjoying the legendary buoyancy of the Dead Sea

1.

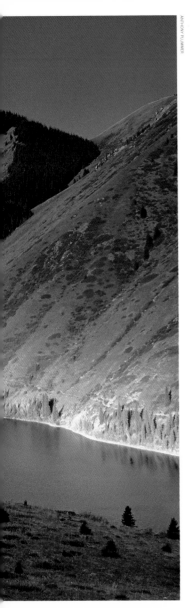

ANTHONY PLUMMER

If you love remoteness, wide open spaces, lunar landscapes, long hypnotic train rides and horse sausage (and who doesn't?), you'll be in your element in Kazakhstan. But it's not all barren steppes – there's also cosmopolitan Almaty and the spectacular spurs of the Tian Shan and Altay mountains to explore. And if it occasionally seems that the landscape has been bombarded by nuclear explosions, well, that's because Soviet rocket scientists began using Kazakhstan as a sandpit in the late 1940s.

BEST TIME TO VISIT

April to June (spring) and September to November (autumn)

ESSENTIAL EXPERIENCES

» Market-hopping in Almaty, the mercantile city that gathers together Chinese, Uzbek, Russian and Turkish traders
» Nature-spotting in Almatinsky Nature Reserve for the super-rare snow leopard and *arkhar* (big-horned wild sheep)
» Gazing at the view across Lake Burabay, also seen on the 10 tenge banknote
» Making the pilgrimage to Kazakhstan's greatest building, the mausoleum of Kozha Akhmed Yasaui
» Trekking the mighty Altay mountains, border to both Russia and China

GETTING UNDER THE SKIN

» **Read** *The Silk Road: A History* by Irene Frank and David Brownstone, a richly illustrated and mapped history of the legendary caravan routes
» **Listen** to pop-folk fusionists Urker's *Made in Kazakhstan*, featuring the string instruments the *dombyra* and *kobyz*

» **Watch** Ali G's mate Borat for cultural clashes when a supposed Kazakhstani visits the UK and US

» **Eat** *qazy*, the smoked horsemeat sausage sometimes served sliced with cold noodles

» **Drink** *shubat*, fermented camel's milk

IN A WORD

» *Asalam aleykum* ('peace be with you' in Kazakh)

TRADEMARKS

» Borat the travelling Kazakhstani TV celebrity; big furry hats; Silk Road traders haggling over a tenge; barren steppes spanning the horizon; Soviet-era service

SURPRISES

» Ever-changing visa and border rules; enjoying a truly great local yogurt

MAP REF F,26

(1.) The sheer hillsides around Nizhny Kol-Say with Alatau mountains in the distance

(2.) Taking it up a notch, speed chess players race against time in Panfilov Park, Almaty

(3.) The imposing Soviet architecture of the television broadcasting centre in Almaty

(4.) Old Russian houses line the deserted streets of Fort Shevchenko

(5.) Cows recline beneath a yurt near the town of Shymbulak

1.

ALEX DISSANAYAKE

Kenya beckons travellers with a magical mix of incredible wildlife, rich cultural heritage, palm-fringed beaches, and coastal towns seeped in Swahili history. Few places can rival Kenya for the safari experience, though these days your big-game hunting will (thankfully) be restricted to capturing trophies on film. Nothing can prepare you for the incredible sight of the annual migration of the wildebeest, and wherever you lay your head you'll be romanced by the star-studded night-sky and your imagination stirred by the noises of the African night.

BEST TIME TO VISIT
January to February, the hottest and driest months

ESSENTIAL EXPERIENCES
» Taking a safari – by minibus, 4WD, truck, camel, small plane or hot-air balloon
» Experiencing the wildebeest mass migration – the sight and sound of a million hoofs on the move with a host of eager predators in hot pursuit
» Winding down a notch or 10 with a lazy spell in other-worldly Lamu
» Taking the Nairobi–Mombasa night train for a taste of the old-colonial experience

GETTING UNDER THE SKIN
» **Read** Isak Dinesen's epic settler account, *Out of Africa*
» **Listen** to *benga*, the contemporary dance music of Kenya, by Shirati Jazz, Victoria Kings and Them Mushrooms
» **Watch** Robert Redford and Meryl Streep in the big-screen version of *Out of Africa* or the equally tear-jerking screen-translation

2.

3.

4.

DAVID WALL

of Kiki Guillman's *I Dreamed of Africa*

» **Eat** *nyama choma*, literally 'roasted meat' of any shape or form, but usually goat

» **Drink** Tusker – the elephant beer

IN A WORD

» *Jambo* (hello)

TRADEMARKS

» Spear-bearing Maasai warriors; wiry marathon runners; strong coffee; man-eating lions; gin-soaked old colonials; Nairobbery

SURPRISES

» Nairobi's cosmopolitan population mix and its western-style skyscrapers and suburban sprawl; the shadowy, medieval architecture of spice-infused Swahili Lamu and old-town Mombasa and Malindi

MAP REF M,24

ANDERS BLOMQVIST

(1.) A bejewelled Maasai mother carries her baby past a village enclosure
(2.) A herd of elephants in the savanna as Mt Kilimanjaro looms over the border in Tanzania
(3.) A Maasai woman loses herself in song
(4.) Maasai cattle and native animals compete for grazing land in Aberdare National Park
(5.) If looks could kill – a Maasai warrior cuts an intimidating figure in the Rift Valley
(6.) An afternoon chat in Watamu

1.

2.

3.

DAVID RYAN

Blessed with billions of stunning fish swarming over myriad coral reefs and plenty of WWII wrecks, Kiribati (pronounced kiri-bahs) is a hidden island paradise. The atolls are scattered either side of the equator so the weather is dependably warm. Modernity is slowly rearing its head, but locals still welcome travellers as rarely seen curios. There are few organised activities on offer, though it's not hard to find diving and game fishing with local people, and the less adventurous will find idyllic beaches are never far away.

BEST TIME TO VISIT

March to October, to avoid the humidity and tropical downpours

ESSENTIAL EXPERIENCES

» Taking part in a traditional dance in a *maneaba* (traditional meeting house)
» Sipping fresh coconut milk in a stilt house over an aqua lagoon in North Tarawa
» Being brought down to size by the enormous WWII guns at South Tarawa
» Salting clams or weaving thatch with locals to enjoy the relaxed pace of the Outer Islands
» Trying bonefishing or birdwatching on Christmas Island

GETTING UNDER THE SKIN

» **Read** Gavin Bell's *In Search of Tusitala: Travels in the Pacific after Robert Louis Stevenson*, which follows Stevenson through Kiribati
» **Listen** to anything by home-grown production company NDTeariki Music Productions, recording in Kiribati
» **Watch** the documentaries of director Dennis O'Rourke, including *Atoll life in Kiribati*

» **Eat** traditional islander fare like taro, sweet potato or coconuts

» **Drink** the unfortunately named sour toddy, brewed from coconut palm

IN A WORD

» *Ko rabwa n rokom* (thank you for your visit)

TRADEMARKS

» Far-flung coral atolls; deep blue ocean; devout Catholics; coconut drinks by the beach; friendly locals; beachcombing the days away

SURPRISES

» The International Date Line used to split Kiribati down the middle, until 1 January 1995 when Kiribati decided to have the same day nationwide

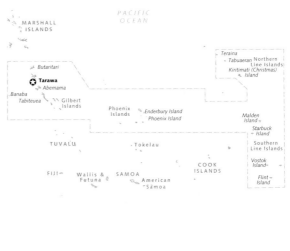

MAP REF M,38

(1.) No diving from the back door, living on the edge in a thatched hut
(2.) A Gilbertese boy hugs his dozing pig
(3.) Chilling outside the local shop
(4.) Always keen on nautical sports, Gilbertese racing canoes compete in Tarawa Lagoon

1.

TONY WHEELER

Continuing to defy the odds stacked heavily against it, North Korea is a land where ancient myths bend to modern political reality, where dictator Kim Jong Il runs the only brand around and is also believed to control the weather. Few are allowed into the hermit state, and then only under constant escort, leaving the country free of commercial tourism and ensuring that the lives of ordinary North Koreans remain as mysterious to outsiders as that of its leader. Behind the propaganda, rumour and weirdness is the real story; the fascination is in finding the truth.

BEST TIME TO VISIT

May, for May Day and the Arirang Mass Games, or any time free of famine

ESSENTIAL EXPERIENCES

» Feeling the full force of North-South tension along the Demilitarised Zone at Panmunjeom
» Taking in pristine mountain views in the stunning resort of Kumgangsan
» Walking (with minders) amid Pyongyang's architectural wealth, and grabbing a few solo moments shopping in Department Store No 1
» Revisiting the past at the ancient Korean capital of Kaesong
» Exploring the far north and Korea's highest peak and holy mountain Paekdusan

GETTING UNDER THE SKIN

» **Read** widely – there's not a lot of factual material in print or on the web, and people are rarely ambivalent about North Korea
» **Listen** to the marching feet of the world's fifth-largest army
» **Watch** *Forever in Our Memory*, a 1999 film that deals with the starvation of up to three million North Koreans during the 1990s

2.

3.

4.

» **Eat** *bibim naengmyeon* (cold noodles), or the Korean menu on any tour
» **Drink** *soju* (rice wine) or *nokcha* (green tea)

IN A WORD

» *Juche* (self-reliance)

TRADEMARKS

» The Great Leader (the late Kim Il Sung) and his son, The Dear Leader (Kim Il Jung, AKA The Great Leader; Confused? So are we.); cult of personality; the 38th parallel; Cold War, 21st-century style: kidnapping, nuclear tests, rapprochement, border tension

SURPRISES

» There's an internet café (just one); the current Great Leader has only uttered six words in public ('Glory to the people's heroic military'), and is said to own 20,000 movies

MAP REF G,33

(1.) Hooping it up at a mass gymnastics display at Pyongyang
(2.) Soldiers dancing at the Arirang Mass Games
(3.) A border guard investigates a demilitarised zone building
(4.) Ballroom décor at the Reconstruction Station in Pyongyang
(5.) Spectacular waterfalls at Rimyongsu
(6.) Women in blue move in sync at the Arirang Mass Games

1.

An Asian economic tiger, South Korea is a mosaic of old and new: rural folk villages and DVD mini-cinemas, ancient stone pagodas and rock music bars, buzzing modern cities and feudal-era fort-resses, densely forested mountains graced by some of Asia's finest Buddhist temples. It's a compact and little-explored country, where Asian traditions, Western fashions, Confucian ideals and democratic ideas mingle to form an identity based on language, national pride and a fondness for nature's beauties.

BEST TIME TO VISIT

September to November (autumn)

ESSENTIAL EXPERIENCES

» Rubbing shoulders with the locals at one of Seoul's boisterous traditional markets
» Hitting the beach at Daecheon, for the best sand and seafood on the west coast
» Exploring the past by visiting Jikjisa, a temple dating back to the 5th century
» Hiking around spectacular Sereoksan National Park

GETTING UNDER THE SKIN

» **Read** *Yi Sang's Wings*, an allegory of adultery, colonialism and the absurdity of life; Rhie Won-Bok's *Korea Unmasked*, which details Korean history, culture and sociology
» **Listen** to Park Dong-jin, leading voice of the *pansori*, traditional storytelling through music
» **Watch** *Chihwaseon* (Painted Fire), by director Im Kwon Taek, about a famous 19th-century painter; Park Chan-wook's *JSA (Joint Security Area)*, a thriller about tensions on the border between North and South Korea

2.

3.

4.

- » **Eat** *bulgolgi* (sweet marinated beef cooked at the table), *bi bim bap* (stir-fried meat, rice, veggies, red pepper paste and fried egg) and *kimchi* (a fiery pickled cabbage concoction traditionally buried during winter to ferment)
- » **Drink** *soju* (clear potato-based alcohol which packs a heck of a kick), or for something more soothing try *nokcha* (green tea)

IN A WORD

- » *Annyeong haseyo* (hello, informal)

TRADEMARKS

- » Big city Seoul; seafood and rice; the 38th Parallel; Confucius drinking in Itaewon; young salary-mad workers; the land between Japan and China

SURPRISES

- » The youngest in the party *always* pours the drinks; when exchanging money, use your right hand – the left signals disrespect

MAP REF H,33

(1.) Ribbons ripple through the air during a Farmers' Dance
(2.) A serene Buddha statue surveys Songnisan National Park
(3.) A bearded gentleman rugs up in *hanbok* (traditional dress) against the winter
(4.) Seoul's bright lights dazzle the shopping districts

1.

With the 1990–91 Gulf War a fading memory, Kuwait is once again the prototypical Gulf oil state. Walking around Kuwait City, it is hard to imagine the destruction of just a decade ago. There has been an obsessive, meticulous re-creation of the country's pre-invasion appearance. Liberation brought a new kind of openness to Kuwaiti life and for those looking for a relaxed entry into the Muslim world, Kuwait offers opportunities to wander around souqs, mosques and other sandy traces of bygone Bedouin days.

BEST TIME TO VISIT
» May (spring) or October (autumn) – or in the early 18th century when Kuwait was nothing more than a few tents clustered around a fort

ESSENTIAL EXPERIENCES
» Taking in the views of the Sief Palace from the Kuwait Towers in Kuwait City
» Sampling Islamic art at the Tareq Rajab Museum in Kuwait City
» Buying Bedouin goods at Sadu House in Kuwait City
» Strolling through the public gardens in Al-Ahmadi
» Wandering among the archaeological ruins on Failaka Island

GETTING UNDER THE SKIN
» **Read** Thomas Friedman's *From Beirut to Jerusalem*, an excellent read for anyone wishing to more fully understand the causes and effects of the region's strife
» **Listen** to *Stars of Kuwait*, a complete taste of Kuwaiti music
» **Watch** *Fires of Kuwait* by David Douglas – shot in Kuwait after the Gulf War, it follows a number of teams who fought to extinguish the hundreds of burning oil wells

2.

3.

4.

- » **Eat** *fuul* – broadbean paste made with garlic, olive oil and lemon; felafel – spiced, fried chickpea balls; *khobz* – Arabic flat bread; hummus – chickpea paste with garlic and lemon
- » **Drink** coffee – served Arabic-style

IN A WORD

- » *Gowwa* (hello, informal)

TRADEMARKS

- » The oil industry; mosques; Kuwait Towers; Bedouin culture; colourful souqs; cloth weaving; museums; coffeehouses; delicious Arab food; archaeological sites; the remarkably easy-going feel of Kuwait City

SURPRISES

- » The temple and archaeological ruins on the island of Failaka Island; informal gatherings *(diwaniya)*, usually at someone's home, where Kuwaitis gather to chat

MAP REF I,25

(1.) Observing the remains of Gathering Station 14, bombed during the Gulf War
(2.) Iconic Kuwait Towers, Kuwait City's most distinctive landmark
(3.) A visitor to the Kuwait Museum shows off his traditional headgear
(4.) Festively decorated water reservoirs outside Kuwait City

1.

What Kyrgyzstan lacks in gracious buildings and fancy cakes, it makes up for with nomadic traditions such as laid-back hospitality, a healthy distrust of authority and a fondness for drinking fermented mare's milk. It is perhaps the most accessible and welcoming of the former Soviet Central Asian republics, and boasts the region's most dramatic mountains – the central Tian Shan and Pamir Alay ranges.

BEST TIME TO VISIT

April to early June (spring) and September to October (autumn)

ESSENTIAL EXPERIENCES

» Hiking in the rugged Ala-Archa Canyon, within sight of the region's highest peak

» Soaking in the thermal springs and spas of Lake Issyk-Kul and wildlife watching for big cats, ibex, bear and wild boar

» Stopping off at Karakol, famous for its apple orchards, Sunday market and backstreets full of Russian gingerbread-style cottages

» Travelling through the Kyrgyz Fergana Valley via the hair-raising Bishkek–Osh Road

GETTING UNDER THE SKIN

» **Read** Chinghiz Aitmatov's novel *Djamila*, which tells of Kyrgyz life and culture

» **Listen** to Kyrgyz traditional music played on a mixture of *komuz* guitars, a vertical violin known as a *kyl kyayk*, flutes, drums, mouth harps (*temir komuz*, or *jygach ooz* with a string) and long horns

» **Watch** Aktan Abdykalykov's *Besh Kumpyr* (Five Old Ladies)

» **Eat** homemade *beshbarmak* (large flat noodles topped with lamb or horse meat or both and cooked in vegetable broth) or snack on *samsa* (a meat pie with flaky puff pastry baked in a tandoori oven)

2.

3.

4.

» **Drink** *kymys* (a mildly alcoholic drink of fermented mare's milk) or settle for a cup of green tea

IN A WORD

» *Salam* (hello)

TRADEMARKS

» Horse sausages; teahouses; yurts; mountains; felt rugs; nomads; horse riding

SURPRISES

» Bishkek, the capital, is named after a wooden plunger – a *bishkek* is a churn used to make fermented mare's milk; the name Kyrgyz is one of the oldest recorded ethnic names in Asia, going back to the 2nd century BC in Chinese sources

MAP REF G,27

(1.) Tash-Rabat Caravanserai, once a popular stop on the old Silk Road in central Kyrgyzstan
(2.) Squinting into the sun, a happy family poses for a portrait outside its summer yurt
(3.) Russian-style apartment buildings dominate Toktogula Road in Karakol
(4.) Graves of nomads form the shape of a yurt for shelter in the afterlife
(5.) Roadside assistance at Lake Song-Kol where a bogged car is towed by hardy horses
(6.) A horse-riding hero wearing a denim jacket and a Kyrgyz hat in Jailoo, south of Kochkor

1.

Life in laid-back Laos is languid and leisurely: watching the morning sun light up the mighty Mekong River, wandering through aromatic markets and kicking back with a beer in hand. It's the simple pleasures that make a visit to this enigmatic country a delight, and what Laos lacks in in-your-face attractions is made up for with lush surrounds, friendly folk and gastronomic treats. The casual grandeur of Unesco World Heritage–listed Luang Prabang and small-town feel of the capital, Vientiane, make Laos one of the highlights of Southeast Asia.

BEST TIME TO VISIT

November to February, as Laos knows how to turn up the sweltering heat, and torrential downpours are a speciality

ESSENTIAL EXPERIENCES

» Circumnavigating Vientiane's revered Pha That Luang stupa
» Shopping nirvana at Luang Prabang's night market
» Floating down Nam Song in Vang Vieng till dusk
» Fine dining at one of Luang Prabang's atmospheric eateries
» Cooling off under the Kuang Si waterfall, near Luang Prabang

GETTING UNDER THE SKIN

» **Read** *Bamboo Palace* by Christopher Kremmer – part travelogue, part mystery, it chronicles the lost dynasty of Laos
» **Listen** to expat Paris-based troupe, Molam Lao
» **Watch** *Bombies,* a documentary probing the legacy of the US carpet-bombing campaign inflicted on Laos
» **Eat** *fŏe,* noodle soup in any variety; *tam màak hung,* deliciously laden spicy papaya salad
» **Drink** Bolaven Plateau brew for coffee aficionados; light and tasty Beer Lao; *lào-láo,* a fiery rice alcohol that is an acquired taste

5.

JULIET COOMBE

IN A WORD

» *Pai talat* (to the market)

TRADEMARKS

» Longtail boats; rice; Buddha-filled pagodas and wats; café culture; rural bandits; unexploded ordnance

SURPRISES

» Laos has one of the lowest population densities in Asia – around 18 people per sq km (about 11 per sq mile); by the end of the Vietnam War, Laos had the dubious distinction of being the most bombed country in the history of warfare

MAP REF J,31

(1.) Working the rice paddies on Khong Island
(2.) A young girl passes blue doors in the restored city of Luang Prabang
(3.) Vang Vieng's markets are the place to haggle for groceries
(4.) Novitiate monks peek out a window
(5.) Lavishly dressed women carry offerings to Vientiane's Pha That Luang

1.

Latvia may be sandwiched between Estonia and Lithuania, but its capital, Riga, is the biggest and most vibrant city in the Baltics. Great day-trip destinations surrounding Riga include the coastal resort Jurmala, the Sigulda castles overlooking the scenic Gauja River Valley, and the Rastrelli Palace at Rundale. Latvia's less-travelled roads are equally rewarding, from the dune-lined coast and historic towns of the Kurzeme region in the west of the country to the remote uplands of the east.

BEST TIME TO VISIT

April to September (spring to summer)

ESSENTIAL EXPERIENCES

» Visiting Rastrelli's lavishly Baroque Rundale Palace outside Riga
» Swinging across the Gauja River Valley in a cable car
» Strolling in the land of the Livonian people at Cape Kolka
» Beachcombing for washed-up amber along Latvia's Baltic coast
» Burrowing in the Riezupe sand caves near Kuldiga
» Wandering through Riga's massive Central Market

GETTING UNDER THE SKIN

» **Read** Latvia's national epic, *Lacplesis* (The Bear Slayer), written by Andrejs Pumpurs in the mid-19th century and based on traditional Latvian folk stories
» **Listen** to AutoBuss Debesis, art rock with a Latvian twist
» **Watch** *Homeland*, a documentary by Juris Podnieks that captures the tumultuous events of the early 1990s
» **Eat** *piragi*, meat pasties baked in the oven – Latvia's answer to fast food
» **Drink** the infamous Balzams, a thick, jet-black, 45% proof concoction – it's best served with coffee or mixed with equal parts vodka

RHONDA GUTENBERG

IN A WORD

» *Sveiks* (hi, or even goodbye)

TRADEMARKS

» Vibrant Riga; drinking sessions; scientists; sports-loving people; singing and dancing troupes

SURPRISES

» Pig's snout is a traditional Christmas dish; Riga is over 800 years old; Latvia is a remnant of the Holy Roman Empire; Latvia became a member of the European Union in May 2004

MAP REF E,22

(1.) A satisfying feline stretch outside a pretty house in Aglona
(2.) The majestic Russian Orthodox Cathedral in Riga
(3.) Patches of snow cling to the roof of a building overlooking the Filharmonijas Laukums
(4.) Freshest pick of the bunch at the Central Market, Riga

1.

Lebanon's modest borders pack in a powerful mix of cultures and traditions: mountain ski resorts and bucolic valleys, Roman ruins and Islamic architecture, bikini-clad beachgoers and women in chadors. After years of civil war, 2006 saw a return to instability as war broke out between Israel and Hezbollah. The prime minister described the resulting level of destruction as unimaginable. However, the Lebanese, famed for their commercial skill, great food and appreciation of a good party, are working hard at rebuilding. Beirut, once the Paris of the Middle East, is a fragile but cosmopolitan city intent on making a comeback.

BEST TIME TO VISIT
» June to mid-September – or before 1918 to experience the reign of the Ottoman Empire

ESSENTIAL EXPERIENCES
» Watching the sunset at Pigeon Rocks, Beirut's most famous natural attraction
» Spending a day viewing the extraordinary Roman ruins at Baalbek
» Driving along the magnificent scenic route to the Biblical Cedars
» Wandering through the ancient ruins at Byblos
» Discovering Mameluk architecture and markets in Tripoli
» Basking in the splendour of the palace at Beiteddine

GETTING UNDER THE SKIN
» **Read** William Dalrymple's *From the Holy Mountain*, a funny, thought-provoking account of the author's journey in the footsteps of a 6th-century monk
» **Listen** to *Fairuz Chante Zaki Yassif*, performed by Fairuz and composed by Zaki Yassif, the father of Lebanese folk music

439

» **Watch** *Le cerf-volant* (The Kite) by Randa Chahal Sabag, about a love affair between a Lebanese girl and an Israeli soldier

» **Eat** *kibbeh* (spiced minced lamb in a fried bulgur-wheat shell); baklava (syrupy sweet filo pastries)

» **Drink** *jellab,* a sweet drink made with raisins and pine nuts; *arak* on ice with a splash of water

IN A WORD

» *Ahalan was sahalan* (hello; literally 'welcome and welcome')

TRADEMARKS

» Dramatic landscapes; delicious food; ancient cities; sunny beaches; Mt Lebanon Range; crusader castles; temple complexes; picturesque port towns; olive groves and vineyards

SURPRISES

» A world-famous arts festival is held every July in Baalbek; there are amazing trekking opportunities

MAP REF H,24

(1.) Restoration work continues at Khan al-Franj (Inn of the Foreigners)
(2.) Palatial ruins of the Ottoman-era bathhouse Hammam al-Jadid
(3.) Looking up to street posters in Tyre
(4.) The so-called Temple of Bacchus at Baalbek

MARK DAFFEY

1.

Appropriately dubbed 'the kingdom in the sky', Lesotho is a mountainous country landlocked in the heart of South Africa. Its forbidding terrain and the defensive walls of the Drakensberg and Maluti ranges gave both sanctuary and strategic advantage to the Basotho (the people of Lesotho), who forged a nation while playing a key role in the manoeuvres of the white invaders on the plains below. Lesotho is an often surprising combination of developing modernity and ancient culture. It has avoided many of the recent wars and much of the political instability that has plagued most of the African continent.

BEST TIME TO VISIT

» May to September, to avoid the rains

ESSENTIAL EXPERIENCES

» Spending a night in a Basotho village on the edge of townships surrounding Maseru
» Hiking along the top of the Drakensberg escarpment
» Climbing Thaba-Bosiu (Mountain At Night), where King Moshoeshoe the Great established his second mountain stronghold
» Riding sure-footed Basotho ponies through the rugged and beautiful interior
» Following in the fossilised footsteps of dinosaurs near Quthing

GETTING UNDER THE SKIN

» **Read** *Stories By and About Women in Lesotho*, edited by K Limakatso Kendall, containing tales by Southern Sotho women and providing insights into women's thought in Lesotho
» **Listen** to the *lekolulo*, a flute-like instrument played by herd boys; the *thomo*, a stringed instrument played by women; and the *setolo-tolo*, a stringed instrument played with the mouth by men

2.

3.

4.

- » **Eat** *frikkadel* (fried meatball) or *koeksesters* (small doughnuts dripping in honey)
- » **Drink** locally made *joala* (sorghum beer) or maize beer

IN A WORD

- » *Dumela* (hello)

TRADEMARKS

- » Poverty; landlocked by South Africa; rainmaking rituals; mountains; the 'kingdom in the sky'

SURPRISES

- » The Basotho are traditionally buried in a sitting position, facing the rising sun and ready to leap up when called; the famous Basotho pony is the result of crossbreeding between short Javanese horses and European full mounts

MAP REF Q,23

(1.) Red Hot Pokers bloom as a grinning mountain trekker rides to Ribaneng Falls
(2.) Children play in the cool waters near Qacha's Nek village
(3.) Green hills form a gentle backdrop to the magnificent Maletsunyane Falls in Maseru
(4.) A Gwa Gwa woman dressed for the day
(5.) A woman and her husband wrapped in oilskins at the edge of Makhaleng valley
(6.) Sharing a joke with a Basotho boy

1.

Diamond-rich Liberia is on the north Atlantic coast of West Africa, bordered by Sierra Leone, Guinea and Côte d'Ivoire. It's in recovery from years of bitter civil strife, but on the security front things are looking up since the election of Africa's first female president, Ellen Johnson-Sirleaf in 2005. A regional peace initiative means one day travellers will again be able to explore this equatorial country, bask on its beautiful beaches, trek across verdant hillsides and explore pockets of magnificent rainforest.

BEST TIME TO VISIT

November to April, in the dry season

ESSENTIAL EXPERIENCES

» Spotting elephants, pygmy hippopotamii, chimpanzees and antelopes
» Exploring Liberia's stunning rainforest, covering around 40% of the country
» Visiting the bustling town of Ganta (Gompa City) in Liberia's mountainous interior
» Dining on collard greens and sweet-potato pie at a tiny roadside 'chop bar'
» Swimming in the vast Atlantic Ocean at Ellen's Beach, near Monrovia
» Experiencing the rich diversity and ceremonial cultures of over a dozen different ethnic groups

GETTING UNDER THE SKIN

» **Read** *Liberia: Portrait of a Failed State* by John-Peter Pham, a sensitive, factual account of African politics and Western intervention
» **Listen** to *Pavarotti & Friends – For The Children Of Liberia*, a collection of extreme musical genres – including Bon Jovi and the Spice Girls – under the uplifting guidance of Luciano Pavarotti

4.

5.

6.

CHRISTOPHER HERWIG

» **Watch** *Liberia: America's Stepchild*, by Nancee Oku Bright, a startling documentary about the settlement of freed American slaves in Liberia and their interactions with the indigenous peoples
» **Eat** goat soup and traditional rice bread
» **Drink** ginger beer, *poyo* (palm wine) and strong coffee

IN A WORD

» Diamonds for sale

TRADEMARKS

» Diamond smugglers; tidal lagoons; lush rainforest; amazing wildlife; rubber plantations; a nation of proud survivors; mangrove swamps; a struggling economy; cassava and sweet potato

SURPRISES

» Monrovia is one of the wettest capitals in Africa with over 4500mm of annual rainfall and humidity of over 90% – phew!

MAP REF L,19

(**1.**) Medical students enjoy watching the ceremony at Liberia's 159th Independence Day
(**2.**) A headful of oranges casually makes its way down a street in Monrovia
(**3.**) Randall Street, downtown Monrovia, at sunset
(**4.**) A boy works hard pounding mud to make bricks
(**5.**) Football fun in a downpour on Gurley Street, Monrovia
(**6.**) A streetside hairdresser looks after a client on Randall Street, Monrovia

1.

The word is out: Libya is the latest travellers' hotspot, and one of the last unspoilt places on the Mediterranean seaboard. Obscured from Western view for the last 30 years under the government of Colonel Mu'ammar Gaddafi, the country has recently begun courting international tourism. Ripe for discovery are Libya's incredible hospitality, beautiful desertscapes, well-preserved classical ruins, prehistoric rock art and palm-fringed oases.

BEST TIME TO VISIT

November to March for cooler temperatures – or during Libya's golden age in the 2nd century AD

ESSENTIAL EXPERIENCES

» Shopping in the bustling medina in Tripoli
» Walking through the streets and souqs of Benghazi
» Viewing the desert architecture and old city at Ghadhames
» Exploring the archaeological site at Leptis Magna, regarded as the best Roman site in the Mediterranean
» Visiting the preserved Greek city of Cyrene
» Hiking through the magnificent Jebel Akhdar mountains

GETTING UNDER THE SKIN

» **Read** Libyan-born Khaled Mattawa's *Ismailia Eclipse*, poetry that speaks across both cultural and political borders
» **Listen** to *Marhab* by Masoud, modern Libyan folkloric tunes
» **Watch** *Lion of the Desert* by Libyan filmmaker Moustapha Akkad, about a Libyan guerilla soldier who tries to stop the invasion of Italian troops during WWII
» **Eat** *cuscus bil-Bosla* – couscous with lamb, beans and tomato; *dolma mshakila* – peppers and zucchinis stuffed with spiced, minced lamb; *shorba bilhout* – spiced fish soup; delicious, sweet local dates

2.

3.

4.

» **Drink** sweet mint tea or the excellent local mineral water

IN A WORD

» *Ahlaan wasahlaan* (welcome)

TRADEMARKS

» Unesco World Heritage–listed sites; ancient Roman and Greek cities; beautiful resort towns; local souqs and medinas; Islamic culture; historic mosques and *hammams*; gorgeous beaches; mud-brick desert architecture

SURPRISES

» Stunning oases nestled in the Saharan desert; Tuaregs – the blue men of the desert; the pottery market at Gharian

MAP REF I,21

(1.) A local man in the Ubari Sand Sea with the mirage-like Unmal Miah Lake behind him
(2.) The honeycombed chambers of a fortified granary store in the Berber village of Kabaw
(3.) Tents gather in an hospitable semicircle at an encampment in the Libyan Sahara desert
(4.) A massive swell of dunes rolls towards the palm-fringed Dawada Lakes
(5.) A Tuareg man from the Ash Shati' region looks out from under his white headscarf
(6.) An elderly man takes an evening stroll past mud-brick houses in Ghadhames

1.

2.

3.

Postage stamp-sized Liechtenstein is sandwiched snugly between Austria and Switzerland, Liechtenstein's domineering elder sibling. The Swiss franc is the legal currency and border regulations are necessary only on the Austrian side. A cross-country walk takes on a new meaning here, as Liechtenstein measures a mere 25km north to south and 6km west to east. It's a prosperous place with a high standard of living, low taxes, numerous banks, the wealthiest royal family in Europe, its own stamps and an enviable unemployment rate of around 1.3%.

BEST TIME TO VISIT

December to April for winter sports, May to October for hiking

ESSENTIAL EXPERIENCES

» Having your passport stamped to earn bonus bragging points
» Tackling the rugged hiking trails that wind through stunning Alpine scenery
» Exploring tiny Vaduz, which sits below historic Vaduz Castle
» Whizzing down the Malbun resort's ski runs
» Collecting stamps at the Postage Stamp Museum in Vaduz

GETTING UNDER THE SKIN

» **Read** *Secrets of the Seven Smallest States of Europe: Andorra, Liechtenstein, Luxembourg, Malta, Monaco, San Marino and Vatican City* by Thomas Ecchardt, which outs Liechtenstein from its historical closet
» **Listen** to Vaduz-born composer Joseph Gabriel Rheinberger
» **Watch** films from countries with less than 10 million inhabitants at the Vaduz Film Festival, held every August
» **Eat** filling soups, cheeses, and Alp-fortifying food such as *rösti* (fried shredded potatoes) and wurst (sausage)

4.

» **Drink** local, rarely exported, wine

IN A WORD

» *Vilech chöi mer üs mal zum Briefmärkele träffe?* (maybe we could swap stamps sometime?)

TRADEMARKS

» A copycat Switzerland; wine producers; obsessive philatelists; a tax haven for enthusiastic entrepreneurs; the Alps; a retreat for expats; tiny mountain villages; crisp air; banks; ski runs and hiking routes

SURPRISES

» Dentures are an important export; there's no military service – the 80-strong army was disbanded in 1868; bank customers can no longer deposit money anonymously

MAP REF F,21

(1.) The village of Balzers offers lush hills, vineyards and a splendid view towards Switzerland
(2.) The sun shines on a bed of flowers in picturesque Balzers
(3.) Tourists are greeted by the royal family from postcard racks around the country
(4.) Members of a uniformed brass band blow their horns on National Day in Mauren

WAYNE WALTON

1.

Rebellious, quirky and vibrant, Lithuania owes much to the rich cultural currents of central Europe. It once shared an empire with neighbouring Poland that stretched from the Baltic almost to the Black Sea. Its capital Vilnius boasts a Baroque Old Town that is the largest in Eastern Europe and praised as the 'New Prague'. Lithuania's natural treasures also glitter – from the forests of the south to the magical Curonian Spit and the Nemunas Delta on the coast.

BEST TIME TO VISIT

May to September (spring and summer)

ESSENTIAL EXPERIENCES

» Wandering through the winding streets of Vilnius and peering into hidden courtyards

» Exploring the Curonian Spit, an isolated thread of sand composed of dunes and lush pine forests inhabited by elk, deer and wild boar

» Savouring fish freshly smoked to an old Curonian recipe

» Soaking up the curative powers of Druskininkai's mineral springs

GETTING UNDER THE SKIN

» **Read** Antanas Skma's semi-autobiographical novel *Balta drobule*, which pioneered the use of stream of consciousness in Lithuanian literature

» **Listen** to the avant-garde jazz of the Ganelin Trio

» **Watch** *Koridorius* (The Corridor) by director Šarcnas Bartas or *The Necklace of Wolf's Teeth* by Algimantas Puipa

» **Eat** *zeppelin cepelinai*, an airship-shaped parcel of thick potato dough, filled with cheese, *mesa* (meat) or *grybai* (mushrooms). It comes topped with a sauce made from onions, butter, sour cream and bacon bits. You also might like to try smoked pig's ears (or not).

2.

» **Drink** the local beer Utenos or potent *stakliskes*, a honey liqueur

IN A WORD

» *Làbas* (hello)

TRADEMARKS

» Winning independence from the Soviet Union; Baltic states; Stalin World; Eurovision Song Contest

SURPRISES

» When visiting a Lithuanian, bring an odd number of flowers – even-numbered bouquets are for the dead! Never shake hands across a doorway, as it is believed to bring bad luck.

MAP REF E,22

(1.) The Hill of Crosses in Siauliai, where devotional crucifixes bristle from the tombstones
(2.) Look at me! The dramatic silhouette of a statue beneath the Belfry of St John's in Vilnius
(3.) Vilnius presents a frosty vista from Gedimino Hill
(4.) Portrait of a homeless man in Vilnius

1.

2.

3.

MARTIN MOOS

Lilliputian Luxembourg may not be big enough to contain the letters of its name on a map of Europe, but it makes up in snazz what it lacks in size. It has a wealth of verdant landscapes crisscrossed by rivers and dotted with the sort of rural hamlets that most people associate with fairy tales. Luxembourg's people are justifiably proud of their heritage: the nation's motto is inscribed everywhere throughout Luxembourg City, the capital – *Mir wëlle bleiwe wat mir sin* – 'We want to remain what we are'. After a visit, you're sure to hope they do.

BEST TIME TO VISIT

March to June, for the most pleasant weather

ESSENTIAL EXPERIENCES

» Feeling claustrophobic in Luxembourg City's fortress casements, a honeycomb of damp chambers and connecting tunnels hewn from the belly of the Bock
» Taking in the superb panoramas from Citadelle du St Esprit in Luxembourg City
» Spending a lazy day visiting the wineries along the Moselle Valley's Route du Vin
» Playing 'king of the castle' at Vianden
» Hiking among the amazing rock formations in the primeval landscape of the Müllerthal 'Little Switzerland' region

GETTING UNDER THE SKIN

» **Read** *How to Remain What You Are*, a humorous look at Luxembourg ways by George Müller, a local psychologist and writer
» **Listen** to Fluyd, an alternative rap 'n' roll group, and Sascha Ley
» **Watch** the excellent animation of *Kirikou et la Sorcière*
» **Eat** *judd mat gaardebounen* (slabs of smoked pork served in a thick cream-based sauce with huge chunks of potato and broad

4.

beans), *ferkelsrippchen* (grilled spareribs) and *liewekniddelen mat sauerkraut* (liver meatballs with sauerkraut)

» **Drink** Moselle wines labelled *'Marque Nationale du Vin Luxembourg'* (which means the wine has passed a few wine-tasting tests)

IN A WORD

» *Moien* (hello)

TRADEMARKS

» Home to the most dramatically situated capital city in Europe; dumplings; stunning castles; beautiful china; proud people

SURPRISES

» Whitsunday is celebrated with a handkerchief pageant in honour of St Willibrord; the Moselle Valley's wine festival is held from August to November's 'New Wine' celebration in Wormeldange

BELGIUM

GERMANY

• Troisvierges

Clervaux •

• Untereisenbach

• Wiltz

• Esch-sur-Sûre

Vianden •

• Diekirch

Reisdorf

Ettelbrück •

Berdorf •

Echternach

• Mersch

Wasserbillig •

• Grevenmacher

Luxembourg City ✪

• Wormeldange

• Pétange

• Remich

• Bettembourg

FRANCE

Esch-sur-Alzette •

Schengen

FRANCE

MAP REF F,20

(1.) The tranquil town of Grund, now a Unesco World Heritage–listed site
(2.) The stark exterior of Grand Theatre de la Ville de Luxembourg in Luxembourg City
(3.) A whimsical monument to nonviolence outside a European Union building in the capital
(4.) Like a vision from a dream, the illuminated Castle of Vianden glimmers in the night

1.

MICHAEL AW

Macau may be firmly back in China's orbit, but its Portuguese patina makes it a most unusual Asian destination. In contrast to nearby Hong Kong its atmosphere is laidback, with Mediterranean-style cafés filled with palm-readers, caged birds and pipe-smokers. Highlights include fabulous architecture, narrow cobbled alleys, grand Baroque churches and balconied colonial mansions. Macau is wooing commerce and tourism like never before, and plans are afoot for all kinds of family-oriented shopping malls and theme parks to counter-balance the peninsula's long-held popularity as a haven for gamblers.

BEST TIME TO VISIT

October to December (winter)

ESSENTIAL EXPERIENCES

» Strolling along Praia Grande and visiting the A-Ma Temple
» Munching on a bowl of *caldo verde* and a plate of *bacalhau* at one of the Portuguese restaurants in Taipa village
» Skywalking around the outer rim of the Macau Tower or climbing to the top of the telecommunications spire
» Swimming and basking on the 'black sand' of Hác Sá Beach on Coloane

GETTING UNDER THE SKIN

» **Read** Austin Coates' *City of Broken Promises* – a fictionalised account of the life of 18th-century Macanese trader Martha Merop
» **Listen** to a heady mix of opera, musicals, visiting orchestras and other musical events at the annual two-week Macau International Music Festival held in October
» **Watch** *The Bewitching Braid* by Macanese director Cai Yuan Yuan

2.

3.

4.

» **Eat** the Portuguese-inspired *porco à Alentejana*, a tasty casserole of pork and clams, or the Macanese *galinha africana* (African chicken), a chicken cooked in coconut, garlic and chillies

» **Drink** *vinho verde*, a crisp, dry, slightly effervescent 'green' wine from Portugal that goes down a treat with spicy Macanese dishes

IN A WORD

» *Nei ho ma?* (hello, how are you?)

TRADEMARKS

» The former Portuguese colony; great food; a shopping haven

SURPRISES

» The Procession of the Passion of Our Lord is a 400-year-old tradition in which a colourful procession bears a statue of Jesus Christ from Macau's St Augustine Church to Macau Cathedral; tourism generates more than 40% of Macau's GDP

Map:
- Kun Iam Temple
- Luís de Camões Grotto & Gardens
- Sun Yatsen Memorial Home
- *Inner Harbour*
- Ruins of the Church of St Paul
- Chapel of St Michael
- Fortaleza de Monte
- Leal Senado
- St Francis Garden
- Jorge Alvares Statue
- *Baía da Praia Grande*
- Ponte Governador Nobre de Carvalho Macau-Taipa Bridge
- A-Ma Temple
- Barra Hill
- *Nam Van Lakes*

MAP REF J,31

(1.) An opera singer gazes heavenward as her powerful voice fills the concert hall
(2.) A heavy nose and a floral finish – the membership criteria for the Wine Society of Macau
(3.) A devotee lights a candle at the temple of Kwan Yin, goddess of mercy
(4.) Some of Macau's wealth of culinary delights are glimpsed in this steaming food stall
(5.) Fragrant smoke wafts from votary incense at the A-Ma Temple
(6.) These delicately prepared dumplings will be eaten in a traditional Chinese banquet

1.

Smack bang in the middle of the mountainous Balkan Peninsula, encircled by Greece, Bulgaria, Albania, Serbia and Montenegro, it's no wonder the Former Yugoslav Republic of Macedonia has been a powder keg of Ottoman and Orthodox influences. These days the opportunities for relaxation and exploration are unexpectedly varied: you can sit in a lively café, experience the time-worn Turkish bazaars, gaze at any number of medieval monasteries, wander in space-age shopping centres and marvel at Lake Ohrid's swag of cultural monuments.

BEST TIME TO VISIT

July and August – the best months to catch Macedonia's festivals

ESSENTIAL EXPERIENCES

» Wandering through Skopje's Oriental bazaar district
» Visiting the City Art Gallery housed in the Daud Paša Baths in Skopje, once the largest Turkish baths in the Balkans
» Making a pilgrimage to the 17th-century Church of Sveti Naum at Ohrid
» Scrambling through the Ruins of Heraclea at Bitola
» Skiing the southern slopes of Šar Planina, west of Tetovo
» Hiking in the Pelister National Park

GETTING UNDER THE SKIN

» **Read** *Black Lamb and Grey Falcon* by Rebecca West, a between-the-wars Balkan travelogue
» **Listen** to the Tavitjan Brothers Trio's self-titled album, featuring some of the most famous jazz musicians in Macedonia
» **Watch** Milcho Manchevski's *Before the Rain*, a visually stunning vision of how inter-ethnic war in Macedonia might begin
» **Eat** Turkish-style grilled mincemeat; *burek* – cheese or meat pies

» **Drink** *skopsko pivo* – the local beer; *rakija* – the national firewater, a strong spirit distilled from grapes

IN A WORD

» *Zdravo* (hello)

TRADEMARKS

» Orthodox churches; splendid mosaics; Lake Ohrid; bazaar districts; smoky cafés and bars; Byzantine monasteries; ski resorts; Roman ruins

SURPRISES

» The gnarled, 900-year-old plane tree at Ohrid; the five-day Balkan festival of Folk Dances and Songs, held at Ohrid in early July

MAP REF G,22

(1.) A comfortable silence reigns in an orthodox reading room
(2.) Glassy lake and mountains viewed from cypress trees around the Church of Sveti Naum
(3.) Finely detailed mosaics adorn the exterior of the Church of St Panteleimon, Ohrid
(4.) Empty wedding dresses hover over the heads of women in a Skopje clothing shop
(5.) The 13th-century Church of Sveti Jovan Bogoslov Kaneo stands guard over Lake Ohrid

1.

Madagascar's teeming fertile forests and geographical isolation have served to preserve and propagate 'nature's design laboratory' in a mix found nowhere else on earth. Sadly, this astounding diversity is threatened by aggressive deforestation. Still, for now, Madagascar's forests are a shimmering, seething mass of a trillion dripping leaves and slithering, jumping, quirky creatures from nature's bag of tricks: lemurs, chameleons, periwinkles and baobabs, aloes, geckos, sifakas and octopus trees.

BEST TIME TO VISIT

April to October (winter) – or for an authentic pirate experience, the 17th century when more than 1000 pirates were based on Madagascar's east coast

ESSENTIAL EXPERIENCES

» Kicking back in Fort Dauphin (Taolagnaro), with its windswept coastline and picturesque mountain backdrop
» Sailing out to Île Sainte Marie – a former haunt of pirates
» Spotting lemurs at Parc National de Montagne d'Ambre
» Exploring the lush rainforests of Parc National de Ranomafana
» Trekking in the beautiful Masoala Peninsula

GETTING UNDER THE SKIN

» **Read** *Madagascar, Island of the Ancestors* by John Mack, a superb ethnographic overview of Malagasy culture
» **Listen** to Paul Bert Rahasimanana ('Rossy') – check out *Island of Ghosts* or *Bal Kabosy*
» **Watch** Raymond Rajaonarivelo's *Quand les Étoiles Rencontrent la Mer* (When the Stars Meet the Sea), the story of a boy born during a solar eclipse; *Angano...Angano...Tales from Madagascar*, a documentary in the oral Malagasy tradition

MADAGASCAR

CAPITAL ANTANANARIVO POPULATION 16,979,744 AREA 587,040 SQ KM OFFICIAL LANGUAGES MALAGASY, FRENCH

2.

3.

4.

» **Eat** *vary hen'omby* (rice served with stewed or boiled zebu) or Malagasy cheeses (made from zebu cow's milk)

» **Drink** *betsa-betsa* (fermented sugar cane juice) or *punch aux cocos* (rum and coconut milk punch)

IN A WORD

» *Manao ahoana ianao* (how do you do?)

TRADEMARKS

» Lemurs; pirates; zebu-drawn carts; fourth-largest island in the world; trekking

SURPRISES

» Over half of the world's chameleon species are found in Madagascar; according to the *vintana* belief, Friday (which is associated with nobility) is considered a good day to be born, while Thursday is associated with servitude

Comoros

Mayotte

Antsiranana
(Diego Suarez)

Sambava

Mahajanga (Majunga)

Mozambique
Channel

Toamasina
(Tamatave)

Antananarivo

Morondava

INDIAN
OCEAN

Morombe

Fianarantsoa

Toliara (Tuléar)

Vangaindrano

Manambondro

Androka

Taolagnaro
(Fort Dauphin)

MAP REF 0,25

(1.) An avenue of stately baobabs in Toliara near Morondava
(2.) A solitary Malagasy tomb on the High Plateaus
(3.) A swashbuckling girl and her piratey parrot in Fianarantsoa
(4.) Pirogues drift into an aimless symmetry off the island of Nosy Nato
(5.) Traditional henna patterns on the face of a young girl in Nosy Be
(6.) Vividly dressed village girls on their way to market in the south of Madagascar

1.

The tourist brochures bill Malawi as 'the warm heart of Africa', and for once the hype is true. Malawi's ever-changing landscape takes you from the top of lofty mountains, down steep escarpments, through woodland, farmland and empty grassland, to the shores of a magnificent lake. Nature lovers will adore the national parks and game reserves, mountain hiking and plateau trekking, lake diving and boating – plus the warm welcome, as Malawians tend to be extremely friendly toward travellers.

BEST TIME TO VISIT

Late April to November (the dry season)

ESSENTIAL EXPERIENCES

» Paddling across Lake Malawi with the shrill call of fish-eagles floating across the waves
» Riding with zebras and antelopes across the rolling plateau of Nyika National Park
» Climbing the steep winding paths of Mt Mulanje to cool grassy plateaus speckled with wildflowers
» Taking a wildlife drive through Liwonde National Park to spot elephants, antelopes, hyenas and lions

GETTING UNDER THE SKIN

» **Read** Malawian poet Steve Chimombo's highly acclaimed *The Rainmaker*, or Paul Theroux's *Jungle Lovers*, a light and humorous take on 1960s Malawi culture and politics
» **Listen** to Lucius Banda, who plays soft ('Malawian-style') reggae, or Ethel Kamwendo, one of Malawi's leading female singers
» **Watch** *Up in Smoke*, a documentary exploring the effects of the tobacco industry in Malawi
» **Eat** *chambo* (a Lake Malawi fish – a local speciality) or *nsima* (maize porridge – the regional staple)

4.

JERRY GALEA

5.

6.

» **Drink** the locally brewed beer Chibuku

IN A WORD

» *Moni* (good morning)

TRADEMARKS

» Baobab trees; Lake Malawi; fish; national parks; trekking; teeming wildlife

SURPRISES

» Lake Malawi covers almost a fifth of Malawi's total area; the remains of settlements of modern humans dating back some 100,000 years have been found on the shores of Lake Malawi

MAP REF N,23

(1.) A sombre-faced fisherman lost in thought on the banks of a lake
(2.) A young villager observes the dry landscape of southern Malawi
(3.) A woman hoists a basket over her head in southern Malawi
(4.) A timid reedbuck stands alone under a brooding sky in Nyika National Park
(5.) The inquiring face of a village child in the Nsasje District
(6.) A spirited afternoon game of volleyball outside the Indaba bar in Cape Maclear

1.

Malaysia is an assault on the senses – a cultural fusion of colours, flavours and dialects combined with sticky tropical heat. It boasts superb beaches, mountains and national parks, plus a heady mix of people – Malay, Chinese, Indian, and the diverse indigenous tribes of Sabah and Sarawak in Borneo. Historical influences loom large in the stately colonial architecture of Georgetown (Penang) and Melaka, and the prosperous nation's love of progress is proclaimed in its gleaming, futuristic buildings.

BEST TIME TO VISIT

May to September (the dry season)

ESSENTIAL EXPERIENCES

» Balancing on the creaky canopy walk over Taman Negara National Park
» Snorkelling with Technicolor fish in crystal-clear waters off the Perhentian Islands
» Sipping a freshly snipped brew of full-bodied Highlands tea in the Cameron Highlands
» Climbing the challenging craggy peak of Mt Kinabalu
» Haggling under the bright lights of Kuala Lumpur's night markets

GETTING UNDER THE SKIN

» **Read** Joseph Conrad's *Lord Jim* – adventure on the South China Seas and the real-life story of Raja Brooke of Sarawak; *The Return* by KS Maniam – contemporary Malaysian fiction exploring the Indian Malaysian experience
» **Listen** to traditional Malay *gendang* (drum) music; kampung-style world music by Zainal Abidin; KL alt-rock band Flop Poppy
» **Watch** Mahadi J Murat's *Sayang Salmah* (1995), a taut family drama set in post-independence Malaya; *Guardians of the Forest* (2001), a documentary about the indigenous Orang Asli people

2.

3.

4.

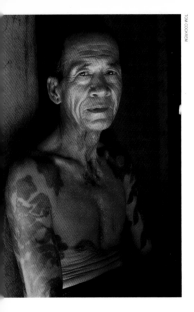

» **Eat** the stinky but delicious durian fruit; laksa (spicy coconut noodle soup)

» **Drink** *air kelapa* (coconut water); *tuak* (Borneo rice wine)

IN A WORD

» *Jalan-jalan* (I'm just travelling around)

TRADEMARKS

» Orang-utans; tea plantations; Mahathir Mohamad; colonial remnants; Petronas Towers; jungle tribes; logging and dams; tropical islands; hawker food; gleaming mosques

SURPRISES

» Malaysia is well on the way to achieving its goal of becoming a fully industrialised nation by 2020; nine state sultans still reign, and they take five-year turns at being chief sultan of Malaysia

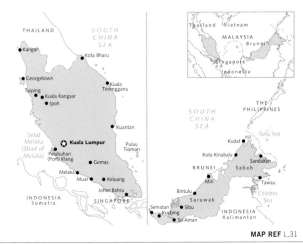

MAP REF L,31

(1.) Hide and seek – a young girl peeks through a broken fence near Lake Batang Ai
(2.) Tea pickers carve patterns through crop fields during harvest in the Cameron Highlands
(3.) The Petronas Towers dominate the skyline of Kuala Lumpur
(4.) A keymaker in Georgetown, Penang, takes a moment to leaf through a newspaper
(5.) A tattooed elderly man rests in the Menyang Sedi Longhouse near Lake Batang Ai
(6.) Fishing boats float languidly under a radiant sky in Tanjong Bunga

1.

This small Islamic nation of fishing and trading people has a history, culture and language all its own. The Maldives is made up of a string of 1190 tiny islands, most of them measuring less than a couple of kilometres and bobbing only a few metres above sea level. If your idea of paradise is a pristine tropical island with swaying palm trees, white-sand beaches and turquoise lagoons, then the Maldives will not disappoint.

BEST TIME TO VISIT

December to April (the dry season)

ESSENTIAL EXPERIENCES

» Swimming in a clear-blue lagoon, strolling on soft white sand and sitting under a coconut tree
» Scuba diving to see turtles, mantas and morays, whale sharks, nurse sharks, hammerheads and rays
» Exploring the underwater shipwreck *Maldive Victory*, alive with corals and home to trevally, snapper, squirrelfish and cod
» Taking a flight over the atolls and watching the free-form patterns of sea, sandbank, reef and island

GETTING UNDER THE SKIN

» **Read** *Mysticism in the Maldives*, which documents Maldivian myths and stories
» **Listen** to popular local bands Mezzo and Zero Degree
» **Eat** *garudia* (soup made from dried and smoked fish, often eaten with rice, lime and chilli) for a main meal and finish off with an *arecanut* (an oval nut chewed with betel leaf, cloves and lime), which is the equivalent of an after-dinner mint
» **Drink** *raa* (a sweet and delicious toddy tapped from the crown of the palm trunk)

5.

IN A WORD

» *A-salam alekum* (hello)

TRADEMARKS

» Pristine tropical islands; swaying palm trees; pure white-sand beaches; brilliant aquamarine water; abundant marine life; gloriously coloured coral; peerless diving

SURPRISES

» Ancient beliefs survive: the islanders fear *jinnis* – evil spirits that come from the sea, land and sky; the full name of the country is Dhivehi Raajjeyge Jumhooriyyaa

Haa Alifu — Dhidhdhoo
Haa Dhaal — Kulhuduffushi
Funadhoo — Shaviyani
Ugoofaaru — Noonu
Manadhoo
Raa — Lhaviyani
Naifaru
Baa — Eydhafushi
Kaafu
INDIAN
OCEAN
Alifu — ⭐ Male'
Mahibadhoo
Felidhoo
Magoodhoo — Vaavu
Faafu
Kudahuvadhoo — Muli
Dhaalu — Meemu
Veymandhoo
Thaa — Laamu
Hithadhoo

Gaaf Alif
Viligili
Thinadhoo
Gaaf Dhaal — Equator

Gnaviyani — Fuamulaku
Seenu — Hithadhoo

INDIAN
OCEAN

MAP REF L,27

(1.) The bow of a dhoni boat appears to hover above calm, ethereal waters
(2.) Thatched bungalows stretch out into the sea off Dhunikolhu island
(3.) Cheeky boys splash about in a rubber tube on Maalhoss island
(4.) A sandy path winds its way through a grove of palm trees
(5.) Fresh-faced students in their brilliant white school uniforms on the streets of Male'

1.

From Bamako to Timbuktu, Mali has desert scenery that may have you believing you're on the set of *Lawrence of Arabia*. And there's so much more, from the fringes of the Saharan desert and the great Niger River, to medieval mud-brick mosques and pink-hued sandstone villages. Malians are a proud and enduring people who have suffered through drought and famine of biblical proportions. There is a wealth of talented musicians and great passion among the people for their traditional culture.

BEST TIME TO VISIT

October to February (before the heat) – or in June 1960 when Mali gained independence from France

ESSENTIAL EXPERIENCES

» Hunting for bargains in Bamako's pavement market stalls
» Trekking through the magnificent Bandiagara Escarpment
» Watching a gorgeous sunset at Gao
» Photographing the mud-brick houses and mosque at Djenné
» Buying colourful handwoven fabrics at the market in Ségou
» Making your way through the desert to enigmatic isolated Timbuktu

GETTING UNDER THE SKIN

» **Read** *The Unveiling of Timbuctoo: The Astounding Adventures of Caillie* by Gailbraith Welch, an account of the first Western explorer to both reach and return from Timbuktu
» **Listen** to the beautiful, intimate tracks on *Je Chanterai pour Toi* by Boubacar Traoré; Ry Cooder and Ali Farka Touré's *Talking Timbuktu*
» **Watch** *Yeleen* by Souleymane Cissé, depicting the struggle of a young warrior to destroy the corruption of an older society
» **Eat** fried Nile perch; *poulet yassa* – chilli-spiced grilled chicken; *riz yollof* – meat or vegetables cooked with tomato

2.

3.

4.

» **Drink** ginger and hibiscus juices sold in plastic bags

IN A WORD

» *Merci* (thank you)

TRADEMARKS

» Castellated mosques; desert landscapes; the Bambara and Dogon cultures; bustling markets; archaeological ruins; faded French colonial glory; ancient rock paintings; the indigo turbans and robes of the Tuareg; griot music; desert elephants

SURPRISES

» The music and dance performances held in local *carrefour* (cultural centres); the riotous football matches; the villages carved into mountain cliffs

MAP REF J,19

(1.) The Great Market in Djenné comes to life in front of the century-old mud-brick mosque
(2.) A young girl crouches at the foot of a tree in a village by the River Niger
(3.) The dusty hands of a Dogon hunter grip an old rifle in Mopti
(4.) Wooden boats known as *pinasse* run between Mopti and Timbuktu along the River Niger
(5.) An indigo-clad Tuareg carpet seller in Timbuktu displays his wares on top of his head
(6.) Desert bloom – a stunning Tuareg woman sits in the sand in the village of Tin Telout

1.

At first glance Malta appears to be steeped in the past. Ancient temples, the oldest free-standing structures in existence, traditions dating back over 2500 years and buses that could have been around when Malta gained independence in 1964 – it all makes you wonder if the country should be declared a living museum. Though Malta has a rich history it also offers beaches, bars, bustling Mediterranean life, friendly locals, a passion for *festas*, water sports and excellent opportunities for scuba diving.

BEST TIME TO VISIT

February to June (before the heat) – or any time outside 1942 when the country was bombed for 154 days and nights

ESSENTIAL EXPERIENCES

» Wandering round the magnificent fortified capital of Valletta, built by the Knights of St John
» Experiencing a *festa*, lasting up to five days and including fireworks, the parade of the patron saint, brass bands, food, drink and general celebration
» Scuba diving at the Azure Window, a giant rock arch in the cliff surrounding the Inland Sea on the island of Gozo
» Swimming at the Blue Lagoon, one of the best bathing spots in the Mediterranean

GETTING UNDER THE SKIN

» **Read** Francis Ebejer's *For Rozina… A Husband*, based on Maltese village life and comprising a collection of short stories. *The Kappilan of Malta* by Nicolas Monserrat tells of a priest's experiences during WWII.
» **Listen** to Charles Camilleri's *Il Weghda* – the first opera written in Maltese, and the Beangrowers' *Beangrowers* – a pop/electro/rock/punk mix

495

5.

6.

7.

» **Watch** Ridley Scott's *Gladiator*, one of the many films shot in Malta; the 1953 movie *The Malta Story*, which plays out events leading up to the island being awarded the George Cross in 1942

» **Eat** *timpana* – baked macaroni with egg, meat and tomatoes; *mqaret* – deep-fried pastries stuffed with chopped, spiced dates

» **Drink** Kinnie – a soft drink flavoured with oranges and herbs

IN A WORD

» *Kif inti?* (how are you?)

TRADEMARKS

» Churches; ancient buildings; crazy drivers; British tourists; crusading knights; the Maltese Cross; pedestrianised Valletta

SURPRISES

» There are no permanent water features on Malta; the country didn't invent Maltesers; it's one of the most densely populated countries in the world

MAP REF H,21

(1.) Golden rays of sunlight illuminate megaliths erected 3600 BC to 3000 BC at Hagar Qim
(2.) A colourful *luzzu* fishing boat sports an 'eye of protection'
(3.) The megalithic Mnajdra temple complex was built to follow the sun's alignment
(4.) A visitor strolls up to a giant snail etched into the stark salt pans around Xwejni Bay
(5.) This domed church and its Maltese cross preside over the water's edge
(6.) A fisherman and his boat posing by St Julian's Harbour
(7.) Rising above Mosta, this church has one of the world's largest unsupported domes

1.

CHRISTIAN ASLUND

The Marshalls are made up of more than one thousand flat coral islands of white-sand beaches and turquoise lagoons. Like other Pacific paradises there's spectacular diving, lush tropical greenery and beautiful beaches. The flipside is that many of the Marshallese still struggle with the after-effects of the 20th-century's Atomic Age. Bikini Atoll is the most famous of the nuclear-testing sites of the 1960s, though inhabitants of other islands also suffer from radiation poisoning. Many islands remain too contaminated to be resettled or visited.

BEST TIME TO VISIT

Diving is at its best May to October, when the water is calmest, though water temperatures are bathlike year-round

ESSENTIAL EXPERIENCES

» Deep-sea fishing off Longar Point on Arno Atoll
» Witnessing the night-time pyrotechnics of missile-testing on Kwajalein Atoll, the world's largest coral atoll
» Relaxing on Majuro Atoll's chilled-out beaches
» Swimming and fishing off Mejit Island
» Discovering history on Maloelap Atoll among the twisted wrecks of WWII bombers

GETTING UNDER THE SKIN

» **Read** *Man This Reef* by Gerald Knight – translated legends of an elderly Marshallese storyteller
» **Listen** to local boy band, County Light – their debut album *Jambo* combines English and Marshallese songs
» **Watch** shocking documentaries about Bikini Atoll including Dennis O'Rourke's definitive *Half Life*
» **Eat** fresh seafood

2.

» **Drink** coconut milk straight from the source

IN A WORD

» *Yokwe yuk* (love to you – the traditional greeting)

TRADEMARKS

» Bikinis; warmly welcoming Marshallese; 'secret' US bases; WWII wrecks, stunning but uninhabitable beaches; big game fishing

SURPRISES

» Visiting the traditional small village of Laura on Majuro Atoll; camping out on the outer islands in absolute serenity

Taongi Atoll

PACIFIC OCEAN

Bikar Atoll

Enewetok Atoll

Bikini Atoll *Rongelap Atoll* *Taka Atoll* *Utrik Atoll*

Ailinginae Atoll *Rongerik Atoll* *Ailuk Atoll*

Mejit Island

Wotho Atoll *Jemo Island*

Likiep Atoll *Wotje Atoll*

Ujelang Atoll *Kwajalein Atoll* *Erikub Atoll* *Maloelap Atoll*

Ujae Atoll *Lae Atoll* *Lib* *Aur Atoll*

Namu Atoll *Jabwot Atoll* **D-U-D** ⚙ *Arno Atoll*

Ailinglaplap Atoll *Majuro Atoll* *Mili Atoll*

Jaluit Atoll *Knox Atoll*

Namorik Atoll *Kili*

Ebon Atoll

MAP REF L,38

(1.) A traditional beach barbecue on Likiep Atoll
(2.) Sun, sand and a comfortable armchair. Who could ask for more?
(3.) Locals take time out for a game of volleyball on Kwajalein Atoll
(4.) Bliss infuses the face of a girl drinking coconut milk straight from the source
(5.) A bronzed snorkeller emerges from the waters of Likiep Atoll

1.

JEAN ROBERT

Martinique is a slice of France set down in the tropics, with islanders wearing Paris fashions and breakfasting on croissants. But the zouk music pouring out of bars and nightclubs are a reminder that Martinicans have a culture of their own, solidly based on West Indian Creole traditions. French may be the official language, but most locals speak Creole, which retains traces of the many tongues spoken by African slaves. Martinique's large towns feel like modern suburbs, but thankfully nearly a third of the island is forested.

BEST TIME TO VISIT
February to March (early spring)

ESSENTIAL EXPERIENCES
» Enjoying the cosmopolitan society of Fort-de-France, with its blend of French and Creole cultures
» Exploring Saint-Pierre's ruins, caused by the 1902 volcanic eruption
» Soaking in the sun on the vast stretches of beach at Les Salines
» Cruising the Route de la Trace, a scenic rainforest drive across the mountainous interior

GETTING UNDER THE SKIN
» **Read** *The Collected Poetry of Aimé Césaire*, the force behind the Black Pride phenomenon known as *négritude*; *Texaco* by Patrick Chamoiseau and *Malemort* by Édouard Glissant are also excellent reads
» **Listen** to *Shades of Black* by zouk band Kassav'
» **Watch** *Sugar Cane Alley*, by Euzhan Palcy, documenting the love and sacrifice of a poor black family living on a sugar plantation in Martinique in the 1930s

2.

» **Eat** *accras* (fish fritters) or delicious French pastries

» **Drink** *ti-punch* (a mixture of white rum, sugar cane juice and a squeeze of lemon) or the local beer, Lorraine

IN A WORD

» *Bonjour* (hello)

TRADEMARKS

» French cuisine; lush mountains; volcanoes; sugar plantations; zouk music

SURPRISES

» Josephine Bonaparte was born in Martinique; Paul Gauguin spent five months on Martinique in 1887

MAP REF K,13

(1.) This fishing boat provides a focal point for beachgoers
(2.) A colourful street corner in Saint-Pierre
(3.) A hurricane sky darkens the bay
(4.) Nets hang out to dry in the pretty fishing village of Anse d'Arlet

Mauritania's biggest attraction is the very desolation that keeps so many people away. In this mysterious, wild, confounding country resources are scarce and sand is plentiful. Among the vast, blank, shifting dune-fields and strange, flat-topped mountain ranges, the only fertile land is found in the oases and along a narrow strip bordering the Senegal River. Set in this severe landscape is a deeply traditional Islamic republic, inhabited by warm, yet reserved, humorous people, measuring out endless amounts of hospitality in glasses of tea with 10 sugars.

BEST TIME TO VISIT

December to March, when it's cooler (but still hot)

ESSENTIAL EXPERIENCES

» Navigating the empty sea of Saharan dunes by camel
» Exploring the ruins of Koumbi Saleh, legendary capital of the medieval empire of Ghana
» Lingering in Chinguetti – the seventh-holiest city of Islam
» Visiting Nouakchott's wharf and fish market, Port de Pêche
» Succumbing to the enchantment of the old quarter of Ouadâne
» Counting two million sandpipers in Parc National du Banc d'Arguin

GETTING UNDER THE SKIN

» **Read** Michael Asher's recounting of the first west-to-east camel crossing of the Sahara in *Impossible Journey: Two Against the Sahara*
» **Listen** to the stunning combination of Arabic melodies and African percussion by diva Dimi Mint Abba
» **Watch** Abderrahmane Sissako's poignant *Hermakano* (Waiting for Happiness), set in Nouâdhibou

» **Eat** at a *méchui*, a traditional nomad's feast, where an entire lamb is roasted over a fire and stuffed with cooked rice (cutlery optional)

» **Drink** glasses of strong, sweet mint tea

IN A WORD

» *Salaam aleikum* (hello)

TRADEMARKS

» Endless sand; oases; desertification; birdlife; 'controlled democratisation'

SURPRISES

» Only in 1980, when there were an estimated 100,000 Haratin slaves in Mauritania, did the government finally declare slavery illegal, although there are regular round-ups of antislavery activists; Mauritania boasts the longest, slowest, dustiest train in the world

MAP REF J,19

(1.) Shy children hide behind one another in the wide open desert spaces of Trarza
(2.) The enchanting greenery of the oasis near Terjit bursts from the surrounding dry rock
(3.) A young Mauritanian girl dressed in rich purple cloth
(4.) A camel caravan picks a path through the dunes near Chinguetti in the Adrar region
(5.) Heavily wrapped locals trudge along the road between Nouâdhibou and Nouakchott

1.

Mauritius boasts endless sugar cane plantations, dramatic mountains, a vibrant cultural mix and some of the finest beaches and aquamarine lagoons in the Indian Ocean. The island has a distinct Indian flavour, seasoned with African, Chinese, French and British elements. You can enjoy a dish of curried chickpeas or a Yorkshire pudding on the outdoor terrace of a French café, sipping imported wine or a thick malty ale while listening to Creole music and the conversation of locals in any number of tongues.

BEST TIME TO VISIT
July to September (winter)

ESSENTIAL EXPERIENCES
» Lazing on the long, casuarina-fringed beach of Belle Mare
» Diving offshore, especially at the northern end of the island
» Hunting for bargains in the downtown market in Port Louis
» Strolling around the beautiful Sir Seewoosagur Ramgoolam Botanical Gardens at Pamplemousses
» Hiking in the Black River Gorges National Park – a must for nature lovers

GETTING UNDER THE SKIN
» **Read** the romantic novel *Paul et Virginie* by Bernardin de St Pierre, or *Petrusmok* by well-known author Malcolm de Chazal
» **Listen** to Ti-Frère, the most popular séga singer, or Creole singer Jean Claude-Monique
» **Eat** *rougaille* (a Mediterranean dish of tomatoes, onions, garlic and any kind of meat or fish) or daube (stew)
» **Drink** lassi (a yogurt and ice-water drink) or *alouda glacé* (a syrupy brew of agar, milk and fruit syrup)

2.

3.

4.

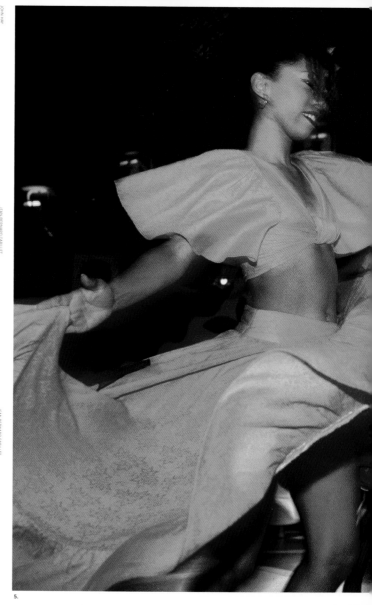

5.

MAURITIUS

IN A WORD

» *Tapeta!* (cheers!)

TRADEMARKS

» Home to the extinct dodo; sugar plantations; coconut palms; pamper-happy beach resorts; Indian-fusion cuisine

SURPRISES

» Undersea walks are becoming increasingly popular – participants don lead boots and diving helmets and stroll along the seabed feeding the fish, while oxygen is piped in from the surface

MAP REF 0,26

(1.) A picturesque rural scene near the oddly named town of Flic en Flac
(2.) A mountain range soars above verdant palm-fringed valleys
(3.) Giggling sisters make their way to school in Mahébourg
(4.) Thatched umbrellas cast cool discs of shade on an idyllic beach near Trou d'Eau Douce
(5.) A séga dancer shakes her booty in Belle Mare

1.

Like its native jalapeño peppers and agave tequila, Mexico embodies a spicy, fiery passion for *la vida*. This same spirit overflows from the country's vibrantly colourful art and music, and its complex culture, history and geography. Mexico's charm is its mix of modern and traditional, the clichéd and the surreal, the ancient and the brand-new. True to the country's contradictory nature, the attitude towards the US, its neighbour to the north, is a combination of both uncertainty and longing.

BEST TIME TO VISIT

October to May, to avoid extreme temperatures

ESSENTIAL EXPERIENCES

» Navigating your way through massive Mexico City, especially the Museo Nacional de Antropología and the large open-air market
» Eating fish tacos at sunset on the beach in Zipolite
» Exploring the awe-inspiring ruins at Teotihuacán and Palenque
» Being immersed in the Mayan world of the Yucatán
» Snorkeling at Isla Mujeres and Cozumel

GETTING UNDER THE SKIN

» **Read** eyewitness accounts of the Spanish arrival in the 'new world' such as *History of the Conquest of New Spain* by Bernal Díaz del Castillo; *The Labyrinth of Solitude* by Octavio Paz, a poetic exploration of Mexican myths and identity
» **Listen** to Vicente Fernandez' *ranchera* ballads, Los Tigres del Norte and Café Tacuba – pioneers of *rock en español*
» **Watch** Mayan peasants fleeing north for a new life in *El Norte*; a taste of magic-realism romance in *Like Water for Chocolate*; the raw edge of Mexican cinema's nuevo wave in *Amores Perros*
» **Eat** a *comida corrida* (the daily special set menu offered in the markets), chocolate *mole*, sweet tamales with milky *atole*; staples

JEFFREY BECOM

2.

3.

4.

like tortillas, beans and chillies, *tunas* (prickly pear cactus fruit), *nopales* (cactus leaves)

» **Drink** *jugos naturales*, especially the bloodlike *vampiro* fruit juice (beet and carrot); all three alcohols from the maguey plant: tequila, mezcal and the less alcoholic pulque; *cerveza* (beer)

IN A WORD

» *¡Que le vaya bien!* (may things go well for you!)

TRADEMARKS

» Mariachis; beaches and coastal resorts; Diego Rivera and Frida Kahlo; *telenovelas*; cliff divers in Acapulco; revolutionary heroes; border towns; margaritas; Día de los Muertos skeletons

SURPRISES

» Seeing pre-Hispanic ruins in the metro stations; the Olmecs were the first people to extract chocolate from cacao beans – 3000 years before anyone else; the Caesar salad was invented in Tijuana

MAP REF I,9

(1.) A villager drags an obstinate pig past a vibrant Tlacotalpan house
(2.) The face of an elderly *campesino* (peasant) in San Blas
(3.) Bright shades and dark shadows converge in a street in Real del Monte
(4.) A human skull adorns a tomb in the town of Muna, Yucatán
(5.) The ancient Mayan temple of Kukulcán dwarfs a group of visitors in Chichén Itzá
(6.) Hanging loose during siesta time in Chichicapa

1.

There's something to be said for a country that has tried to outlaw ties and baseball caps. Despite being firmly tied to the USA's economic and political apron strings, each of the four island states has maintained its own culture: Kosrae remains a casual backwater; Pohnpei a jungle paradise; bright, bubbly Chuuk attracts divers with its sunken WWII wrecks; and unconventional Yap is a traditional centre, famous for its massive stone money.

BEST TIME TO VISIT

Temperatures hover around 27°C (81°F) year-round, but it's a little less humid December to June

ESSENTIAL EXPERIENCES

» Diving the sunken Japanese fleet resting in Chuuk lagoon
» Bashing through thick rainforest interiors or snorkelling the fringing reef of Kosrae
» Staying amongst the hibiscus flowers and jungle hillsides on Pohnpei
» Rocking on at Nan Madol, Pohnpei's ancient stone city
» Embracing traditional life in Yap, where some people still wear loincloths and everyone has a bulge of betel nut in their cheek
» Collecting seashells on Nukuoro, an uninhibited Polynesian haven

GETTING UNDER THE SKIN

» **Read** *Islands Islands: A Special Good,* by Bernadette V Wehrly – a collection of poems, songs and legends
» **Listen** to Randall Mathias' album *Little Refonuwach*, a blend of contemporary and traditional Chuukese melodies
» **Watch** *The Paradise Islands, Micronesia* – a video designed to show off the islands as a tourist destination
» **Eat** (or rather chew) *buw* (betel nut), sometimes with tobacco added on Yap

» **Drink** *sakau* (kava), a narcotic drink made from the roots of pepper shrubs, which is hugely popular on Pohnpei

IN A WORD

» *Mogethin* (Yapese), *Kaselehia* (Pohnpeian), *Ran annim* (Chuukese) – greetings from the respective islands

TRADEMARKS

» Giant stone money; red-stained lips from betel nut chewing; diving in underwater maritime 'museums'; bountiful seafood feasts; dark jungle interiors; friendly villagers; empty beaches

SURPRISES

» Micronesian societies are made up of clan groupings, with descent traced through the mother (except on Yap, where descent is patrilineal); the head clan on each island can trace its lineage back to the island's original settlers

MAP REF L,36

(**1.**) Glistening in the sun, a girl whistles through her hands on the island of Yap
(**2.**) The river carves a green corridor through the rainforests of Pohnpei
(**3.**) A snorkeller investigates what lies beneath the palm fronds of Satawal Atoll
(**4.**) In a blur of grass skirts, traditional dancers on Yap boogie to frenzied beats
(**5.**) The Sleeping Lady mountain range reclines by glassy waters in Kosrae

1.

One of Europe's smallest yet most divided nations, Moldova is a country of multiple personalities. The nation claims some of the most fertile soil in the former Soviet Union with forests and vineyards stretching to every corner of its landlocked borders. Yet the natural splendour of Moldova conceals a population torn by political and ethnic tensions. Civil strife has given rise to two break-away republics: Transdniestr and Gaugauz. With a history as colourful as its landscape, Moldova is an intriguing place to visit; a post-Soviet enigma waiting to be unveiled.

BEST TIME TO VISIT

May to August, or whenever you can – Moldova's Kafkaesque bureaucracy makes obtaining a visa a virtual lottery

ESSENTIAL EXPERIENCES

» Strolling along the leafy boulevards of the capital Chişinău, stopping to smell the roses at the 24-hour flower stalls
» Finding a taste of the Orient by bargaining your way up and down the exotic central market
» Heading underground to the subterranean wine village at Cricova and sampling Moldova's most successful export: dry white Sauvignons and gaudy sparkling reds
» Getting a feel for the austerity of religious life at the magnificent 13th-century monastery of Orheiul Vechi carved into a remote cliff face

GETTING UNDER THE SKIN

» **Read** Tony Hawkes' travelogue *Playing the Moldovans at Tennis*, the product of an unlikely bet involving the Moldovan football team; for a deeper cultural perspective read Charles King's *The Moldovans: Romania, Russia and the Politics of Culture*

MOLDOVA

CAPITAL CHIŞINĂU POPULATION 4,439,502 AREA 33,843 SQ KM OFFICIAL LANGUAGE MOLDAVIAN

3.

DAN HERRICK

4.

JEFF GREENBERG

5.

» **Watch** *The Last Month of Autumn*, winner of the Cannes Grand Prix in 1967, a poetic tale of a Moldovan peasant and his family

» **Eat** *mamaliga*, a maize porridge served with cheese, cream and diced fried meat; in Gagauz try the very savoury *sorpa*, a spicy soup made from ram's meat

» **Drink** Sauvignon, Cabernet and Muscat wines produced in local vineyards, plus local varieties such as Feteasca and Black Rara

IN A WORD

» *La revedere!* (goodbye)

TRADEMARKS

» Fine wine; sunflowers; tin-pot republics; oriental carpets

SURPRISES

» The separatist republic of Transdniestr created its own state currency by sticking a postage stamp of Suvorov, a local war hero, on obsolete Russian roubles

MAP REF F,23

(1.) The All Saints Church of Chişinău blends seamlessly into the sky
(2.) Punk's not dead in Moldova
(3.) The majestic Soroca Fortress dates from the 15th century
(4.) A honey vendor plies his trade at the Kishinev covered market
(5.) Newlyweds about to embark on a taxi journey in Chişinău

1.

Although it's more a pre-breakfast stroll than a country, Monaco packs a lot of living into a little land. Most of the people who dwell here come from somewhere else, drawn by the sun, glamorous life-style and – most importantly – tax-free income. This is the playground of Europe's elite, a country where Lady Luck might clean you out at the casino one day and put you on the Grimaldi guest list the next. It's a glittering, preening, swanking opportunity for people-watching that shouldn't be passed up by amateur anthropologists.

BEST TIME TO VISIT

April/May and September/October (spring and autumn)

ESSENTIAL EXPERIENCES

» Losing money in the over-the-top splendour of the Monte Carlo Casino
» Visiting the Musée Océanographique, probably the best aquarium in Europe, with 90 seawater tanks and a display of living coral
» Wandering around Monaco's Palais du Prince, which was built in the 13th century
» Checking out the spectacular views from the Jardin Exotique, which has 7000 varieties of cacti and succulents
» Sailing off Monaco in a glass-bottomed boat

GETTING UNDER THE SKIN

» **Read** Peter Mayle's *Anything Considered*, a novel about Monaco featuring monks, crime and truffles; *The Bridesmaids: Grace Kelly and six intimate friends*, in which Judith Balaban Quine persuades Grace's best buddies to spill the beans
» **Listen** to the prize-winning Monte Carlo Philharmonic
» **Watch** Grace Kelly in the Hitchcock classic *To Catch a Thief* – she met Prince Rainier while filming; *Golden Eye*, with Pierce Brosnan

527

4.

as 'Bond, James Bond', and location shots including the Grand Corniche and Monte Carlo Casino

» **Eat** finger food (if you want to compete with the wannabe starlets on Monte Carlo's beach)

» **Drink** martinis or mineral water

IN A WORD

» *Très chi-chi*

TRADEMARKS

» Princess Grace; the casino; the Formula One Grand Prix; endless gossip about princesses Caroline and Stephanie; a tax-free haven; Ferraris

SURPRISES

» James Bond really does live in Monaco (well, Roger Moore does); the citizens of Monaco (known as Monégasques) only number about 5000 out of the total population; Monaco's territory only covers 1.95 sq km

MAP REF G,20

(1.) A harbour view of the city of dreams: Monte Carlo
(2.) A warm welcome from a valet at Monte Carlo Casino
(3.) With its cannons and cannonballs, the Prince's Palace is an imposing sight
(4.) Monaco's architecture oozes grace and presence

1.

Mongolia has always stirred up visions of the untamed: Genghis Khan and his hordes, and wild horses galloping across the Steppes. Even today, outside of Ulaan Baatar you may get the feeling you've stepped into another century rather than another country. The 'Land of Blue Sky' is a place where Siberian forests, rolling Steppes, the vast Gobi Desert, glacier-wrapped mountains and crystal-clear lakes meet. It is also one of the last unspoiled travel destinations in Asia.

BEST TIME TO VISIT
May to October, to avoid the cold

ESSENTIAL EXPERIENCES
» Exploring the museums and monasteries of Ulaan Baatar, which offer a fascinating glimpse into the culture of pre-Soviet Mongolia
» Riding a horse along the Steppes
» Camping out under the stars in the Gobi Desert
» Visiting a *ger* – the large white felt tents symbolic of Mongolia's nomadic heritage
» Fishing in the vast beautiful lake Khövsgöl Nuur, with water so pure you can drink it

GETTING UNDER THE SKIN
» **Read** *The Secret History of the Mongols*, recording the life and deeds of Genghis Khan
» **Listen** to *Spirit of the Steppes: Throat Singing from Tuva & Mongolia,* featuring *khoomi*, the unique vocal artform with no analogue in the West
» **Watch** *The Story of the Weeping Camel,* about a camel who abandons her calf – the surprise hit of film festivals in 2004
» **Eat** mutton: mutton with noodles, mutton with rice, or mutton disguised as something else

2.

» **Drink** *airag*, fermented mare's milk, or *süütei tsai,* salty tea

IN A WORD

» *Za* (a catch-all term said at the conclusion of a statement)

TRADEMARKS

» Ghengis Khan; savage hordes; *gers*; horses; archery; barbecues and hotpots; scantily clad wrestlers; endless plains

SURPRISES

» No-one was more surprised than the Mongolians when the Soviet Union collapsed, leaving them without an international patron, and spectacularly broke

RUSSIA

Ulaangom
Ölgii
Khovd
Uliastai
Altai
Bayankhongor
Amarbayasgalant Khiid
Mörön
Sükhbaatar
Darkhan
Bulgan
Ulaan Baatar ☼
Kharkhorin
Arvaikheer
Mandalgovi
Choibalsan
Öndörkhaan
Baruun Urt
Sainshand
Dalandzadagad

CHINA

MAP REF F,31

(1.) A group of Buddhists perform an impromptu ritual on the Mongolian Steppes
(2.) Happiness is your own reindeer
(3.) A wrestler warms up before his bout by dancing *devekh* (eagle dance)
(4.) A weather-worn Kazakh in his fox-fur hat

1.

PATRICK HORTON

Victorian travellers to the Balkans touted Montenegro as some kind of Utopia. From its heartbreakingly beautiful Adriatic waterfront to its ruggedly mountainous interior, Montenegro – one of the world's newest countries – certainly crams a lot of beauty into its diminutive territory. With picturesque fishing villages, pristine alpine vistas, a dramatic history and rich culture, it has plenty to offer. Having bloodlessly detached itself from Serbia it is revelling in its newfound independence. And the proud Montenegrins are striding ahead confidently, eager to share their little corner of Utopia.

BEST TIME TO VISIT
May, June and September – or 1878 when Prince Nikola Petrović was in the ascendant

ESSENTIAL EXPERIENCES
» A white-knuckle ride up the switchback mountain road to Cetinje
» Pondering the piratical history of Ulcinj from the sandy beach at Velika Plažua
» Driving around the Boka Kotorska, threading between the opal waters and the lavender-tinged mountains
» The alpine beauty of Durmitor, skiing in winter and trekking or white-water rafting in summer
» Getting wonderfully lost in the alleyways of Kotor, then climbing the 1300 steps to enjoy the view from the ramparts

GETTING UNDER THE SKIN
» **Read** *Wild Europe*, Božuidar Jezernik's compendium of travellers' accounts of the Balkans including snippets of lore and quirky observations from Montenegro

2.

3.

4.

» **Listen** to the keening of the *gusle*, a one-stringed fiddle that is played to accompany epic poetry

» **Watch** *Casino Royale* – this Bond flick has some scenes supposedly set in Montenegro

» **Eat** a grilled fish picnic (on the coast); roast lamb (in the mountains)

» **Drink** the local brew Nikšićko, or *rakija* (local brandy)

IN A WORD

» *Dobro došli* – Welcome!

TRADEMARKS

» Adriatic coastline, imposing mountains, towns built entirely of stone, orthodox churches and sombre icons, terracotta rooves and grapevines growing over verandas, moustachioed fishermen and shepherds, coffee (and obligatory cigarettes) in the town plaza

SURPRISES

» Wild pomegranates in September, Mediterranean *joie de vivre*; Montenegro avoided much of the trauma that engulfed the Balkans in the 1990s

MAP REF G,22

(1.) Local boys hanging out together on the streets of Bar
(2.) A line of washing adds character to a cheery mural in Kotor
(3.) The former fishing village St Stefan in Budva now attracts high fliers and high prices
(4.) The Monastery of Saint Peter of Cetinje (Sveti Petar Cetinjski) in Cetinje
(5.) The Ostrog Monastery near Nikšić, in the stony fissure of a cliff face in Montenegro
(6.) Hungry? Fill up at a traditional hamburger shop in Podgorica

1.

JOHN ELK III

SARA-JANE CLELAND

JOHN BRETTELL

Tangier, Casablanca, Marrakesh…just the names of these cities stir a hint of spice in the nostrils. Morocco has been thoroughly mythologised, and for good reason – the light is shimmering, the art extraordinary, and the region's history comes alive in its medieval cities, Roman ruins, Berber kasbahs and Islamic monuments. If you can survive the touts it's also heaven for shoppers, with open-air markets throughout the country piled high with rugs, woodwork, jewellery and leather – said to be the softest in the world.

BEST TIME TO VISIT
October to April for pleasant temperatures countrywide

ESSENTIAL EXPERIENCES
» Indulging in Moroccan café culture – fresh croissants, mint tea and olives all round
» Trekking in the mountains and sleeping at a home-stay to enjoy the legendary Berber hospitality
» Exploring the medinas of Fèz and Marrakesh – two of the world's largest intact medieval towns
» Visiting the Roman ruins and mosaics at Volubilis
» Soaking in a *hammam* (traditional bathhouse) – every town has at least one
» Wandering past the snack stalls and entertainers of Marrakesh's Djemaa el-Fna

GETTING UNDER THE SKIN
» **Read** *Year of the Elephant* by Leila Abouzeid, or Leonora Peet's *Women of Marrakesh*, in which Peets gets about as close as a non-Muslim can to the lives of local women
» **Listen** to Berber group Master Musicians of Joujouka

5.

» **Watch** *Le Coiffeur du Quartier des Pauvres* by Mohammed Reggab, an insight into the plight of the poor in a working-class suburb of Casablanca. The classic *Lawrence of Arabia* includes scenes filmed in the fabulous kasbah of Aït Benhaddou.

» **Eat** *seksu* (couscous) with a *tagine* (casserole)

» **Drink** sweet mint tea or fresh orange juice

IN A WORD

» *Ssalamu 'lekum* (hello)

TRADEMARKS

» Mint tea; Berbers; Fès; couscous; quality rugs; Bogart and Bergman in *Casablanca*

SURPRISES

» The last Barbary lion, a species indigenous to Morocco and used in ancient Roman amphitheatres for disposing of Christians, died in captivity in the 1960s

MAP REF H,19

(1.) Two boys from Er-Rachidia bask in the glow of the desert sun on the Merzouga dunes
(2.) Oriental arches recur like a hall of mirrors at the Tin Mal Mosque prayer hall in Tiznit
(3.) A Berber woman stands out in the lunar landscape of the High Atlas Mountains
(4.) Steam wafts invitingly from food stalls at the market in Place Djemaa el-Fna, Marrakesh
(5.) Ait Benhaddou, redolent with the romance of *The Thousand and One Nights*

1.

While Mozambique has had more than its share of difficulties – not least of which was a long, horrific civil war – the atmosphere is upbeat, and reconstruction has proceeded at a remarkable pace. The country's modern face reflects a unique blend of African, Arabic, Indian and European influences. Its cuisine is spicier, its music more tropical, and its pace more laid-back than its formerly British neighbours. Mozambique's coastline is one of the longest on the continent, with endless stretches of white-sand beaches and unexplored offshore reefs.

BEST TIME TO VISIT

June to August, when rainfall and temperatures are at their lowest

ESSENTIAL EXPERIENCES

» Visiting Pemba, a coastal town at the mouth of a huge bay with a great beach, some interesting buildings and a lively atmosphere
» Exploring Ilha de Moçambique, the northern half of which is a Unesco World Heritage–listed site
» Swimming at the Bazaruto Archipelago National Park
» Seeing the grand Zambezi River dammed by the Barragem de Cahora Bassa
» Lazing on the long, beautiful beaches of Tofo and Barra

GETTING UNDER THE SKIN

» **Read** *Dumba-Nengue – Histórias trágicas do Banditismo* by politician, journalist and environmentalist Lina Magaia
» **Listen** to Léman's *Automy dzi Txintxile* (Changes of Life) and *Katchume* by Kapa Dêch
» **Watch** *Borders of Blood* and *Mueda, Memory and Massacre*
» **Eat** *matapa* (cassava leaves cooked in a peanut sauce, often with prawns) in the south and *galinha á Zambeziana* (chicken with

a sauce of lime juice, garlic and hot pepper) in Quelimane and Zambézia province

» **Drink** *sura* (palm wine) or *nipa*, a local brew made from the fruit of the cashew

IN A WORD

» *lixile* (good morning)

TRADEMARKS

» Friendly people; guerrilla war; beautiful beaches; land mines

SURPRISES

» Large mammals believed to be extinct or on the verge of extinction in Mozambique include the black rhino, white rhino, giraffe, roan antelope and the African wild dog

MAP REF 0,24

(1.) A young student of Islam studies in the sunlight outside a mosque in Vilankulo
(2.) Handmade clay pots, a speciality of Ponta da Barra, for sale by a dusty roadside
(3.) A pedal-powered peddlar outside his shop on Ibo Island
(4.) Fishermen mend their nets outside the Catholic church on Ilha de Moçambique

1.

Myanmar (Burma) still wears its traditional *longyi* even as its neighbours abandon their saris and sarongs for Levis and miniskirts. Its holy men are more revered than its rich or its famous, and in the countryside, where rice paddies are still farmed using water buffalo, it might be the 16th century as easily as the 21st. These romantic images are a traveller's dream, but they exist in the presence of oppression and hardship. Myanmar is ruled by a harsh military regime, and human rights abuses are widespread, despite resistance by democracy activists. Many travellers choose not to travel to Myanmar because of the current political situation there.

BEST TIME TO VISIT

November to February (the cool season)

ESSENTIAL EXPERIENCES

» Taking a trip to Bagan, where thousands of ancient temples rise spectacularly out of a vast, treeless plain
» Joining the pilgrimage to Kyaiktiyo, a shining golden boulder stupa perched on a mountaintop cliff
» Drifting on pristine Inle Lake, home to floating villages, water gardens and monasteries
» Browsing the rollicking night market in riverside Pathein

GETTING UNDER THE SKIN

» **Read** *Freedom from Fear & Other Writings* – essays by and about Aung San Suu Kyi; George Orwell's *Burmese Days* – a classic novel of British colonialism; Paul Theroux's *The Great Railway Bazaar* – a funny account of the author's train trip through 1970s Burma
» **Listen** to traditional rhythmic Burmese music or original compositions by Burmese rocker Zaw Win Htut

» **Watch** John Boorman's *Beyond Rangoon*, which dramatised the 1988 pro-democracy uprising and its brutal suppression; Kon Ichikawa's *The Burmese Harp*, a beautiful 1950s black-and-white film
» **Eat** *thouq* (spicy salad with lime juice) or *peh-hin-ye* (lentil soup)
» **Drink** Mandalay Beer or *htan ye* (fermented palm juice)

IN A WORD

» *Bama hsan-jin* ('Burmese-ness', a quiet, modest and cultured quality)

TRADEMARKS

» Golden buddhas; jade; opium; Aung San Suu Kyi; ethnic embroidery; the military regime; the road to Mandalay

SURPRISES

» Myanmar's other famous dissidents (with jail time to prove it) are side-splitting comedians The Moustache Brothers; Myanmar's opium crop is rivalled only by Afghanistan's

MAP REF J,30

(1.) Three novice monks stand at a window at the Shwe Yaunghwe monastery, Inle Lake
(2.) A monk embarks on the long walk over Taungthaman Lake on the U Bein's Bridge
(3.) Temple ruins scattered like boulders amid the cultivated plains of Bagan, Mandalay
(4.) Laden with goods, a barge eases its way through the morning mist in Nyaungshwe
(5.) The silhouette of a tree is etched against the red sky as a boat enters Taungthaman Lake

549

1.

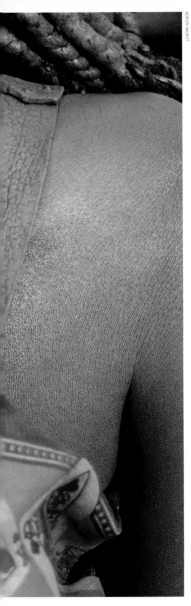

It's hard to imagine how the German colonisers of Namibia coped with the unlimited elbow room, vast deserts and annual quota of 300 days of sunshine, but that's exactly what draws travellers nowadays. Wedged between the Kalahari and the chilly South Atlantic Ocean, it's a land of deserts, seascapes, wildlife reserves, ancient rock art, gentle bush-walking terrain and an exhilarating sense of sheer boundlessness.

BEST TIME TO VISIT

May to October (the dry season)

ESSENTIAL EXPERIENCES

» Wandering around Windhoek, Namibia's attractive capital city
» Camping at Etosha National Park, one of the world's best wildlife-viewing venues
» Heading to the 'dune sea' of the Namib Desert, home to the country's enigmatic emblem, the dunes of Sossusvlei
» Driving through Khaudom Game Reserve, a wild and hard-to-reach park packed with wildlife
» Luxuriating in the hot springs at Ai-Ais in the Fish River Canyon
» Soaking up the European vibe of Swakopmund, Namibia's most German town

GETTING UNDER THE SKIN

» **Read** *Born of the Sun*, the largely autobiographical first novel by local author Joseph Diescho
» **Listen** to the heavenly voices of Namibia's renowned ensemble the Cantare Audire Choir
» **Watch** *Sophia's Homecoming,* which tells the story of an Owambo woman who goes to work as a domestic in Windhoek
» **Eat** a cooked breakfast with bacon and *boerewors* (farmer's sausage)

2.

3.

4.

» **Drink** the light and refreshing Windhoek Lager, or try a traditional brew such as *mataku* (watermelon wine)

IN A WORD

» *Hallo* (hello)

TRADEMARKS

» Sand dunes; diamond mining; German beer gardens and coffee houses; vast deserts; limitless sunshine; rock art; wonderful wildlife

SURPRISES

» The word of elders should not be questioned and they should be accorded utmost courtesy; in areas where individual sand dunes are exposed to winds from all directions, a formation known as a star dune appears

MAP REF P.22

(1.) Riding in style, a Himba baby snoozes against its mother's back
(2.) A regiment of Himba children stands to attention in the village of Okangwati in Kunene
(3.) Hardy quiver trees take root in rocky terrain
(4.) With stealth, cunning and a charming smile, a Kalahari man stalks his prey
(5.) A zebra crossing in Etosha National Park
(6.) One of the massive Sossusvlei sand dunes of central Namibia

1.

2.

3.

Nauru was once the rich kid of the Pacific, wealthy through phosphates. But now the stocks of bird poop have been exhausted, mining has utterly destroyed the landscape, and the island survives on handouts from Australia in return for hosting a detention centre for asylum seekers. With fresh water, vegetables and power in short supply, and a new detention centre being built on Christmas Island, Nauru's future is in the balance.

BEST TIME TO VISIT

March to October, to avoid the cyclone season

ESSENTIAL EXPERIENCES

» Slumbering under shady palms at Anibare Bay, Nauru's best beach
» Deep-sea fishing off Yaren
» Shuddering at Nauru's 'topside' in the central plateau – a burning wasteland of searing white rock, bizarre coral pinnacles and ugly, deep pits

GETTING UNDER THE SKIN

» **Read** *Nauru: Phosphate and Political Progress* by Nancy Viviani, an authoritative history of the mining that has crippled the island
» **Listen** to the strange cry of the noddy bird
» **Watch** *The Reef: Our Future, Our Heritage,* a documentary about the deteriorating reefs around the island
» **Eat** Chinese food, common on the island
» **Drink** *demangi,* the island's traditional take on fermented toddy

IN A WORD

» *Kewen* (gone, dead)

TRADEMARKS

» Mined-to-exhaustion plateaus; a quick-fix asylum for Australia's

4.

refugees; wealthy islanders with guano-stained wallets; satellite TV in most homes; weightlifting world champions pumping iron in every gym

SURPRISES

» Nauruans still hunt on the bald plateau for black noddy birds, often using stereos that play taped pre-recorded bird calls; most meals served on the island consist of imported junk food

MAP REF M,37

(1.) A divine sunset tempers the industrialism of phosphate loading
(2.) Birds flock to a young boy at feeding time
(3.) A family has fun cooling down among the rockpools
(4.) The entrancing beauty of Anibare Bay always catches the breath

1.

Draped along the heights of the Himalaya, Nepal's sublime scenery, time-worn temples and peerless walking trails leave visitors spellbound. Rich in spirituality and spectacular scenery, the country is the quiet cousin of neighbouring powerhouses China and India. Nothing compares to being amongst some of the world's tallest peaks for a natural high, but while there are grand feats to be enjoyed in Nepal, part of the country's appeal lies in simple pursuits: witnessing age-old rice harvesting or relishing the cultural cul-de-sac of Bhaktapur.

BEST TIME TO VISIT

October to November, for balmy days and crystal-clear visibility

ESSENTIAL EXPERIENCES

» Being stuck in traffic amid bikes, cows, cars, beggars, pilgrims and vendors in Kathmandu
» Taking on the high tides of Bhote Kosi for the ultimate whitewater rafting adventure
» Pondering the universe in Buddha's tranquil birthplace, Lumbini
» Being amused by Swayambhunath's tribes of garrulous monkeys
» Navigating a boat on Pokhara's sublime lake, Phewa Tal
» Riding an elephant on safari in Royal Chitwan National Park
» Pushing your body to the limits on an extended trek, whether it's in the all-encompassing Langtang or once-in-a-lifetime Mt Everest region

GETTING UNDER THE SKIN

» **Read** *Tenzing and the Sherpas of Everest* by Judy and Tashi Tenzing, a compelling tale about Nepal's national hero
» **Listen** to *Nepal: Ritual and Entertainment,* Nepalese sounds from *damai* ritual music to *panchai baja* ensembles

2.

3.

4.

» **Watch** *Darpan Chhaya*, an emotionally charged musical high-lighting the Nepalese fascination with all things romantic, patriotic and theatrical

» **Eat** *dal bhaat tarkari* – it's what you get if you combine lentil soup, rice and curried vegetables, and is the staple Nepalese diet

» **Drink** a refreshing lassi (curd and water in any number of flavours) or *chang*, a hearty Himalayan brew made from barley

IN A WORD

» *Namaste* (hello/goodbye)

TRADEMARKS

» Maoist rebels; prayer flags; *om* chanting; chai tea; mandalas; shopping for Buddhas

SURPRISES

» Nepal's most significant celebration, Dasain (October), involves the biggest animal sacrifice on the calendar; always remove your shoes before entering a Nepali home

MAP REF I,29

(1.) A Rai tribeswoman sitting amidst the exotic vegetation of Sagarmatha province
(2.) A sword-bearing Hindu holy man materialises from a pool of flowers, Kathmandu
(3.) The village of Panauti rises and shines in the glow of early morning, Bagmati province
(4.) The jagged edge of Mt Machhapuchhare rises into the empty morning sky in Annapurna
(5.) A *mahout* (elephant keeper) prepares lunch for his herd in Royal Chitwan National Park
(6.) Wisdom creases the kind face of an elderly woman in Ghandruk

1.

One of the chief pleasures of the Netherlands is its lively contrast between pragmatic liberalism and the buttoned-up, just-so primness of a culture founded on Calvinist principles. In Dutch society, ostentation is anathema and fuss of any kind is regarded as undignified. The towns are surrounded by canals and castle walls, the endlessly flat landscape which inspired the nation's early artists still stretches unbroken to the horizons, and the dykes still occasionally threaten to give way.

BEST TIME TO VISIT

April to September (spring through summer)

ESSENTIAL EXPERIENCES

» Exploring Amsterdam's many neighbourhoods, from red-light sleaze and bohemian chic to stately grandeur
» Visiting Hoge Veluwe National Park, the country's largest, which also houses works by Van Gogh, Picasso and Mondriaan in the Kröller-Müller Museum
» Riding a bicycle around the Randstad region to see the spectacular bulb fields, which explode into colour between March and May
» Wandering around the labyrinth of tunnels on Maastricht's western outskirts

GETTING UNDER THE SKIN

» **Read** *The Diary of Anne Frank*, a moving journal that describes her life in hiding in Nazi-occupied Amsterdam; *The Fall* by Albert Camus, an existential monologue that uses Amsterdam's canal system as an analogy for the rings of Hell
» **Listen** to Tiësto, the undisputed trancemeister, or for something more highbrow, pianist Ronald Brautigam
» **Watch** *Stromenlied* (Song of the Rivers) by acclaimed documentary filmmaker Joris Ivens

4.

5.

6.

» **Eat** *stamppot* (potatoes mashed with kale, endive or sauerkraut, and served with smoked sausage or strips of pork) or *Vlaamse frites* (chips with mayonnaise) for a quick snack

» **Drink** Heineken beer or try Dutch gin *(jenever),* which is often drunk with a beer chaser; the combination is known as a *kopstoot* ('head butt')

IN A WORD

» *Een pils/bier, alstublieft* (a beer, please)

TRADEMARKS

» Bikes; dykes; windmills; clogs; tulips; red-light district; pot smoking; Van Gogh

SURPRISES

» Dutch ovens were invented in Pennsylvania; the Dutch are reputedly the tallest people in the world

MAP REF E,20

(**1.**) One of Amsterdam's 550,000 bikes parked in front of a graffiti mural
(**2.**) Unesco World Heritage–listed windmills at Kinderdijk
(**3.**) Tulip fever lives on in Amsterdam
(**4.**) Kids imagining life as a cannonball in the Scheepvaartmuseum, Kaltenburgerplein
(**5.**) A mannequin set in a sultry pose attracts attention in a shop window
(**6.**) Den Haag's ivy-covered, red-shuttered cop shop

1.

JEAN-BERNARD CARILLET

VINCENT TALBOT

JEAN-BERNARD CARILLET

Kanaks and *café au laît,* blackbirding and barrier reefs, Melanesian massacres and *menus du jour* – New Caledonia exemplifies that one person's bread is another person's *pain*. It's still very much a colony of France, and the motherland has sent in the marines more than once to keep the local population from rioting. Political unrest aside, New Caledonia attracts divers and tourists who flock to experience the Pacific with a taste of France.

BEST TIME TO VISIT

May to October, to avoid the cyclones and mosquitoes

ESSENTIAL EXPERIENCES

» Canoeing down a river by moonlight through a drowned forest in Parc de la Rivière Bleue
» Watching the sun set across a tranquil lagoon from anywhere along Ouvéa's white-sand beach
» Sailing in the glittering bay around Île des Pins
» Delving into the architectural masterpiece that is Noumea's Jean-Marie Tjibaou Cultural Centre
» Scuba-diving the world's second-largest reef
» Discovering the tiny raised coral atoll of Tiga with deserted beaches and great diving

GETTING UNDER THE SKIN

» **Read** Jean-Marie Tjibao's *Kanaké – the Melanesian Way*, an insight into Kanak culture featuring colour photographs, poems and legends
» **Listen** to OK! Ryos, a Mare band known for their harmonies and soaring vocals – try *Wa Coco*, their 'best of'
» **Watch** *Le Bal du Gouverneur,* a romance set in 1950s New Caledonia

5.

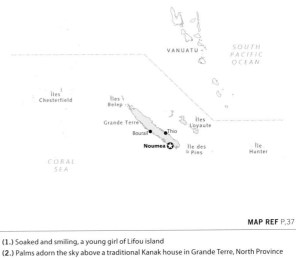

» **Eat** *bougna*, a delicious combination of taro, yam, sweet potato, banana, and pieces of chicken, crab or lobster cooked in banana leaves in a ground oven

» **Drink** kava sold from private houses called *nakamal*

IN A WORD

» Kanaks traditionally refer to themselves as Ti-Va-Ouere ('Brothers of the Earth')

TRADEMARKS

» Dispossessed Kanak community; French tourists in abundance; idyllic grass huts on the beach; colonial strife; stunning beaches; clan societies

SURPRISES

» New Caledonia's economy centres around mining and metallurgy; cricket has been the favourite sport of Kanak women since the missionaries introduced it to the Loyalty Islanders in the 1850s

VANUATU

SOUTH PACIFIC OCEAN

Îles Chesterfield

Îles Belep

Grande Terre

Îles Loyaute

Bourail ● ● Thio

Noumea ⊗ Île des Pins

Île Hunter

CORAL SEA

MAP REF P.37

(1.) Soaked and smiling, a young girl of Lifou island
(2.) Palms adorn the sky above a traditional Kanak house in Grande Terre, North Province
(3.) Washing day on Lifou island where colourful Kanak dresses line up to dry in the sun
(4.) A corridor of blue stretches out to the horizon at Ouvéa lagoon in the Îles Loyaute
(5.) A weird and wonderful wood-carved palisade in Vao

1.

One could be forgiven for thinking that Mother Nature decided to take her best features and exhibit them all in this South Pacific island nation. All the classics are there – awe-inspiring Alps, plunging fjords, expanses of pristine beach, dense rainforests, active volcanoes – but what makes this such a stellar performance is the sheer concentration of it all. Top it off with lively indigenous culture, cosmopolitan cities and a people with a distinctly Kiwi lust for life, and you know this is one special country.

BEST TIME TO VISIT

November to April, when the weather is warmest

ESSENTIAL EXPERIENCES

» Traversing the South Island on the TranzAlpine train
» Throwing yourself off something high – bungee jumping is as compulsory here as seeing the Eiffel Tower in Paris
» Enjoying a gourmet feast of fresh fish and chips on a deserted Northland beach
» Seeing the marine life off the coast of Kaikoura
» Spending a culture-filled weekend in one of the cities – the Polynesian bustle of Auckland, creative current of Wellington or European feel of Christchurch

GETTING UNDER THE SKIN

» **Read** Witi Ihimaera's *The Whale Rider* – a moving insight into the spirituality, tradition, and culture of the Maori people
» **Listen** to Salmonella Dub's *Killer Vision*, which displays influences quintessential to the new wave of New Zealand music
» **Watch** Peter Jackson's *Lord of the Rings* trilogy – the stunning landscape dominates the films
» **Eat** whitebait – a seasonal delicacy; hu hu grubs – slug-like and not for the faint-hearted, but delicious off the grill

2.

3.

4.

ANDERS BLOMQVIST

» **Drink** a 'boutique beer' – independent breweries are providing delicious variations on the traditional varieties

IN A WORD

» Sweet as, bro

TRADEMARKS

» Sheep; Maori; the All Blacks; clean and green; nuclear-free; extreme sports; the end of the earth; Middle Earth; Neil Finn; Janet Frame; pohutukawa blossoms

SURPRISES

» Not everyone plays rugby; there's a thriving food and wine culture; much more than just two islands

DENNIS JOHNSON

MAP REF S,38

(**1.**) Mist above the bubbling surface of the Champagne Pool, Waiotapu Thermal Reserve
(**2.**) Virgin snow sheathes the peak of Mt Taranaki, a dormant volcano in the North Island
(**3.**) A snowboarder prepares for a spectacular wipe-out in the Cardrona ski fields, Otago
(**4.**) Sleek boulders and rock formations create an eerie atmosphere on the West Coast
(**5.**) Nosy neighbours greet each other with a traditional hongi in Rotorua
(**6.**) Under a forbidding cloak of cloud, a volcano broods in Tongariro National Park

1.

Tucked between Costa Rica's mammoth ecotourism scene and Honduras' dazzling displays of indigenous history, Nicaragua is all too often ignored by travellers. Their loss. The warm, inclusive pride of the Nicaraguan people suffuses the country with an intoxicating energy that captivates visitors. For the cognoscenti, Nicaragua is inspiring landscapes, colonial beauty, weeklong parties, stunning wildlife, beautiful beaches, rollicking reggae and long nights spent with friends in the plaza – all rolled up in a neat little package that carries a discount price tag.

BEST TIME TO VISIT
June to March, to avoid the dusty end of the dry season – or in the 13th century, before the Spanish arrived

ESSENTIAL EXPERIENCES
» Watching the moon rise over the cathedral in colonial Granada
» Climbing the volcanoes on Isla de Ometepe and cooling off by swimming in the Lago de Nicaragua
» Kicking back in a beach hammock in San Juan del Sur
» Spotting a quetzal at the Reserva Natural Miraflor
» Buying handicrafts at Masaya's Mercado Viejo
» Enjoying perfect snorkelling off Little Corn Island

GETTING UNDER THE SKIN
» **Read** Rubén Darío's *Stories and Poems* – works by the founder of Spanish modernism; Salman Rushdie's *The Jaguar Smile: A Nicaraguan Journey* – revealing personal experiences of a visit
» **Listen** to Duo Guardabaranco's *Antología* of collected pop works; Los Mejía Godoy's *Loving in Times of War* – legendary Nicaraguan brothers sing folk
» **Watch** *Nicaragua Was Our Home* – a documentary about Miskito Indians and Sandinistas that purportedly influenced Reagan's

5.

foreign policy; *Alsino and the Condor* – a boy's struggle to escape the realities of his war-torn homeland

» **Eat** *baho* – beef, yucca, plaintains and vegetables slowly simmered; *sopa de albondiga* – cornmeal-ball soup

» **Drink** Flor de Caña rum; *pinolio* – dissolved ground corn (add some sugar!)

IN A WORD

» *¡Va pue'!* (all right!)

TRADEMARKS

» Contras and Sandinistas; dusty farms and towns; rickety buses with chickens; earthquakes and hurricanes; US intervention in politics

SURPRISES

» Amazing biodiversity; there are no ruins; the unique Caribbean culture on the Atlantic coast; the friendliest people in Central America

MAP REF K,11

(1.) A teacher competes for the undivided attention of her pupils in a village school
(2.) Macho *muchachos* wrestle on the paving stones of León
(3.) A blinkered beast of burden plods through the vibrant streets of Granada
(4.) The little women of Río San Juan fitted out for their First Communion
(5.) A cavalcade of cowgirls salute the crowd at a rodeo in Estelí

1.

Niger sits precariously on the edge of the Sahara, a barren windswept land ravaged by drought and colonial conquest, yet somehow surviving against the odds. It's a country of aristocratic desert nomads, skilled artisans and a race of tall, lithe people so physically beautiful that even the men enter beauty contests. With unmissable sights like the stark beauty of the Ténéré Desert and the ancient caravan town of Agadez, Niger is a vital element of the Saharan experience.

BEST TIME TO VISIT

November to February, when it's cooler

ESSENTIAL EXPERIENCES

» Exploring the labyrinthine old mud-brick quarters of Zinder and Agadez
» Enjoying the bustle and colour of Zinder's weekly market
» Searching for wildlife in Parc National du W
» Hearing the stories of the Tuareg around the campfire or beneath the rock art of the Aïr Mountains
» Watching the sun set over the mighty Niger River from a pirogue in Niamey
» Seeking out the silent gravitas of deserted villages and vast sand dunes of the Ténéré Desert and Djado Plateau in the Sahara

GETTING UNDER THE SKIN

» **Read** *In Sorcery's Shadow: A Memoir of Apprenticeship Among the Songhay of Niger* by Paul Stoller – a readable, often humorous, and detailed account of his fieldwork
» **Listen** to the impassioned vocals and masterful musicianship of Yacouba Moumouni in his album *Alatoumi*
» **Watch** *The Sheltering Sky,* directed by Bernardo Bertolucci, which was filmed in Niger

4.

5.

6.

- » **Eat** dates, yogurt, rice, mutton, rice with sauce, couscous and ragout
- » **Drink** tea or a Flag beer

IN A WORD

- » *Bonjour* (hello)

TRADEMARKS

- » Desert nomads; camels; uranium mining; dinosaur bones; the Tuareg; the Fulani

SURPRISES

- » There are five principal tribal groups: the Hausa, Songhaï-Djerma, Wodaabé, Tuareg and Kanouri; camel racing is a favourite Tuareg sport

MAP REF J,21

(1.) Beautiful Wodaabé bachelors line up to be admired at the annual Salt Festival in Agadez
(2.) A baby in a pouch enjoys a spot of traditional dancing in Maradi
(3.) Tuareg women in Niamey robed in traditional blue and black mantles
(4.) Swords come out for celebration during a Ramadan festivity in Niamey
(5.) A devotee hangs hip outside the Grande Mosquée of Niamey
(6.) Builders prepare all-natural construction materials in the waters near Diffa

1.

JANE SWEENEY

In Nigeria hundreds of different peoples, languages, histories and religions all sit shoulder to shoulder in a hectic, colourful and often volatile republic. It is a country struggling to contain the sum of its parts within a democratic framework. A chronic crime problem, religious intolerance, large-scale unemployment and overcrowding in poor living conditions regularly push the rule of law to the brink. Despite this, there is still an unfaltering optimism among Nigerians that their proud nation will indeed make it to the party.

BEST TIME TO VISIT

December to March

ESSENTIAL EXPERIENCES

» Viewing wildlife at Yankari National Park
» Club-hopping in Lagos
» Visiting the ancient mud-walled city in Kano
» Shopping for rare books at the Onitsha Writers' Market
» Exploring the Niger Delta

GETTING UNDER THE SKIN

» **Read** anything by Nobel Prize winner Wole Soyinka, internationally acclaimed writer Chinua Achebe or Ben Okri, a crowd-pulling favourite on the Western literary circuit
» **Listen** to world-renowned musician, the late Fela Kuti, whose eclectic fusion of traditional Yoruba call-and-response chanting with freestyle jazz (Afrobeat) was always in demand. Other favourites are king of juju music Sonny Ade, the granddaddy of afro-reggae, Sonny Okosun and soul singer, Sade.
» **Watch** *A deusa negra* (Black Goddess) by Nigerian director Ola Balogun

2.

3.

4.

» **Eat** *egusi* (a fiery-hot yellow stew made with meat, red chilli, ground dried prawns and green leaves) or palm-nut soup (a thick stew made with meat, chilli, tomatoes, onions and palm-nut oil)

» **Drink** palm wine (a favourite drink all over Nigeria, especially in the south where the palm trees grow wild)

IN A WORD

» *Sannu* ('hello' in Hausa)

TRADEMARKS

» Fantastic music; money scams; masochistic travellers; violence; corruption; oil-rich economy; Niger Delta

SURPRISES

» Nigeria is home to 20% of Africa's entire population; juju, the native magic that was the original basis for Caribbean voodoo, is still an important element in many tribal cultures

MAP REF L,21

(1.) Muskets bristle amongst a rabble of celebrating men at the Durbar Festival, Kano
(2.) Traditional mud huts huddled on stilts in Sokoto
(3.) Ornately dressed Hausa-Fulani horsemen pay annual homage to the emir in Kano
(4.) Street scenes of Kano
(5.) A well-attired woman of Katsina
(6.) Pink-and-yellow cloth frames the face of a woman in Zaria

CHRISTIAN ÅSLUND

Europe's 'wild west', Norway has a ruggedly beautiful frontier character, with easy access to wild outdoor country and forested green belts circling even the largest cities. Its mountains, fjords and glaciers are highly prized, along with its cultured cities, unspoiled fishing villages and rich historic sites, from Viking ships to medieval churches. North of the Arctic Circle, the population thins, the horizons grow wider, and seals, walruses and polar bears sun themselves on ice floes.

BEST TIME TO VISIT

May to September (late spring to summer)

ESSENTIAL EXPERIENCES

» Being overawed by the grand fjords of Arctic Norway, which dwarf anything in the south
» Wandering the streets of colourful, historic Bergen
» Visiting the virtually intact 9th-century *Oseberg* Viking ship and museum in Oslo
» Touring the stave churches at Borgund, Heddal and Urnes
» Viewing the midnight sun from Nordland
» Spotting walruses, polar bears and whales in the high Arctic

GETTING UNDER THE SKIN

» **Read** *A Doll's House* by quintessential Norwegian dramatist Henrik Ibsen, or Jostein Gaarder's bestseller *Sophie's World*
» **Listen** to composer Edvard Grieg or indigenous Sami artist Ailu Gaup
» **Watch** *The Pathfinder*, based on a medieval legend and presented in the Sami language, or Anja Breien's *Jostedalsrypa*, about a 14th-century girl who survived the Black Death
» **Eat** *lapskaus* (a hearty meat stew with vegetables) or *lutefisk* (dried cod soaked in potash lye)

2.

3.

4.

CHRISTIAN ASLUND

» **Drink** the national spirit, *aquavit* (or *akevitt*) – a potent potato and caraway liquor. The standard Norwegian beer is pils lager.

IN A WORD

» *Vær så god* (an all-purpose expression of goodwill)

TRADEMARKS

» Vikings; fjords; the aurora borealis; stave churches; skiing; the midnight sun; whaling

SURPRISES

» Lemmings don't throw themselves off cliffs in mass suicide; the legal drinking age is 18 years for beer and wine, but 20 for spirits

ANDERS BLOMQVIST

MAP REF D,21

(1.) The Antmands Dottir bar promises warmth and wine to a local in Tromsø
(2.) Caution: Reindeer Crossing – a buck traverses an icy road in Arctic Norway
(3.) A lonely rowing boat floats beneath a heavy sky in the town of Flåm
(4.) Pale northern light beams down on bronzed bodies in Stryn
(5.) Local sniffs the wax on a visiting surfer's board in the coastal village of Unstad in Lofoten
(6.) Autumn colours fringe the foothills near Skjak

1.

Previously regarded as the hermit of the Middle East, Oman is slowly coming out of its shell. One of the more traditional countries in the region, it has become more outward-looking in recent years. Once an imperial power that jostled with both Portugal and Britain for influence in the Gulf, its development since 1970 is striking, given that its oil reserves are greatly limited. An ever-increasing number of travellers are discovering its friendly people, dramatic mountain landscapes and vast unspoiled beaches.

BEST TIME TO VISIT
Mid-October to mid-March, to avoid the monsoon season

ESSENTIAL EXPERIENCES
» Visiting the Omani–French Museum in Muscat
» Browsing through the early-morning fish market in Mutrah
» Visiting the dramatically sited forts of Nakhal and Jabrin
» Bargain-hunting at Nizwa's colourful souq
» Exploring the archaeological sites around Salalah
» Discovering Wadi Ghul, the Grand Canyon of Arabia
» Hiking and caving in the Hajar Mountains

GETTING UNDER THE SKIN
» **Read** Phillip Ward's *Travels in Oman: On the track of the Early Explorer*, a combination of modern travelogue and historical traveller accounts
» **Listen** to *Symphonic Impressions of Oman* by Lalo Scifrin, per-formed by the London Symphony Orchestra, which captures the mood, scenery and traditions of Oman
» **Eat** *balaleet* – a popular breakfast dish of sweet vermicelli with egg, onion and cinnamon; *machboos* – slow-cooked meat and

rice with onion, spices and dried limes

» **Drink** *laban* – salty buttermilk; cardamom-infused yogurt drinks

IN A WORD

» *Tasharrafna* (nice to meet you)

TRADEMARKS

» Impressive forts; sandy beaches; beautiful mountain scenery; vibrant bazaars; groves of frankincense trees; men in bright blue *dishdashas* (shirt dresses); ancient ruins; traditional dance and music; silver jewellery; desert motoring; remote villages

SURPRISES

» Camel racing is a traditional sport, as is bull-butting – pairing Brahmin bulls to fight (no injury or bloodshed is involved); nomadic Bedouin tribes still live in the interior

MAP REF J,26

(1.) Men flock to the market on the edge of the desert in Sanaw
(2.) Dressed for devotion, four men march past a Burami mosque
(3.) A weathered local man in his workshop in the historical town of Bahla
(4.) A donkey and scooter share a car park outside a building in Nizwa

Media impressions of Pakistan are a jumble of Islamic fundamentalism and martial law, while for overland travellers the country is often seen as the last hurdle before reaching India. In fact Pakistan offers some of Asia's most mind-blowing landscapes, extraordinary trekking, the spectacular Karakoram Highway, a multitude of cultures, and a long tradition of hospitality. It's the site of some of the earliest human settlements and the crucible of two of the world's major religions: Hinduism and Buddhism.

BEST TIME TO VISIT

November to April in the south (when it's cooler), May to October in the north (before winter sets in)

ESSENTIAL EXPERIENCES

» Trekking among giants in Baltistan, where the Karakoram erupts in an unequalled display of peaks and twisting glaciers
» Exploring the ancient site of Moenjodaro, relic of an Indus Valley civilisation
» Soaking up the frontier atmosphere of Quetta, a desert outpost with buzzing bazaars
» Rambling through the tangle of twisting alleyways in Lahore's Old City en route to the historic Lahore Fort

GETTING UNDER THE SKIN

» **Read** *Pakistan: The Eye of the Storm*, by former BBC correspondent Owen Bennett-Jones; Salman Rushdie's *Shame*, whose characters are a metaphor for Pakistan
» **Listen** to the late Nusrat Fateh Ali Khan, the revered Qawwali singer, who collaborated on soundtracks for *Dead Man Walking* and *The Last Temptation of Christ*
» **Watch** the second film in the *Earth*, *Fire* and *Water* trilogy, directed by Deepa Mehta and depicting the tragic upheaval of Partition

» **Eat** meat and vegetable curries; hot and spicy samosas

» **Drink** fresh fruit juices, milky tea, buttermilk flavoured
with pistachios

IN A WORD

» *Ap khairiyat se hai?* (how are you?)

TRADEMARKS

» Trekking the Karakoram Highway; totally obsessed cricket fans;
Shoaib Akhtar, one of the world's fastest bowlers; General
Musharraf; nuclear weapons; oily, spicy curries

SURPRISES

» In the tribal areas bordering Afghanistan federal law applies only
to the roads and 10 yards on either side – elsewhere tribal
law applies

MAP REF I,27

(1.) The majestic mausoleum of Bibi Jawindi looms over passers-by in Uch Sharif, Punjab
(2.) Bus drivers break for morning tea at the Rajah bazaar in Punjab
(3.) A young boy dwarfed by the towering doorways of the Badshahi Mosque, Lahore
(4.) Old-timers hang out in Peshawar's old city district

1.

2.

3.

CASEY MAHANEY

The Republic of Palau is becoming a byword for an underwater wonderland, showcasing Micronesia's richest flora and fauna, both on land and beneath the waves. It's a snorkeller's paradise, with an incredible spectrum of coral, fish and sumo-sized giant clams. There's a good chance this bounty will survive, as Palauans are active on environmental issues, particularly regarding overtourism, overfishing, erosion, litter and pollution.

BEST TIME TO VISIT

September to July, avoiding stormy August

ESSENTIAL EXPERIENCES

» Sailing through the twisty maze of the Rock Islands
» Keeping a respectful distance from a traditional *bai* (men's meeting house) on Micronesia's second-largest island, Babeldaob
» Climbing Malakal Hill on Koror Island for great views of the Rock Islands
» Diving into history around Peleliu, the WWII-ravaged paradise
» Chowing down on seafood at Koror's smorgasbord of eateries

GETTING UNDER THE SKIN

» **Read** Arnold H Leibowitz's *Embattled Island: Palau's Struggle for Independence*, a US-friendly take on Palau's postwar political history
» **Listen** to *Natural...*, the first album by the Paluan band, InXes
» **Watch** *Palau – The Enchanted Islands*, a scuba adventure by filmmaker Avi Klapfer
» **Eat** cassava, betel nut, tuna, sushi, lobster
» **Drink** abundant and fresh coconut milk

IN A WORD

» *Alii* (hello)

TRADEMARKS

» Giant clams; maverick politicians taking on Uncle Sam; red-mouthed betel-nut chewers; WWII wrecks and ruins; storyboard art; outrigger canoes

SURPRISES

» The draft Palauan constitution of 1979 – it created the world's first nuclear-free state... until the US asked for amendments; the thousands of crab-eating macaques on Angaur island

Ngeruangel

Palau Islands

Kayangel

Kossol Reef

Kossol Passage

Philippine Sea

Sonsorol Islands

Pulo Anna

South-West Islands   Merir

Philippine Sea

Babeldaob

Palau Islands

Tobi   Helen

PACIFIC OCEAN

Arakabesang   **Koror**
Malakal   Auluptagel
Ulong   Urukthapel
Rock Islands
70 Islands   Eil Malk
Ngemelis   Ngerchong
Ngesebus   Carp Island   *PACIFIC OCEAN*
Peleliu

Angaur

MAP REF L,34

(1.) A well-illustrated chief's house with painted gables and a steeply pitched thatched roof
(2.) An orange-fin anemone fish lights up the surroundings
(3.) Threads of local history are woven into the tales enacted in Yapese dancing
(4.) Viewed from above, the islands of Palau present a vision of pristine splendour

1.

Today 'Palestine' is two territories of Israel: Gaza in west Israel and the West Bank bordering Jordan. It's the birthplace of Christ, the Holy Land of the medieval Crusades, a landscape of striking contrasts and a travel agent's worst nightmare. Despite ongoing efforts by the UN, the long-fought struggle for independence, characterised by terrorism, has resulted in a land ravaged by violence. The religious significance of the area to Arabs, Jews and Christians, combined with its strategic location, has made the Palestinian Territories among the most hotly disputed bits of real estate in the modern world.

BEST TIME TO VISIT

September to November and March to May are best, but check the political climate rather than the temperature

ESSENTIAL EXPERIENCES

» Visiting the Byzantine mosque at Hisham's Palace in ancient Jericho, the world's oldest town
» Experiencing the kitsch 'mangerfication' of Bethlehem by taking a trip to Shepherds' Fields and a look at Milk Grotto Chapel – a shrine to the Virgin Mary's lactations
» Floating in the eerie tranquillity of the Dead Sea

GETTING UNDER THE SKIN

» **Read** *Gaza: Legacy of an Occupation* by Dick Doughty and Mohammed El-Aydi, which gives an emotive, gritty view of Palestinian life in the Strip. And of course, the Bible.
» **Listen** to tinny Arabic pop VERY LOUDLY from street-traders' cassette decks
» **Watch** the Palestinian version of a 'road trip' movie, *Route 181 – Fragments of a Journey to Palestine-Israel*. Directed by Michel

Khleifi (Palestinian) and Eyal Sivan Route (Israeli), it charts the UN-imposed borders decided in Resolution 181, 1947.

» **Eat** a street-stall *swharma* (grilled meat served in pita bread)
» **Drink** juice made from tamarind, dates and almonds

IN A WORD

» *Al-hamdu lillah 'al as-salāma* (thank God for your safe arrival)

TRADEMARKS

» Birthplace of Christ; armed checkpoints; Yasser Arafat; massive concrete 'peace walls' covered with razor wire; Turkish baths; suicide bombers; mosques; minarets

SURPRISES

» Cash, what's that? In Palestine people buy everything, right down to their morning coffee, with a credit card. Occasionally, though, you might stumble on a coin bearing the name Palestine, dating from the Ottoman Empire or British Mandate period.

MAP REF H,24

(**1.**) A line of trees sits in the cliffs of Wadi Qelt near the Monastery of St George of Koziba
(**2.**) Children peer inquisitively down on the crowd below
(**3.**) Just another stroll for two local women
(**4.**) This boy carries a staff in procession
(**5.**) A congregation of holy men gather in formation

HANAN ISACHAR

LEBANON
UNDOF Zone
Quneitra
The Golan Heights
Sea of Galilee
Ein Gev SYRIA
MEDITERRANEAN SEA
Jenin
Nablus
West Bank
Ramallah
Jerusalem
Jericho JORDAN
Bethlehem
Gaza
Gaza Strip
Hebron
Dead Sea
ISRAEL
EGYPT
Red Sea

1.

Its name may be synonymous with a canal and a hat, but this little-visited isthmus nation has some of the finest birdwatching, snorkelling and deep-sea fishing in the Americas. Proud Panama celebrates its Spanish heritage with frequent and colourful festivals, seasoned with the influences of the seven remaining indigenous groups and the West Indian culture of its black population. It's difficult to leave the country without feeling you're in on a secret the rest of the travelling world has yet to discover.

BEST TIME TO VISIT

Mid-December to mid-April (the dry season)

ESSENTIAL EXPERIENCES

» Birdwatching at Cana, deep in the heart of Parque Nacional Darién
» Watching a huge ship nudge its way through the Panama canal
» Sampling the coffee in the cool mountain town of Boquete
» Diving with the sea turtles on Archipiélago de Bocas del Toro
» Photographing the Spanish colonial architecture of Península de Azuero
» Going hiking in search of the elusive quetzal

GETTING UNDER THE SKIN

» **Read** *When New Flowers Bloomed*, a collection of stories by women writers from Panama and Costa Rica. *Tekkin' a Waalk* by Peter Ford includes a stroll along Panama's Caribbean coast.
» **Listen** to Panamanian folk music on Samy and Sandra Sandoval's *Grandes Exito*
» **Watch** the Academy Award–winning documentary *The Panama Deception* by Barbara Trent, which investigates the US invasion of Panama
» **Eat** *sancocho* (a spicy chicken and vegetable stew) or *carimañola* (a deep-fried roll of yucca filled with chopped meat)

» **Drink** *chicheme* (a delicious concoction of milk, sweet corn, cinnamon and vanilla) or *seco* (distilled from sugar cane, served with milk and ice)

IN A WORD

» *Vamos, pues* (let's go)

TRADEMARKS

» The umbilical cord between Central and South America; the world's most famous shortcut; Manuel Noriega; Swiss banks; corrupt politicians; Panama hats

SURPRISES

» The Kuna Indians of the San Blas Archipelago run the 378 islands as an autonomous province, with minimal interference from the national government. They maintain their own economic system, language, customs and culture, with distinctive dress, legends, music and dance.

MAP REF L,11

(1.) A girl and her parrot out for a stroll in Bocas del Toro
(2.) Teribe children play near the village of Sicyic in Bocas del Toro Province
(3.) A stone angel watches over the skyline of Panama City
(4.) Houses jumbled at unusual angles along the main street of Bocas del Toro on Isla Colón
(5.) A Choco Indian family posing on the porch of their home in Darién

1.

Kundus and *garamut* drums beat out dizzying rhythms in the sweet sticky heat. The sound of insects rings in the air, and frogs and geckos bark as night falls, silenced only by a sudden deluge of tropical rain. The vegetation surrounding you is on growth hormones – an overproductive superabundance of greenery. This is PNG, a raw, remarkably untamed land, filled with great mountain ranges, mighty rivers and stunning beaches, and five million people living much the way they have for thousands of years.

BEST TIME TO VISIT

June to September is cooler, drier and takes in the majority of the provincial celebrations and Highlands *sing sings*

ESSENTIAL EXPERIENCES

» Standing atop snowflecked Mt Wilhelm on a clear morning, taking in the coasts of the world's second-biggest island
» Attending a Highlands *sing sing* to watch tens of thousands of people gather bedecked in *bilas* (finery) of body-paint, masks and headdresses of bird-of-paradise feathers
» Snorkelling over the teeming reef-life – millions of fish in impossible colours, giant clams, monster gropers and WWII shipwrecks
» Travelling up the Sepik River into the powerhouse of Pacific art
» Visiting the ghost town of Rabaul, buried in Tuvurvur's volcanic ash

GETTING UNDER THE SKIN

» **Read** Tim Flannery's *Throwim Way Leg,* an account of his field trips into the interior's remotest parts in search of tree kangaroos
» **Listen** to Telek's *Serious Tam* CD (Real World), showcasing the extraordinary voice and music of Rabaul's most famous son

» **Watch** Robin Anderson and Bob Connelly's cinematic triptych *First Contact, Joe Leahy's Neighbours* and *Black Harvest*, an outstanding exposition of Highlanders' first encounters with the outside world and their emergence into modern times

» **Eat** fresh fish, lobster and market gardeners' produce

» **Drink** SP Lager

IN A WORD

» *Em nau!* (fantastic! right on!)

TRADEMARKS

» Penis-gourds; betel nut; *sing sings*; tropical islands; bilum bags; tribal art; laid-back 'PNG time'; beautiful beaches; Kokoda Trail; Asaro mud men; yam worship; rascals

SURPRISES

» Women suckling pigs; *mumus* (underground ovens); shell-money; shark-calling; ancestor worship; altitude sickness; bats, birds-of-paradise

MAP REF M,35

(1.) A lone fisherman punts home as dusk settles near Maliwai
(2.) A Southern Highlands man includes a woolly hat in his traditional headdress
(3.) A Christian mother and child attending church in Madang
(4.) Traditional dancers shake it up in grass skirts and matching anklewear

1.

The tourist trail largely bypasses this small subtropical country and therein lies much of Paraguay's charm. Travellers who visit with an open heart and mind are rewarded with unspoiled natural beauty, an abundance of wildlife and some of the friendliest and most unaffected people in the world. Conversing in a blend of Spanish and Guaraní that epitomises the country's unique cultural interweaving, the Paraguayans are most certainly the highlights of this *Paraíso Perdido* (Paradise Lost).

BEST TIME TO VISIT

May to September (winter)

ESSENTIAL EXPERIENCES

» Surviving a ride in one of Asunción's wooden-floored buses
» Visiting the Jesuit Missions of Trinidad and Jesús – impressive colonial remains where missionaries and Guaraní Indians once lived and learned harmoniously together
» Exploring the vast, thorny wilderness of the Chaco – host to exotic and endangered animals and birds
» Heading up the Río Paraguay on a local passenger boat

GETTING UNDER THE SKIN

» **Read** Augusto Roa Bastos' *Son of Man*, which ties together several episodes of Paraguayan history, or for travel literature try *At the Tomb of the Inflatable Pig: Travels Through Paraguay* by John Gimlette
» **Watch** Hugo Gamarra's *The Gate of Dreams* about Augusto Roa Bastos' life and literature; Claudio MacDowell´s *The Call of the Oboe,* set in a forsaken Paraguayan village; Enrique Collar's *miramenometokéi: Espinas del Alma* (Thorns of the Soul), about a girl marked by family secrets, set in modern-day Asunción

615

» **Listen** to harp and guitar-based folk music and its interpretations by guitarists such as Agustín Barrios Mangoré and Berta Rojas

» **Eat** *chipa* (cheese-bread sold everywhere); *sopa paraguaya* (corn-bread); freshly boiled *mandioca* (cassava); *borí borí, sooyo sopy* and *locro* (stew-like soups that bear the brunt of many local jokes)

» **Drink** *tereré* (ice-cold *yerba mate* – herbal tea, best shared with the locals), Pilsen (the national beer), *caña* (sugar cane alcohol)

IN A WORD
» *Mba'eichapa?* (how are you?)

TRADEMARKS
» Jaguars in the jungle; dictators, corruption and contraband; duty-free electronic goods; handicrafts; horse-drawn carts

SURPRISES
» The German-speaking Mennonite community in dusty Filadelfia; Nueva Australia, named after a short-lived attempt by Australians to set up Utopia in Paraguay

MAP REF P.14

(1.) Portrait of a young local boy in a Paraguay village
(2.) An early fresh bread delivery passes by the pastel pink Congressional Palace in Asunción
(3.) The Paraguay military on parade stand to attention in dress uniform
(4.) The domed tower and walls of the colonial Iglesia de la Encarnacion church, Asunción

1.

WES WALKER

If Peru didn't exist, travel guidebooks would have to invent it. It's a land of lost cities and ancient ruins, brooding Andean peaks and trashy urban beaches. It's dense jungles and overcrowded cities, mysterious Inca rites and Roman Catholic masses, practising shamans and dashboard Virgin Marys, Shining Path guerillas and ex-shoeshine-boys for president. It's like the whole world in a snowdome.

BEST TIME TO VISIT

June to August (the dry season)

ESSENTIAL EXPERIENCES

- » Arriving at Huayna Picchu just as the sun rises
- » Sinking into the hot springs at Aguas Calientes after hiking to Machu Picchu
- » Getting a bird's-eye view of the Nazca Lines
- » Visiting the islands of Lake Titicaca
- » Hiking in the Cordillera Blanca
- » Walking through Cuzco over ancient cobblestones and past walls built by the Incas

GETTING UNDER THE SKIN

- » **Read** *The Bridge of San Luis Rey,* by Thornton Wilder, an examination of 18th-century colonial Peru
- » **Listen** to *Afro-Peruvian Classics: The Soul of Black Peru,* on David Byrne's Luaka Bop label
- » **Watch** *Fitzcarraldo,* directed by Werner Herzog and featuring a particularly maniacal Klaus Kinski in an epic film about an obsessed opera lover who wants to build an opera in the jungle
- » **Eat** *ceviche* – fresh seafood marinated in lemon juice and chilli peppers, and served with corn on the cob or yucca
- » **Drink** Inka Kola, bubble-gum flavoured fizz; *chicha morada,* a non-carbonated sweet drink made from purple corn; papaya fruit juice

2.

3.

4.

IN A WORD

» *La noche es larga* (the night is long)

TRADEMARKS

» Pan pipes; quirky hats; religious iconography; Incan ruins; llamas; the Andes; colourful textiles; old black Dodges with Madonnas painted on the side; jungles; mysterious biomorphs and geo-glyphs etched into the land; 16th-century Spanish architecture and artefacts

SURPRISES

» Snow and skiing, sand boarding, multiple petticoats under brightly coloured taffeta dresses, village squares filled with schoolchildren and marching bands

MAP REF N,12

(1.) Glamour llamas in the freezing Alto Plano region
(2.) The 500-year-old city of Machu Picchu, a dazzling survivor of the Inca kingdom
(3.) Aymará women weaving mats by the shores of Lake Titicaca
(4.) The soaring peaks of Alpamayo dramatically slice into the sunset in Cordillera Blanca
(5.) Ready to roll – an Aymará boy about to race his old bicycle tyre
(6.) Two colourfully garbed Aymará girls share a joke

621

1.

ERIC WHEATER

Closer to Spain and Mexico via the fabled galleon trade, and some say to Hollywood by way of its showbiz politics, the Philippines remains Southeast Asia's destination of surprises along routes less travelled. There are more than 7000 shimmering islands to choose from, plus endless fiestas, but the best thing is the sense that there are still discoveries to be made. With so many islands and comparatively few visitors, the Philippines is one of the last great frontiers in Asian travel.

BEST TIME TO VISIT

September to the middle of May (the typhoon off-season) – or before Magellan arrived in 1521

ESSENTIAL EXPERIENCES

» Landing on Boracay beach by boat
» Absorbing the 17th-century atmosphere of Unesco World Heritage–listed Vigan
» Joining in the Mardi Gras fun at Iloilo's Dinagyang festival
» Rubbing elbows with Pontius Pilate and Barabbas at Crucifixion re-enactments in Pampanga
» Losing one's sanity in Manila but finding reasons to return

GETTING UNDER THE SKIN

» **Read** *Great Philippine Jungle Energy Cafe*, a magical novel by the award-winning Alfred A Yuson, or Pico Iyer's bittersweet insights in the Philippines chapter of his travelogue *Video Nights in Kathmandu*
» **Listen** to *Anak* (Child), the international hit by Freddie Aguilar
» **Watch** *Back to Bataan*, a wartime film about WWII, starring John Wayne and Anthony Quinn, with a Filipino cast

2.

3.

4.

» **Eat** *dinuguan*, a thick, black soup made of pig's blood with either pork or chicken entrails

» **Drink** *guyabano* juice, a refreshment made from the soursop fruit

IN A WORD

» *Okey, pare ko* (It's cool, man)

TRADEMARKS

» Jeepneys; San Miguel beer; *barong* shirts; Latin-soulled Asians with Californian accents; Imelda Marcos' shoes; ultra-hospitable people

SURPRISES

» Guimaras Island, for its delectable mangoes, ethereal islets and Trappist monastery where you might meet T-shirted and denim-clad monks

MAP REF K,33

(1.) Kids surf the nets in Tamontaka
(2.) A colourful mob of Ati-Atihan Festival celebrants on Panay Island
(3.) Public transport is slow but reliable in Santo Tomas, Mindanao Island
(4.) Enduring character traits of the nation witnessed in the expression on a child's face
(5.) Every hour is peak hour in the Blumentritt district of Manila
(6.) Mt Mayon rises dramatically above rice paddies in Albay

1.

Beautifully green and lush, tiny Pitcairn is most famous as the hideaway settlement for the notorious HMS *Bounty* mutineers. Ironically, more than 200 years later, it's one of the last remnants of the British Empire that Fletcher Christian and his gang rebelled against. With points of interest with names like John Catch-a-Cow and Bitey Bitey, the antiquated language of the mutineers' descendants is an attraction in itself. In October 2004, a third of the island's adult male population was arrested on child sex abuse charges. This reduction of the labour force threatens the island's long-term economic viability.

BEST TIME TO VISIT

April to October (the dry season)

ESSENTIAL EXPERIENCES

» Catching up with the HMS *Bounty* mutineers on Pitcairn – there are several relics, along with Fletcher Christian's cave
» Beachcombing by the beautiful lagoon on Ducie Atoll
» Birdwatching on Henderson Island with its unique *makatea* (raised coral island) geology
» Reading pre-European history in the mysterious Polynesian petroglyphs carved into the rocks at Down Rope

GETTING UNDER THE SKIN

» **Read** *Fragile Paradise* by Glynn Christian (Fletcher's great-great-great-great-grandson), an investigation of the mutiny and the mutineers' fate on Pitcairn
» **Watch** the original film about the mutiny, *In the Wake of the Bounty* (1933) – filmed in Pitcairn, Tahiti and Australia, and starring a young Errol Flynn, or any of the three later versions, starring Clark Gable, Marlon Brando and Mel Gibson respectively as the good guy

627

5.

» **Eat** breadfruit, the miracle fruit the HMS *Bounty* was sent out to collect

» **Drink** water

IN A WORD

» *Whutta-waye?* (how are you?)

TRADEMARKS

» Fletcher Christian descendants; beaches that you'd jump ship for; coral atolls; pirate hideaways; beautiful Tahitians; seafaring language

SURPRISES

» The people of Pitcairn really are descendants of the HMS *Bounty* mutineers and their Tahitian companions: HMS *Bounty* family names – Adams, Young and Christian – are still common

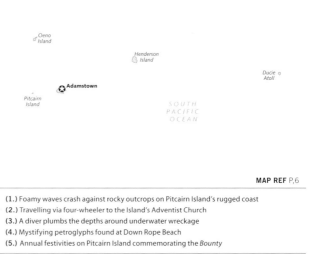

MAP REF P,6

(1.) Foamy waves crash against rocky outcrops on Pitcairn Island's rugged coast
(2.) Travelling via four-wheeler to the Island's Adventist Church
(3.) A diver plumbs the depths around underwater wreckage
(4.) Mystifying petroglyphs found at Down Rope Beach
(5.) Annual festivities on Pitcairn Island commemorating the *Bounty*

1.

Poland is a country of striking contrasts: contemporary city slickers fill the capital, Warsaw, while in the countryside horse-drawn carts negotiate peaceful lanes where the new millennium is just a rumour. Nestled in the heartland of Europe, Poland has been both a bridge and a front line between Eastern and Western Europe. Today the country has bounced back from the turmoil of the 20th century and reinvented itself as a must-do fixture on every traveller's map.

BEST TIME TO VISIT
» May to June (late spring) and September to mid-October (autumn) – or the 16th century, Poland's golden age

ESSENTIAL EXPERIENCES
» Seeing Warsaw change before your eyes
» Exploring Kraków's beautiful old town and staying up late to hit the cellar bars
» Strolling around Gdańsk's historic streets and then heading to the haunting sands of the Baltic coast
» Hiking and climbing the Tatras, home to some of Europe's finest mountain scenery
» Visiting Auschwitz and praying that such tragedies never happen again

GETTING UNDER THE SKIN
» **Read** The Heart of Europe: A Short History of Poland by Norman Davies, a readable, fascinating insight into the development of the nation
» **Listen** to Krzysztof Komeda's jazz piano compositions, icons of Polish culture
» **Watch** anything by Roman Polanski, Poland's most famous film export – try Knife in the Water, his first feature film

» **Eat** *bigos* (sauerkraut with a variety of meats) and *pierogi* (stuffed dumplings), both essential to your Polish experience

» **Drink** *wódka* (vodka), the drink of choice – *zubrówka* (bison vodka) is flavoured with a blade of bison grass, a local wild herb

IN A WORD

» *Na zdrowie!* (cheers!)

TRADEMARKS

» Lech Walesa and striking shipbuilders; Pope John Paul II; bleak Communist architecture; heroic goalkeepers and toasts of *wódka* to all of the above

SURPRISES

» The country has some of Europe's best mountain, coastal and lake scenery; Poland is staunchly Catholic

MAP REF E,22

(1.) Feisty folk singers let it rip at a music festival in Kazimierz Dolny

(2.) A street scene in the old quarter of Warsaw, frozen in the frame of a pale blue archway

(3.) Colourful gabled buildings line the old town square of Jelenia Gora

(4.) Snow blankets a spruce forest in the foothills of the Tatra Mountains

1.

JOHN KING

Savouring life slowly is a Portuguese passion, and much of the best pleasures are humble: traditional folk festivals; simple, honest food drowning in olive oil; music that pulls at the heart strings, recalling past love and glory; and markets overflowing with fish, fruit and flowers. The landscape is wreathed in olive groves, vineyards and Unesco World Heritage sites, while Portugal's delightfully laid-back capital, Lisbon, is an architectural time warp, with Moorish, medieval, Manueline and Art Nouveau.

BEST TIME TO VISIT
Mid-June to September (summer)

ESSENTIAL EXPERIENCES
» Enjoying the nightlife of Bairro Alto, Lisbon
» Exploring the revitalised medieval district of the Alfama in Lisbon
» Sunbathing on the sandy beaches of Costa da Caparica
» Discovering Neolithic standing stones in the wild countryside near Évora, Elvas and Castelo de Vide
» Wandering around the beautifully preserved hill-top villages of Monsaraz and Marvão

GETTING UNDER THE SKIN
» **Read** *Fernando Pessoa & Co: Selected Poems by Fernando Pessoa,* a collection of work by Portugal's greatest poet; Nobel Prize winner José Saramago's *O Evangelho segundo Jesus Cristo,* a unique reinterpretation of the biblical gospels
» **Listen** to *O Melhor* by Amália Rodrigues, who brought *fado* (bittersweet Portuguese folksongs) international recognition, or *Film* by rock band The Gift
» **Watch** *O Fantasma* directed by João Pedro Rodrigues, which recounts the tale of a sex-obsessed trash collector, or Wim Wenders' *A Lisbon Story*

2.

3.

4.

BILL WASSMAN

» **Eat** *sardinhas asadas* (charcoal-grilled sardines) or *pasteis de nata* (custard tarts)
» **Drink** *vinho* (wine) or tawny port

IN A WORD

» *Tudo bem* (all's good)

TRADEMARKS

» Cork plantations; golf courses; Lisbon nightlife; football fanatics; wild ocean beaches; late-bottled vintage port; the Lisbon earthquake of 1755

SURPRISES

» Many historians believe that it was Portuguese explorers who first reached Australia, some 250 years before its 'official' discovery by Captain James Cook; some 15 thousand million corks a year come from Portugal – around 60% of world output

JEFFREY BECOM

MAP REF G,19

(1.) Shoppers stride past the blue-and-white tiled walls of the Capela das Almas in Porto
(2.) Festival decorations strew the town of Campo Maior with dappled shadows
(3.) A swarthy sea dog treats both himself and his fish with salt and sun
(4.) Dusk tinges the harbour at Ferragudo in unusual hues of pink and blue
(5.) An elderly widow in Lisbon dressed in the sombre clothes characteristic of her age
(6.) Washing day in Loule, Algarve

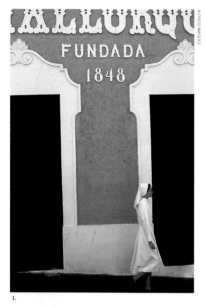

1.

2.

3.

Puerto Rican culture is a mixture of Spanish, African and Taíno traditions topped with a century-thick layer of American influence – and consequently nothing in Puerto Rico is one-dimensional. Spanish is the island's main language, but people also use many English, Amerindian and African words. Roman Catholicism reigns, but is infused with spiritualism and folkloric traditions. The music keeps time with African *bomba* and also 'Nuyorican' salsa that hails from émigrés in New York. Puerto Rico is uniquely a part of, and apart from, the US and the rest of the Caribbean.

BEST TIME TO VISIT

To avoid crowds and inflated prices, come during hurricane season (May-November) – but keep an eye on weather reports!

ESSENTIAL EXPERIENCES

» Drinking *café con leche* near dawn after a night of dancing
» Taking sunset walks at El Morro when the evening breeze picks up
» Enjoying the lush rainforest at El Yunque
» Swimming in the bioluminescent bay at Vieques
» Lazing in a hammock or dipping into the crystalline waters on Culebra
» Sampling fine rums native to Puerto Rico
» Winter whale-watching or surfing in Rincón
» Wandering through Ponce's historic district brimming with criollo architecture

GETTING UNDER THE SKIN

» **Read** Rosario Ferre's revisionist stories in *Sweet Diamond Dust*. Christina Duffy Burnett's *Foreign in a Domestic Sense* is an examination of American imperialism.

» **Listen** to *coquís*, Puerto Rico's native frogs; the infamous sounds of Tito Puente and Willie Colon; the compilations *Viva Salsa* and *Salsa Superhits* by Fania Records

» **Watch** the acclaimed *West Side Story* which represents stateside Puerto Ricans of the day. See Rachel Ortiz' heartfelt documentary *Mi Puerto Rico*.

» **Eat** plantain dishes such as *mofongos* and *tostones, sofrito* and *asopao de pollo* (traditional meals), *carrucho* (conch), *tembleque* (coconut pudding)

» **Drink** piña coladas, *Cuba libres*, *mojitos* or any other rum drink, *batidos* (milkshakes) made with *mamey* (a sweet, fragrant fruit) or *guanábana* (soursop)

IN A WORD

» *Ay, bendito!* (poor thing/what a shame/oh dear!)

TRADEMARKS

» Living *la vida loca*; the 51st state; Nuyorican poets; rum cocktails

SURPRISES

» The immensity of the cruise ships that come and go like mobile cities; the incongruity of using the US dollar

MAP REF J,13

(1.) A passing nun adds the finishing touch to a Spanish colonial tableau in old San Juan
(2.) Palm trees reach out to the ocean on Isla Verde
(3.) Patriotism is to wear your banner on your balcony at Casa Borinquen in Old San Juan
(4.) A pair of girls sizes up an accordian player at the Castillo de San Cristóbal

1.

Best known for being unknown, Qatar has a habit of falling off the world's radar – in fact, it only started issuing tourist visas in 1989. Travel to this thumb-shaped country in the Gulf and you'll find a a land of ritzy hotels, ancient rock carvings, enormous sand dunes and distinctive architecture. There's the opportunity for amazing desert excursions, or if greenery and shade are what you're after, you can stroll along the lovely 7km coastal corniche in Doha.

BEST TIME TO VISIT
» November to March for milder weather

ESSENTIAL EXPERIENCES
» Marvelling at the sea turtles at the Aquarium in the Qatar National Museum in Doha
» Looking at a restored traditional Qatari house at the Ethnographic Museum in Doha
» Taking in the amazing ocean views from the mosque in Al-Khor
» Wandering through the ancient fort at Al-Zubara
» Watching the locals haggling at the markets

GETTING UNDER THE SKIN
» **Read** *Arabian Time Machine: Self-Portrait of an Oil State* by Helga Graham, a collection of interviews with Qataris about their lives, culture and traditions
» **Listen** to *The Music of Islam: Volume 4*, recorded in Qatar and featuring traditional melodies played on the oud, a traditional stringed-instrument
» **Watch** *Qatar: A Quest for Excellence* made by Greenpark Productions, exploring the life and culture of Qatar through evocative visual images and music

2.

3.

4.

» **Eat** *labneh*, a kind of yogurt cheese often made from goat's milk; *matchbous*, rice served with spiced lamb; or *wara enab*, stuffed vine leaves

» **Drink** *qahwe*, spiced Turkish coffee; or fruit juices

IN A WORD

» *Salaam* (hello)

TRADEMARKS

» Traditional houses; the Arabian oryx; sand dunes; ancient forts; traditional Bedouin weaving; old watchtowers; palm-lined sea-shores; rambling souqs; easy-going people; sandstorms; fierce heat; Islamic culture; coastal towns; historical museums

SURPRISES

» Aladdin's Kingdom – the only amusement park in the gulf with a serious roller coaster; camel races at Al-Shahhainiya

MAP REF I,25

(1.) Wild camels traverse the forbidding sand dunes of Jarayan al-Batnah
(2.) Bedouin men chilling on a wall
(3.) Stark lines and contrasts mark the geometry of a mosque in Doha
(4.) The Barzan Tower's modern architecture meets classical styles at the Corniche, Doha
(5.) In the harbour of Al-Khor, a fishing dhow looks towards a distant mosque
(6.) The rippled surface of a sand dune swells into an inland sea near Khor al-Adaid

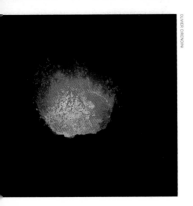

Réunion is so sheer and lush, it looks as if it has risen dripping wet from the deep blue sea – which it effectively has, being the tip of a massive sub-merged prehistoric volcano. The island is run as an overseas *département* of France, making it one of the last colonial possessions in the world. French culture dominates every facet of life, from the coffee and croissant in the morning to the bottle of Evian and the carafe of red wine at the dinner table. However, the French atmosphere of the island has a firmly tropical twist, with subtle traces of Indian, African and even Chinese cultures.

BEST TIME TO VISIT
May and June

ESSENTIAL EXPERIENCES
» Hiking the three extraordinary cirques, the active Piton de la Fournaise volcano, and Piton des Neiges – Réunion's highest peak
» Soaking up the breathtaking and varied scenery, from austere mountains to intriguing amphitheatres
» Mixing in with the colourful cultural melting pot *à la Réunionnais* of Creoles, Europeans, Indians and Chinese
» Feasting on the delicious diversity of food, from traditional Creole curries to *haute cuisine française*
» Strolling down Le Barachois, a park lined with cannons and cafés

GETTING UNDER THE SKIN
» **Read** Catherine Lavaux's *La Réunion: Du Battant des Lames au Sommet des Montagnes*
» **Listen** to Compagnie Creole, a Caribbean group originally from Réunion but now based in Paris
» **Eat** *carri poulpe* (octopus curry) and, if you want to spice things up, add some *rougaile* (a spicy tomato, ginger and vegetable chutney)

5.

» **Drink** *rhum arrangé* (a mixture of rum, fruit juice, cane syrup and a blend of herbs and berries) or a bottle of French red wine

IN A WORD

» *Bonjour* (hello)

TRADEMARKS

» Volcanoes; trekking; lush forests; bad beaches; fantastic food; a French colony

SURPRISES

» Early settlers developed a taste for the apical bud of the palmiste palm (unfortunately once the bud is removed, the palm dies); the Plaine-des-Palmistes, a green plateau filled with flowers, was stripped bare in a few generations; there are still people searching for the treasure of pirate Olivier Levasseur (or 'La Buse' – the Buzzard) in Mauritius, the Seychelles and Réunion

MAP REF P.26

(**1.**) Street beats and bright bandanas at a festival in St-Louis
(**2.**) Some of the hottest items on sale at the market in St-Paul
(**3.**) A tide of heavy cloud washes around the peak of La Roche Ecrite
(**4.**) The scalding crater of the Piton de la Fournaise broods and boils
(**5.**) The jagged peaks of the Bras des Merles in the awesome Cirque de Mafates

1.

Romania is the Wild West of Eastern Europe, a country where tourism means you and a horse and cart. But it's certainly chasing the dreams of the West. Straddling the rugged Carpathian Mountains, Romania offers an extraordinary kaleidoscope of cultures and sights, including majestic castles, medieval towns, superb hiking and skiing; and Bucharest has a charm all of its own. Romania's greatest asset is its diversity, whether you want to stray off the beaten tourist track or stay well and truly on it.

BEST TIME TO VISIT
May and June, followed by September and early October

ESSENTIAL EXPERIENCES
» Descending underground to a cave or salt mine in Transylvania, Crişana or Banat
» Sharpening your fangs and practising saying 'I vant to suck your blurd' at Dracula's castle in Bran
» Experiencing 'cart-rage' when trying to overtake a horse-drawn cart on a winding mountain road
» Slapping on some smelly, curative mud on the Black Sea coast
» Braving a vigorous drinking session of 60-proof moonshine *palincă* (brandy) with exuberant locals
» Marvelling at the striking baroque architecture at Braşov and castle-spotting at Râsnov

GETTING UNDER THE SKIN
» **Read** Norman Manea's *The Hooligan's Return: A Memoir*, relating the return of the author to his homeland in the late 1990s
» **Listen** to Pasărea Colîbrî, a very popular contemporary band with great folk-inspired soft rock and pop tunes
» **Watch** *Cold Mountain*, directed by Anthony Minghella, which was filmed at the Carpathian Mountains

2.

3.

4.

» **Eat** *ciorbă de burtă,* a lightly garlicky soup made of tripe

» **Drink** wine, wine and more wine – among the best are Cotnari, Murfatlar, Odobeşti, Târnave and Valea Călugărească

IN A WORD

» *Bună* (hello)

TRADEMARKS

» A film-set for cheap horror flicks; mountain festivals; Dracula and all things Transylvanian; Queen Marie of Romania; imposing castles; medieval villages; wine producers; rolling green countryside; a country that's ripe for discovery

SURPRISES

» Romania is usually in the top five countries in the world for having the highest marriage rates

MAP REF F,22

(1.) An eerie glow on the cobbled streets of Sighişoara
(2.) Arges valley near Poienari and the defensive fortress of Vlad Ţepeş
(3.) Tiny barns dot the gently rolling slopes in the green countryside
(4.) Forest workers and their wives travel on flat-bed wagons along the Vişeu de Sus railway
(5.) Headscarves and coloured striped aprons are worn in this part of the Maramureş
(6.) A man climbs the stairs to his Sighişoara apartment

1.

Winston Churchill famously described Russia as a 'riddle wrapped in a mystery inside an enigma', and this remains an apt description of a place most outsiders know very little about. A composite of the extravagant glories of old Russia and the drab legacies of the Soviet era, Russia is a country that befuddles and beguiles but never bores.

BEST TIME TO VISIT

May to October

ESSENTIAL EXPERIENCES

» Experiencing imperialist extravagance at the Hermitage in St Petersburg
» Sweating it out in a *banya* – the combination of dry sauna, steam bath and plunges into ice-cold water is a regular feature of Russian life
» Taking one of the world's great train journeys across Siberia
» Learning to drink vodka the Russian way
» Paying your respects to Lenin's mummified body in Red Square
» Gazing at the crystal-clear blue waters of Lake Baikal from an old wooden cottage in lovely Listvyanka

GETTING UNDER THE SKIN

» **Read** Tolstoy's *War and Peace,* if you're feeling brave; otherwise have a go at Dostoevsky's *Crime and Punishment*
» **Listen** to anything by Tchaikovsky or Rachmaninoff
» **Watch** the Oscar-winning *Burnt by the Sun,* a poignant treatment of the Stalinist purges
» **Eat** *bliny* (pancakes with savoury or sweet fillings) and, of course, caviar
» **Drink** vodka – what else?

IN A WORD

» *Za vashe zdarov'e!* (to your health!)

5.

TRADEMARKS

» Vodka; corrupt billionaires; Soviet-era architecture; *babushkas* in scarves; queues; dachas; shopping at GUM; *matryoshka* dolls; cabbage and cabbage

SURPRISES

» St Petersburg is a beautiful city of canals, sometimes known as the 'Venice of the North'

MAP REF D,28

(1.) The candy-striped Chesma Church in St Petersburg built for Catherine the Great
(2.) The distinctive Soviet architecture of the colossal Hotel Rossiya in Moscow
(3.) A cabin attendant wears elegant furs on the Irkutsk to Moscow express
(4.) The famous Trans-Siberian snakes through a winter wonderland
(5.) Figures traverse the frozen surface of the River Neva in St Petersburg

1.

Rwanda is often called *Le Pays des Milles Collines* (the Land of a Thousand Hills) for the endless mountains in this scenically stunning little country. Nowhere are the mountains more majestic than the peaks of the Virunga volcanoes in the far northwest of the country, forming a natural frontier with the Democratic Republic of Congo (Zaïre) and Uganda. Hidden among the bamboo and dense jungle of the volcanoes' forbidding slopes are some of the world's last remaining mountain gorillas. A beautiful yet brutalised country, Rwanda is all too often associated with the horrific genocide that occurred here in 1994, but the country has taken giant strides towards recovery in the years since.

BEST TIME TO VISIT

Any time except mid-March to mid-May when the long rains set in

ESSENTIAL EXPERIENCES

» Visiting the rare mountain gorillas in the dense forest of Parc National des Volcans
» Soaking up the sun, sand and stunning scenery at Gisenyi, on Lake Kivu, Rwanda's answer to the Mediterranean
» Tracking down huge troops of colobus monkeys in Nyungwe, the country's largest tropical rainforest
» Exploring one of Africa's best ethnographical and archaeological museums in Butare, Rwanda's intellectual capital
» Checking out the nightlife in Kigali

GETTING UNDER THE SKIN

» **Read** *We Wish to Inform You That Tomorrow We Will Be Killed with Our Families* by Phillip Gourevitch, an account of the killings and how the international community failed Rwanda in 1994 and beyond

2.

3.

4.

» **Listen** to the queen of Rwandan music, Cecile Kayirebwa
» **Watch** *Gorillas in the Mist* – the story of Dian Fossey's years with the mountain gorillas of Rwanda
» **Eat** *tilapia* (Nile perch), goat meat and beef brochettes
» **Drink** the local beers, Primus and Mulzig, or try the local firewater, *konyagi*

IN A WORD

» *Muraho* ('hello' in Kinyarwanda) – use unsparingly

TRADEMARKS

» The horrific 1994 genocide; Dian Fossey; volcanoes; dense jungles; gorilla tracking; mountains

SURPRISES

» Tiny, landlocked Rwanda has 340 people per square kilometre; there are thought to be around only 700 mountain gorillas left in the world today

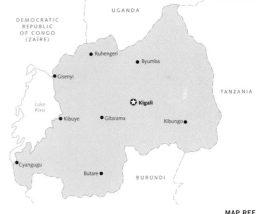

UGANDA

DEMOCRATIC
REPUBLIC
OF CONGO
(ZAÏRE)

● Ruhengeri
● Byumba
● Gisenyi

TANZANIA

Lake Kivu

✿ **Kigali**

● Kibuye
● Gitarama
Kibungo ●

● Cyangugu

Butare ●

BURUNDI

MAP REF M,23

(1.) Holding the house together, a woman stands at the entrance to a homestead in Nyanza
(2.) A reconstruction of the ancient palace of the Mwami (King) in Nyanza
(3.) A boy launches his dugout canoe for a day's fishing on the lake, Gisenyi
(4.) Gaudy shopfronts in the capital, Kigali
(5.) Pretty in green, a muslim girl of Cyangugu
(6.) Nyakarimbi, a village home to creators of brilliant cow-dung paintings in geometric design

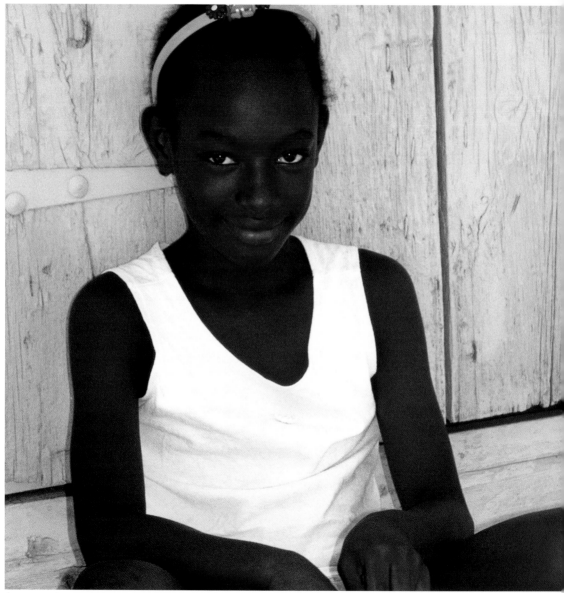

1.

The islands of St Kitts and Nevis are two of the sleepiest places in the Caribbean, and one of the few countries in the region where agriculture is still a larger part of the economy than tourism. The islands have mountainous interiors, patchwork cane fields, salt ponds and deeply indented bays. The culture of the islands draws upon a mix of European, African and West Indian traditions. While three quarters of the population live on St Kitts, both islands are small, rural and lightly populated.

BEST TIME TO VISIT

Year-round

ESSENTIAL EXPERIENCES

» Staying in cosy, atmospheric plantation inns
» Strolling the expansive coconut-lined Pinney's beach on Nevis
» Enjoying St Kitts' southeast peninsula, with its fine scenery and beaches
» Exploring Brimstone Hill Fortress National Park with its historic significance and coastal views
» Diving amongst rays, barracuda, garden eels, nurse sharks, sea turtles, sea fans, giant barrel sponges and black coral
» Wandering around the seaside village of Old Road Town to see vintage sugar cane trains hauling loads of freshly cut cane from the fields to the mills

GETTING UNDER THE SKIN

» **Read** *Historic Basseterre: The Story of its Growth* by Sir Probyn Inniss, which recounts the growth of the capital. Read Sir Fred Phillips' memoirs *Caribbean Life and Culture: A Citizen Reflects* for a more personal account.
» **Listen** to West Indian and African influenced music

4.

5.

6.

RICHARD CUMMINS / WAYNE WALTON

RICHARD CUMMINS

WAYNE WALTON

» **Eat** fresh fish and seafood until bursting point
» **Drink** Cane Spirit Rothschild (CSR), a clear sugar cane spirit, by itself or with Ting, a grapefruit soft drink

IN A WORD

» Put your feet up

TRADEMARKS

» Sugar; snorkelling; laid-back attitude; plantation estates; fine beaches; cricket

SURPRISES

» The federation of the two islands forms the smallest nation in the western hemisphere. While Kittitians and Nevisians amicably coexist – they share essentially the same culture, and most Nevisians live on St Kitts – they are fierce rivals. Their annual cricket match is an intense affair.

MAP REF J,13

(1.) A young girl smiles for the camera from outside a doorway in Basseterre
(2.) An essential mode of transport in Charlestown
(3.) The citadel's interior makes an inviting retreat in Brimstone Hill Fortress National Park
(4.) Time to paint the house blue again soon
(5.) The catch of the day dries out in front of Bloody Point Restaurant
(6.) Palm trees watch yet another fuschia and red sunset over the Caribbean

1.

Resort developments on St Lucia have made this high, green island one of the Caribbean's trendy package-tour destinations, but it's still a long way from being overdeveloped. Bananas are still bigger business than tourism in this archetypal island heaven, and much of the island is rural: small coastal fishing villages give way to a hinterland of banana and coconut plantations folded within deep valleys topped by rich, mountainous jungle. The rugged terrain continues offshore in a diving heaven of underwater mountains, caves and drop-offs.

BEST TIME TO VISIT
January to April

ESSENTIAL EXPERIENCES
» Hobnobbing with the yachties at Marigot Bay
» Playing pirates on Pigeon Island, a base used by 'Wooden Leg' de Bois for raiding passing Spanish galleons
» Keeping your eyes peeled in the Frigate Islands Nature Reserve for frigate birds, herons, and (gulp!) boa constrictors
» Holding your nose to investigate the stinky Sulphur Springs bubbling mud and gases from underground volcanoes
» Heading for the extremes on Moule à Chique, the southernmost point of the island, with views of the Maria Islands and St Vincent

GETTING UNDER THE SKIN
» **Read** Derek Walcott's *Collected Poems, 1948–1984*, an anthology by St Lucia's favourite son and Nobel Prize winner
» **Listen** to calypso, reggae and dub, especially at a Friday night 'jump-up' party
» **Watch** the many movies that have used St Lucia as a backdrop including *Superman II* and the 1967 original *Doctor Dolittle*

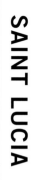

SAINT LUCIA

CAPITAL **CASTRIES** POPULATION **162,157** AREA **616 SQ KM** OFFICIAL LANGUAGE **ENGLISH**

2.

3.

4.

» **Eat** West Indian and Creole dishes from across the Caribbean

» **Drink** the local beer, Piton, brewed in Vieux Fort

IN A WORD

» *Bon jou* – good day (in Kwéyòl, which the French Creole islanders sometimes use)

TRADEMARKS

» Pirate hideouts; yachties recruiting for their next voyage; pristine beaches; impenetrable jungles; the Pitons towering over the island; bananas aplenty

SURPRISES

» In these idyllic surroundings, swimming isn't always a good idea as Bilharzia (schistosomiasis) is endemic to St Lucia (but only in fresh water)

CARIBBEAN SEA

★ Castries

Anse La Raye

Canaries

Soufrière

Micoud

Choiseul

Vieux Fort

ATLANTIC OCEAN

MAP REF K,13

(1.) There's never a dull moment when strolling down Brazil Street
(2.) The Cathedral of the Immaculate Conception's interior depicts colourful biblical scenes
(3.) A fisherman sits on a jetty, tending his boat
(4.) This woman carries brooms to market
(5.) Rainforest in the Morne Coubaril Plantation with the peak of Petit Piton looming behind
(6.) A portrait of a smiling girl

1.

St Vincent and the Grenadines form a multi-island nation well known to wintering yachties, aristocrats and rock stars, but off the beaten path for most other visitors. The 30 islands and cays that comprise the Grenadines reach like stepping stones between St Vincent and Grenada and are surrounded by coral reefs and clear blue waters. Fewer than a dozen are inhabited, and even these are lightly populated and barely developed. St Vincent and the Grenadines share traditional West Indian culture, giving it a multi-ethnic twist of African, Black Carib, French and British influences.

BEST TIME TO VISIT

January to May

ESSENTIAL EXPERIENCES

» Trekking up St Vincent's La Soufrière volcano and passing through banana estates and rainforest before reaching the scenic summit
» Enjoying the pristine beaches and reefs of the Tobago Cays
» Diving to find colourful sponges, soft corals, great stands of elkhorn coral, branching gorgonian and black corals, and a few sunken wrecks
» Relaxing on the black-sand surf beaches of St Vincent's Atlantic coast
» Drinking with Mick Jagger in Mustique
» Hanging out with lizards after climbing Fort Duvernette

GETTING UNDER THE SKIN

» **Read** the history of St Vincent's Black Caribs in *Wild Majesty: Encounters with Caribs from Columbus to the Present Day* by Peter Hulme and Neil Whitehead

4.

» **Listen** to reggae, calypso, steel bands and local boy made good, Kevin Lyttle

» **Watch** *Pirates of the Caribbean*, which was mostly shot in St Vincent

» **Eat** *bul jol* (roasted breadfruit and saltfish with tomatoes and onions) and feast on the plentiful tropical fruits

» **Drink** the locally distilled Captain Bligh Rum or the local lager, Hairoun

IN A WORD

» Pass me the sunscreen, please

TRADEMARKS

» Rock stars and royalty; tropical island paradise; exclusive resorts; yachts; volcanoes

SURPRISES

» Mick Jagger lived on Mustique; the sweet, juicy St Vincent orange is ripe while still green

MAP REF K,13

(1.) Shopping for fresh vegetables on Union Island
(2.) A bubbly spirit delivers a crate of cola across a street in Kingstown
(3.) The distinguished *Royal Clipper* proudly pushes its way out to sea
(4.) A diver spots a barrel sponge in the waters off Bequia Island

1.

Samoa is so laid-back it's only a kava session away from being comatose. Palm-fringed beaches, booming white surf and lush rainforests wreathed in misty clouds make it the kind of place that Hollywood location scouts go gaga over. The Samoan Islands comprise two entirely separate entities: the independent country of Samoa and the US territory of American Samoa. Over the years it's been visited by trading ships and served as a bolt hole for the homeless riffraff of the seas – ex-whalers, escaped convicts, bawdy traders and retired pirates. After such a tumultuous history, this is a place that has earned a little time in the sun.

BEST TIME TO VISIT

May to October, when the weather is perfect and the events calendar is full

ESSENTIAL EXPERIENCES

» Spending the night in a 225-year-old banyan tree amid fruit bats and birds on Falealupo Peninsula
» Discovering Pulemelei Step Pyramid, Polynesia's largest and most mysterious ancient monument
» Gazing into Olemoe Falls, Samoa's most beautiful waterfall and tropical pool
» Blowing your mind at Alofa'aga Blowholes, one of the world's largest marine blowholes
» Getting volcanic at Sale'aula Lava Field, a vast expanse of black basalt formed by flowing lava enveloping a village

GETTING UNDER THE SKIN

» **Read** *Where We Once Belonged* by Sia Figiel, a local author's first novel about dispossession in modern Samoa

WILL SALTER

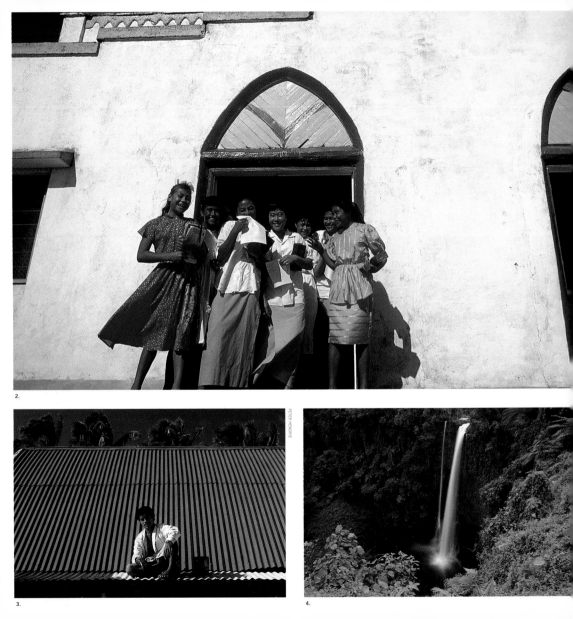

2.

3.

4.

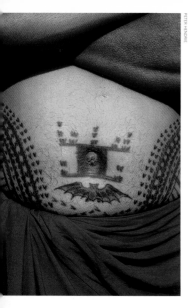

PETER HENDRIE

» **Listen** to world-renowned Samoan hip hop such as the Boo Ya Tribe and King Kapisi

» **Watch** *Fa'a Samoa: The Samoan Way*, an amusing video portraying everyday life in Samoa

» **Eat** a traditional Polynesian feast cooked in an *umu* (below-the-ground oven)

» **Drink** kava, the ceremonial drink made from the ground roots of pepper plants

IN A WORD

» *Malo* or *Talofa* – traditional greetings

TRADEMARKS

» Hefty rugby-playing locals; kava ceremonies; palm-fringed beaches; ornate traditional tattoos; volcanoes periodically blowing their tops; Robert Louis Stevenson

SURPRISES

» The International Dateline makes Samoa the last place on earth to see the sun set and means many travellers arrive the day before they left

SOUTH
PACIFIC
OCEAN

Savai'i
Salelologa
SAMOA &**Apia**
Upolu

Manu'a
Islands

Pago Pago
Aunu'u
Tutuila AMERICAN
SAMOA

SOUTH
PACIFIC
OCEAN

MAP REF N,1

JOHN BORTHWICK

(1.) Released from church, children prepare to sully their Sunday best in Apia
(2.) Cheerful churchgoers at the entrance to the Vaiusu Catholic Church, Upolu Island
(3.) Painting himself into a corner, a man crouches on a corrugated iron roof
(4.) The Fuipisia Falls cascade on the Edenic trail of the Mulivaifagatola River
(5.) Traditional tummy tattoos on Savai'i Island
(6.) A young adventurer crosses the canopy walkway in the Falealupo Rainforest Reserve

1.

2.

3.

It might be geographically part of Italy, but the Most Serene Republic of San Marino is miraculously the world's oldest surviving republic. If you're into the experience of extreme kitsch, this is the place for you – it's packed to the gills with 'genuine reproductions' of medieval relics. A dozen or so kilometres inland from Rimini, it's not much bigger than two or three suburbs strung together but has its own distinctive flavour and proud identity, boasting three grand fortresses and some of the most stunning views of the Adriatic.

BEST TIME TO VISIT
July to September for the best weather

ESSENTIAL EXPERIENCES
» Paying a visit to the Basilica del Santo – the heart and spirit of both the city and the republic
» Roaming unhindered around La Rocca, the First Tower
» Descending into the deep dungeon in the tower fortress Montale
» Wandering around the richly, carved stone Palazzo Publico
» Marvelling at the views from the Piazza della Libertà
» Walking in the relative calm and quiet of the Appennines

GETTING UNDER THE SKIN
» **Read** *Secrets of the Seven Smallest States of Europe: Andorra, Liechtenstein, Luxembourg, Malta, Monaco, San Marino and Vatican City* by Thomas Ecchardt
» **Listen** to *Live in San Marino*, by Lino Patruno & His Jazz Star of Italy – an excellent album of popular jazz standards recorded live in the republic
» **Watch** Darryl Zanuck's *The Prince of Foxes*, filmed in San Marino (he 'rented out' the entire republic!)

CAPITAL **SAN MARINO** POPULATION **28,119** AREA **61.2 SQ KM** OFFICIAL LANGUAGE **ITALIAN**

SAN MARINO

4.

» **Eat** brioche for breakfast, pasta with *carciofi* (artichokes), mushrooms or *vongole* (clams), grilled seafood or *bustrengo* (a sweet cake made with polenta, apples, honey, raisins and lemon zest)

» **Drink** frothy cappucinos or grappa (spirits distilled from grape residue)

IN A WORD

» *Buongiorno* (literally 'good day')

TRADEMARKS

» Stamp and coin collecting; stupendous fortresses; rampant postcard production; the smell of frankincense and myrrh on holy days; Mount Titano; bell towers; amazing architectural design; jam-packed streets full of tourists

SURPRISES

» The Museo di Auto d'Epoca – a museum of cars, both old and new; Chiesa di San Francesco – the oldest building in the republic

ITALY

- La Dogana
- Serravalle
- Domagnano
- Acquaviva
- Borgo Maggiore
- ✪ **San Marino**
- Faetano
- Chiesanuova
- Fiorentino

ITALY

MAP REF G,21

(1.) Uniformed guard outside the fortress of La Rocca
(2.) The neoclassical Basilica del Santo is said to be the most important church in San Marino
(3.) Castles in the air: La Rocca o Guaita fortress rises like an apparition from clearing mists
(4.) Ristorante Bolognese, a culinary haven in San Marino's historic centre

1.

2.

3.

Never heard of this little slice of the Caribbean in the Gulf of Guinea? You're not the only one. The two islands of São Tomé and Príncipe comprise the smallest country in Africa, and one of the newest. These sleepy islands boast miles of pristine beaches, crystal-blue waters, rolling hills, jagged rock formations and lush rainforests. The Portuguese may have left little infrastructure after independence in 1974, but they did leave a strong cultural legacy. Portuguese (as well as Forro, a form of Creole) is spoken throughout the islands and Roman Catholicism is the major religion.

BEST TIME TO VISIT
June and September

ESSENTIAL EXPERIENCES
» Swimming at the secluded white-sand beaches with a lush jungle backdrop on the East Coast
» Exploring São Tomé town – a friendly, quiet capital city with scenic side streets and colonial architecture
» Snorkelling on the true tropical paradise of Príncipe
» Straddling the equator at Ilhéu das Rolas
» Sipping on some of the best coffee you'll ever taste
» Visiting the pleasant town of Trindade in the island's interior where you can experience the Waterfall Cascadas de São Nicolau nearby
» Hiking through rainforest and birdwatching
» Kicking back and relaxing under the palm trees

GETTING UNDER THE SKIN
» **Read** *Former Portuguese Colonies* by Herb Boyd which includes an historical overview of São Tomé and Príncipe

» **Listen** to Gilberto Gil Umbelina, the most famous popular recording artist from São Tomé and Príncipe

» **Eat** fantastic fresh fish and a wonderful assortment of fresh fruit

» **Drink** excellent coffee or the local beer, Creola

IN A WORD

» *Olá* (hello)

TRADEMARKS

» Where is this place?

SURPRISES

» The illiteracy rate on the islands is 90%; the islands became the biggest sugar producers in the world shortly after the Portuguese founded the town of São Tomé in 1485

Príncipe · Santo António
· Don Infante
Henrique

GULF OF GUINEA

Guadalupe
Neves · · ✪ **São Tomé**
Santa · · Ribeira
Catarina · Afonso
ATLANTIC São Tomé
OCEAN · Porto Alegre

MAP REF L,21

(1.) I've got a lovely bunch of coconuts, São João dos Angolares
(2.) São Toménse women sift the dust from cocoa beans at a cocoa plant in Agua Ize
(3.) Actors perform a play called Ferrabras, an annual event in Santo António
(4.) The monolithic Pico Cão Grande dominates the verdant landscape

1.

Once an exclusive club for the chosen few, such as pilgrims bound for Mecca, oil sheiks from Texas, contract workers from everywhere else, and the odd asylum-seeking dictator, Saudi Arabia now welcomes visitors on special visas. The cost is stiff, the restrictions intimidating, but the thrill of just being there is unbeatable. Delights for the intrepid, moneyed traveller include ancient souqs in urban landscapes, antiquities half-buried in the desert, a biblical sea and the heady taste of Arabian hospitality.

BEST TIME TO VISIT

November to February

ESSENTIAL EXPERIENCES

» Exploring the spectacular rock tombs of Medain Salah
» Witnessing the sword dance *ardha*
» Sculpture-spotting along Jeddah's corniche
» Judging the camel beauty contest near Hafar al-Batin
» Sighting dugongs in the Red Sea around the Farasan Islands
» Admiring rock art around Najran
» Visiting the ancient Masmak Fortress in Riyadh

GETTING UNDER THE SKIN

» **Read** *Sandstorms, Days and Nights in Arabia*, Peter Theroux's memoir of the Middle East, or the delightful coffee-table book *The Kingdom of Saudi Arabia*
» **Listen** to *Arabian Masters*, featuring Umm Kolthum, Fairouz, Abdel Halim Hafez, and other Arabic singers and musicians
» **Watch** *Lawrence of Arabia*, David Lean's 1962 epic, not quite Saudi Arabia (shot in Jordan) but many similarities

SAUDI ARABIA

CAPITAL **RIYADH** POPULATION **24,293,844** AREA **1,960,582 SQ KM** OFFICIAL LANGUAGE **ARABIC**

2.

3.

4.

» **Eat** with your fingers (but never with the left hand). Try a boiled young camel on steaming rice.

» **Drink** cardamon-flavoured coffee

IN A WORD

» *Is-salaam 'alaykum* (peace be upon you)

TRADEMARKS

» Old souqs and camel markets; Aramco (Arabian American Oil Company); dates and carpets; millions of expatriate workers in thousands of construction sites and camps; bearded men in robes greeting one another with hugs and kisses; Mecca and Medina

SURPRISES

» Stumbling onto a back lot in Jeddah, where, according to the locals, one will find the tomb of Eve; for women, wearing an all-encompassing *abaya* is essential for visiting Saudi Arabia

MAP REF J,24

(1.) The lion tomb is an imposing sight at the Al-Khuraibba Tombs near Al-Ula

(2.) The Diwan, or meeting room, of Madain Salah is a sight to be admired

(3.) Locally made baskets and ceramic bowls for sale in Najran Basket Souq

(4.) The Auto Cube is one of many modern artworks in Jeddah

(5.) The Faisaliah Tower in Riyadh, designed by Sir Norman Foster

(6.) Traditional balconies and decorative façades in Jeddah's old town

1.

Given the long list of influential Scottish inventors and scientists, you would think that the Scots would have come up with something to tame the weather. But, as comedian Billy Connolly said, 'there's no such thing as bad weather, only the wrong clothes'. Weather aside, Scotland, like a fine malt, is a connoisseur's delight – a complex mix of history, festivals galore, feisty people and a wild and beautiful landscape – it should be savoured slowly.

BEST TIME TO VISIT

» May to September – or before the Act of Union in 1707 when the English stayed south of the border

ESSENTIAL EXPERIENCES

» Taking in the magnificent view of the Firth of Forth from the top of Edinburgh Castle
» Viewing the aurora borealis on a clear winter's night from the shores of Loch Tay
» Walking around Neolithic homes at Skara Brae, Orkney, built before the Egyptians thought of pyramids
» Climbing Ben Nevis to experience the remote beauty of Scotland's Highlands
» Hitting a very small ball into a very small hole, with a very tall flag in it, at St Andrews

GETTING UNDER THE SKIN

» **Read** anything by Robert Burns, or *Trainspotting* by Irvine Welsh, for an incomparable but often incomprehensible insight into Scotland
» **Listen** to the Proclaimers, or The Corries for true Scottish folk
» **Watch** *Whisky Galore*, adapted from Compton MacKenzie's novel. MacKenzie is known for the adage 'Love makes the world go round? Not at all! Whisky makes it go round twice as fast'.

» **Eat** haggis, *neeps* and *tatties* (haggis, turnips and potatoes) or try some *cranachan* (whipped cream flavoured with whisky, and mixed with toasted oatmeal and raspberries)

» **Drink** whisky, Deuchars IPA (beer) or Irn-Bru (soft drink)

IN A WORD

» *Och aye tha noo* (how are you?/I'm fine; the meaning is not very easy to translate)

TRADEMARKS

» Hogmanay and ceilidhs; castles, kilts and tartanalia; Highland Games; bagpipers; haggis; deep-fried Mars Bars; whisky; serious drinkers; heart disease; the Loch Ness Monster; Sean Connery

SURPRISES

» More redheads are born in Scotland compared to the rest of the world. Some of the oldest mountains in the world can be found in the Highlands of Scotland.

MAP REF D,19

(**1.**) The desolate ruins of Dunnottar Castle, Stonehaven
(**2.**) These punters enjoy a drink in Edinburgh's The Honeycomb
(**3.**) It may be called Greensleeves, but the dresses are red
(**4.**) A Highland Cow stares right back
(**5.**) The magnificent Salisbury Crags give a different perspective on Edinburgh

1.

Lush Senegal is known for its great natural beauty and gorgeous tropical climate. Surrounded by desert, it offers a rich landscape, great beaches for soaking up the sun and some excellent scuba diving opportunities. Dakar, its capital city, is raw, crowded and exciting, and more favoured by travellers than many of the other larger African cities. Senegal has a rich musical culture with many internationally recognised musicians. Best of all is a slow wander through its streets.

BEST TIME TO VISIT

November to February – or in the 13th and 14th centuries when the Djolof kingdom flourished

ESSENTIAL EXPERIENCES

» Experiencing West African culture at Dakar's IFAN Museum
» Basking in the sun on the beaches of Cap Skiring
» Soaking up the atmosphere in Kaolack
» Viewing the grand houses of the old European quarter in St-Louis
» Purchasing trinkets at the Marché St-Maur in Ziguinchor
» Driving through Niokolo-Koba park to see hippos, baboons, buffalo and more
» Admiring the breathtaking scenery of the Siné-Saloum Delta

GETTING UNDER THE SKIN

» **Read** *God's Bits of Wood* by Senegalese writer Sembene Ousmane, the story of adversity faced by strikers on the Dakar-Niger train line in the 1940s
» **Listen** to the amazing voice of Youssou N'Dour on *Eyes Open*
» **Watch** Safi Faye's *Mossane*, the story of a beautiful young girl promised to an arranged marriage but carrying on a secret, chaste love affair

SENEGAL

CAPITAL DAKAR POPULATION 10,580,307 AREA 196,190 SQ KM OFFICIAL LANGUAGE FRENCH

» **Eat** *maffé saloum* (beef cooked with peanuts, tomato, yams and carrots) or *yassa* (chicken cooked with olives, lemon and onions)

» **Drink** *bissap* juice, a popular local drink with lots of zing, or spicy ginger juice

IN A WORD

» *Asalaa-maalekum* (greetings, 'peace be with you' in Arabic)

TRADEMARKS

» The Wolof and Mandinka tribes; a thriving groundnut industry; beautiful mosques; lively fishing communities; colourful birdlife; vibrant markets; mangrove swamps; gorgeous handicrafts; amazing wildlife; excellent beaches; *marabouts* (holy men)

SURPRISES

» Stunning tapestries at the famous, cooperative-run Manufactures Sénégalaises des Arts Décoratifs in Thiès; the Maison des Esclaves (Slave House) on Gorée Island

MAP REF K,18

(1.) A pointy-shoed pedestrian hits the pavements of St-Louis
(2.) Children playing on the beach at Yoff
(3.) A young girl of Dakar looks after her baby brother
(4.) A child cavorts in front of a crumbling colonial building in St-Louis

DOUG MCKINLAY

Serbia is rapidly losing its dubious reputation from the 1990s, and is instead becoming renowned for a great nightlife, fabulous eating and a taste for high (and low) culture. The hip and gritty capital, Belgrade, takes the spotlight as a haven for party-lovers, with Novi Sad's Exit and the raucous Guča festivals as the musical highlights on Europe's party calendar. Ottoman atmosphere is dished up in the southern region of Sandžak, while monasteries and peaceful vineyards stretch across Fruška Gora in the north. The southern province of Kosovo declared independence in early 2008.

BEST TIME TO VISIT

July to September

ESSENTIAL EXPERIENCES

» Dancing under the stars in Novi Sad's baroque citadel during Exit music festival

» Braving the potent *šljivovica* while brass bands blare at the rural 'n' wild Guča festival

» Exploring the placid monasteries and Austro-Hungarian architecture of Fruška Gora

» Swimming at Ada Ciganlija, and frolicking with the Belgraders on the banks of the Danube

GETTING UNDER THE SKIN

» **Read** Tim Judah's *The Serbs: History, Myth and the Destruction of Yugoslavia*, a comprehensive account of Serbia's part in Yugoslavia's demise. To understand the region's complexities, read Ivo Andric's *Bridge on the Drina.*

» **Listen** to *Dragačevci*, brass band tradition that mixes Roma, Turkish and Balkan styles; Belgrade's electro-fusion band *Darkwood Dub*

2.

3.

4.

» **Watch** Srdjan Dragojevic's *Rane (Wounds)* – a gritty, humorous depiction of Belgrade in the 1990s; Emir Kusturica's *Underground* – a whirlwind vision of life in communist Yugoslavia

» **Eat** *Ćevapi* (little meat rolls); *pljeskavica* (spicy, thin burger); *ražnjiçi* (shish kebab–style meat)

» **Drink** *rakija*, the local grape firewater; the ubiquitous *šljivovica*, a strong plum brandy

IN A WORD

» *Nema problema* (no problem)

TRADEMARKS

» Crazy brass bands; old accordions; mullets and tracksuits; the Danube; nationalist fervour; pavement cafés

SURPRISES

» Wonderful mountains and National Parks; good skiing; great food; excellent nightlife

MAP REF G,22

(1.) A lady in red ascends a graffiti-covered stairwell in Belgrade
(2.) City-dwellers emerge onto Belgrade's neon-lit streets at night
(3.) Workers take a well-earned break from building at Trg Republike, Belgrade
(4.) The beautiful town square of Novi Sad
(5.) An ancient cemetery lies in front of the Church of St Peter, Novi Pazar
(6.) Pester power prevails at a popcorn stand in Kalemegdan Park, Belgrade

1.

2.

3.

RALPH HOPKINS

Among the 115 coral islands that make up the Seychelles are some of the most idyllic island getaways in the Indian Ocean, or indeed the world. Here you will find the luxuriant, tropical paradise that appears in countless advertisements and glossy travel brochures. But however seductive the images, they simply can't compete with the real-life dazzling beaches and crystal-clear waters of Praslin and La Digue, or the cathedral-like palm forests of the Vallée de Mai. There are more shades of blue and green in the Seychelles than it is possible to imagine.

BEST TIME TO VISIT
March to May and September to November

ESSENTIAL EXPERIENCES
» Lazing on some of the most beautiful beaches on the planet
» Exploring the secluded islands for sensational snorkelling, diving and marine life
» Meandering through the wild and wonderful Valleé de Mai
» Relaxing on La Digue – renowned for its laid-back ambience, idyllic beaches and friendly folk
» Visiting Aldabra, one of the world's largest coral atolls and the original habitat of the giant land tortoise
» Hunting for hidden pirate treasure on the eerie and mystical large granite island of Silhouette

GETTING UNDER THE SKIN
» **Read** *Aldabra Alone* by Tony Beamish, which looks at life among the giant tortoises during an expedition to the Aldabra group
» **Listen** to Creole pop and folk musician Patrick Victor
» **Watch** Jacques Cousteau's documentary *The Silent World*, much of which was shot on Assumption Island

RALPH HOPKINS

» **Eat** *carri coco* (a mild meat or fish curry with coconut cream) and *nouga* (a sweet, sticky coconut pudding) for dessert

» **Drink** the local lager, Seybrew, or try a fresh fruit juice

IN A WORD

» *Bonzour. Comman sava?* ('Good morning. How are you?' in the local language)

TRADEMARKS

» Palm-fringed beaches; land tortoises; coral atolls; upmarket resorts; diving enthusiasts

SURPRISES

» Giant tortoises are endemic to only two regions in the world: Seychelles and the Galápagos Islands; the famously erotic nut of the *coco de mer* palm grows only on the female tree and can weigh up to 20kg

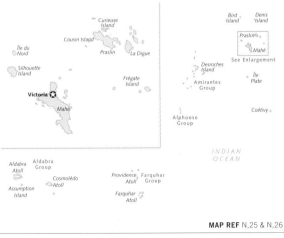

MAP REF N,25 & N,26

(**1.**) A young girl takes a break from shopping
(**2.**) The Taj Denis Island Resort chef proudly holds up a whopper of a red snapper
(**3.**) A liner cruises under a pearly sky off Aldabra Atoll
(**4.**) Unusual granite formations on Anse Source D'Argent beach, La Digue Island

705

1.

VANESSA WRUBLE

ERIC WHEATER

Despite its rich diamond mines, Sierra Leone's development has been challenged by political instability since independence in 1961. Throughout the 1990s it was gripped by a savage civil war between the government and Revolutionary United Front. Freetown, pumped full of international aid, has a happy-go-lucky and vibrant atmosphere and Freetown Peninsula has some of West Africa's most magical beaches. In the interior are lush landscapes, jungle, and reserves abundant with wildlife.

BEST TIME TO VISIT

» November to April, but in the future when stability is restored

ESSENTIAL EXPERIENCES

» Splashing and partying at the stunning beaches – brilliant white sand backed by thick jungle
» Admiring spectacular views from Mt Bintumani, West Africa's highest point
» Reflecting on history at Freetown's famous 500-year-old cotton tree, under which slaves were sold until 1787
» Diving and snorkelling in the crystal waters near Banana Islands
» Spotting elephants, pygmy hippos and rare bongo antelopes at Outamba-Kilimi National Park
» Being charmed by Sierra Leone's wonderfully friendly people

GETTING UNDER THE SKIN

» **Read** *Blood Diamonds: Tracing the Deadly Path of the World's Most Precious Stones* by Greg Campbell
» **Listen** to *A Chapter of Roots* by Sierra Leonean singer/songwriter Freddy Shabaka, or the Brooders playing a jammin' mix of roots, rock and reggae
» **Watch** the disturbing and moving documentary, *Cry Freetown*, filmed by local cameraman Sorius Samura after the battle of 1999

VANESSA WRUBLE

VANESSA WRUBLE

4.

5.

6.

- » **Eat** groundnut stew (meat and ground-peanut stew); pepper soup; steamed yam; and roasted corn
- » **Drink** light and fruity *poyo* (palm wine) and local Star beer

IN A WORD

- » Which way to the beach?

TRADEMARKS

- » Gem smugglers; hot and humid equatorial weather; diamond mines; colourful markets; a country with indomitable spirit recovering from civil war; chaotic traffic jams; beach, beach and more beach; rare wildlife; okra-based meals

SURPRISES

- » At a Sierra Leone market you can buy anything, from enormous saucepans to always-handy monkey skulls

MAP REF L,18

(1.) A young photographer against the red backdrop of his streetside studio in Bo
(2.) Traditional circle huts in a village near the northern town of Binkolo
(3.) A young girl from Masonga
(4.) Fetching water from the well in Koidu
(5.) Men fix their boat on the banks of the prosaically named River No 2
(6.) A group of traditional musicians and dancers perform at festivities in Freetown

GLENN BEANLAND

Many people dismiss the island-city of Singapore as the McDonald's of Southeast Asia – blandly efficient and safe, boringly unadventurous and overwhelmingly corporate. It's true that Singapore has traded in its steamy rickshaw image for towers of concrete and glass, but a sultry heart still beats beneath the surface. This is an undeniably Asian city with a unique mix of Chinese, Malay and Indian traditions, where fortune tellers, calligraphers and temple worshippers are still a part of everyday life.

BEST TIME TO VISIT

February to October, during the dry season

ESSENTIAL EXPERIENCES

» Discovering the region's arts and culture at the Asian Civilisations Museum
» Exploring Little India – on Sunday evening it's like the set of a Bollywood musical
» Tucking into a bowl of noodles at a hawker-style food centre
» Watching the fabulously glitzy drag diva cabaret shows at the Boom Boom Room
» Taking in the sky-high views on the cable-car ride to the grand-daddy of amusement parks, Sentosa Island
» Eyeballing beasties at Singapore's excellent zoo, or after dark on the Night Safari

GETTING UNDER THE SKIN

» **Read** *Foreign Bodies* and *Mammon Inc* by Hwee Hwee Tan, two modern morality tales about Singaporean youth. Suchen Christine Lim's *Fistful of Colours* captures the tensions between modern and traditional Singapore.
» **Listen** to Chinese opera, or local bands the Boredphucks and Force Vomit

2.

3.

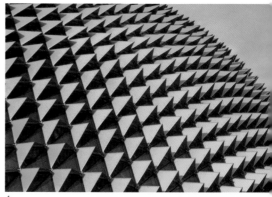

4.

» **Watch** Eric Khoo's *Mee Pok Man*, internationally acclaimed as a truly Singaporean film, and Tay Teck Lock's *Money No Enough*, which was a huge local box-office hit

» **Eat** Hainanese chicken-rice (Singapore's signature dish) or *kaya* toast (toast with egg and coconut topping)

» **Drink** Tiger beer or a healing herbal tea in Chinatown

IN A WORD

» *Kiasu* ('afraid to lose' – Singaporeans are very competitive)

TRADEMARKS

» Orchard Road shops; Changi airport; hawker-stall food; litter-free streets; Singapore Slings at Raffles Hotel; efficient public transport; Lee Kuan Yew; rogue traders; Changi Prison; Hello Kitty

SURPRISES

» It's not all concrete – gardens and greenery are everywhere; many Singaporeans are deeply religious and superstitious

MAP REF M,31

(1.) Behind the scenes at a *wayang kulit* (shadow play) puppet show
(2.) Bright lights and lanterns illuminate North Bridge Road to celebrate Chinese New Year
(3.) Impassive mannequins remain unfazed by hefty pricetags on Orchard Road
(4.) The tactile walls of Esplanade – Theatres on the Bay, dubbed 'the durians' by locals
(5.) Body-piercing made even more painful by dangling pawpaws at the Thaipusam Festival
(6.) A modern Singaporean girl checks her look before taking on the busy streets

713

RICHARD NEBESKY

Slovakia, the Czech Republic's less glamorous partner, emerged dishevelled and sleepy after the 'velvet revolution' of 1989. Although it's now holding its own in a rebuilding Eastern bloc, there's a refreshing absence of Prague-style glitz and glamour. It is a land of real spirit, where folk traditions have survived the domination of foreign rulers and where a plethora of castles and chateaux pay testament to untold wars and civil conflicts. Perhaps the biggest draw for travellers, however, is the friendly, funny and intelligent Slovak people themselves.

BEST TIME TO VISIT

May to June (for sunny weather) – or before Bratislava becomes sold as 'the new Prague'

ESSENTIAL EXPERIENCES

» Roaming the crumbling ruins of Spiš, Slovakia's largest castle
» Discovering Levoca, a medieval walled town and a treasure-chest of Renaissance architecture
» Wandering, wining and dining in the bustling, renovated old town of Bratislava
» Luxuriating in the spa at Bardejovské Kúpele after exploring the *skansen* (open-air museum) in the spa's foothills
» Exploring the caves of Slovak Karst
» Following the crowd to Bojnice, the most visited chateau in Slovakia

GETTING UNDER THE SKIN

» **Read** the brilliant village tales of Bozena Slancikova and the poetry of Ivan Krasko
» **Listen** to Dezider Kardoš's second symphony, *Hero's Ballad*, and Jana Kirschner

2.

3.

4.

» **Watch** the seminal vampire chiller *Nosferatu*, set in spooky Orava Castle
» **Eat** *bryndzové halušky* (small potato dumplings, similar to Italian gnocchi, topped with sheep's cheese and a sprinkling of fried bacon bits) and cakes that would be three times the price in a Viennese cake shop
» **Drink** homemade *slivovice* (plum brandy) and Zlatý Bažant (Golden Pheasant beer) made in Hurbanovo

IN A WORD
» *Ahoj* (hello)

TRADEMARKS
» The poor sister of the Czech Republic; Stalinist architecture; high-rise apartment blocks; farmers; villages; mountains

SURPRISES
» The largest meteor ever to hit Europe landed near the East Slovakian town of Zboj in 1866, its flight was visible from the High Tatras, over 200km away

MAP REF F,22

(1.) Cheap downhill thrills – skiing in the Low Tatras
(2.) A Slovakian-style boutique hotel – a gypsy caravan rests near Spiš
(3.) Bojnice Castle presides over the fairy-tale township
(4.) Caught wearing the same outfit, Slovak girls dance up a storm
(5.) A façade in Bardejov, a township that time-capsules Gothic and Renaissance styles
(6.) Velvet locomotion – a train speeds towards the High Tatras

1.

It's a tiny place, half the size of Switzerland, and numbers less than two million people, but Slovenia (Slovenija) is blessed with rich resources and natural good looks. Persistently peaceful, Slovenia has been doing just fine since breaking from Yugoslavia, and its many delights belie its small stature: the Venetian harbour towns on the Adriatic coast and the *Sound of Music* scenery of the Julian Alps, the concert halls of Ljubljana and the countless opportunities for adventure in its national parks. And just to place it for you, Slovenia is bordered by Italy, Austria, Hungary, Croatia and the Adriatic Sea.

BEST TIME TO VISIT

May to September for summer sun

ESSENTIAL EXPERIENCES

» White-water rafting on the turquoise rapids of the Soča River
» Daydreaming while boating on the fairy-tale Lake Bled
» Marvelling at the world-renowned Lipizzaner horses strutting their stuff at Lipica
» Attempting to conquer the dramatic Predjama Castle
» Partying Slovenia-style at the Kurentovanje festival in Ptuj

GETTING UNDER THE SKIN

» **Read** *Questions about Slovenia* by Matjaž Chvatal – this explains the differences between Slovenia, Slovakia and Slavonia, describes what *koline* (pig-slaughters) are, and pinpoints the things that make Slovenes laugh. *Slovenia: My Country* by Joco Žnidaršič is a heartfelt paean to the photographer's homeland.
» **Listen** to anything by Vita Mavric – a classic Slovene chanteuse, or *Pulover Ljubezni – Jumper of Love* by Terra Folk, modern Slovene folk music

» **Watch** Maja Weiss' *Varuh Meje*, which follows three women on a break from college as they take a perilous journey down the Kolpa River, crossing national, political and sexual boundaries
» **Eat** *žlikrofi* – ravioli of cheese, bacon and chives; *gibanica* – layered flaky pastry with fruit, nut, cheese and poppy seeds
» **Drink** *žganje* – a strong brandy or *eau de vie* distilled from a variety of fruits. *Zlata Radgonska Penina* is an excellent sparkling wine based on Chardonnay and Beli Pinot.

IN A WORD
» *Dober dan* (good day/hello)

TRADEMARKS
» Fairy-tale castles; virgin forests; cobalt-blue rivers

SURPRISES
» Slovenia is NOT Slovakia; this tiny country has produced several world ski champions; and it has been making high-quality wine since the time of the Romans

MAP REF F,21

(1.) A man steers a boat through the gentle waters of Lake Bled, Gorenjska
(2.) A lantern casts a stark shadow against a bright wall in Maribor
(3.) Ljubljana's Franciscan Church of the Annunciation rises above the Triple Bridge
(4.) Ghostly church spires in the twilight, Ljubljana
(5.) Fierce dancers dressed as mythical figure Kurent, Kurentovanje festival, Ptuj

1.

PETER HENDRIE

Those lured to the Solomon Islands by the promise of extraordinary natural features will not be disappointed. Pristine beaches, dense tropical jungle, coral atolls, lagoons and reefs that see almost no tourists abound in the Solomons. Unfortunately, the deteriorating security situation and rise in political unrest has seen a sharp drop in tourist numbers and the Solomon Islanders face a tough future.

BEST TIME TO VISIT
July to November (the drier season)

ESSENTIAL EXPERIENCES
» Riding a boat across Marovo Lagoon
» Chillin' on Uepi Island for a few days and snorkelling in the lagoon
» Seeing Malaita's lagoons where artificial islands support hundreds of villagers
» Visiting skull caves – macabre and fascinating shrines to ancestor worship
» Watching a shiver of reef-sharks hunting fish in a frenzy of boiling water
» Diving over the WWII wreckage from the famous Battle of Guadalcanal

GETTING UNDER THE SKIN
» **Read** *Ples Bilong Iumi – The Solomon Islands, the Past Four Thousand Years* by Sam Alasia et al. *Lightning Meets the West Wind – The Malaita Massacre* by Keesing & Corris relates the story of a district officer's killing by Kaiwo tribesmen in 1927.
» **Watch** Terrence Malick's *The Thin Red Line*, a grim war film based on James Jones' 1963 novel about the WWII battle for Guadalcanal
» **Eat** crayfish, coconuts and tropical fruits; the islanders were eating sweet potatoes long before it was fashionable
» **Drink** Honiara's own Solbrew beer – 'lets get fresh!'

IN A WORD

» *Apinun!* (good afternoon)

TRADEMARKS

» Spear-fishing from outrigger canoes; deep-sea fishing; snorkelling and scuba diving; fresh fish at Honiara market; tide shifts under stilt-house villages; getting around by boat; incredible friendliness

SURPRISES

» Great T-shirt art, skull caves and ossuaries; blonde-haired Melanesians; the sound of falling coconuts; weird wares in trade stores; night-time coconut-crab spotting; racing flying fish in trade boats; *very* early morning mass; crowds gathering at grass airstrips

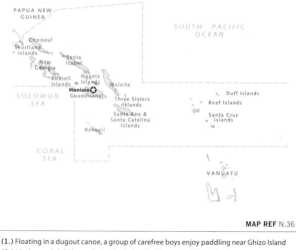

MAP REF N,36

(1.) Floating in a dugout canoe, a group of carefree boys enjoy paddling near Ghizo Island
(2.) Mother and child leave their stilted, thatched home on Ghizo Island
(3.) A Malaita Islander plays a traditional bamboo panpipe
(4.) A spear-fisherman prepares to strike off Sikaiana Atoll

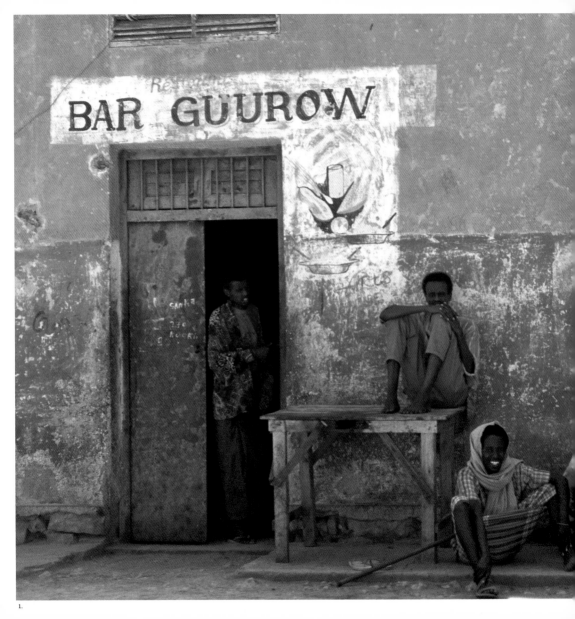

1.

CLAVER CARROLL

Situated in the Horn of Africa, Somalia has had a long history of internal conflict that continues to this day. It also has some of the longest beaches that Africa has to offer, plateaus and mountains, a continuously hot climate and a rich nomadic culture. The friendly people, often dressed in long, flowing robes, are regal and striking. Despite a high rate of criminal activity, there is a growing sense of hope for a more peaceful future.

BEST TIME TO VISIT

From July to August or from January to February for the dry season

ESSENTIAL EXPERIENCES

» Buying henna and frankincense on the streets of Mogadishu
» Observing the rich culture in Hargeisa
» Splashing in the reportedly shark-free waters of Gezira beach
» Visiting the tannery at Brava
» Journeying in the beautiful mountains from Hargeisa to Berbera
» Watching herders bringing their livestock to the watering hole at Liboi
» Staying right on the beach in the old Arab town of Merca
» Wandering amongst the friendly people of Berbera

GETTING UNDER THE SKIN

» **Read** *Aman: The Story of a Somali Girl* by Janice Boddy and Virginia Lee Barnes, a first-person account of life for a Somali girl
» **Listen** to *Waaberi 'New Dawn'* by Maryam Mursal and the Waaberi ensemble – gentle singing and sounds from one of Somalia's greatest treasures
» **Watch** *Black Hawk Down* by Ridley Scott, an account of the flawed events surrounding a US military combat mission in Somalia

» **Eat** a breakfast of fried onions and sheep liver with bread, *baasto* (spaghetti) or rice with sauce, or *soor* (porridge made from sorghum)
» **Drink** fresh mango or papaya juice

IN A WORD
» *Ma nabad baa?* (greeting; literally 'Is it peace?')

TRADEMARKS
» A large rural population; goats and camels; lively teahouses; tasty, traditional food; women with hennaed hands and feet; wide valleys; street traders; chewing khat; tropical fruit; beautiful old Arab towns; colourful robes; magnificent sunsets

SURPRISES
» Camel trading at the livestock market; the satin-draped green Sheik Madar's tomb in Hargeisa; goat herds on the runway at Mogadishu airport

MAP REF L,25

(1.) A group of young men, pleased to see their local watering hole start trading for the day
(2.) An overloaded mule carts brushwood into town
(3.) Rocking out the crustaceans – musical men use large shells as instruments
(4.) Two local boys chat with Australian troops at a newly constructed windmill

A huge variety of landscapes, climates and cultures are crammed into Africa's southern tip – there are 11 official languages, for a start. It's a truly spectacular, friendly and rewarding place for all visitors, offering something for even the most experienced of travellers. You can find yourself sipping a superb wine on majestic Table Mountain, catching a perfect wave on an unspoiled subtropical beach, tracking a lion on an African safari, or exploring for diamonds in the vast flat expanses of Kimberley.

BEST TIME TO VISIT
February and March for warm, sunny weather

ESSENTIAL EXPERIENCES
» The stunning views from the top of Table Mountain, overlooking the 'fairest cape' of them all
» Learning to surf in the warm waters of KwaZulu-Natal
» Touring along the spectacular garden route to go whale-watching in Hermanus
» Visiting the 'Big Hole' diamond mine in Kimberley
» Exploring the spectacular Drakensberg Mountains

GETTING UNDER THE SKIN
» **Read** Nelson Mandela's autobiography, *Long Walk to Freedom*. A truly compelling book, and a compulsory read of the epic life story of the man who won freedom for his people.
» **Listen** to the South African national anthem, a uniting chant containing words from 4 of the 11 official languages
» **Watch** *Cry Freedom*, Richard Attenborough's powerful film detailing the moving story of black activist Steve Biko; or *Egoli*, the most popular soap opera showing a modern, multicultural and vibrant South Africa

2.

3.

4.

» **Eat** a *braai* (barbecue), with local meats including *boerewors* (hearty farmers sausage). *Biltong* (dried and cured meat) is also a favourite throughout the country.

» **Drink** some of the best wines in the world from the Cape Winelands, or the local brew, Castle Lager

IN A WORD

» Howzit…

TRADEMARKS

» Cape Town; rugby Springboks; Biltong; Table Mountain; *braai*; beaches; diamond and gold mines; the township of Soweto; Kruger National Park; Nelson Mandela

SURPRISES

» With such climatic diversity, it's guaranteed to be summer somewhere in South Africa all year round; the Kruger National Park has the greatest diversity of animals in the whole of Africa, and is the size of Wales

MAP REF Q,22

(1.) A family of elephants gathers at a water hole
(2.) A white rhino examines the horizon at Hluhuwe-Umfolozi National Park
(3.) Catching the curl at Noordhoek, one of Cape Town's best surfing beaches
(4.) Sunset over the quiver trees on the plains of South Africa
(5.) A Zulu woman flaunts her traditional earplugs and elaborate headdress
(6.) A Zulu chief proffers a pipe to visitors to his village

1.

Spain has been the home of some of the world's great artists and has museums and galleries to match. In the cities, narrow twisting old streets suddenly open out to views of daring modern architecture, while spit-and-sawdust bars serving wine from the barrel rub shoulders with blaring, glaring discos. There are endless tracts of wild and crinkled sierra to explore, as well as some spectacularly rugged stretches of coast. Culturally, the country is littered with superb old buildings, from Roman aqueducts to Gothic cathedrals, and almost every second village has a medieval castle.

BEST TIME TO VISIT

May, June and September

ESSENTIAL EXPERIENCES

» Exploring the amazing, whimsical architecture of Gaudí's Parc Güell in Barcelona
» Bargain-hunting in El Rastro flea market in Madrid
» Partying through the night during Valencia's Las Fallas
» Pouring over the fascinating Romanesque relics of medieval Aragón at Huesca and San Juan de la Peña
» Visiting the wonderful Museo Guggenheim in Bilbao
» Sipping summertime *cañas* (beers) and enjoying the magnificent views to the Sierra de Guadarrama at Las Vistillas
» Walking the Camino de Santiago to Santiago de Compostela

GETTING UNDER THE SKIN

» **Read** the 17th-century novel *Don Quijote de la Mancha* by Miguel de Cervantes; or *For Whom the Bell Tolls*, a terse tale of civil war by Ernest Hemingway
» **Listen** to Andrés Segovia, who established classical guitar as a genre; or flamenco guitarist Paco de Lucia

2.

3.

4.

» **Watch** Pedro Almodóvar's *Todo Sobre Mi Madre* (All About My Mother), which portrays the lives of an improbable collection of women

» **Eat** paella, or *fabada asturiana* (a heavy white-bean–based stew)

» **Drink** red wine from the Ribera del Duero region

IN A WORD

» *Buenos días* (good day)

TRADEMARKS

» Flamenco; bull-fighting; drunken Brits on Ibiza; Picasso; football; the Spanish Inquisition; the Running of the Bulls festival

SURPRISES

» In Catalunya, devil and dragon figures run through the streets spitting fireworks at crowds during the *correfoc* (fire-running). Leading *gaiteros* (bagpipers) are heroes in Galicia.

MAP REF G,19

(1.) This picturesque clifftop belltower resides at Guadalest in the Alicante region
(2.) Appreciative art-lovers flock to the Museo del Prado
(3.) A detail of Galathea's tower, part of the Teatre-Museu Dalí, Figueres
(4.) Symbolic billboards of bulls guard the hillside
(5.) Joan Miró's vibrant Dona i Ocell sculpture, housed at the Parc Joan Miró in Barcelona
(6.) A flamenco dancer and her guitarist whip up some nightclub action

1.

Marco Polo dubbed Sri Lanka the finest island in the world, and visitors continue to be seduced by the heavy warm air, the endless rich green foliage, the luxuriant swirls of the Sinhalese alphabet, the multicoloured Buddhist flags, and the variety of saris, fruit, jewellery and spices on sale in the markets. Sri Lankan festivals announce themselves with sparkling lights strung over town clock towers and bazaar alleys.

BEST TIME TO VISIT
» December to March (the driest time of the year) – or around the 7th century, to flog your wares to the Arab traders

ESSENTIAL EXPERIENCES
» Sharing the first rays of the morning sun with pilgrims at the summit of Adam's Peak
» Lazing the day away on the beach in sleepy Mirissa
» Wandering through tea plantations in the hills around Nuwara Eliya
» Climbing the spectacular rock fortress of Sigiriya
» Experiencing a puja (offering of prayer) at the Temple of the Tooth in Kandy

GETTING UNDER THE SKIN
» **Read** Michael Ondaatje's *Running in the Family*, a humorous account of returning to Sri Lanka after growing up there in the 1940s and '50s
» **Listen** to www.labaila.com, web-streamed Sri Lankan radio from Los Angeles
» **Watch** Prasanna Vithanage's *Death on a Full Moon Day*, a film about a father who refuses to accept the death of his soldier son
» **Eat** coconut *sambol*, a hot accompaniment to curry made of grated coconut, chilli and spices

» **Drink** *arrack*, the local spirit, which is usually fermented from coconuts or palm trees

IN A WORD

» *Ayubowan* (may you live long)

TRADEMARKS

» Beautiful beaches lined with palm trees; tea plantations; coconuts; friendly, smiling faces; elephants; rice and curry; batik; three-wheelers winding in and out of traffic; good cricketers and enthusiastic supporters; Kandyan dancers

SURPRISES

» Buddhist temples that depict images of Hindu gods; serious traffic accidents are rare despite the apparent lack of road rules

MAP REF L,28

(1.) The stilt-fishermen of Weligama cast their lines into the perilously high tide
(2.) A novice monk pauses from his daily chores for a smiling snap
(3.) Vibrant water lilies in bloom outside Kandy
(4.) In the early-morning light train tracks snake into the capital, Colombo
(5.) Women engage in the back-breaking harvest of tea near Nuwara Eliya

1.

ERIC WHEATER

SUDAN

CAPITAL **KHARTOUM** POPULATION **38,114,160** AREA **2,505,810 SQ KM** OFFICIAL LANGUAGE **ARABIC**

The ancient Egyptians knew Sudan as the Land of Cush – a source of ivory, gold, spices and incense. It was power and the promise of great hidden treasures that made Sudan – the largest country in Africa – the object of invasion and exploration for much of its long and tumultuous history. This land that stretches from the Sahara to the Red Sea to the swamps of the Sudd, is a diverse and fascinating melange. Yet today much of it remains unexplored – one of the last frontiers of travel.

BEST TIME TO VISIT

» November to March (the dry season)

ESSENTIAL EXPERIENCES

» Riding the ferris wheel in Khartoum, from where you can see the two Niles, Blue and White, meet and meld after their lengthy journeys from the African hinterland

» Visiting the pyramids and hieroglyphs of Meroe, all that remains of Africa's southernmost pharaohs

» Losing yourself in the atmospheric souqs (markets) and camel markets of Omdurman

» Getting dizzy from the spinning of the whirling dervishes of Halgt Zikr

» Wandering the melancholy ruins of abandoned Suakin, once a thriving Red Sea port full of coral houses

GETTING UNDER THE SKIN

» **Read** Tayeb Salih's *Season of Migration to the North*, a compelling tale of a Sudanese man torn between the West and his homeland; or *Emma's War* by Deborah Scroggins, the true and moving story of a British aid-worker who married a Sudanese warlord

» **Listen** to Abdel Gadir Salim's *Merdoum Kings* – big band arrangements of Sudanese songs

2.

3.

4.

» **Eat** *fuul* (stewed brown beans), *ta'amiya* (the local equivalent of felafel), and fresh Nile perch

» **Drink** *shai* (tea), always served sweet and sometimes with mint; or coffee scented with cardamom and cinnamon

IN A WORD

» *Tamam* (good, well or right)

TRADEMARKS

» Bedouin in flowing robes; the untouched beauty of the Red Sea coast; Khartoum, a great city at the confluence of rivers amid the desert; Dinka, Nuer and Nuba tribespeople – tall and proud

SURPRISES

» Diverse landscapes and accompanying diverse cultures from the arid north to the lush and mountainous south; overwhelming hospitality – a national point of pride

MAP REF K,23

(1.) With the Kassala Hills as a stunning backdrop, a camel train crosses Eastern Sudan
(2.) Two brilliantly dressed girls pose for a portrait against a mud-brick wall
(3.) A man re-thatches his home in hope of rain in the dry northern region around Kassala
(4.) A boy bears grain around the souq, Kassala
(5.) Madhi's Tomb, re-built in 1947 to commemorate the nation's greatest Muslim leader
(6.) A goat-seller shows off one of the herd's finest at a market in Omdurman, Khartoum

1.

2.

3.

Suriname is a unique cultural enclave whose extraordinary ethnic variety derives from indigenous cultures, British and Dutch colonisation, the early importation of African slaves and, later, workers from China and indentured labourers from India and Indonesia. Paramaribo, the capital, retains some fine Dutch colonial architecture, but the country's greatest attractions are the extraordinary nature parks and reserves, notably the enormous Central Suriname Nature Reserve.

BEST TIME TO VISIT

» Early February to late April or mid-August to early December. Sea turtles come ashore to nest March to July.

ESSENTIAL EXPERIENCES

» Reaching the top of the Voltzberg at sunrise for a breathtaking panorama
» Visiting Galibi Nature Reserve, one of the world's few nesting sites for giant leatherback turtles
» Mooching around Paramaribo (Parbo), a curious hybrid city of northern Europe and tropical America
» Taking a stroll through Brownsberg Nature Park tropical rainforest
» Conquering Mt Kasikasima after days of canoeing, trekking and becoming one with nature
» Venturing into the interior in a small plane to survey the mind-boggling expanse of the unspoiled rainforest

GETTING UNDER THE SKIN

» **Read** *Tales of a Shaman's Apprentice* by Mark Plotkin, or *Suriname: Politics, Economics & Society* by Henk E Chin and Hans Buddingh
» **Listen** to 'the most swinging flautist' Ronald Snijders
» **Watch** the documentary *Cowboys and Indians* about the Guiana Shield, directed and produced by Ray Kril and Terry Roopnaraine

4.

» **Eat** salt fish, *bami goreng* (fried noodles) or *petjil* (a type of green bean)

» **Drink** a *djogo* of Parbo beer; Borgoe and Black Cat, local rums

IN A WORD

» *Tof* ('cool' in Dutch); *vissa* ('party' in Sranang Tongo, the lingua franca)

TRADEMARKS

» The interior; bauxite; the second-worst national football team in South America

SURPRISES

» Under the Treaty of Breda (1667), the Dutch retained Suriname and their colonies on the Guyanese coast in exchange for a tiny island now called Manhattan; Paramaribo's Javanese neighbourhood, Blauwgrond, features people cooking in their kitchens and serving dinner to customers on their patios

MAP REF L,14

(1.) An idyllic spot in Galibi Nature Reserve
(2.) Chewing the fat on the streets of Paramaribo
(3.) A trio of charming white houses
(4.) Like animated branches of this old tree, boys leap after a ball into the river

1.

ARIADNE VAN ZANDBERGEN

The smallest country in the southern hemisphere is also one of the most easy-going – laid-back Swazis are more likely to celebrate for fun than demonstrate for reform. A progressive and hands-on attitude towards wildlife preservation has endowed it with a striking bunch of national parks. Black and white rhinos, elephants, and more recently lions, have been reintroduced into the collection of national parks and game reserves. In the rich and vigorous culture of the Swazi people, significant power is vested in the monarchy. The kingdom is highly conservative, and in many ways illiberal; the popular support it has enjoyed is wavering.

BEST TIME TO VISIT
June to August

ESSENTIAL EXPERIENCES
» Walking around the Malolotja Nature Reserve – one of Africa's most enchanting wilderness areas
» Wildlife-watching in the excellent private Mkhaya Game Reserve
» Bunking down in a beehive hut in Mlilwane Wildlife Sanctuary
» Witnessing the spectacular annual Umhlanga dance and Incwala ceremony in the Ezulwini Valley, Swaziland's royal heartland
» Shooting white-water rapids, including a 10m waterfall, on the Usutu River
» Shopping for Swazi arts and crafts, including stunning tapestries

GETTING UNDER THE SKIN
» **Read** *The Kingdom of Swaziland* by D Hugh Gillis, a history of the kingdom
» **Listen** to gospel singer France Dlamini
» **Watch** anything by film pioneer Hanson Ngwenya

2.

ARIADNE VAN ZANDBERGEN

3.

4.

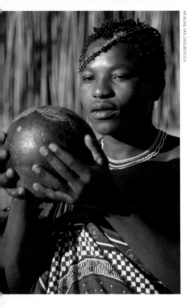

» **Eat** fantastic seafood – seafood kebabs, seafood curry, grilled trout with almonds…
» **Drink** home-produced beer, often made from sorghum or maize

IN A WORD

» *Sawubona* (hello in Swati; literally 'I see you')

TRADEMARKS

» Casinos; sugar cane; speed bumps; lions; rare black rhinos

SURPRISES

» Mkhulumnchanti is the name of the Swazis' deity; respect for both the aged and ancestors plays a large part in the complex structure of traditional Swazi society; most Swazis rely at least partly on traditional medicine: there are two types of practitioners, the *inyanga* (usually a man) and the *sangoma* (usually a woman)

MAP REF P.23

(1.) Women gather for a village meeting amid the austere landscape of Ezulwini Valley
(2.) Nervous young dancers prepare for ceremonial dancing to honour the king in Mbabane
(3.) A Swazi woman sits outside a traditional 'beehive' hut
(4.) Sun-like floral forms and bold colours dominate local art, Ezulwini Valley
(5.) A hungry Swazi boy drinks his morning porridge from a traditional clay bowl
(6.) A *sangoma* (traditional spiritual doctor) fixes his patients with an examining gaze

1.

Sweden is a land of contradictions that make an unexpectedly pleasing whole. Starkly beautiful lake and forest landscapes contrast with stylish, modern cities; the country is as famous for its Viking-era sites as it is known for its cutting-edge technology; even the flat, relatively balmy south contrasts with the mountainous, Arctic north. It's a place where you can get away from it all in quiet forests or be right in the thick of things in busy towns.

BEST TIME TO VISIT
» Late May to late July for sunshine; December to March for skiing

ESSENTIAL EXPERIENCES
» Drifting around Stockholm and its archipelago by boat
» Skiing Dalarna's slopes or watching Vasaloppet, the world's biggest cross-country skiing race
» Ambling around the historic town of Lund
» Taking advantage of *allemansrätten* (public right to the countryside) and hiking Sweden's superb forest
» Exploring the ruins of Visby's chuches
» Touring the glassworks of Glasriket (the Kingdom of Crystal) in Kalmar Län

GETTING UNDER THE SKIN
» **Read** Charlotte Rosen Svensson's *Culture shock! Sweden: A Guide to Customs and Etiquette*, for a guide to Swedish cultural behaviour
» **Listen** to ABBA, the Hives, Tobias Froberg, the Cardigans and José González
» **Watch** anything by Ingmar Bergman, or *Mitt Liv Som Hund* (My Life as a Dog)
» **Eat** a lot of fish and the ubiquitous potato – try *sill och nypotatis* (pickled herring and new potatoes), *pytt i panna* (fried diced potatoes, sausage and onion served with diced beetroot and a fried

4.

egg), *Janssons frestelse* (baked potato, onion, cream and anchovy dish), and, if you're really brave, *sürströmming* (fermented herring)

» **Drink** *kaffe* (coffee), which the Swedes love and do surprisingly well, but they love their aquavit and their *öl* (beer) even more. Try Absolut vodka, and Spendrups or Pripps beer

IN A WORD

» *Jättebra!* (fantastic!)

TRADEMARKS

» Beautiful blondes of both genders; Saabs and Volvos; cheap but impossible-to-assemble furniture; Vikings; tennis players; meat-balls and schnapps; sexually liberated socialists; Ericsson; skiing

SURPRISES

» Not all Swedes are blonde; Sweden is not completely covered in snow in winter; alcohol can only be bought through the state-run alcohol retailing monopoly, Systembolaget

MAP REF D,21

(1.) Cows kick back in comfort in rural Vejbystrand
(2.) The ornate cast-iron spire of Riddarholmskyrkan church, Stockholm
(3.) Flowers in her hair for Midsummer celebrations in Skepparkroken
(4.) The peak of a farmhouse roof peers over a bright yellow field on the Kulla Peninsula

1.

It's not much of a problem finding scenes of devastating beauty in Switzerland. The clichés are all here: soaring peaks, tumbling waterfalls, sparkling lakes, quaint rural houses and, of course, cows grazing contentedly in their verdant Alpine meadows. Towns and cities offer picture-perfect medieval centres and colourful parades and festivals. Trains wind through the mountains and, to complete this fairy tale, everything runs, well, like clockwork.

BEST TIME TO VISIT

Anytime

ESSENTIAL EXPERIENCES

» Getting in amongst it in the Alps – by train, funicular, cable car or postal bus, or on foot, skis, snowshoes or dog sled
» Relaxing in a centuries-old Roman spa
» Wine tasting inside a glacier atop Klein Matterhorn
» Rising above it in a hot-air balloon
» Following Lord Byron's footsteps through Château Chillon
» Sleeping in the straw of a farmer's empty barn in summer

GETTING UNDER THE SKIN

» **Read** Johanna Spyri's *Heidi* – the classic children's story of an orphan girl living in the Swiss Alps, and Anita Brookner's *Hotel du Lac* – a novel centred on a group of out-of-season hotel guests around Lake Geneva
» **Listen** to Appenzeller Echo – a traditional Swiss group, featuring yodelling and Alphorn, or Yello – groundbreaking '80s electronica
» **Watch** Alain Tanner's *Messidor* – a grim feminist road-movie (think *Thelma & Louise* with Alps); or Krzysztof Kieslowski's *Three Colours: Red* – the story of a relationship between a model and a judge, set in Geneva

2.

3.

4.

5.

» **Eat** *rösti* (fried, shredded potatoes) and chocolate
» **Drink** Rivella (lactose-based soft drink) or absinthe (wormwood grows in the Val de Travers)

IN A WORD

» *Röstigraben* (literally 'rösti trench'); refers to the cultural divide between German- and French-speaking Switzerland

TRADEMARKS

» Clocks; banks; cows; mountains; edelweiss; fondue; blondes; Swiss Army knives; Matterhorn; mercenaries

SURPRISES

» Diverse architecture (La Chaux-de-Fonds is Le Corbusier's home town); Valais cow fights; snow golf

MAP REF F,21

(1.) Youngsters make the most of a wintry day by skating on frozen Lake Zürich
(2.) Birch trees bloom with late-autumn colour in the Graubünden countryside
(3.) Switzerland's most photographed mountain, the Matterhorn, reflected in a tranquil lake
(4.) Half-timbered façades meet the rustic style of Kloster St Georgen in Stein am Rhein
(5.) On the way up – in January Château d'Oex hosts its annual hot-air balloon festival

1.

JOHN ELK III

Syria's location at a geographical crossroads has resulted in a history that is rich and varied. From the ancient cities of Alexander the Great and the Romans, to the castles of the Crusaders and the bustle of modern-day Damascus and Aleppo, Syria is truly unique. Full of hidden treasures and surprisingly easy to get around, Syria is a gem for travellers looking to get off the beaten track and go somewhere on a budget.

BEST TIME TO VISIT

March to May (spring)

ESSENTIAL EXPERIENCES

» Experiencing the sun setting over the ruins of Palmyra, an ancient Roman city in a desert oasis

» Taking in the sweeping views from the impregnable battlements of Crac des Chevaliers

» Haggling for authentic Bedouin jewellery in Aleppo's Ottoman-era souq

» Visiting the early Christian monastery where Simeon the Stylite perched on a pillar for 32 years

» Escaping the bustle of Damascus' streets to the tranquil porticos of the Umayyad Mosque

» Catching a performance at Bosra's superbly preserved Roman theatre

GETTING UNDER THE SKIN

» **Read** Agatha Christie's *Come Tell Me How You Live* – a study of archaeology and life in the desert in the mid-20th century

» **Listen** to Farid al-Atrache – the Arabic Sinatra, a famous crooner of the 1940s and '50s – or George Wasouf, the country's biggest pop export

» **Watch** *Dreams of the City*, an evocative fictional study of Damascus,

2.

3.

4.

and *The Nights of the Jackal*, an engrossing study of the impacts of war and westernisation on a Syrian family

» **Eat** *mahalabiyeh* – a dessert similar to a blancmange, laced with orange-blossom essence, almonds and pistachios

» **Drink** *chai* (tea), served in small glasses and incredibly sweet

IN A WORD

» *Marhaba* (hello)

TRADEMARKS

» Call to prayer; hair-raising taxi rides; men in *galibeyahs*; women in *abayas*; Carlos the Jackal; ancient ruins; posters of the president

SURPRISES

» Syria has the oldest continually occupied cities in the world; families with 10 children or more get free public transport for life; vintage American cars in good condition fill the streets

MAP REF H,24

(1.) Camel guides await visitors to Palmyra, a city dating back to the 2nd century AD
(2.) The old Arab fort of Qala'at ash-Shmemis dominates the surrounding plains
(3.) A local shepherd girl tends her flock near the Phoenician temple of Amrit
(4.) Tea for two brewed fresh and sweet in the Souq al-Hamidiyya, Damascus
(5.) Two smiling friends reunited in the walled city of Tartus
(6.) Reverential worshippers pray at Sayyida Ruqayya Mosque, Damascus

1.

TONY WHEELER

PAUL KENNEDY

Ever since French explorers landed on the island in the 18th century, Tahiti has almost singularly represented the tropical-paradise myth for Europeans. It's French Polynesia's biggest, most famous and historically interesting island, but the glossy pictures in travel agents' windows are almost certainly of other unspoiled French Polynesian islands. People come to French Polynesia to live it up in stylish resorts, scuba dive in lagoons teeming with tropical fish, gorge on the unique mix of French and Polynesian cuisine and, basically, experience a little French chic mixed with South Pacific charm.

BEST TIME TO VISIT

The drier, cooler months from June to October, or in July for the *Heiva i Tahiti* festivities

ESSENTIAL EXPERIENCES

» Approaching the impossibly beautiful, rugged coastline of the Marquesas under sail
» Gazing at the amazing tiki and other archaeological artefacts at Hiva Oa
» Snorkelling the gorgeous lagoon at Bora Bora
» Partying in Pape'ete
» Daydreaming on Mo'orea, an accessible yet still traditional island
» Browsing and bargaining at Marché du Pape'ete on a busy Sunday

GETTING UNDER THE SKIN

» **Read** *The Marriage of Loti*, by Pierre Loti, a romance that reinforced the romantic myth of Tahiti
» **Listen** to *Echo Des Iles Tuamotu Et De Bora Bora*, an authentic slice of Paumotu music by Marie Mariteragi
» **Watch** the 1962 remake of *Mutiny on the Bounty*, starring Marlon Brando as Christian – much of this film was shot in Tahiti

4.

PAUL KENNEDY

» **Eat** from *les roulottes*, the cheap roadside snack bars

» **Drink** a local Maitai, a Polynesian take on the cocktail (there's a hefty wallop of coconut liqueur in every drink)

IN A WORD

» *Aita pe'a pe'a* (no problems)

TRADEMARKS

» Paul Gauguin's depictions of island beauty; green mountains leaping from sapphire lagoons; surfing championships; tiki ornaments hanging over every dashboard; colourful *pareu* (fabric) worn by men and women; lascivious dancing that outraged missionaries

SURPRISES

» Even the 'always-smiling' Tahitians get the 'blues' (a mood they call *fiu*), when they can seem distant or incommunicative

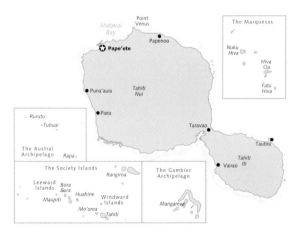

MAP REF 0.4 & 0.5

(**1.**) Displaying traditional *tatau* (tatoo) patterns, which pre-date Christian colonisation
(**2.**) Young dancers preparing to welcome disembarking visitors at Pape'ete harbour
(**3.**) A boogie-boarder rides the wave of popularity making body boarding all the rage
(**4.**) Children dive from a roof into an idyllic lagoon on Tahiti

CAPITAL TAIPEI POPULATION 22,500,000 AREA 35,563 SQ KM OFFICIAL LANGUAGE MANDARIN CHINESE

Taiwan is a modern industrialised megalopolis clinging to the fringes of an ancient culture; a string of teeming cities at the foot of a glorious mountain range. It's traditional noodles from a 7-Eleven, aboriginal tribes in miniskirts and a day of temple rituals followed by waterslide rides. If you step outside chaotic Taipei, you'll discover why Taiwan is known as Ilha Formosa, 'the beautiful island'. Mountain peaks puncture a sea of clouds, slick black volcanic rock wraps the coastlines and waterfalls shroud themselves in mist. Taiwan is a computer-generated Chinese watercolour.

BEST TIME TO VISIT

Autumn weather from September to November is the most pleasant

ESSENTIAL EXPERIENCES

» Discovering the finest collection of Chinese artefacts in the world at Taipei's National Palace Museum

» Indulging in the pleasures of Tainan, famous for fine weather, wonderful food and a multitude of riotously colourful temples

» Being overawed by Toroko Gorge, one of the world's great natural spectacles: sheer limestone and marble cliffs towering over a fast-flowing jade-green river

GETTING UNDER THE SKIN

» **Read** *Harmony in Conflict* by Richard Hartzell, an often-recommended primer for Westerners considering living in Taiwan

» **Listen** to Mando-pop, the soothing, soft-pop schmaltz with Mandarin lyrics, epitomised by singers S.H.E. and Sun Yan Zi

» **Watch** *Betelnut Beauty* by Lin Cheng-sheng – a raw film dealing with the mean streets of Taipei and the city's second-most

771

5.

notorious occupation (the betel nut vendor)

» **Eat** anything you can find on the mainland, as well as Taiwan's own Fujian-Taiwanese cuisine. The adventurous must try 'stinky tofu': ubiquitous in Taiwanese food stalls.

» **Drink** the national brew, Taiwan Beer – it won second prize at the Brewing Industry International Awards 2002

IN A WORD

» *Wei?* (used when answering your mobile phone)

TRADEMARKS

» Sabre-rattling with the PRC; English teaching; Chiang Kai-shek

SURPRISES

» Taiwan's aborigines are only 2 % of the population. They are most numerous in the mountainous regions in the east of the island, where they still preserve vestiges of their original Australoid culture (with many making a living from tourism).

MAP REF I,33

(1.) An elderly man completes a Buddhist ceremony in Tainan
(2.) Young girls about to dance in the Double 10th Day parades, Taipei
(3.) A brief hike from Tienhsiang leads to a stunning pagoda in Taroko Gorge
(4.) Trainspotting in Taipei – the MRT (Mass Rapid Transit) speeds over gridlocked traffic
(5.) A child practises people-watching through a torn mesh screen

ERIC WHEATER

1.

A Persian-speaking outpost in a predominantly Turkic region, Tajikistan is the odd man out in Central Asia. The country is a patchwork of self-contained valleys and regional contrasts, forged together by Soviet nation-building and shared pride in a Persian cultural heritage that is claimed as the oldest and most influential in the Silk Road region. That Tajikistan was the most artificial of the five Soviet-fashioned Central Asian republics is tragically illustrated by the bloody way it fell apart as soon as it was free of Moscow rule.

BEST TIME TO VISIT
April to June or September to November

ESSENTIAL EXPERIENCES
» Driving from Khojand to Dushanbe through a vertical world of towering peaks with high-altitude lakes and deserts
» Hiking in the Fan Mountains
» Visiting the turquoise Iskander-Kul lake
» Being overwhelmed by the Wakhan Corridor, a remote and beautiful valley peppered with forts, Zoroastrian ruins and spectacular views of the Hindu Kush
» Wandering in Istaravshan's backstreets and attending the Tuesday bazaar

GETTING UNDER THE SKIN
» **Read** works by Tajikistan's most popular living writer, Taimur Zulfikarov, or *Kim* by Rudyard Kipling – the story of the Raj during the 19th-century cold war between Russia and Britain in which the region became embroiled
» **Listen** to *Falak*, a popular form of melancholic folk music
» **Watch** *The Beginning and the End* directed by Tajikistan's Sayf Rahim

» **Eat** *Krutob* (a wonderful rural dish of bread, yogurt, onion and coriander in a creamy sauce) or snack on a *nahud sambusa* (chickpea samosa)

» **Drink** the sickly sweet cola and luminous lemonades manufactured in Dushanbe or Khorog

IN A WORD

» *Assalom u aleykum* (peace be with you)

TRADEMARKS

» Mountains; civil war; the Silk Road; Persian culture

SURPRISES

» Sogdian, the lingua franca of the Silk Road widely spoken in the 8th century, is still heard in the mountain villages of the Zeravshan Valley; most Tajiks are Sunni Muslims, but Pamiri Tajiks of the Gorno-Badakhshan region belong to the Ismaili sect of Shia Islam, and therefore have no formal mosques

MAP REF G,27

(1.) A horse struggles in the rush during a game of Buzkashi, over Naurus day celebrations
(2.) A vividly mosaiced theatre in Dushanbe
(3.) Two girls get their kicks on a thrilling swing ride during the Muslim festival of Navrus
(4.) The desolate landscape of Gombezkol Pass leads to northern Gombezkol Valley
(5.) A young hopeful checks out his favourite Bollywood stars

777

1.

STEVE DAVEY

Dig below the heat and dust, and Tanzania will take your breath away – literally, if you dare to climb Kilimanjaro. The Great Rift Valley, Ngorongoro Crater, Lake Victoria, the Serengeti and Zanzibar are legendary. Fearless explorers, proud warriors and mighty beasts have roamed across this unassuming land, but history and politics have not always been kind and successive self-serving rulers have left their mark. Crumbling façades reflect the crumbling economy, and today Tanzania is a fascinating land of eclectic contradictions, remaining faithful to its heritage while bravely struggling to adapt to the present.

BEST TIME TO VISIT

Late June to October – or before 1498, when the first European arrived

ESSENTIAL EXPERIENCES

» Conquering altitude, cold and fatigue on Kilimanjaro
» Rediscovering some of the world's oldest hominid fossils
» Wandering lost in the alleys and mayhem of Zanzibar's Stone Town
» Basking in a superb Serengeti sunset
» Succumbing to the beating drums on a steamy African night
» Forgetting time under the billowing sail of an ancient dhow
» Seeing the mass migration of wildebeest

GETTING UNDER THE SKIN

» **Read** Emily Said-Ruete's *Memoirs of an Arabian Princess* – an autobiographical glimpse into the life of a Zanzibari princess who eloped to Europe
» **Listen** to *Music from Tanzania & Zanzibar, Vol 2* by various artists – a reflection of Zanzibar's Afro-Arab culture

2.

3.

4.

» **Watch** the spectacular IMAX documentary *Kilimanjaro – To the Roof of Africa* directed by David Breashears
» **Eat** pilau (a tasty meat and rice dish full of the Spice Island's aromatic produce) or *ugali* (a bland staple made from maize or cassava flour, eaten with a sauce)
» **Drink** *konyagi* – a potent white-rum–style drink

IN A WORD
» *Hakuna matata* (no worries, not a problem)

TRADEMARKS
» Cunning baboons; mosquito nets; the Big Five; fragrant spices; Arabian palaces; wildlife safaris; endless dusty plains; traditional Maasai; grinning children; white beaches

SURPRISES
» Some local buses don't break down; large bottoms are considered beautiful

MAP REF N,24

(1.) Flamingos are a splash of colour on Lake Magadi
(2.) A black rhinoceros surveys the stark Ngorongoro National Park
(3.) A Barabaig girl wears a goatskin garment distinctive of her tribe
(4.) A game warden protects the diverse wildlife of the Serengeti National Park
(5.) Stocking up on food before a long train journey
(6.) A Maasai woman wears the multicoloured beaded fan neckwear

1.

2.

3.

CHRIS MELLOR

Thailand is the total package: jaw-dropping natural beauty, eye-catching architecture, an intricately woven culture and downright fabulous cuisine. Southeast Asia's most accessible and instantly appealing country gets under your skin. Your taste buds start to crave their daily dose of *phàt thai* noodles, your senses revel in the neon-lit delights of Bangkok, and artfully dodging traffic becomes second nature. Whether you're barefooting it on a budget or going five-star ritzy, dive in!

BEST TIME TO VISIT

Thailand is a year-round destination, but the rainy season falls between June and August

ESSENTIAL EXPERIENCES

» Visiting Thailand's former capital, Ayuthaya, which lives up to its World Heritage–listed status
» Chilling out in delightful Chiang Mai before trekking in the Golden Triangle region
» Dancing under the full moon to thumping electronic beats on Ko Pha-Ngan
» Escaping to Thaleh Ban National Park, satisfying any naturalist
» Exploring all things exotic in Thailand's turquoise waters
» Shopping: anywhere, anytime

GETTING UNDER THE SKIN

» **Read** Chart Kobjitti's *Pan Ma Ba* (Mad Dog & Co) – an account of Thailand's *farang* (foreigner) scene. Stir-fry up a storm with David Thompson's sumptuous *Thai Food*.
» **Listen** to Carabao's *Made in Thailand,* a *pleng pue cheevit* (song for life) classic
» **Watch** the sweet essence of Thai culture in *Fan Chan* (My Girl)

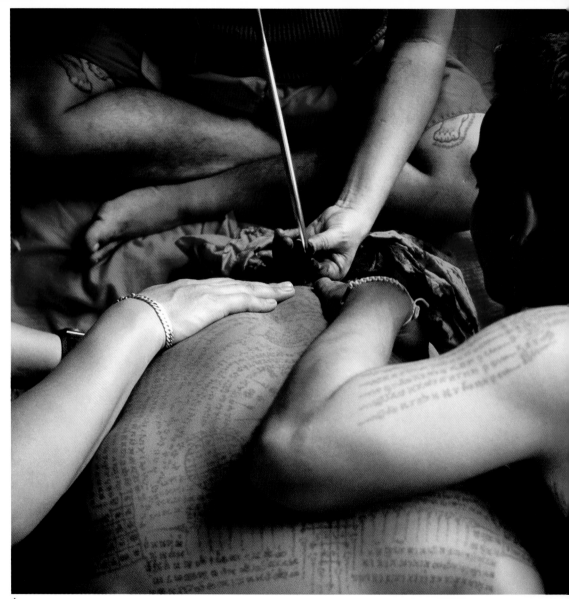

4.

» **Eat** *tôm yam kûng* (spicy prawn and lemongrass soup) or taste sensational *mîang kham* (an appetiser of coconut, ginger, lime, peanuts and dried shrimp)

» **Drink** sugar cane juice or rice whisky

IN A WORD

» *Mai pen rai* (it's all right/never mind)

TRADEMARKS

» Technicolor Thai silk; Bangkok pollution; nomadic hair-braiders; exquisite beaches; noisy *túk túks*; Singha beer; heartwarming hospitality; pampering spas and silky pools

SURPRISES

» In Thai, the word for 'meal', *méu*, is a close homonym with the word for 'hand', and Thais extend a hand towards a bowl of noodles with amazing frequency; every Thai house, office building or rice field has to have a spirit house to go with it – a place for *phrá phum* (earth spirits) native to this site to live in

MAP REF K,30

(1.) A boy flies his kite down the street on the predominantly Muslim island of Ko Panyi

(2.) Young monks begin early morning prayers in Nong Khai

(3.) Heavy trading at the Damnoen Saduak Floating Market, Ratchaburi Province

(4.) A tattooist monk carves emblems of luck and protection into the flesh of another monk

1.

RICHARD I'ANSON

Tibet is a land of stark, arid beauty, where snow-capped mountains guard sacred turquoise lakes, and centuries-old monasteries are pervaded by the smell of yak-butter lamps, the chanting of mantras by monks in saffron robes, and the prostrations of the pious. Throughout the country, faded, wind-torn prayer flags flutter from the roofs of whitewashed brick-and-mud homes. While the Chinese occupation remains an intrinsic and oppressive part of everyday life, the unwavering faith of the Tibetans gives them strength to protect their culture and heritage.

BEST TIME TO VISIT
May, June, September and October

ESSENTIAL EXPERIENCES
» Cleaning away all the sins of your lifetime by walking the circuit of Mt Kailash
» Gazing up at the Potala, an architectural masterpiece and structural centrepiece of Lhasa
» Spending a low-oxygen night at Rongphu Monastery, the world's highest monastery
» Bumping along the Friendship Highway, which, despite its name, is not hospitable or fast
» Witnessing raucous monastic debates – despite occasional looks of terror, the monks generally seem to enjoy them

GETTING UNDER THE SKIN
» **Read** Mary Craig's *Tears of Blood: A Cry for Tibet*, a riveting account of Tibet since the Chinese takeover; or Heinrich Harrer's *Seven Years in Tibet*, an engaging account of Harrer's sojourn in Tibet during the mid-20th century
» **Listen** to *Chö*, by Choying Drolma & Steve Tibbets, a stunning introduction to Tibetan religious music

2.

3.

4.

» **Watch** *Himalaya*, directed by Eric Valli, an epic story of Tibetan herders, with an all-Tibetan cast and spectacular cinematography; *Kundun*, directed by Martin Scorsese, beautifully chronicles the life of His Holiness the Dalai Lama until his exile from Tibet

» **Eat** *tsampa*, a dough of roasted-barley flour and yak butter mixed with water, tea or beer; *momos* are small dumplings filled with meat or vegetables

» **Drink** yak-butter tea – drink it hot, because it's even worse cold

IN A WORD

» *Tashi delek!* (in Tibetan, used as a greeting, literally 'good fortune')

TRADEMARKS

» Pious pilgrims and saffron-clad monks; spiritual home of the Dalai Lama; Chinese occupation; Han immigration; sky burials

SURPRISES

» Tibetans stick their tongues out to show respect; thumbs up is a sign of begging

MAP REF H,29

(1.) The Potala remains Lhasa's architectural highlight
(2.) Street sharks – local hustlers play a mean game of pool on the quiet streets of Lhasa
(3.) A well-dressed monk lights ritual incense in the town centre
(4.) Mass transit for the faithful – a group of monks are taken across Lhasa in a truck
(5.) Keeping the faith – a villager holds up an image of the exiled Dalai Lama
(6.) Girls visiting Sera Monastery

Tiny Togo, a thin sliver of land wedged between Ghana, Burkina Faso and Benin, is blessed with deserted beaches, a fascinating culture and friendly people. Upcountry are beautiful hills and plateaus, while the region around Kpalimé, near the Ghanaian border in the southwest, is particularly scenic and is known for its butterflies. The famous fortress-like mud-brick houses of the Tamberma people can be seen in the Kabyé region, a place that has withstood the onslaught of modernisation.

BEST TIME TO VISIT
Mid-July to mid-September

ESSENTIAL EXPERIENCES
» Hiking the beautiful hill country surrounding Kpalimé, well known for its butterflies
» Gazing at the extraordinary *tata* compounds, built without tools, in the Tamberma Valley
» Browsing through the bewildering collection of traditional medicines and fetishes on offer at the Marché des Fétishes in Lomé
» Discovering the crumbling colonial charm of Aného, the former capital, set on a picturesque lagoon
» Enjoying Lake Togo's water sports, including windsurfing and water-skiing
» Having fun bargaining with Mama Benz, the smart wealthy women traders of Lomé's Grand Marché

GETTING UNDER THE SKIN
» **Read** the autobiography *An African in Greenland* by Tété-Michel Kpomassie, who was raised in a traditional Togolese family
» **Listen** to Bella Bellow for a hybrid of traditional music fused with the contemporary sounds of West Africa, the Caribbean and South America

4.

» **Watch** Togolese director Anne-Laure Folly's *Femmes aux yeux ouverts* (Women with Open Eyes), which explores the problems facing women in West Africa

» **Eat** *koklo mémé* (grilled chicken with chilli sauce) or *abobo* (snails cooked like a brochette)

» **Drink** *tchakpallo* (fermented millet with a frothy head) or palm wine

IN A WORD

» *Un-lah-wah-lay* ('good morning' in Kabyé, one of the major indigenous languages)

TRADEMARKS

» Beaches; clay houses of the Tamberma; voodoo; great food

SURPRISES

» The Ewe consider the birth of twins a great blessing, but the Bassari consider it a grave misfortune; of the Togolese population, 59% are animists

MAP REF L,20

(1.) Wearing their wares on their heads, local women march to market in Vogan
(2.) What are you looking at? The curiosity of a young boy in the village of Klouto
(3.) An elderly Muslim man smiles in silence, Lomé
(4.) Umbrellas sprout amongst a crowd gathering for a festival in Sansanne Mango

1.

Since Captain Cook first landed here, Tonga has charmed travellers with its wild feasts, friendly people and awe-inspiring natural beauty. The modern world has crept into the kingdom with LA gangster wear more common than traditional waist mats on the streets of Tongatapu. Still, the islands remain visually spectacular with rainforest crater lakes and volcanic peaks. After riots in November 2006, which damaged much of the capital, Tonga has worked hard to get travellers to return to the islands.

BEST TIME TO VISIT

May to October is the best time to visit as summer (November to April) is the hurricane season

ESSENTIAL EXPERIENCES

» Gorging yourself at a Tongan feast, especially on Tongatapu and Vava'u
» Dodging the spray at the Mapu'a 'a Vaca Blowholes, Tongatapu – a 5km stretch of geyser-like blowholes with fountains of sea-water up to 30m high
» Spotting breeding humpback whales who call the ocean around Ha'apai and Vava'u their boudoir
» Climbing eerie, uninhabited (but still active) volcanoes that rise out of the ocean on Tofua and Kao

GETTING UNDER THE SKIN

» **Read** *Tonga Islands: William Mariner's Account* by Dr John Martin, published in 1817 and still one of the best books on pre-Christian Tonga
» **Listen** to *Dance Music of Tonga – Malie! Beautiful*, a sampler of various artists of traditional music
» **Watch** *The Other Side of Heaven*, a Disney story of a 1950s missionary preaching in Tonga

PETER HENDRIE

TONGA

CAPITAL NUKU'ALOFA POPULATION 108,141 AREA 748 SQ KM OFFICIAL LANGUAGES TONGAN, ENGLISH

» **Eat** a genuine Tongan feast served in an *umu* (underground oven), taro and sweet potato, roasted suckling pig, chicken, corned beef, fish and shellfish

» **Drink** kava (Piper methysticum), the all-purpose forget-your-cares-and-stare-at-the-sunset tipple that's widely available

IN A WORD

» *Malo e lelei* (hello)

TRADEMARKS

» Friendly indigenous people; migrating humpback whales; kings and queens ruling an island paradise; tapa adorning the walls of every building; packed churches on Sunday

SURPRISES

» Despite the sackloads of tourist dollars whale-watching brings in, Tonga has a prominent whaling lobby that believes hunting the sea mammals is a long-honoured part of Tongan culture. The king, however, outlawed whaling in the 1970s.

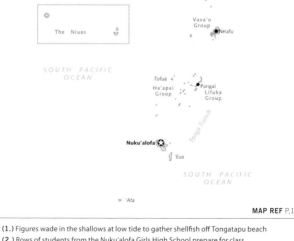

MAP REF P,1

(1.) Figures wade in the shallows at low tide to gather shellfish off Tongatapu beach
(2.) Rows of students from the Nuku'alofa Girls High School prepare for class
(3.) Two shy girls peek around a tree on Lifuka Island
(4.) A woman paints a traditional tapa on Tongatapu Island

1.

Tobago and its twin island, Trinidad, are the Caribbean's odd couple. 'Little sister' Tobago is relaxed, slow-paced and largely undeveloped. Trinidad is a densely populated, thriving island with a cosmopolitan population and strong regional influence. It's famous for hosting the loudest and wildest Carnival in the Caribbean, whereas on Tobago the reefs are calm and protected and the beaches are good.

BEST TIME TO VISIT

Mid-April to mid-December, or go two days before Ash Wednesday for Carnival

ESSENTIAL EXPERIENCES

» Partying the night away at Port-of-Spain's spectacular Carnival festival
» Swimming and snorkelling at palm-fringed, white-sand beaches on Tobago
» Spotting birds at Trinidad's Caroni Swamp
» Diving at Buccoo Reef off Tobago
» Exploring Trinidad's wild and rural east coast – a mix of lonely beaches, rough Atlantic waters and mangrove swamps

GETTING UNDER THE SKIN

» **Read** *A House for Mr Biswas* by VS Naipaul – dig deep into the country's multi-ethnic culture by reading this vivid portrait of life as an East Indian in Trinidad
» **Listen** to long-time king of calypso, The Mighty Sparrow
» **Watch** *Hosay Trinidad*, about the observance of Shia Muharram rites on Trinidad
» **Eat** *callaloo* (a thick green soup made with okra, onions, spices and the leaves of the dasheen plant), or head to a beachside eatery for a shark & bake (a sandwich made with a slab of fresh shark and deep-fried bread)

ANDREW MARSHALL

TOM BOYDEN

4.

5.

6.

» **Drink** ginger beer or sorrel (made from the blossoms of a type of hibiscus and mixed with cinnamon and other spices)

IN A WORD

» Carnival!

TRADEMARKS

» Twin islands; cricket matches; white-sand beaches and crystal-clear water; birdwatching enthusiasts

SURPRISES

» The oddest attraction in Trinidad is Pitch Lake, a continually replenishing lake of tar, which is the world's single largest supply of natural bitumen; Tobago has only 4% of the country's population

MAP REF K,13

(1.) Bundles of beans all strung up for sale on the streets of Port-of-Spain
(2.) The creation of a new steel pan (drum) in the Blue Diamonds panyards, Port-of-Spain
(3.) A green honeycreeper sings on a branch in the rainforest
(4.) Wooden fishing boats vacation among palm trees in Tobago
(5.) A cheerful street vendor pushes past offering chilled delights
(6.) Dancers strut their stuff in a swirl of colour and movement at Trinidad Carnival

Tunisia is an ancient land moving to a modern beat where millennia of history come alive: in the astonishing Roman colosseum at El-Jem; in the ancient cities of Dougga and Sufetula; in charming medinas surrounded by crenellated walls; and in the fairy-tale architecture of the Berbers. In Kairouan, the fourth-holiest city in Islam, foundation myths and towering mosques connect Tunisia to the heart of Islam. Infinitely hospitable, Tunisians have their feet firmly planted in tradition while rushing head-long into the modern world.

BEST TIME TO VISIT
Mid-March to mid-May

ESSENTIAL EXPERIENCES
» Exploring the archaeological site of Carthage, rich in mythology and sea views
» Navigating the mirages of the Chott el-Jerid causeway
» Bathing in the hot springs of Ksar Ghilane as the sun sets over the dunes
» Spelunking the underground Roman villas of Bulla Regia
» Haggling with Kairouan's skilled carpet salesmen

GETTING UNDER THE SKIN
» **Read** Mustapha Tlili's novel *Lion Mountain*, or *Pillar of Salt* by Albert Memmi
» **Listen** to the El-Azifet Ensemble, fine purveyors of *malouf,* a traditional Arab-style music form
» **Watch** the backgrounds of international films such as *Star Wars* and *The English Patient* (both set in Tunisia)
» **Eat** couscous with vegetables and harissa (a red chilli concoction made from dried red peppers, garlic, salt and caraway seeds)

CRAIG PERSHOUSE

2.

3.

4.

» **Drink** coffee, mint tea or, for an alcoholic tipple, try *boukha* – a gloopily sweet, aromatic spirit made from distilled figs, served at room temperature or chilled, and often mixed with Coke

IN A WORD

» *Bari kelorfik* (thank you – a blessing)

TRADEMARKS

» Carthage; the Land of the Lotus Eaters; the Sahara desert; pristine white-sand beaches

SURPRISES

» Tunisian proverbs include: 'Good reputation is better than wealth' and 'High prices attract buyers'; Tunisia was the first predominantly Islamic independent state to ban polygamy (1956); Ibadism as practised in Jerba is one of Islam's smallest sects, found elsewhere only in the M'Zab Valley in central Algeria and in Oman

MAP REF H,21

(1.) Death-defying horsemen display astonishing skill and courage at a festival in Douz
(2.) A hive of stairways and storage holes make up the *ghor*fas (grain storerooms) of Medenine
(3.) Knocking on heaven's door – the superb craftsmanship of a door in Tunis
(4.) Boats bob at their moorings at the harbour of Bizerte
(5.) Suspicious eyes peer from the distinctive blue headscarf of a Tuareg man in Douz
(6.) A girl smiles generously from beneath her flashy garments at the Sahara Festival, Kebili

Turkey is Asia's foothold in Europe, a melting pot of cultures and a bridge between continents. It is modernising rapidly – sometimes so fast you'd swear you can actually see it happening in front of your eyes. It's secular and Western-oriented and boasts a vigorous free-enterprise economy. The cuisine is to die for, the coastline a dream, and many Turkish cities are dotted with spectacular old mosques and castles. To top it off, Turkey remains the Mediterranean coast's bargain-basement travel destination.

BEST TIME TO VISIT
Spring (late April to May) and autumn (late September to October)

ESSENTIAL EXPERIENCES
» Haggling your way to a bargain in the Grand Bazaar in İstanbul
» Floating over the spectacular landscape of Cappadocia in a hot-air balloon
» Taking in the history of the eerily peaceful Gallipoli Peninsula
» Exploring Ephesus, the best-preserved ancient city in the eastern Mediterranean
» Letting yourself be scrubbed clean and invigoratingly massaged in a *hammam* (steam bath)
» Wandering the cobbled lanes of the beautifully preserved Ottoman city of Safranbolu
» Sailing the blue waters of Turkey's southwest coast in a traditional *gûlet* (wooden yacht)

GETTING UNDER THE SKIN
» **Read** Irfan Orga's *Portrait of a Turkish Family*, which tells of a family struggling to survive the collapse of the Ottoman Empire and the birth of the Turkish Republic

» **Listen** to Tarkan, the undoubted king of Turkish pop for much of the 1990s and early 2000s

» **Watch** Peter Weir's *Gallipoli* – an Australian's account of the Anzac experience during the Gallipoli campaign of WWI

» **Eat** Turkish bread – no Turkish meal would be complete without it. *Pide* or flat bread is the most famous variety.

» **Drink** *raki* – a clear, strong spirit made of grapes infused with aniseed

IN A WORD

» *Merhaba!* (hello!)

TRADEMARKS

» Turkish delight; the place where East meets West and commercialism meets tradition; kebabs in a dozen different varieties; whirling dervishes; delicious Turkish bread; *raki*; carpet sellers; tea offered in a shop immediately prior to a sales pitch

SURPRISES

» Turkey has its very own pop industry and it's hugely successful; it gets so cold in some parts of the country that you can ski in winter

MAP REF G,23

(1.) A man sits amid the stately Rüstem Paşa Camii Mosque in İstanbul
(2.) Rose tea for the taking at a street market in Bosphorus
(3.) The dreamlike volcanic rock formations of the Göreme Open-Air Museum
(4.) A wizened beadseller and his daughter, İstanbul
(5.) Men relax on heated marble in the Galatasaray Baths, İstanbul

1.

JOHN NOBLE

JANE SWEENEY

MARTIN MOOS

The most curious of the Central Asian republics, Turkmenistan resembles a Gulf state without the money. Most of the country consists of an inhospitable lunar-like desert called the Karakum, which conceals unexploited oil and gas deposits. Turkmenistan is sparsely populated and its people, the Turkmen, are only a generation or two removed from being nomads. Turkmenistan is as much a culture as a country, since the Turkmen have never formed a real nation and have allowed their cities to become predominantly populated by other peoples.

BEST TIME TO VISIT

Spring (April to June) and autumn (September to November)

ESSENTIAL EXPERIENCES

» Staying in a traditional yurt in the village of Darvaza and going to the nearby Darvaza Gas Craters – an enormous inferno like a volcano at ground level

» Visiting the vast Karakum desert

» Enjoying some of the best scenery in the country at the Kugitang Nature Reserve – complete with dinosaur footprints and caves

» Taking a tour around the historic city of Merv – a huge site of vast complexity, which juxtaposes time scales and cultures

» Avoiding the thousand-plus indigenous species of insects, spiders, reptiles and rodents at the Repetek Desert Reserve

GETTING UNDER THE SKIN

» **Read** poems by Magtymguly Feraghy. *Sacred Horses: The Life of a Turkmen Cowboy* by Jonathon Maslow is a good, if abrasive, account of this naturalist's visits to the Karakum desert.

» **Listen** to *City of Love* by Ashkhabad, a five-piece ensemble

» **Eat** *diorama* (bread with pieces of boiled meat and onions), shashlyk (lamb kebab) and *plov* (rice, meat and carrots)

» **Drink** *chal* (fermented camel's milk) for breakfast in the desert, and tea, which you'll be offered at every juncture throughout the day

IN A WORD

» *Salam aleykum* ('peace be with you' in Turkmen)

TRADEMARKS

» 'Bukhara' rugs; camels; deserts; hardcore trekkers; yurts; the personality cult of late leader President Turkmenbashi (Turkmenbashi translates as 'leader of the Turkmen')

SURPRISES

» Merv is Turkmenistan's only Unesco World Heritage site; the Karakum desert has recorded air temperatures of over 50°C (122°F), and the surface of the sand sizzling at a soul-scorching 70° (158°F)

MAP REF G,26

(1.) Her hand heavy with jewellery, a bride in a dazzling veil covers her face
(2.) The mausoleum of Sultan Tekesh stands beside the Kutlug Timur tower, Konye-Urgench
(3.) A high-rise housing façade displays traditional architectural styles
(4.) A man and his mule prepare to cross the road (with mausoleum in the background)
(5.) Cheerful children gather outside a yurt in the wide open spaces around Darvaza

TURKS & CAICOS ISLANDS

Oddly named, a little misshapen and often covered with cactus and thorny acacia trees, this archipelago is the often-neglected stepsister to the neighbouring Bahamas. But this is the Caribbean, so this British crown colony still has many charms. Several islands are fringed with exquisite beaches and for divers there are several hundred miles of coral reef that make it a hot destination.

BEST TIME TO VISIT

Mid-April and July (avoid sweltering August to November)

ESSENTIAL EXPERIENCES

» Bonefishing at Sapodilla Bay or on South Caicos
» Dodging the resort crowds at Providenciales and lazing on incredible beaches
» Picnicking with iguanas and flamingos on West Caicos
» Hiking the well-designed paths of Middle Caicos
» Exploring the underground caverns of Conch Bar Caves National Park, complete with lagoons, stalactites and stalagmites, colonies of bats and petroglyphs by Lucayan Indians
» Wall diving or windsurfing off Grand Turk
» Shaking up the Salt Cay, a fascinating blend of historic buildings and amazing beaches

GETTING UNDER THE SKIN

» **Read** J Dennis Harris's *A Summer on the Borders of the Caribbean Sea*, a classic 19th-century travelogue. *Water and Light* by Stephen Harrigan is a splendid memoir by a Texan about diving off Grand Turk.
» **Watch** *Extraordinary People*, a TV documentary about a world-record attempt at free diving off Turks and Caicos
» **Eat** conch, which can often be better than in the Bahamas
» **Drink** rum – in a cocktail, shot or slipper

IN A WORD

» TIs or Belongers (the islanders' names for themselves)

TRADEMARKS

» Shady expats living off 'investments' or involved in 'exports'; lavish resorts; cocktails sipped in casinos; excellent birdwatching; terrific year-round tans; excellent diving

SURPRISES

» Technically, the Turks and Caicos (like the Bahamas) lie outside the Caribbean Sea; they are washed on the north and east by the Atlantic and on the south and west by the Gulf Stream

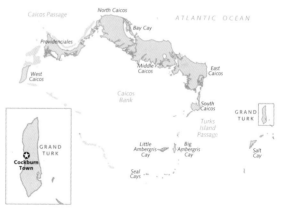

MAP REF J,12

(1.) A green turtle explores Turks and Caicos' watery underworld
(2.) Cycling past sky-blue houses in Columbus Plaza, Cockburn Town
(3.) Men relaxing in the afternoon sun outside a house in Salt Cay
(4.) A prickly close-up of a Turks Head Cactus

1.

If you want to disappear for a while, head to Tuvalu. On average, it receives fewer than a thousand tourists a year, so you're likely to have the beach to yourself. The tiny group of islands, however, are seriously endangered by rising sea levels caused by global warming, so you'd better be quick.

BEST TIME TO VISIT

May to September, when the easterly trade winds spring up

ESSENTIAL EXPERIENCES

» Joining in a game of soccer on Funafuti's pitch, which doubles as the airport landing strip
» Snorkelling in Funafuti Marine Conservation Area to gawp at tropical fish and cavorting turtles
» Wreck-spotting on Nanumea Atoll for remains of several US landing craft and a B-24 bomber
» Worshipping at the only remaining pre-Christian altar buried in the bush of Nukulaelae Atoll
» Training in the Tuvaluan martial art of wielding the *katipopuki* (hardwood spear) on the island of Niutao

GETTING UNDER THE SKIN

» **Read** *The People's Lawyer* by Philip Ells – an amusing and insightful account of a young Voluntary Service Overseas lawyer's spell in Tuvalu, or *The Happy Isles of Oceania – Paddling the Pacific*, by the notorious Paul Theroux
» **Listen** to *Tuvalu: A Polynesian Atoll Society* – a good sampler with chants from several different islands
» **Watch** *Pacific Women in Transition,* featuring a Tuvaluan woman adapting to the changes of modern life on the island
» **Eat** your fill of seafood at a *fatele,* the mega-feast that always involves dancing
» **Drink** toddy, the fermented coconut sap that delivers an alcoholic kick

PETER BENNETTS

IN A WORD

» *Se fakamasakoga fua o fai se fatele* (any excuse for a *fatele*)

TRADEMARKS

» Fine-sand beaches on clear seas; indigenous dot.tv millionaires; first-rate snorkelling around atolls; isolation; rising sea levels

SURPRISES

» Although Tuvalu literally means 'cluster of eight', there are nine islands in the nation; the highest point on Tuvalu is just 4.6m (15ft) above sea level

Nanumea Atoll

Niutao

Nanumaga

SOUTH PACIFIC OCEAN

Nui Atoll

Vaitupu

Nukufetau Atoll

Funafuti Atoll
Funafuti

SOUTH PACIFIC OCEAN

Nukulaelae Atoll

Niulakita

MAP REF N,39

(1.) A proctective grandmother looks after the children in an airy house on Funafuti Atoll
(2.) Traditional Tuvaluan handicrafts, Funafuti
(3.) The impossibly idyllic Tepuka Islet set like an emerald between sea and sky
(4.) Harvesting toddy from a dwarf coconut palm on Vaitupu Island
(5.) The late Honourable Ionatana Ionatana, former prime minister of Tuvalu, with his son

Uganda's remarkable transformation from tragic, war-torn nation into one of the fastest growing economies in Africa is drawing increasing numbers of resourceful travellers to the erstwhile 'Pearl of Africa'. Downtown Kampala has a contagious buzz and bustle, but can be quickly left behind for beautiful mountains, trekking opportunities and some of the few remaining communities of endangered mountain gorillas.

BEST TIME TO VIST

January to February (when the weather is hot but generally dry) or June to September (the dry season)

ESSENTIAL EXPERIENCES

» Staying up to enjoy Kampala's vibrant, fast-changing nightlife
» Trekking Mt Elgon's cliffs, caves, gorges and waterfalls without another soul in sight
» Spectacular wildlife-watching at Murchison Falls
» Penetrating the Impenetrable Forest (Bwindi National Park), home to half of the world's surviving mountain gorillas
» Roaming through the mystical snow-capped Rwenzori 'Mountains of the Moon'

GETTING UNDER THE SKIN

» **Read** *The Last King of Scotland* by Giles Foden, a page-turner chronicling the experience of Idi Amin's personal doctor-turned-confidant; or *The Abyssinian Chronicles* by Ugandan Moses Isegawa, a coming of age story of a boy and of a country during Idi Amin's dark reign and its chaotic aftermath
» **Listen** to *Ngoma: Music from Uganda,* a cultural preservation project by the multi-ethnic Ndere Troupe
» **Watch** *Raid on Entebbe*, the Charles Bronson classic about the Israeli rescue mission of a Palestinian-terrorist hijacked plane

ANDREW VAN SMEERDIJK

UGANDA

CAPITAL KAMPALA POPULATION 25,632,794 AREA 236,040 SQ KM OFFICIAL LANGUAGE ENGLISH

823

2.

3.

4.

» **Eat** *matoke* (mashed plantains) and groundnut sauce – food for fuel rather than food for fun

» **Drink** Bell Beer, infamous for its 'Great night, good morning!' ad-jingle, or try *waragi*, the local grain-distilled spirit (watch out for the kick!)

IN A WORD

» *Mazungu!* (white man!)

TRADEMARKS

» The tragedy of HIV/AIDS (one in five of the population is afflicted); a freshwater lake bigger than Ireland (Lake Victoria)

SURPRISES

» In spite of all they've endured, Ugandans are some of the most open and outgoing people in the world; proof that the number of people, pieces of baggage and chickens that can be squeezed into a *matatu* (minibus taxi) is far more than the 14 it was built for

MAP REF M,23

(1.) A group of exhausted porters at Mt Elgon not far from the Uganda–Kenya border
(2.) Mountaineers brave the icy wasteland of Stanley Plateau, Rwenzori National Park
(3.) Two smiling siblings out for a stroll
(4.) A herd of Uganda Kob, a rare breed of impala, gathers beneath the Rwenzori Mountains
(5.) With an innocent expression, a boy leans against a broad tree trunk
(6.) A boy in simple pink robes leans against a wall in the capital, Kampala

1.

JONATHAN SMITH

A country whose national anthem is 'Ukraine Has Not Yet Died' may not seem the most uplifting destination, but Ukraine rewards travellers with hospitable people, magnificent architecture and miles of gently rolling steppes. Nearly every city and town has a centuries-old cathedral, exquisite mosaics, and many have open-air museums of folk architecture. The last few years have been quite dramatic for Ukraine. The euphoria following the Orange Revolution (where people united in a peaceful protest against the election outcome) soon abated as inflation, slow economic growth and disputes with Russia over gas brought the people back down to earth.

BEST TIME TO VISIT

April to June

ESSENTIAL EXPERIENCES

» Seeing mummified monks in Kyiv's Caves Monastery
» Being dazzled by St Sophia Cathedral's sparkling domes
» Discovering Europe's only virgin beech forest at the Carpathian Biosphere Reserve
» Living like royalty in Lviv's early-20th-century hotels; don't miss a night at the opera
» Cutting a hole in the icy crust of the Black Sea in winter and catching your dinner

GETTING UNDER THE SKIN

» **Read** *Everything is Illuminated* by Jonathan Safran Foer, which recounts the US author's journey to find his family in the Ukraine
» **Listen** to the all-male Ukrainian Bandura Chorus, a professional orchestra who perform traditional choral and *bandura* music

UKRAINE

CAPITAL **KYIV** POPULATION **48,055,439** AREA **603,700 SQ KM** OFFICIAL LANGUAGE **UKRAINIAN**

2.

» **Watch** *Zemlia* (the Earth), a 1930 classic by Alexander Dovzhenko
» **Eat** bowls of soul-warming borsch, or the addictive *varenyky* (boiled dumplings served with cheese or meat)
» **Drink** vodka, the word comes from *voda* (water), and translates as 'a wee drop'

IN A WORD

» *Dobry den'* (hello, literally 'good day')

TRADEMARKS

» Cossacks; *pysanky* – the beautifully painted eggs; proud singers; lax anti-money laundering laws; ice fishing; pristine, isolated ski slopes; Chernobyl; Soviet architecture; borsch; Orthodox churches; rugged mountains; icy temperatures; big, furry hats

SURPRISES

» Nearly 3000 rivers flow through Ukraine; chicken Kiev was invented in New York

MAP REF F,23

(1.) Who says size matters? Traditional *matryoshka* dolls for sale in Odesa
(2.) Dormition Cathedral's onion domes glint impressively in the sun
(3.) Ornate, blue interior of the sculpted corbelled dome of the Boyim Chapel
(4.) Women dressed elegantly in traditional costume at The Khan's Palace in Bakhchysaray

1.

CHRIS MELLOR

Once an obscure corner of Arabia, the United Arab Emirates has transformed itself into an Arabian success story through a mix of oil profits, stability and a sharp eye for business. Visitors are attracted by beaches, deserts, oases, camel racing, Bedouin markets and the legendary duty-free shopping of Dubai – all packed into a relatively small area. Dubai is the Singapore of the Gulf, with bustling harbours, gigantic shopping malls and bold architecture. Each of the seven emirates bears a unique character.

BEST TIME TO VISIT

November to April

ESSENTIAL EXPERIENCES

» Mixing with mobile-phone–toting sheikhs, pint-sized jockeys and punters of every nationality at Nad al-Sheba racecourse in Dubai
» Exploring the cool date-palm plantations in the heart of Al-Ain
» Crossing dunes, riding camels and flying falcons at the luxurious Al-Maha Desert Resort
» Looking at the enormous waves of peach-tinged dunes at Liwa oasis
» Watching a bullfight on a Friday afternoon in Fujairah
» Spending a luxurious night at the architecturally renowned Burj al-Arab hotel, built in the shape of an Arabian dhow sail

GETTING UNDER THE SKIN

» **Read** *Arabic Short Stories*, translated by Denys Johnson-Davies, an excellent primer with tales from all over the Middle East
» **Listen** to a performer playing an ancient oud, a carefully constructed wooden instrument, which sounds similar to a mandolin
» **Watch** contemporary Arab cinema at the Dubai International Film Festival

2.

3.

4.

» **Eat** *fuul* (paste made from fava beans, garlic and lemon) and felafel (deep fried balls of chickpea paste served in a piece of Arabic flat bread)

» **Drink** copious quantities of strong *shai* (tea) with *na'ana* (mint), and dark muddy *qahwa* (coffee)

IN A WORD

» *Marhaba* (hi)

TRADEMARKS

» Wadi-bashing (four-wheel driving around UAE's oases); a duty-free shopper's paradise; the Trucial states; carpet merchants and Bedouin souvenirs; Pakistani, Indian and Iranian expats; international racehorses

SURPRISES

» The United Arab Emirates is the cheapest place outside Iran to buy Iranian caviar

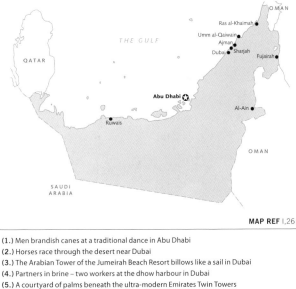

MAP REF I,26

(1.) Men brandish canes at a traditional dance in Abu Dhabi
(2.) Horses race through the desert near Dubai
(3.) The Arabian Tower of the Jumeirah Beach Resort billows like a sail in Dubai
(4.) Partners in brine – two workers at the dhow harbour in Dubai
(5.) A courtyard of palms beneath the ultra-modern Emirates Twin Towers
(6.) A dazzling veil on the face of a Muslim woman

1.

ROB BLAKERS

A gloriously defiant work in progress, the US isn't a place that you come to and stand still. America has always been about the journey, and calls out for exploration and discovery. Some head to the cities, from the grand canyons of Manhattan to Los Angeles' sun-drenched boulevards, while others choose solitary contemplation of the country's awesome natural beauty. Some come to revel in America's kitsch and pop culture. But if the journey across America never fails to be rewarding, it's because of her people, whose energy and restless reinvention never cease.

BEST TIME TO VISIT
March to July

ESSENTIAL EXPERIENCES
- » California beaches at sunset
- » Camping the Great American West
- » Pounding the pavement in always-bustling New York City
- » Crunching New England leaves in autumn
- » Cruising the neon madness of the Las Vegas strip
- » Enjoying live music festivals in Austin, Memphis or Seattle

GETTING UNDER THE SKIN
- » **Read** Jack Kerouac's *On the Road*, the classic Beat Generation paean to restless roadtripping; Don DeLillo's *Underworld*, an ambitious novel of the Cold War and American culture
- » **Listen** to Johnny Cash's *American Recordings*, fusing blues, rock, country, and punk; *James Brown's Greatest Hits* – you'll feel good with the Godfather of Soul
- » **Watch** Francis Ford Coppola's *The Godfather* trilogy, a saga of family, capitalism and violence; or Sam Mendes' *American Beauty*,

2.

3.

4.

which captures the zeitgeist of 21st-century angst

» **Eat** steak and potatoes – T-bones or rib eyes; vegetarian burritos; pizza – deep dish or thin crust

» **Drink** Craft microbrews (pale ales, porters, pilsners and stouts), or double decaf non fat soy lattes with a shot of vanilla, to boot

IN A WORD

» Thank you, come again

TRADEMARKS

» Burgers, fries and Budweiser; red-white-and-blue T-shirts, sneaker and jeans; yuppies in SUVs, cowboys in pickups; loud people; gun-lovers; dangerous cities

SURPRISES

» New Yorkers love to help strangers; half the citizens don't vote; in American football, you're *supposed* to use your hands

MAP REF G,9

(1.) Startlingly pristine wilderness of Yosemite Valley, California
(2.) Sun Studios, the world's most famous recording studio where Elvis cut his first record
(3.) Subway entrance, 51st and Lexington Avenue
(4.) A blues-hound jamming at the annual June Chicago Blues Festival
(5.) The renowned circular Guggenheim Museum, designed by Frank Lloyd Wright
(6.) All-American boys sipping on iconic soft drink outside Dick's Drive Inn

1.

2.

3.

Uruguay may be pint-sized, but it's certainly big-hearted when it comes to attractions. It contains Montevideo, one of South America's most interesting and diverse capitals; charming colonial towns such as Colonia; the hilly interior (true gaucho country); and a cluster of internationally renowned beach resorts.

BEST TIME TO VISIT

December and January, when the beautiful people flock to the beach and are a sight to behold

ESSENTIAL EXPERIENCES

- » Exploring Montevideo's architectural diversity and multi-cultural character
- » Scaling the battlements of the beautiful city of Colonia
- » Sailing, fishing and basking at Punta del Este on the Uruguayan Riviera
- » Heading to the quiet interior towns of Tacuarembo, the country's monument to the gaucho

GETTING UNDER THE SKIN

- » **Read** Juan Carlos Onetti's *Tierra de Nadie* (No Man's Land)
- » **Listen** to *La Cumparsita*, one of the best-known tangos, composed by Uruguayan Gerardo Matos Rodriguez. Uruguayans consider Montevideo to be as much the birthplace of the tango as Buenos Aires.
- » **Eat** beef. Uruguayans are cow crazy, consuming more beef per capita than almost any other nation. The *parrillada* (beef platter) is standard fare.
- » **Drink** maté, the brew of choice. Uruguay also produces some excellent wines.

IN A WORD

- » *Tranquilo* (chilled out)

4.

TRADEMARKS

» The Switzerland of South America; a buffer between rival regional powers; a haven for other country's unwanted rogues; sizzling sun-worshipping humans at Punta del Este

SURPRISES

» Many shops and museums in Uruguay close when it rains; Montevideo's late summer carnival includes dance troupes beating out spirited African-influenced rhythms on large drums

MAP REF Q,14

(1.) Mirror-image living in Plaza Cagancha, Montevideo
(2.) Maté gourds among the hordes at Feria de Tristan Narvaja market, Montevideo
(3.) Is turquoise the new black? Punta del Este
(4.) In safe hands – 'El Mano' beach sculpture on Playa Brava, Punta del Este

1.

Sharing borders with all five of the other 'Stans, Uzbekistan lies at the heart of Central Asia. It was here that the ancient Silk Road traversed, that Alexander the Great conquered, that the great warlord Timur was born. Such a crossroads could not be anything but a cultural melting pot, and so it is that Uzbekistan boasts a proud artistic history and diverse culture, exemplified by the most magnificent cities in Central Asia.

BEST TIME TO VISIT

April to June (spring) – or 1370 when Timur reigned and the arts blossomed

ESSENTIAL EXPERIENCES

» Visiting the Registan, a fantasy of majolica and azure, in Samarkand
» Strolling through Khiva's perfectly preserved historic heart
» Taking a break in the shaded plaza of Labi-Hauz in Bukhara
» Stopping off in laid-back Shakrisabz, the hometown of Timur
» Photographing the melancholy fishing boats left high and dry by the shrinking Aral Sea at Moynaq
» Crossing the Ferghana Valley, a fertile corridor beneath the majestic Pamir mountains

GETTING UNDER THE SKIN

» **Read** Tom Bissell's *Chasing the Sea* – a journey to the Aral Sea and an insightful look at modern Uzbekistan, or *The Ruba'iyat of Omar Khayyam* – penned by a one-time resident of Samarkand
» **Listen** to *The Best of Yulduz*, by Yulduz Usmanova, Uzbek diva
» **Eat** shashlyk, barbecued mutton at its smoky best, and *pulao*, seasoned rice with mutton
» **Drink** black tea by the bottomless glass cup, and *ayran* – a salty yet thirst-quenching yogurt drink

UZBEKISTAN

CAPITAL TASHKENT POPULATION 25,981,647 AREA 447,400 SQ KM OFFICIAL LANGUAGE UZBEK

CHRISTINE OSBORNE

IN A WORD

» *Yöl bolsin* (may your travels be problem free)

TRADEMARKS

» White-bearded old men whiling away the day in the shade; cotton fields, bustling covered bazaars; unnecessary red tape; lofty domes and minarets; nomad-designed carpets; the marriage of apricot brickwork and azure tile work

SURPRISES

» Sunset in oasis towns; fresh watermelons on hot summer afternoons; spontaneous welcomes; invitations into family homes

MARTIN MOOS

MAP REF G,27

(1.) Like a giant sand castle, the walls of Khiva's old town rise out of the surrounding terrain
(2.) A local sits casually on a prayer rug at the Shahr-I-Zindakh mausoleum
(3.) Flower power in Bukhara where a local displays fine hand-embroidered silk
(4.) Ancient domes and stern walls watch over a row of giggling children in Khiva

1.

The ni-Vanuatu, as the peoples of Vanuatu are known today, are among the most welcoming people in the Pacific – despite colonialists who came for sandalwood and left with slaves. Vanuatu's fractured terrain of volcanoes and lush forests has produced a kaleidoscope of cultures and more than 100 indigenous languages. After last century's coups, Vanuatu now enjoys its independence. An increasing number of travellers contribute to the local economy by exploring the jungle above and below the water.

BEST TIME TO VISIT

April to October (the southern winter)

ESSENTIAL EXPERIENCES

» Witnessing a very old extreme sport as the islanders on Pentecost land-dive to guarantee their yam harvest
» Keeping your eyes peeled for dugongs while snorkelling
» Watching from the haven of a beach hut on Vila as hundreds of fruit bats cloud the metallic sky before a wild storm
» Finding the beach you've always dreamt of, only to discover there's an even better one on the next island (there are 83 islands)
» Joining in local volleyball games with the owners of the biggest smiles and blondest afros in the world (ni-Vanuatu children)

GETTING UNDER THE SKIN

» **Read** Jeremy McClancy's *To Kill a Bird with Two Stones* – an exceptional history of Vanuatu right up to its independence in 1980
» **Listen** to the *tamtam* or slit-drums –still crafted from traditional designs, they were once used to send coded messages between communities
» **Watch** *Finding Nemo* – to see the film that has had a devastating effect on Vanuatu's sea life due to the demand for pet fish

847

4.

5.

6.

» **Eat** a banana as long as your arm, baked sweet in the oven and sliced like a steak on your plate
» **Drink** *aelan bia* (island beer), otherwise known as kava, the becalming brew which most island men imbibe at the end of a long day. Women can drink it at Port Vila's kava bars.

IN A WORD
» *Tank yu tumas* ('thank you very much' in Bislama)

TRADEMARKS
» Jungle; local dances; atmospheric drumming; wild boars; carvings and spears; aqua water; snorkelling and scuba diving; big bananas; 'cooking pots'; wild cyclones

SURPRISES
» This laid-back place is uptight about magic; the cuisine is well regarded throughout the Pacific

Torres
Islands
Vanua Lava
Island
Gaua   The Banks
Island   Islands

Espiritu
Santo   Ambae Maewo
Island   Island Island
Luganville
Malo Island   Pentecost
Island

Malekula   Ambrym
Island   Island
Epi
Island

Coral   SOUTH
Sea   Port Vila Efate   PACIFIC
Island   OCEAN

Erromango
Island

Tanna
Island

Aneityum
Island

MAP REF 0,37

(1.) Father and son get together at a ritual pig-killing site on Malekula Island
(2.) Kava tied up in woven baskets for sale at a city market on Efate Island
(3.) Designer denim influences the traditional *namba* (penis wrapper) on Tanna Island
(4.) Chief Willie Orion of Salap poses beneath a land-dive tower on Pentecost, Penama
(5.) Villagers on Tanna Island, dressed to impress
(6.) Dense vapour billows from the smoking vents of Mt Marum volcano on Ambrym Island

1.

The world's smallest state, and home to the world's largest church, the Vatican City is the central authority of the Catholic Church, a fact which pervades every street, every brick and every grain of sand encompassed within its borders. Whether you want to check out the sheer volume of art treasures stored here, get in to see the Holy Father himself or simply take advantage of the tranquil atmosphere, the Holy See inspires awe in its visitors for good reason.

BEST TIME TO VISIT

April to June (the low season) – or Wednesday, when the Pope meets his flock

ESSENTIAL EXPERIENCES

» Craning your neck memorising every detail of Michelangelo's Sistine Chapel ceiling
» Attending an audience with the Holy Father
» Climbing to the roof of St Peter's Basilica on a clear day (warning: it's a fair hike!)
» Tracking down the works of Bernini, Michelangelo and Raphael (for starters) in the Vatican palaces and museums
» Rubbing the worn-down foot of St Peter for luck
» Perusing the Vatican Library with more than one million bound volumes

GETTING UNDER THE SKIN

» **Read** Robert J Hutchinson's *When in Rome: A Journal of Life in Vatican City* for an in-depth look at Vatican nitty gritty; Thomas J Reese's *Inside the Vatican: The Politics and Organization of the Catholic Church. The Sistine Chapel* by Fabrizio Mancinelli charts the history of the chapel's great artworks.
» **Watch** *Inside the Vatican*, a National Geographic documentary giving detailed insight into the Holy See; *The Scarlet and the Black,*

2.

3.

4.

5.

starring Gregory Peck, is based on a true story of Vatican official, Father O'Flaherty, who hid POWs during WWII

» **Eat** pasta favourites *carbonara* (egg yolk, cheese and bacon) and *alla matriciana* (tomato, bacon and chilli)

» **Drink** local wines such as Frascati and Torre Ercolana

IN A WORD

» *Silenzio* (silence)

TRADEMARKS

» Arias and sermons; Catholic masses; your favourite saint produced as a tacky plastic souvenir; priceless artwork everywhere you look

SURPRISES

» It's easy to lose a whole day to the museums; the Swiss Guard *do* take their job (and their uniforms) very seriously – you will be turned away if you are not dressed modestly

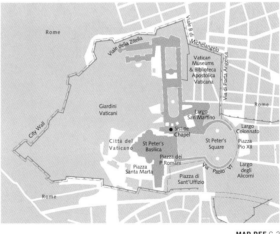

MAP REF G,21

(1.) Visitors reel downwards in the ornate spiral staircase in the Vatican Museum
(2.) A Pope's-eye view of the Holy Roman Empire from the heights of the Basilica
(3.) The Swiss Guards in ultra-sleek battle gear patrol a strategic corner of the city state
(4.) Papal pigeons peck at the cobbles of Piazza San Pietro
(5.) Shafts of heavenly light filter into the cavernous interior of St Peter's Basilica

1.

Venezuela has epic proportions: it has South America's largest lake and third-longest river, the highest waterfall in the world, and longest of all snakes. It also has jaguars, armadillos and some of the most spectacular landscapes on earth. There are the snow-capped peaks of the Andes in the west; steamy Amazonian jungles in the south; the hauntingly beautiful Gran Sabana plateau, with its strange flat-topped mountains, in the east; and miles of white-sand beaches fringed with coconut palms on the Caribbean coast.

BEST TIME TO VISIT

Year-round

ESSENTIAL EXPERIENCES

» Hiking to the top of Roraima, a giant flat-topped mountain with moonscape scenery of blackened rock, pink-sand beaches and bewildering plant life
» Driving from Maracay to Puerto Colombia – a short but dramatic ride through fabulous scenery
» The world's highest waterfall, Salto Angel (Angel Falls), sheltered in a spectacular natural setting
» Los Roques, the beautiful archipelago of coral islands and reefs
» Wildlife-watching in Los Llanos – an immense savanna filled with birdlife, caimans, capybaras, piranhas and anacondas

GETTING UNDER THE SKIN

» **Read** *Doña Bárbara* by renowned author Rómulo Gallegos
» **Listen** to the undisputed king of Venezuelan salsa, Oscar D'León, or get funky with the irreverent Amigos Invisibles
» **Watch** Elia Schneider's *Huelepega* (literally meaning glue-sniffer),

5.

which pulls no punches in its portrayal of the lives of Caracas street children

» **Eat** *empanadas* (deep-fried cornmeal turnovers filled with ground meat, cheese, beans or baby shark) or *pabellón criollo* (shredded beef, rice, black beans, cheese and fried plantain)

» **Drink** *guarapita* (a cocktail made from sugar cane spirit and fresh juices) or the smooth, dark rum Ron Añejo Aniversario Pampero

IN A WORD

» *Rumba!* (party!)

TRADEMARKS

» Oil; beauty queens; *tepuis* (table mountains); Simón Bolívar; salsa; Caracas nightlife; Angel Falls

SURPRISES

» Whole bottles of spirits are commonly poured over coffins and coffin-bearers at Venezuelan funerals; almost half of the total population of Venezuela is younger than 19 years

MAP REF L,13

(1.) The thunderous beauty of Hacha Falls, deep in the jungle of Canaima National Park
(2.) An ocelot at the Hato El Frio, a large cattle ranch in Los Llanos
(3.) Dancing demons about to perform at Festival de Los Diablos Danzantes
(4.) No neighbours to bother you in this traditional thatched stilt house on Orinoco Delta
(5.) A renovator's delight: façade paintwork completed, walls and roof still to come

1.

Vietnam's landscape is sublime: the Red River Delta in the north, the Mekong Delta in the south, and a seemingly endless patchwork of brilliant-green rice paddies in between. Long, sandy beaches grace the coast, while inland there are soaring mountains and lush forests. A country of traditional charm and rare beauty, Vietnam is rapidly opening up to the outside world. Despite the pressures of rapid development, this dignified country has preserved its rich civilisation and highly cultured society.

BEST TIME TO VISIT
» Anytime – the dry season is December to April in the south, and May to October on the central coast

ESSENTIAL EXPERIENCES
» Riding a motorcycle through North Vietnam's stunning high country and staying at remote hill-tribe villages
» Climbing to the top of little-visited Dao Titop (Titop Island) for sweeping views of magnificent Halong Bay
» Selecting an outfit from the latest fashion catalogues and having it tailor-made in the delightful city of Hoi An
» Floating your boat along the Mekong
» Grabbing a bicycle and taking the ride of your life through the streets of Ho Chi Minh City

GETTING UNDER THE SKIN
» **Read** *The Sorrow of War* by Vietnamese writer Bao Ninh. Flogged on every street corner of Hanoi and Ho Chi Minh City, this cynical take on the Vietnam War won a literature prize in Vietnam in 1993.
» **Listen** to US-based Khanh Ly, a contemporary pop music icon
» **Watch** *The Quiet American*, based on Graham Greene's 1954 novel and starring Michael Caine. It's set during the last days of French colonial rule and filmed throughout Vietnam.

VIETNAM

CAPITAL **HANOI** POPULATION **81,624,716** AREA **329,560 SQ KM** OFFICIAL LANGUAGE **VIETNAMESE**

2.

3.

4.

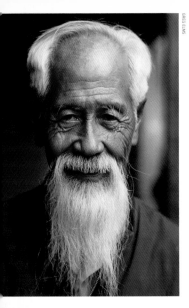

» **Eat** the staple *pho* (noodle soup) or *banh cuon*, delicious steamed rice rolls with minced pork and Vietnam's famous *nouc mam* (fish sauce)

» **Drink** the cheap and widely available *bia hoi* (draught beer). *Ca phe* (coffee) served with condensed milk is deliciously sweet.

IN A WORD

» *Dep qua, phai khong!* (beautiful, isn't it!)

TRADEMARKS

» Postcard sellers; scooter gridlocks; drivers constantly honking their horns; silk shops; tailors; conical hats; rice paddies; limestone cliffs and BOBs (boys on buffalos)

SURPRISES

» North Vietnam gets very cold in December and January! The latest fashions have replaced the elegant *ao dai* (traditional dress).

MAP REF J,31

(1.) Basket boats bob on the waters of Nha Trang
(2.) A passing cyclist blends into the background of decaying buildings in Hoi An
(3.) Sheets of sweet candy hang out to dry in Ho Chi Minh City
(4.) Looking cool on a scooter in the chaotic traffic of Ho Chi Minh City
(5.) An elderly man smiles knowingly in Hoi An
(6.) A weaver of webs repairs his nets in Quang Nam province

1.

2.

3.

Once the hideaway of buccaneers and brigands, the Virgin Islands now attract a more salubrious yachting crew drawn by steady trade winds, well-protected anchorages and a year-round balmy climate. Tourist development has been limited by enlightened environmental policy, and the islands have thoroughly different characters: while the US Virgin Islands have pursued the tourist dollar, the British Virgin Islands are keen to stay limey and out of the limelight.

BEST TIME TO VISIT

The peak tourist season is December to May, but there's dreamy weather year-round

ESSENTIAL EXPERIENCES

» Hiking between beaches and great snorkelling sites in the Virgin Islands National Park
» Mountain biking around Water Island
» Exploring the days when 'King Cane' ruled and sugar was the major crop at the Estate Whim Plantation Museum, St Croix
» Retreating to the mountains and beaches of Jost Van Dyke
» Getting historical with the largest concentration of colonial buildings in Charlotte Amalie
» Chartering a yacht to Anegada – the 'Mysterious Virgin' with a tranquil coral beachfront

GETTING UNDER THE SKIN

» **Read** Martha Gellhorn's *Travels with Myself and Another*, observing the changes between her two visits in 1942 and 1977 to the British Virgin Islands
» **Listen** to a popular *quelbe* (a blend of local folk music) group, such as Stanley and the Ten Sleepless Knights

» **Watch** *The Big Blue* set in Hurricane Hole on St John, US Virgin Islands, with lots of atmospheric diving and rich images
» **Eat** a hearty bowl of *callaloo*, the legendary thick green soup
» **Drink** a well-brewed bush tea, believed to cure all your ills

IN A WORD

» If yo put yo ear a mango root, yo will hear de crab cough (roughly translated: patience is a virtue)

TRADEMARKS

» Wide unspoiled beaches; crystal-clear waters; flamingos aplenty; reggae rhythms; swimming in rum; yachties enjoying an on-deck G&T

SURPRISES

» The Virgins aren't owned by Richard Branson – they're both an unincorporated territory of the USA and crown colony of the United Kingdom

MAP REF J,13

(1.) Radiant as the sun, the magnificent headdress of a Carnival dancer flashes in the street
(2.) The shopkeeper of a boutique in Tortola leans out of a colourful doorway
(3.) Massive boulders form sanctuaries for bathers outside the town of The Baths
(4.) Loud drums and louder shirts at the Carnival parade on St Thomas

1.

EDIN CLARKE

With its craggy sculptures of stone and ruined castles rising above the valley mist, otherworldly Wales is where legend and history merge. Armed with hiking boots or a bicycle, lose yourself in the region's timeless scenery laced with waterfalls, lakes and jagged peaks, winding roads and sandy beaches. Tour villages with tongue-twisting names and gorge yourself on medieval castles and ruins, or join the adrenaline junkies searching for the ultimate thrill.

BEST TIME TO VISIT

Spring (March to May), when the countryside is in bloom and Wales is at its driest

ESSENTIAL EXPERIENCES

» Touring the castles at Conway, Caernarfon and Harlech
» Riding the electric cliff railway at Aberystwyth
» Visiting the Victorian seaside resort of Llandudno
» Hiking, biking, mountaineering, canoeing or caving the Brecon Beacons National Park
» Trawling through Hay-on-Wye's record-breaking number of secondhand bookshops
» Strolling along the cliff-top Pembrokeshire Coast Path from St David's to Cardigan past tiny fishing villages, secluded coves and plenty of pubs

GETTING UNDER THE SKIN

» **Read** Dannie Abse's *Journals from the Antheap*, a humorous account of his trips through Wales, or the novel *Work, Sex and Rugby* by Lewis Davies
» **Listen** to *Generation Terrorists* by the Manic Street Preachers, or some lighter music by a Welsh male choir

- **Watch** *Solomon and Gaenor* or *Hedd Wynn*
- **Eat** *bara brith* (rich, fruited tea-loaf) or *cawl* (a meat-and-vegetable broth)
- **Drink** Brains (beer)

IN A WORD

- *Iechyd da!* (good health!)

TRADEMARKS

- The coal mines of the South; male voice choirs; castles everywhere; the Welsh dragon; leeks; Tom Jones

SURPRISES

- The most famous of Welsh gastronomic specialities is laver bread, which is not bread at all but boiled seaweed mixed with oatmeal and served with bacon and toast for breakfast; vegetarians should head straight for the famous Glamorgan sausage, made from a heady mixture of cheese, breadcrumbs, herbs and chopped leek

MAP REF E,19

(1.) Twilight, when the sky is dusky blue and lights twinkle over Tenby Harbour
(2.) An ancient stone bridge in the typical Welsh countryside around Llanwrst, Conway
(3.) A pleasant stroll through the light-filled Castle Arcade, Cardiff
(4.) An architectural meeting of old and new in Swansea, Wales

1.

Known to the Romans as Arabia Felix – Happy Arabia – Yemen remains the most untouched corner of Arabia. It's here amid the bustling souqs, the desert oases, the traditional Arabian architecture and the remote mountain eyries that you feel you might meet Aladdin or Sinbad or any of the characters of *The Thousand and One Nights*. And while much of Yemen seems untouched by modern events, life continues to unfurl for the locals at a languid pace.

BEST TIME TO VISIT

October to March (when the daytime temperatures are pleasant and the rain infrequent) – or 950 BC when the Queen of Sheba still held sway

ESSENTIAL EXPERIENCES

» Exploring the old quarter of San'a – one of the largest preserved medinas in the Arab world, and home to mud-brick skyscrapers built to a 1000-year-old design
» Visiting Al-Makha, the first important coffee port on the Red Sea
» Meandering through the covered alleys of the Friday market at Bayt al-Faqih
» Marvelling at the ruins of the great dam at Ma'rib, a feat of engineering that watered the desert for 1000 years
» Following in the footsteps of Rimbaud in Aden
» Enjoying the hospitality of the historic cities of Shibam, Sayun and Tarim in the fertile Wadi Hadramawt

GETTING UNDER THE SKIN

» **Read** Tim Mackintosh-Smith's *Yemen, Travels in Dictionary Land* – wry observations of Yemeni life from a long-time San'a resident
» **Listen** to *Yemenite Songs* by Ofra Haza – rhythmic fusion by the well-known Israeli of Yemeni origin

2.

3.

4.

» **Watch** Pier Paolo Pasolini's *Arabian Nights*, a racy adaptation of the age-old tale, which includes scenes shot in Yemen

» **Eat** lentil or lamb *shurba* (soup), or *salta* (a fiery stew of lamb, beans, peppers and coriander)

» **Drink** tea scented with cardamom, or coffee (always sweet) with ginger

IN A WORD

» *Mumkin ithnayn shai* (two teas please)

TRADEMARKS

» Frankincense; silver jewellery; date palms; stony villages precariously perched on lofty mountaintops; broadly smiling Bedouin tribesmen sporting bandoliers and *jambiyas* (curved daggers); dhows bobbing on the Red Sea; daily sessions of chewing mildly intoxicating khat – a national obsession

SURPRISES

» Figs and peaches; deliciously spontaneous approach to life; Yemenis are renowned in the Middle East for their senses of humour

5.

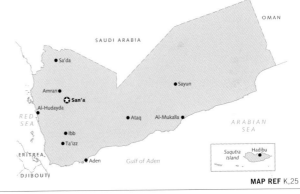

MAP REF K,25

6.

(1.) The Little Bo-Peep of Ta'izz coaxes her goats uphill
(2.) Business is slow and stress-free at Cafe Aden in Aden
(3.) The famous 17th-century limestone bridge of Shaharah spans a deep gorge
(4.) A building in the ancient town of Shaharah perches precariously above a deep valley
(5.) The stunning buildings of San'a are slowly illuminated by the morning light
(6.) Nose wrinkled in the glare of the sun, a local man of Hajja smiles gently

1.

2.

3.

4.

Land-locked Zambia shares its borders with eight other African countries, yet it remains a remote place with untamed wilderness areas, tranquil scenery and friendly, easy-going people. There are natural wonders such as the majestic Victoria Falls, which it shares with neighbouring Zimbabwe; the serene Zambezi River; and great national parks brimming with masses of wildlife. Zambia's remoteness has preserved the strong culture of its people, who still observe ancient traditional ceremonies.

BEST TIME TO VISIT
» May to August when the weather is cool and dry

ESSENTIAL EXPERIENCES
» Heading out to the Zimbabwe boarder to Victoria Falls – don't forget your raincoat
» Bungee jumping off the Zambezi bridge
» Paddling down the tranquil Zambezi River past yawning hippopotamii and getting great views of the riverside wildlife
» Playing a round of golf at Ndola in the Copperbelt district
» Driving out to the Salvation Army–run hospital in Chikankata to see the amazing work being done in the community

GETTING UNDER THE SKIN
» **Read** the collection of home-grown short stories in *A Point of No Return* by Fawanyanga Mulikita or writer-politician Dominic Mulaisho's *The Tongue of the Dumb* and *The Smoke That Thunders*
» **Listen** to *Zambiance*, or for a more traditional collection try *Sounds of Zambia*
» **Eat** *nshima* (dough made from maize), *chibwabwa* (pumpkin leaves), *inkoko* (cooked chicken) and *ifungo* (wild plum-like fruit)
» **Drink** *chai* (tea), *chibuku* (local beer) and stick to *amenshi yakunwa* (drinking water)

5.

DENNIS JONES

IN A WORD

» *Muli shani* ('hello' in Bemba)

TRADEMARKS

» The mighty Zambezi; amazing Victoria Falls; wildlife parks; religious outposts; the lovely, smiling Zambian people

SURPRISES

» For a country that has gone through so much upheaval during the last century the Zambian people have kept a strong sense of pride in both themselves and their country; these people are very friendly and offer hospitality beyond your expectations

ZAMBIA

MAP REF 0,23

(1.) The fearsome and impressive sight of Zambia's massive Victoria Falls
(2.) A family of elephants guzzles water in South Luangwa National Park
(3.) Three Zambian men watch the total eclipse of the sun pass over southern Africa
(4.) A young Burchell's zebra prepares for a safari in South Luangwa National Park
(5.) A pod of hungry hippopotamii splashing about in Lower Zambezi National Park

1.

Zimbabwe is a visually stunning and fascinating place. There's the grandeur of Victoria Falls, incredible wildlife, amazing ruins, the Zambezi River and the unmistakeable warmth and friendliness of the Zimbabwean people. You can spend the night in a tent listening to snuffling hippopotamii in a nearby river, or dance the night away at a percussion jam. Despite internal conflict, soaring inflation and ongoing drought, Zimbabwe offers an incredibly rich and diverse range of tours, activities and scenery.

BEST TIME TO VISIT
May to October (dry season)

ESSENTIAL EXPERIENCES
» The incredible displays of art at the National Gallery of Zimbabwe in Harare
» Joining a *pungwe,* an all-night drinking, dancing and music performance
» Taking in the enormous dimensions of the ruins of the ancient city of Great Zimbabwe
» Spotting lions, giraffes and zebras at Hwange National Park
» Watching a full moon rise over majestic Victoria Falls
» Enjoying the natural beauty of Mana Pools National Park
» Hiking through the fascinating Mavuradonha Wilderness
» Visiting the remote sculptors' community at Tengenenge Farm

GETTING UNDER THE SKIN
» **Read** Doris Lessing's *The Grass is Singing*, a critique of race relations in Rhodesia
» **Listen** to *Viva Zimbabwe* by various local artists, a good introduction to Zimbabwean pop music
» **Watch** *Cry Freedom* by Richard Attenborough or *The Power of One* by John G Avildsen, both filmed in Zimbabwe

ZIMBABWE
CAPITAL **HARARE** POPULATION 12,576,742 AREA 390,580 SQ KM OFFICIAL LANGUAGE ENGLISH

» **Eat** *sadza ne nyama*, a white maize-meal porridge with meat gravy; grilled trout in the Eastern Highlands; *biltong*, a salty dried meat snack; or gem squash, a type of delicious marrow

» **Drink** *chibuku*, the beer of the masses that's not particularly tasty but has a knockout punch

IN A WORD

» *Mhoro* ('hello' in Shona)

TRADEMARKS

» National parks; incredible wildlife; World Heritage sites; remote villages; just about every kind of safari you can think of; the bustle of Harare; mesmerising music; canoeing down the Zambezi River; world-champion soccer player Bruce Grobbelaar

SURPRISES

» Being invited to share in a local festivity; the massive bulk of Zimbabwe's biggest tree in the Chirinda Forest Reserve

MAP REF 0,23

(1.) Traditional healers offer cures outside the Great Zimbabwe National Monument
(2.) A schoolgirl takes a cheerful break from classes
(3.) A tobacco picker tends her child and crops
(4.) A weary boy manages a smile on the road to Masvingo
(5.) The next Bruce Grobbelaar? Zimbawean boys play soccer on a dry plain

DEPENDENCIES, OVERSEAS TERRITORIES, DEPARTMENTS & ADMINISTRATIVE DIVISIONS/REGIONS

AUSTRALIA
» Ashmore & Cartier Islands (northwest of Australia in the Indian Ocean)
» Christmas Island (south of Indonesia in the Indian Ocean)
» Cocos (Keeling) Islands (south of Indonesia in the Indian Ocean)
» Coral Sea Islands (northeast of Australia in the Coral Sea)
» Heard Island & McDonald Islands (southwest of Australia in the southern Indian Ocean)
» Norfolk Island (east of Australia in the South Pacific Ocean)

CHINA
» Hong Kong (see pp350–3)
» Macau (see pp466–9)

DENMARK
» Faroe Islands (east of Norway in the North Atlantic Ocean – see p884)
» Greenland (see pp310–13)

FRANCE
» Bassas da India (west of Madagascar in the Mozambique Channel)
» Clipperton Island (southwest of Mexico in the North Pacific Ocean)
» Europa Island (west of Madagascar in the Mozambique Channel)
» French Guiana (see pp282–5)
» French Polynesia (east of Tahiti in the Pacific Ocean)
» French Southern & Antarctic Lands (southeast of Africa in the southern Indian Ocean)
» Glorioso Islands (northwest of Madagascar in the Indian Ocean)
» Guadeloupe (see pp318–21)
» Juan de Nova Island (west of Madagascar in the Mozambique Channel)
» Martinique (see pp502–5)
» Mayotte (in the Mozambique Channel in southern Africa, between Mozambique and Madagascar)
» New Caledonia (see pp566–9)
» Réunion (see pp646–9)
» Saint Pierre & Miquelon (see p885)
» Tromelin Island (east of Madagascar in the Indian Ocean)
» Wallis & Futuna (see p887)

NETHERLANDS
» Aruba (see pp46–9)
» Netherlands Antilles (see pp46–9)

NEW ZEALAND
» Cook Islands (see pp186–9)
» Niue (east of Tonga in the South Pacific Ocean – see p885)
» Tokelau (see p886)

NORWAY
» Bouvet Island (southwest of South Africa in the South Atlantic Ocean)
» Jan Mayen (east of Greenland in the Norwegian Sea)
» Svalbard (see p886)

UK
» Anguilla (see pp26–9)
» Bermuda (see pp94–7)
» British Indian Ocean Territory (see p883)
» British Virgin Islands (see pp862–5)
» Cayman Islands (see pp150–3)
» Falkland Islands (see pp266–9)
» Gibraltar (see p884)
» Guernsey (northwest of France in the English Channel)
» Jersey (northwest of France in the English Channel)
» Isle of Man (Irish Sea)
» Montserrat (see p884)
» Pitcairn Islands (see pp626–9)
» Saint Helena (see p885; includes Ascension – see p883, Tristan da Cunha – see p887, Gough, Inaccessible and the three Nightingale Islands)
» South Georgia & the South Sandwich Islands (see p886)

» Turks & Caicos Islands (see pp814–17)

USA
» American Samoa (see pp674–7)
» Baker Island (North Pacific Ocean)
» Guam (see pp322–5)
» Howland Island (North Pacific Ocean)
» Jarvis Island (South Pacific Ocean)
» Johnston Atoll (southwest of Hawaii in the North Pacific Ocean)
» Kingman Reef (North Pacific Ocean)
» Midway Islands (west of Hawaii in the North Pacific Ocean)
» Navassa Island (west of Haiti in the Caribbean Sea)
» Northern Mariana Islands (see pp322–5)
» Palmyra Atoll (North Pacific Ocean)
» Puerto Rico (see pp638–41)
» Virgin Islands (see pp862–5)
» Wake Island (North Pacific Ocean)

DISPUTED TERRITORIES
» Antarctica (see pp30–3), Gaza Strip, Paracel Islands, Spratly Islands, West Bank, Western Sahara

OTHER PLACES OF INTEREST TO TRAVELLERS

The following destinations don't fit neatly elsewhere in this book. They are officially dependencies of other nations, but they are not large enough or on a road well enough travelled to warrant a full and separate entry. Despite this, at Lonely Planet we believe that these destinations are of special interest, whether that be due to wildlife or history or geography, and they are generally considered to have a strong independent identity and to be quite different from their parent countries. Tony Wheeler, Lonely Planet's founder and perennial explorer, has compiled this section.

» Volcanic mountains of Ascension

ASCENSION (UK)

CAPITAL GEORGETOWN POPULATION 1000
AREA 88 SQ KM OFFICIAL LANGUAGE ENGLISH

Wideawake Airfield is the RAF's intermediate stop on the long flight from England to the Falkland Islands and is also an important USAF base. The island is noted for its 44 volcano craters, all of them dormant, and for its popularity as a breeding site for green turtles. The island is officially a dependency of St Helena, 1100km to the south.

MAP REF N,18

» The atoll of Diego Garcia from the air

DIEGO GARCIA – BRITISH INDIAN OCEAN TERRITORY (UK)

POPULATION 3500 AREA 60 SQ KM OFFICIAL LANGUAGE ENGLISH

Diego Garcia and the islands of the Chagos Archipelago make up the British Indian Ocean Territory. Technically it's uninhabited – in the 1970s the island's British administrators deported the entire population and most of them now live in less than happy circumstances on Mauritius. They were replaced by military personnel as Diego Garcia became a military base. It also functions as an Indian Ocean alternative to Guantanamo Bay in Cuba, a handy place to keep prisoners well out of sight of the outside world.

MAP REF M,27

FAROE ISLANDS (DENMARK)

CAPITAL **TÓRSHAVN** POPULATION **46,962** AREA **1,399 SQ KM**
OFFICIAL LANGUAGES **FAROESE (DERIVED FROM OLD NORSE) & DANISH**

Halfway between Scotland and Iceland the Faroe Islands also sit
halfway between colonial status and independence. Fishing has
been the mainstay of the economy but, like other places involved in
North Atlantic fishing, the outlook has not been good in recent years.
Fortunately, dramatic scenery – soaring cliffs, crashing surf and
stormy North Atlantic are all words that creep into the descriptions –
plus huge numbers of seabirds have made the islands something of a
tourist attraction.

MAP REF D,19

» The seat of the Løgting (Parliament) in Tórshavn on Steymoy

GIBRALTAR (UK)

POPULATION **27,000** AREA **7 SQ KM** OFFICIAL LANGUAGE **ENGLISH**

Strategically situated guarding the Straits of Gibraltar, the narrow
entrance to the Mediterranean from the Atlantic Ocean, the Rock
makes an interesting stumbling block for British-Spanish relations.
The Spanish want it back and the British would probably be happy to
hand it over, but there's no way the citizens of Gibraltar will go. They
like their little corner of England on the shores of the Mediterranean.
Towering over the town, the upper Rock offers spectacular views and
houses the colony of Barbary macaques, which are Europe's only
primates. If they ever depart, so the legend goes, so will the British.

MAP REF H,19

» View of the Rock of Gibraltar from the top cable-car station

MONTSERRAT (UK)

CAPITAL **PLYMOUTH** POPULATION **5000**
AREA **100 SQ KM** OFFICIAL LANGUAGE **ENGLISH**

In 1997 a volcanic eruption devastated Montserrat. There had been
plenty of warning that after 400 sleepy years the Soufrière Hills
Volcano was about to wake up, but there were still 19 deaths. Half
of the island is now a no-go zone and the population has halved. In
2000 poor Montserrat lost again: while Brazil and Germany were
playing for the World Cup football final in Tokyo, the Montserrat
national team was in Bhutan playing for the position right at the
bottom of the world rankings. Bhutan won.

MAP REF J,13

» A goatherd leads his flock along a rural Montserrat road

NIUE (NEW ZEALAND)

CAPITAL ALOFI POPULATION 1700
AREA 259 SQ KM OFFICIAL LANGUAGES NIUEAN & ENGLISH

Midway between Tonga and the Cook Islands, Niue is a classic example of a makatea island, an upthrust coral reef. It rises often vertically out of the ocean so there's very little beach, but in compensation there are amazing chasms, ravines, and caves all around the coast. Some of them extend underwater, giving the island superb scuba-diving sites. Like a number of other Pacific nations, the world's smallest self-governing state has been suffering a population decline: today there are more Niueans in New Zealand than on 'the Rock of Polynesia'.

MAP REF 0,40

» A humpback whale glides through the waters off Niue

SAINT HELENA (UK)

CAPITAL JAMESTOWN POPULATION 7000
AREA 121 SQ KM OFFICIAL LANGUAGE ENGLISH

From 1815 until he died in 1821, St Helena had one very famous resident, Napoleon Bonaparte. This remote island, halfway between South America and Africa, was where the British shipped the European conqueror after he met his Waterloo. Longwood House, where Napoleon died, is maintained as a museum by the French government. Visitors to the island might also climb the 699 steps of Jacob's Ladder or search out the island's oldest inhabitant, the tortoise Jonathan, which was thought to be 50 years old when it arrived on the island in 1882.

MAP REF 0,19

» Jamestown, nestled snugly in a valley

SAINT PIERRE & MIQUELON (FRANCE)

CAPITAL SAINT-PIERRE POPULATION 7000
AREA 242 SQ KM OFFICIAL LANGUAGE FRENCH

The French lost Canada to the British after the Seven Years' War in 1763, but 20 years later the British decided to let them keep these two islands off Newfoundland. Later they changed their minds before handing them over permanently in 1815. As the only French territory remaining in North America, the island's main industry, after the dramatic decline of cod fishing off Newfoundland, is tourism. In Montréal you may be able to speak French, drink French wine and eat baguettes, but here you can also spend euros.

MAP REF F,14

» A windswept island church and cemetery yard

SOUTH GEORGIA (UK)

CAPITAL **GRYTVIKEN** POPULATION **10 TO 20**
AREA **3755 SQ KM** OFFICIAL LANGUAGE **ENGLISH**

Aptly described as an Alpine mountain range soaring straight out of
the ocean, South Georgia's spectacular topography is matched only
by its equally spectacular wildlife. Its human population may drop as
low as 10 during the winter, but there are two to three million seals, as
many penguins and 50 million birds, including a large proportion of
the world's albatrosses. Add spectacular industrial archaeology in the
shape of the island's abandoned whaling stations, and it's no wonder
this is one of the most popular destinations for Antarctic tourists.

MAP REF T,16

» The abandoned Grytviken Whaling Station in King Edward Point

SVALBARD (NORWAY)

CAPITAL **LONGYEARBYEN** POPULATION **2500**
AREA **61,229 SQ KM** OFFICIAL LANGUAGE **NORWEGIAN**

Far to the north of Norway, the archipelago of Svalbard has become a
popular goal for Arctic travellers, keen to cruise the ice floes in search
of whales, seals, walruses and polar bears. Apart from wildlife there
are also some terrific hiking possibilities on the main island where
you might encounter reindeer and Arctic foxes. The main town, the
engagingly named Longyearbyen, has a long history of coal mining.

MAP REF A,22

» The St Fritiofsbreen glacier in Svalbard

TOKELAU (NEW ZEALAND)

POPULATION **1400** AREA **12 SQ KM**
OFFICIAL LANGUAGES **TOKELAUN, ENGLISH & SAMOAN**

Tokelau consists of three tiny atolls, each of them laid out on classic
atoll design principles: a necklace of palm-fringed islands around a
central lagoon. Off to the north of Samoa, the islands are not only
a long way from anywhere, but also a long way from each other;
it's 150km from Atafu past Nukunonu to Fakaofo. They're also very
crowded: there may be only 1400 people but they've got very little
land to share; none of the islets is more than 200m wide and you've
got to climb a coconut tree to get more than 5m above sea level.

MAP REF N,40

» Tokelau elders perform a traditional wedding dance

» The grass-topped cliffs of the northwest coast of Tristan da Cunha

TRISTAN DA CUNHA (UK)

CAPITAL **EDINBURGH** POPULATION **300**
AREA **98 SQ KM** OFFICIAL LANGUAGE **ENGLISH**

Officially a dependency of St Helena, Tristan da Cunha is frequently cited as the most remote populated place in the world. The island is a simple, towering volcano cone, and an eruption in 1961 forced the complete evacuation of the island. The displaced islanders put up with life in England for two years but most of them returned as soon as the island was declared safe in 1963 and went straight back to catching the crawfish which are the island's main export. Nightingale, Inaccessible and two smaller islands lie slightly southeast of the main island.

MAP REF Q.19

» The striking Sausau Church, Sigave

WALLIS & FUTUNA (FRANCE)

CAPITAL **MATA'UTU** POPULATION **15,500** AREA **274 SQ KM**
OFFICIAL LANGUAGES **WALLISIAN, FUTUNAN & FRENCH**

Luckily for Tahiti, Samuel Wallis, its European 'discoverer', didn't attach his name to the island – he was saving it for his visit to what is now half of another French Pacific colony. The two islands are remarkably dissimilar. Wallis is low lying with a lagoon fringed by *motu*s (islets) while Futuna is mountainous and paired with smaller Alofi. The populations are equally dissimilar: Futuna has connections to Samoa while the Wallis links were with Tonga. Wallis has one of the Pacific's best archaeological sites at Talietumu and an unusual collection of crater lakes.

MAP REF O.39

THE TRAVEL BOOK
A JOURNEY THROUGH EVERY COUNTRY IN THE WORLD

SEPTEMBER 2008

PUBLISHED BY
Lonely Planet Publications Pty Ltd
90 Maribyrnong St, Footscray,
Victoria 3011, Australia
www.lonelyplanet.com
ABN 36 005 607 983

Printed through Colorcraft Ltd, Hong Kong
Printed in Malaysia

ISBN 978 1 741040 050

Statistical information including population, area and official languages for each country was sourced from the Central Intelligence Agency.

PUBLISHER Roz Hopkins

PROJECT MANAGER Ellie Cobb

DESIGN Mark Adams

LAYOUT DESIGNERS Mik Ruff, Indra Kilfoyle

IMAGE RESEARCHERS Gabrielle Clark, Indra Kilfoyle

EDITORS Chris Girdler, Alison Ridgway, Laura Crawford

MANAGING EDITOR Brigitte Ellemor

CARTOGRAPHER Wayne Murphy

PRINT PRODUCTION Graham Imeson

PRE-PRESS PRODUCTION Ryan Evans

PHOTOGRAPHS
All images supplied by Lonely Planet Images **www.lonelyplanetimages.com** except the following:

Alamy.com p29 No 3, p131 No 2, 3, 4, p132 No 5, p182 No 1, p184 No 2, p185 No 3, 4, p250 No 1, 2, 3, p252 No 4, p286 No 1, p330 No 3, p332 No 4, p682 No 1, 2, 3, p684 No 4, p685 No 4, p700 No 4, p746 No 1, 2, p800 No 5, 6, p885 No 2, p887 No1

Corbis p29 No 4, p 627 No 2, p628 No 5, p748 No 4, p883 No 1, 2, p884 No 3

Photolibrary p886 No 3

LONELY PLANET OFFICES

AUSTRALIA
Locked Bag 1, Footscray, Victoria, 3011
Phone 03 8379 8000
Fax 03 8379 8111
Email talk2us@lonelyplanet.com.au

USA
150 Linden St, Oakland, CA 94607
Phone 510 250 6400
Toll Free 800 275 8555
Fax 510 893 8572
Email info@lonelyplanet.com

UK
2nd fl, 186 City Rd, London, EC1V 2NT
Phone 020 7106 2100
Fax 020 7106 2101
Email go@lonelyplanet.co.uk